D1715442

LIBERTY AND LOCALITY IN REVOLUTIONARY FRANCE

Six Villages Compared, 1760–1820

This book examines the interface between the old and the new France in the period 1760–1820. It adopts an unusual 'comparative micro-historical' approach in order to illuminate the manner in which country dwellers cut themselves loose from the congeries of local societies that made up the *ancien régime*, and attached themselves to the wider polity of the revolutionary and Napoleonic state.

The apprehensions and ambitions of six groups of villagers located in different parts of the kingdom are explored in close-up across the span of a single adult lifetime. Contrasting experiences form a large part of the analysis, but the story is ultimately one of fusion around a set of values that no individual villager could possibly have anticipated, either in 1760 or in 1789. The book is at once an institutional, social and political history of life in the village in an epoch of momentous change.

PETER JONES is Professor of French History at the University of Birmingham. His previous publications include *Politics and Rural Society* (1985), *The Peasantry in the French Revolution* (1988), and *Reform and Revolution in France* (1995).

NEW STUDIES IN EUROPEAN HISTORY

Edited by
PETER BALDWIN, *University of California, Los Angeles*
CHRISTOPHER CLARK, *University of Cambridge*
JAMES B. COLLINS, *Georgetown University*
MIA RODRÍGUEZ-SALGADO, *London School of Economics and Political Science*
LYNDAL ROPER, *Royal Holloway, University of London*

This is a new series in early modern and modern European history. Its aim is to publish outstanding works of research, addressed to important themes across a wide geographical range, from southern and central Europe, to Scandinavia and Russia, and from the time of the Renaissance to the Second World War. As it develops the series will comprise focused works of wide contextual range and intellectual ambition.

Books in the series

Royalty and Diplomacy in Europe, 1890–1914
RODERICK R. MCLEAN

Catholic Revival in the Age of the Baroque
Religious Identity in Southwest Germany, 1550–1750
MARC R. FORSTER

Helmuth von Moltke and the Origins of the First World War
ANNIKA MOMBAUER

Peter the Great
The Struggle for Power, 1671–1725
PAUL BUSHKOVITCH

Fatherlands
State Building and Nationhood in Nineteenth-Century Germany
ABIGAIL GREEN

The French Second Empire
An Anatomy of Political Power
ROGER PRICE

Origins of the French Welfare State
The Struggle for Social Reform in France, 1914–1947
PAUL V. DUTTON

Liberty and Locality in Revolutionary France
Six Villages Compared, 1760–1820
PETER JONES

LIBERTY AND LOCALITY IN REVOLUTIONARY FRANCE

Six Villages Compared, 1760–1820

PETER JONES

University of Birmingham

WITHDRAWN

PUBLISHED BY THE PRESS SYNDICATE OF THE UNIVERSITY OF CAMBRIDGE
The Pitt Building, Trumpington Street, Cambridge, CB2 1RP, United Kingdom

CAMBRIDGE UNIVERSITY PRESS
The Edinburgh Building, Cambridge, CB2 2RU, UK
40 West 20th Street, New York, NY 10011-4211, USA
477 Williamstown Road, Port Melbourne, VIC 3207, Australia
Ruiz de Alarcón 13, 28014 Madrid, Spain
Dock House, The Waterfront, Cape Town 8001, South Africa

http://www.cambridge.org

First published 2003

Printed in the United Kingdom at the University Press, Cambridge

Typeface Adobe Garamond 11/12.5 pt   *System* LaTeX 2$_\varepsilon$ [TB]

A catalogue record for this book is available from the British Library

ISBN 0 521 82177 0 hardback

For Betty and Jonah

Contents

Illustrations

Plates

Figures

Maps

Tables

Acknowledgements

This book has been some time in the making and would not have been completed but for the financial assistance of the Humanities Research Board (subsequently the Arts and Humanities Research Board) of the British Academy bestowed in 1995 and in 1999. Material assistance was also provided by the Institut Francophone de Paris in 1995, and by the Ecole des Hautes Etudes en Sciences Sociales, Marseille, in 1999. I owe these bodies a debt that I am happy to acknowledge here.

Material help of a rather different kind was provided by several individuals as the typescript was being readied for the press. Mr Graham Norrie in the Department of Ancient History and Archeology of Birmingham University applied his photographic skills in order to enhance the quality of the illustrations, and Ms Noelle Plack, also a colleague, took time from her own Ph.D. studies in order to read through and correct the typescript from beginning to end.

Archival research in provincial France is a voyage of discovery punctuated by surprises, occasional setbacks and unanticipated friendships. The debts I have incurred are almost too numerous to mention, but I should like particularly to thank the following individuals and the public services that they head. In the Archives Départementales de la Drôme, Mme Michèle Nathan-Tilloy gave permission for documents to be brought to me while I was immobilised in Valence by transport strikes in November and December 1995. A member of her reading-room team even took me to where I wanted to go in her car. In Versailles M. Arnaud Ramière de Fortanier enlisted the help of the entire staff of the Archives Départementales des Yvelines and others besides (notably M. Philippe de Bagneux) in the search for materials relating to the village of Villepreux. He also entertained me royally in his apartment overlooking the Palace of Versailles. Madame Hélène Duthu, until recently the head of the Archives Départementales de la Lozère, provided commensurate help in respect of the village of Saint-Alban. On my frequent visits to Mende it was especially pleasant to meet other old acquaintances, too; in particular M. Benjamin Bardy and M. Alain Laurans, whose unrivalled knowledge of the history of the Lozère I was able to tap. M. Hubert Collin, Directeur des Archives Départementales de Meurthe-et-Moselle, deserves a mention in this context as well. Although we met infrequently, he eased my passage through his *dépôt* in all sorts of much appreciated ways. The same applies to Mme Anne Lejeune who heads the Archives Départementales des Côtes-d'Armor, perhaps the most agreeable working environment that I visited during my travels in provincial France. Thanks to the efforts of Mme Lejeune, I was able to secure a microfilm copy of the municipal deliberations of Châtelaudren and thus save valuable time.

The real heroes of my research forays, however, were the mayors of rural France, together with their collaborators and *bénévoles*. I worked for extended periods in four out of the six villages covered in this study and encountered only kindness and eagerness to help. In Roville M. Jacques Champouillon escorted me around his native village and taught me more in a couple of hours than I had learned in a couple of weeks in the local record office. M. Jean Renaux, mayor of Neuviller, not only gave me unfettered access to the archival records surviving within his *mairie*, but also invited me into his home. Moreover, he arranged for me to visit the parish church in the company of Mme Thérèse Cadiot, and as an indirect consequence of his hospitality I was able to meet and converse with Mlle Didry, the current owner of the chateau of Neuviller. In the village of Saint-Alban, the Office de Tourisme served as my chief point of contact, and I am glad of the opportunity to thank Cédric Planul, Laure Castel and Gabriel Nurit for the interest they showed in my project and the material help they provided (notably plate 4). Although I never had the good fortune to meet the mayor of Roquelaure, I owe to him the photograph reproduced in plate 6. In Châtelaudren my personal contacts were confined to the Office de Tourisme, which nevertheless provided a rich harvest of information. In Villepreux, by contrast, I was greeted on my arrival by a host of individuals from the *adjoint* of this substantial *mairie* downwards. I would like particularly to acknowledge the help provided by Mme Jousse, by the trainee archival assistant Mlle Lalanne, and above all by Mme Annick Bouffil, who provided 'tea breaks' in her office.

Four names remain to be mentioned: individuals who have succoured me during my stays in France for longer than I care to remember. Jean-Michel and Hélène Chevet in Paris and Jean and Arundhati Boutier in Marseille, I hope that you will find in this book some recompense for your unstinting friendship and hospitality over many years.

Introduction

This book explores one of the great moments of transition in modern history – the French Revolution – through the lives and experiences of the inhabitants of six villages. It joins together the problem-oriented approach of the comparative historian and the craft skills of the micro-historian to produce an unusual, authentic and above all decentred analysis of the way a generation of French country dwellers responded to the pressures threatening to alter their lives fundamentally from the 1760s onwards. The reader will judge how far this project has been successful. The practice of comparative history is usually confined to large-scale social phenomena, and it is an open question whether a genre that might be described as 'comparative micro-history' can – or should – exist. The research for this book commenced under no particular theoretical or methodological banner. As anyone who has worked at the grass roots will testify, the availability or non-availability of source materials tends to overshadow all other considerations. Nevertheless, it would be wrong to give the impression that the book simply evolved in a random and haphazard manner. Three guiding ambitions served to direct and structure my investigations: a desire to improve the 'reach' of social history in an area that historians of France think they know rather well; a desire to transcend the ubiquitous village monograph; and finally a desire to try to avoid a composite or 'synthetic' history of the experiences of country dwellers in which examples are culled from far and wide in order to illustrate propositions that have usually been formulated in advance. Most history writing is synthetic in this sense, of course, and we could not manage without such accounts. However, its explanatory capacity – in the field of rural history particularly – is fairly modest and there comes a time when our knowledge and understanding of the past can only be enhanced by adopting alternative strategies.

The issue can be put quite simply: how are the limitations of traditional village monographs to be overcome whilst at the same time unlocking the potentially valuable information they contain? Long ago Albert Soboul urged writers of single village histories to abandon description and adopt a problem-solving approach.[1] The continuing vigour of 'vie quotidienne' styles of history writing within France may indicate that most consumers do not want their history 'problematised'. Nevertheless, it is advice that this study takes to heart: the smaller the entity the bigger the questions that need to be asked. Big questions confined to small localities only make sense within a wider frame of reference, however, and so it became clear almost from the outset that my research presupposed a comparative approach. Comparison can be achieved in several different ways, though, and social historians tend to be too nervous about disturbing the unities of time and place to apply the methodology rigorously. Most commonly, they rely on juxtaposition in which the comparison is implicit and has to be inferred by the reader. Sometimes they blend together the 'synthetic' and the 'comparative' approaches in a manner disquieting to fellow investigators – sociologists and political scientists in particular.

As the subtitle of this study indicates, it is an attempt at rigorous comparison, in the sense that the book is structured around six village histories. Despite sore temptation on occasion, the evidence adduced and the arguments formulated derive almost entirely from these sources. It aspires to a degree of rigour unusual within the field of social and political history in another sense, too. Every effort is made to ensure that the case studies 'talk' to one another. Juxtaposition is usually adequate to the purpose of testing hypotheses or general propositions, but it will not ensure interaction between the subjects of study. By far the most interesting conclusions of my research emerged from the comparing and contrasting of individual village 'situations' – their institutional architecture, their economic characteristics, their elites, the hopes and fears of their ordinary inhabitants and so on. Near total reliance on case studies and a comparative mode of investigation creates its own problems, though. The reader is entitled to ask whether the case studies are representative. If not, why not? If not, how were they chosen and for what purpose? And if they were not selected for their typicality, how do they contribute to the general sum of historical understanding?

The answer to the first objection will help to provide answers to the others. The life histories of six groups of villagers cannot be expected to encapsulate the experiences of a whole generation of country dwellers who grew up during the *ancien régime* and grew old in the aftermath of the

---

[1] A. Soboul, 'Esquisse d'un plan de recherches pour une monographie de communauté rurale', *La Pensée*, July–August 1947, 34–48.

Revolution and the Napoleonic Empire. The case studies on which this book is based are not representative, therefore. Yet nor are they palpably unrepresentative. 'Que la France se nomme diversité,' Lucien Febvre was once moved to exclaim, and his remark can be taken as an implied reproof to would-be schematisers.[2] In a context of a little over 40,000 rural parishes at the end of the *ancien régime*, it would not have made very much difference had I studied sixteen, sixty or six hundred villages. The solutions most commonly espoused in order to address the dilemma of typicality are twofold: either the historian narrows his attention to a particular region, or he constructs a 'village typology'. Georges Lefebvre's *Les Paysans du Nord*, which is based on an investigation of 208 villages, is the classic example of the former approach,[3] whereas the latter has many exemplars. Yet neither 'solution' has been adopted in this case. Why not?

Regional rural histories are legion; indeed, it is by this route that most of our knowledge of the 'early modern' and the 'modern' French countryside has been adumbrated. True, regional histories that span the divide of 1789 are still quite rare,[4] but I have no wish to add to their number. Invaluable though the corpus of regional rural histories may be, it does not allow much scope for comparison and bears a close methodological resemblance to the 'synthetic' style of analysis that I am keen to avoid. The problem with the 'village typology' as an answer to the challenge of diversity is that it frequently becomes an exercise in self-deception. Two traps lie in wait for the unwary: the illusion of representivity and the illusion of objectivity. Constructing a balanced sample of French villages for the purpose of in-depth and cross-regional analysis is not an easy objective to achieve, as most rural historians would acknowledge. However, it is all too easy to construct a self-validating sample of village types which, upon analysis, turns out to vindicate the criteria employed in the initial choice. Even within the confines of a profession that makes no bones about its inability to achieve scientific levels of objectivity, this seems an unsound method. Yet practitioners of the typological approach constantly lay themselves open to the criticism of tautology.

My six villages constitute a selection rather than a sample, then. But how were they chosen? Whilst some care was taken to seek out cases for study in the major historic regions of *ancien-régime* France, it would be foolish to make any larger claim to representivity. They represent themselves, and,

[2] L. Febvre, 'Que la France se nomme diversité: à propos de quelques études jurassiennes', *Annales: économies, sociétés, civilisations*, 3 (July–September 1946), 271–4.
[3] G. Lefebvre, *Les Paysans du Nord pendant la Révolution française* ([condensed version] Bari, 1959).
[4] See, however, J.-P. Jessenne, *Pouvoir au village et révolution: Artois, 1760–1848* (Lille, 1987).

on the whole, I have refrained from treating them as 'tokens' except where overwhelming evidence came to light which indicated that they could usefully perform this role. From the outset the aim was to compare and contrast without too many preconceptions as to what would emerge from the exercise. In my mind I likened the six subjects to laboratory animals brought together for experimental purposes. While each would require prodding and poking in order to disclose individual characteristics under varying laboratory conditions, it was the interactions that I particularly wished to observe. When applied to suitable subject matter, the comparative method has a formidable potential to cut through the opacity that screens off rural history from all but the most persistent observers.

Can a small and 'unrepresentative' selection of country dwellers gathered together in a handful of villages serve as an adequate base for generalisation? The answer has to be negative, of course, even though one might doubt whether the conclusions of 'synthetic' history writing are any better rooted. Yet this does not amount to an admission that the study of villages contributes nothing to the general sum of historical understanding. Micro-historians rightly point out that the explanatory premium dangled in return for 'thinking big' has not lived up to expectations by and large; if the reach of social history is to be improved it might in fact be better to begin by 'thinking small'. As I hope my study will show, village history – properly conceived – restores the complexity to individual lives and the events enfolding those lives. Moreover, as a tool for reconstructing popular mentalities it is unsurpassed. Indeed, micro-historians such as Giovanni Levi make larger claims, professing to believe that in-depth analysis of small social formations will uncover the existence of a specific form of peasant rationality.[5] Comparative micro-history provides a swift antidote for such essentialist modes of thinking, however. On the evidence of the case studies I shall be examining, rationality is not a given but a commodity apprehended differently both within and between villages. The main contribution that the comparative study of the village can make to the sum total of historical knowledge lies not in the discovery of a deep stratum of social truth, then, but in a better understanding of the historic reasons for difference, and sameness.

All of these theoretical and methodological considerations must yield to the question of source availability, though. Village history requires source materials of exceptional quality, and a comparative village history demands sources of comparable quality replicated six times over. With more than 40,000 villages to choose from, one might suppose that the task of selecting

---

[5] G. Levi, *Inheriting Power: The Story of an Exorcist* (Chicago, 1988), p. xv.

sites for study would be relatively straightforward, but, on the contrary, the fully documented French village is the stuff of historians' dreams. For the purposes of this study it was necessary to examine the credentials of around fifty small localities. Even so, the six villages (not to mention several hamlets) that were eventually retained for in-depth analysis proved to be of uneven quality, as will shortly become apparent. In the absence of any assurance that further searching in the archives would result in an improved selection, I decided that the satisfactory geographical distribution of my sites of study (see maps 1 and 2), together with their contrasting ecological and cultural characteristics, should count for more than the imperfections in the documentation. Nevertheless, it was disappointing to discover that one of the villages selected for analysis had lost its municipal *délibérations* – the prime source for this kind of study – relatively recently (see figure 1). Availability cannot be taken as tantamount to accessibility in any case. In four out of the six candidate villages it proved necessary to consult sources *in situ*, that is to say in communal archive depositories, and even in private homes.

Moreover, the question of sources cannot be tackled in isolation. For this book has a quite explicit frame of reference. As stated at the beginning, the aim is to identify and explore some of the processes that altered the habitual trajectory of country dwellers' lives across a span of six decades linking the *ancien régime* to the Restoration. If a rigorous comparison is to be sustained, it is therefore essential that the sources provide chronological continuity. A village whose pre-1789 (or post-1800) history remains shrouded in mystery for want of adequate documentation does not make a suitable candidate for comparative analysis. Yet it would be disingenuous to present the search for sources, or rather for adequately documented villages, as an entirely dispassionate exercise. The question 'sources for what purpose?' is bound to intrude at an early stage, and so it proved in this case. I did not set about gathering my material and thinking about what I might do with it as two completely separate operations. The availability (and non-availability) of sources has therefore helped to structure what follows, and so, too, have certain questions that I have brought to bear on the subject matter. But a constant, contextual interrogating of the sources to see what they might yield of relevance to the central problematic should not be confused with hypothesis formulation and testing, which is a rather different methodology of comparative history. Where *a priori* lines of enquiry proved unenlightening or inappropriate to the evidential context I have not hesitated to abandon them. Instead I have allowed questions suggested by the case studies themselves to order the agenda.

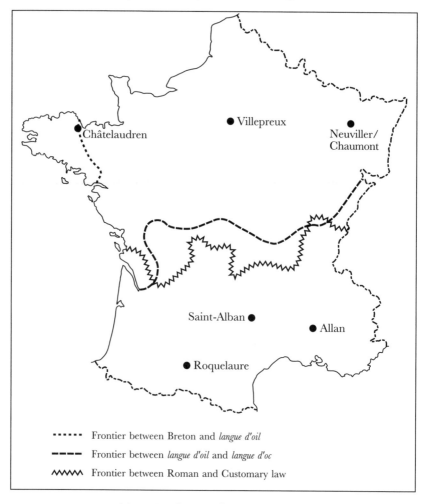

Map 1. Localisation of case-study villages

The result – of necessity – is a study that explores some themes but not others. For instance, I had expected to pursue an argument that would illuminate the substantial militarisation of civil society between 1792 and 1814, but my case studies proved to be reluctant witnesses on this subject and I abandoned the idea at an early stage. A problem of sources no doubt, but perhaps also a salutary reminder that 'thinking small' can offer correctives to grand narratives. On the other hand, I had not expected the theme of seigneurialism – or rather anti-seigneurialism – to bulk as

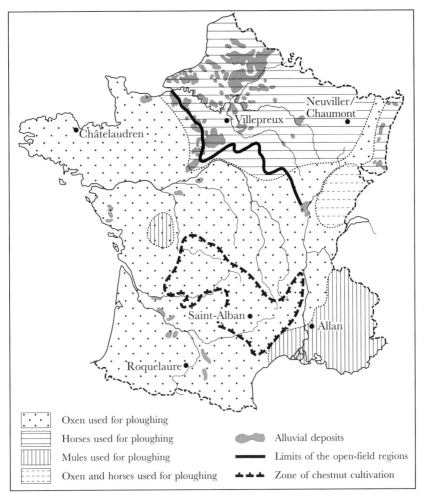

Map 2. The rural economy of France in the eighteenth century

large as it does. When villagers raise an issue time and time again it would be a churlish historian who refused to listen. Nevertheless, the point that this book is not a *total* history of the village between 1760 and 1820 bears repeating. Apart from anything else, the rigorously comparative approach that I have adopted precludes any such undertaking.

What questions are addressed in the pages that follow, then? After an initial presentation of the sites of study, the reader will find (in chapter 2) an extended discussion of the internal architecture and power structuring

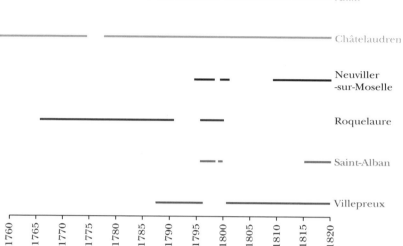

Figure 1. Extant civil deliberations of case-study villages (by year)

of *ancien-régime* villages which queries Alexis de Tocqueville's classic depiction of local institutions and social life etiolated by state centralisation. The awakening of village elites to the possibility of substantial institutional change and the rapid enlargement of social and political horizons within the space of just three or four years (1787–90) is the theme of chapter 3. 'What changes did villagers want to see happen?' and 'To what degree were they able to exert control over the pace and direction of change?' are the basic questions tackled at this stage. Chapter 4 explores how, and how far, villagers came to terms with the psychological landscape of citizenship that successive regimes sought to construct from 1789 onwards. Were the symbolic practices of the Revolutionary era absorbed internally? And what evidence can be marshalled to indicate that the transition from the old order to the new accomplished a durable transformation of collective identities? In view of the paucity of research devoted to the micro-politics of the village, chapter 5 occupies a key position in terms both of content and of method. By constant juxtaposition and comparison, it sets out to illuminate the way local power arenas functioned, and the way they evolved over time. Some of the vectors stimulating politicisation at the grass roots are identified, as are the different types of 'argument' going on at village level. Chapter 6 explores the spiritual dimension of village belief systems, before turning to examine the implications of changes in the relationship between the state and the church for devotional habits and practices. It must be acknowledged that, in the near total absence of sources that might shed light on the religious convictions of villagers, the latter investigation makes more headway than the former. More precision is on offer in chapter 7, however, which assesses the repercussions of six decades of administrative interventionism on the rural economy. It pursues answers to questions arising out of the impact of libertarian and egalitarian ideologies in the realm of land use and ownership.

CHAPTER I

Mise-en-scène

This study first encounters the village in the culminating decades of the *ancien régime*, a period of some thirty or forty years during which a totalising vision of administrative monarchy took hold of France. From the 1760s country dwellers in general and rural communities in particular became the focus of attention of reformers to a degree which historians have only recently begun to understand. While most of the reforms that were mooted received little more than piecemeal application, their reverberations would be far reaching. By 1789, when instructions were issued for parish assemblies to draw up *cahiers de doléances*, life in many, perhaps the majority of, French villages was already caught in a spiral of accelerating change. These changes – at once institutional, cultural and socio-economic – signal the direction in which it would be most profitable to press our enquiries.

At the most fundamental level we will need to ask whether Alexis de Tocqueville's argument that rural communities had become moribund by the end of the *ancien régime* can be accepted. We will need to determine whether such administrative structures as villagers did possess were subscribed, that is to say developed from within, or imposed from the outside. The former invites a comparison of villages equipped with 'municipal' institutions in emulation of the towns with those lacking independent organs of collective expression and reliant still upon the resources of the seigneurie or the parish. The latter raises questions pertaining to the power of the state in the second half of the eighteenth century. Did the monarchy perform a normative role in successfully fashioning the institutions of village life around a common template, or did it compete uneasily and, in the final analysis, unsuccessfully with sectional providers of administrative *tutelle*: the Provincial Estates, the *parlements* and the sundry *cours des aides* and *chambres des comptes*? The policies of successive reform ministers are known in some detail, as are those pursued by a number of provincial intendants. The outlook of the Estates and of the various sovereign courts in the face of perceived encroachments by 'ministerial' power are not too difficult to fathom either, although it is true that the attitudes of bodies such as the Cour des Aides of Montauban or the Chambre des Comptes of Nancy remain shrouded in a good deal of uncertainty. The point at which the policies of all of these agencies intersected was the village. How did one group of villagers accommodate such multiple and often competing forms of interventionism by comparison with another? And how much freedom of manoeuvre remained to them at the end of the day? Of these things we know almost nothing. But first we must acquaint ourselves with the villages that provide the frame of reference for this study.

NEUVILLER-SUR-MOSELLE

The unremarkable Lorraine village of Neuviller is situated midway between Charmes and Flavigny at a point where the road executes an abrupt 90-degree turn before continuing in a straight line (see map 9). Nancy, the historic capital of Lorraine and present-day capital of the Meurthe-et-Moselle department, is roughly twenty-five kilometres to the north, and Epinal, the capital of the department of the Vosges, forty kilometres to the southeast. Linking all of these places is the Moselle, a fast-flowing river with a tendency to flood. It bounds the territory of Neuviller to the east and, until recent times, posed a constant threat to low-lying meadows. For part of the period of interest to us the village bore another name. The significance of this name change, and also of the abrupt turn in the road, will be explored in chapter 2; but in most other respects the configuration of the village has not changed greatly since the late eighteenth century. Then as now the territory of the parish and commune coincided and, until very recently, covered some 440 hectares, an area well below the norm for modern-day French communes (see table 1). This physical area can be divided roughly into three: a portion marked out on the shallow valley floor ('la plaine'), a portion stretched along the flanks ('les coteaux'), and a plateau portion raised about 100 metres above the Moselle river ('le plateau'). The village proper is located on the floor of the valley and in common with the prevailing habitat pattern of Lorraine is highly nucleated: no hamlets and no outlying farms. Within easy walking distance of our village, however, are two smaller settlements whose eighteenth-century history was closely, almost inextricably, entwined with that of Neuviller: Roville-devant-Bayon in the plain and Laneuveville-devant-Bayon on the plateau. At intervals they too will feature in this study.

The provinces of Alsace and Lorraine led the demographic recovery of the eighteenth century, and the *généralité* of Nancy recorded no less

Plate 1. The modern village of Neuviller-sur-Moselle

Table 1. *Physical area of case-study villages*

Village	Territory c. 1760	c. 1820	Present
Allan	12,919 *sétiers de Provence* [2,871 hectares]	2,871 hectares	2,881 hectares
Châtelaudren	287.2 *arpents de Plélo* [46.53 hectares]	46.53 hectares	46.53 hectares
Neuviller-sur-Moselle	1,974 *jours de Lorraine*[a] [394.8 hectares]	440.4 hectares	440.4 hectares[b]
Roquelaure	1,192.5 *arpents d'Auch*[c] [1,824.5 hectares]	1,852.8 hectares	2,123.2 hectares[d]
Saint-Alban	4,560.7 dextres [7,244 hectares]	7,244 hectares	5,386 hectares[e]
Villepreux	2,432.2 *arpents communs* [1,026.5 hectares]	1,026.5 hectares	1,039 hectares
Averages [*communes*]	1,200–1,300 hectares	1,200–1,300 hectares	1,400 hectares

Notes
[a] Cultivated area in 1771
[b] Recently augmented to 648 hectares
[c] Cultivated area in 1741
[d] Arcamont added in 1950
[e] Lajo detached in 1837

than a twofold increase in population by the century's end.[1] However, this headlong rush to make good the biological shortfall of Louis XIV's reign seems scarcely to have registered in the villages overlooking the Moselle. In 1771, the earliest date for which we can determine a figure, the population of Neuviller hovered at a little over 400 souls (see figure 2). Not until the period of Napoleonic consolidation did it climb above 500, by which time the new road constructed at the cost of so much hardship some forty-five years earlier (see pp. 80–1) had established Neuviller as a 'lieu de passage'. An increasing volume of haulage traffic helped to push the numbers living in the village to 612 by 1856.[2] But that was the peak: with the opening of the Nancy–Epinal railway the population started to ebb away. Roville's demographic profile displayed similar characteristics, with the main phase of growth beginning during the Empire (189 inhabitants in 1789, 379 in

[1] M. Morineau, *Pour une histoire économique vraie* (Lille, 1985), p. 125.
[2] Bibliothèque Municipale [hereafter B. M.] de Nancy, Monographies communales: Neuviller-sur-Moselle, 1888.

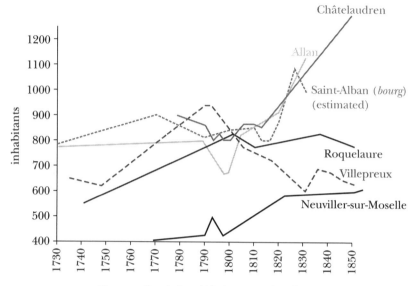

Figure 2. Population shifts in case-study villages

1836), and the same applies to Laneuveville (259 inhabitants in 1789, 388 in 1823).

How did the several hundred households grouped in these modest-sized settlements make a living? Lorraine was noted, then as now, for its open-field landscape and the inhabitants of all three villages derived their liveli-hood from this land. Cottage industrial activity was negligible and can be discounted as a source of income. Yet only Laneuveville, situated on the plateau, conformed closely to the regional model of a 'pays de grande cul-ture' producing wheat and oats. In 1796 the villagers admitted to owning fifty-four plough horses (a ratio of 1:5 inhabitants), and since the figure was volunteered for the purposes of a military levy it can be treated as an underestimate.[3] Neuviller's farmers produced wheat and oats in abundance, too, but barely half of the quantities harvested by their neighbours on the plateau to judge from the agricultural *statistique* of 1836. Instead they had discovered a vocation for viticulture: from 1770, or thereabouts, an accel-erating process of converting arable strips into vineyards had been under way, with the result that by 1818 the inhabitants would describe themselves as *vignerons* rather than farmers. By the end of the *ancien régime*, the vil-lage territory (*finage*) no longer produced enough bread grain to satisfy

---

[3] Archives Départementales [hereafter A. D.] de Meurthe-et-Moselle, L2943^bis, 20 Thermidor IV.

domestic consumption needs; by 1836 almost half of the surface available
for cultivation had been switched to viticulture. Viewed from an ecological
perspective, the tiny village of Roville might also have found a vocation
in vine cultivation, but the 1836 *statistique* suggests otherwise inasmuch
as it records a mere twentieth of the cultivable land planted under vines.[4]
Rather, the village appears to have adopted a more flexible pattern of arable
husbandry geared to the production of lesser grains (rye, barley, buckwheat)
alongside wheat and oats. Meadows, and in particular sown meadows, covered nearly a quarter of the territory of the village by 1836. This relative
absence of vines combined with a substantial investment in fodder crops
hints at social forces at work. It serves as a reminder that the agricultural
vocation of a village is not a 'given', but is shaped by a variety of factors,
among which the pattern of land holdings figures prominently.

All three villages possessed extensive common land (wooded and pasture)
at the start of our period, that is to say around 1760. Indeed, somewhat more
than a third of Roville's territory was open access pasture and heath, which
helps to explain how the majority of the inhabitants – officially described
as 'landless' in 1768 – were able to survive. At Laneuveville the figure was
lower (around one-fifth), and at Neuviller lower still (between one-sixth and
one-seventh). In each locality, moreover, the villagers would be subjected
to the process known as *triage* in the decades before the Revolution. As
a result they lost a third of these precious assets to their titular seigneurs.
Such transactions between unequals left bitter memories, as the *cahiers
de doléances* would testify. Who owned the remaining 'freehold' property,
and in what proportion, is more difficult to ascertain. But at Neuviller,
the village that is the chief focus of our interest, twenty-eight households
(21 per cent) were entirely without land, and only two resident farmers
owned sufficient to maintain a plough team.[5] There were several absentee
or institutional landowners, notably the prior, but their holdings paled
into insignificance when compared with that of the seigneur (also absent
from his chateau for much of the time). In 1771, that is to say after the
strip consolidation operation and concomitant *triage* (see chapter 7), the
seigneur owned some 238 hectares or, to put it another way, a little over
half of the *finage*. Moreover, his holdings were now grouped into relatively
compact blocks of arable, vines and forest. Significantly, the 'chateau' would
still hold the title to approximately one-third of the territory of the village
more than a hundred years later.

[4] A. D. de Meurthe-et-Moselle, 7M 122*, Statistique, 1836, arrondissement de Nancy.
[5] A. D. de Meurthe-et-Moselle, B 11928.

Plate 2. The modern village of Villepreux

VILLEPREUX

Situated barely 10 kilometres from the royal seat of Versailles, the village of Villepreux lived in the shadow of its large neighbour in more ways than one. Indeed, this close proximity to a large centre of population which would undergo severe problems of social, economic and political read-justment in the years following the outbreak of the Revolution and the departure of the Court makes this case study of more than usual interest. The inhabitants of Villepreux worked a territory that, at 1026 hectares, was more than twice the size of that of Neuviller. Forming part of the Plain of France, it was a 'pays de grande culture' and as such intrinsi-cally fertile. The villagers could be forgiven, however, if they felt alien-ated from this bounteous landscape, which had been altered significantly by the hand of man over the previous century. In 1670 the young king Louis XIV projected the creation of a vast game reserve extending west-wards from his new palace. By 1684 the forty-three-kilometre wall enclosing this 'Grand Parc' was more or less complete and it neatly dissected the ter-ritory of Villepreux into roughly equal halves, as well as enclosing eight other parishes in their entirety. Three of the twenty-three gates in the wall opened directly onto the farmland of Villepreux, including the principal portal, the Porte de Paris, which was located at the entrance to the village (see map 3).

The village itself was nucleated in keeping with the pattern of settlement commonly found in the open-field zones of northern and eastern France. Residual defensive fortifications constructed in the early sixteenth century had no doubt served to reinforce this character, although by the eighteenth century the small *faubourg* of Les Bordes had come into being. The only other inhabited places were four farmsteads located a short distance from the village, two of which had chateaux attached to them. Les Grand' Maisons was the seigneurial abode, but not since 1766 had there been a seigneur in residence, and in any case both the title and the fief of Villepreux passed into the Royal Domain from 1776. Not much further away, albeit on the other side of the wall, lay Rennemoulin, a tiny settlement in its own right despite a population that barely exceeded 100 even at its peak. The inhabitants of Rennemoulin lived in daily contact with those of Villepreux and at different times both the civil and the ecclesiastical authorities considered merging the two villages. Indeed, the parish status of Rennemoulin would succumb in the post-Concordat reorganisation of 1804, although the commune has survived until the present day. Since the farmers and wage workers of Rennemoulin faced problems and sought solutions to those problems that

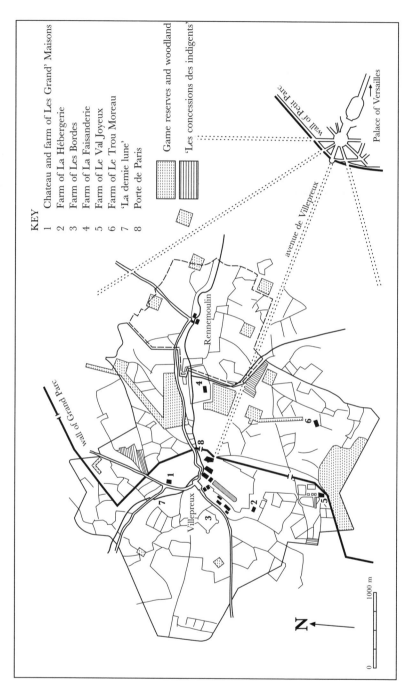

KEY

1 Chateau and farm of Les Grand' Maisons
2 Farm of La Hébergerie
3 Farm of Les Bordes
4 Farm of La Faisanderie
5 Farm of Le Val Joyeux
6 Farm of Le Trou Moreau
7 'La demie lune'
8 Porte de Paris

Game reserves and woodland

'Les concessions des indigents'

Wall of Grand Parc

Villepreux

Rennemoulin

avenue de Villepreux

Wall of Petit Parc

Palace of Versailles

N

0   1000 m

Map 3. Villepreux and Rennemoulin (based on the Carte des Chasses du Roi of 1767–8)

were in every way comparable to the experiences of their close neighbours, they too will feature in this study from time to time.

Although the countryside around Paris exhibited a generally healthy demographic profile (net increase of between 25 per cent and 50 per cent across the eighteenth century),[6] that of Villepreux displayed the symptoms of a fragile and easily undermined social structure. During the first half of the century the population of the village actually declined, a phenomenon that may have been linked to the rerouting of traffic on the main Normandy–Brittany highway. Growth resumed in the second half and carried the population to a peak of around 940 during the early years of the Revolution (see figure 2). But the removal of the Court from Versailles and the collapse of that city's wage-earning economy hit the satellite villages hard. Villepreux would never again see the numerical buoyancy of the 1780s and early 1790s: under-employed labourers and craftsmen drained from the village in search of work in the capital, or else they signed up for service in the army. The economic crisis (inflation followed by deflation) of 1795–8 hit particularly hard and reduced the population to 661, or 711 if soldiers serving on the frontiers are added to the total. Towards the end of the decade a recovery that was sustained into the early years of the Empire took place, but the village remained desperately vulnerable to the slightest economic downturn, as in 1817 when the population plummeted once more to 727.[7] In Rennemoulin, too, the events of the Revolution brusquely curtailed the demographic cycle: from 1791 its population sagged and then stagnated.

Villepreux produced wheat, fodder crops (oats, luzerne) and dairy produce (milk, eggs and butter) in quantities well in excess of those required to feed its resident population. By 1787 some 74 per cent of its territory was given over to arable cultivation, and that figure would rise by a further 6 per cent during the revolutionary decade. Even by the standards of the *généralité* of Paris, therefore, the village was a major player in the market for agricultural produce. Why then were the majority of its inhabitants so poor and vulnerable? The answer is to be found in the pattern of land holding, although the lack of commons and the underdevelopment of cottage industry must count for something as well. Nearly all of the arable land in the parish was grouped into six large farms, four of which were owned by the Royal Domain and leased to tenant farmers. If forest and game covers are included, the king's share alone amounted to a little over half of the territory of the village (522 hectares). This left about fifty

---

[6] Morineau, *Pour une histoire économique vraie*, p. 125.
[7] A. D. des Yvelines, 2LR 111, 2LX 183, 23L 2, 23L 16, 9M 984.

hectares distributed among the remaining two hundred or so households. Needless to say, the majority (72 per cent) owned no land whatsoever.

Compared with those of Neuviller, most of the inhabitants of Villepreux had but a small stake in their own community. Nor could they fall back on the commons, or still vigorous traditions of collective rights, like their counterparts in Lorraine. Yet this kind of loosely meshed and highly polarised social structure was not untypical of villages in the Ile-de-France. On the eve of the Revolution most Versaillais villages contained similar percentages of landless. In Rennemoulin on the other side of the wall, the Royal Domain controlled 69 per cent of the territory (144 hectares) leaving the bulk of the population to manage as best they could on a mere thirteen hectares. In fact most of that which remained belonged to the miller, and 65 per cent of households had no land that they could call their own. There was, moreover, a further factor complicating the lives of tenant farmer and plot holder alike. The Grand Parc teemed with game; indeed, it existed primarily in order to raise and protect game for royal pleasure. Hunting was forbidden and anyone farming land enclosed within the Parc expected higher cultivation costs and yields lower than those applicable to land of equivalent quality located beyond the wall. Indeed, the leases negotiated by the *régisseur* of the Royal Domain acknowledged as much. Arable land in the enclaved portion of Villepreux fetched between a quarter and a third of its intrinsic rental value on the eve of the Revolution owing to the problem of *gibier*.

CHÂTELAUDREN

This village contrasts with those discussed so far in almost every respect. For a start, it lies in Brittany, a province still culturally and institutionally distinct from the rest of northern France at the end of the *ancien régime*. Situated on the linguistic frontier between the 'pays gallo' and the 'pays bretonnant', the medium of day-to-day intercourse for many of its inhabitants was Breton. It is therefore likely that they identified more readily with their locality in its Breton incarnation: Kastel-Aodren. But French influence was never far away: the main Rennes–Brest highway passed their doorsteps and the unmistakably French town of Saint-Brieuc was only fourteen kilometres along the road in an easterly direction. Yet Châtelaudren differed from all the other places covered in this study in another and perhaps more cogent way. It was not an agricultural village, a fact reflected in its meagre territorial base of just forty-seven hectares. Arguably, indeed, it was not even a village, since the vast majority of households made a living from trade and

Plate 3. The village of Châtelaudren, *c.* 1900

industry, or from the supply of professional services. Nevertheless, while the status-conscious elite of Châtelaudren clearly aspired to higher things as the Breton Pre-Revolution got under way, none of the surrounding towns was prepared to grant it civic recognition.

The demography of Brittany reveals some unusual features as well. While the population of the province certainly expanded in keeping with the trend observed nearly everywhere else, the rate of increase was modest (around 10 per cent). That increase, moreover, was chiefly registered during the middle decades of the century: after 1770 it came to a halt and even went into reverse as waves of epidemic disease traversed the province.[8] The lack of hard-and-fast population data for Châtelaudren prior to the Revolution makes it difficult to translate these trends into a local context, but certain facts stand out. A catastrophic flood in 1773 claimed the lives of over thirty villagers, while in the last months of 1779 a widespread outbreak of dysentery decimated their ranks afresh. Certainly, if we reason from the experience of the nearby town of Guingamp, it seems likely that Châtelaudren's population was either stagnant or in regression on the eve of the Revolution. The not particularly reliable census of 1790 recorded around 900 inhabitants (861 plus the *faubourg*), and for the rest of the decade the figure hovered closer to 800 (see figure 2). This decline can probably be attributed to the loss of an important seigneurial jurisdiction whose clientele helped to sustain the shopkeepers and craftworkers of the village. Here as elsewhere, however, matters improved during the period of Napoleonic stabilisation. Traffic started to move more freely along the highway following the cessation of *chouan* activity, and the growth of a relay function brought benefits in terms of investments in village infrastructure. By 1806 the population had climbed back to 867.[9]

Tightly packed onto a pocket-handkerchief of territory carved from the adjacent parish of Plélo, under constant threat of inundation from a pool of water held in place by a grossly inadequate embankment, hemmed in by semi-*bocage* farmland dotted with isolated farmsteads in the manner characteristic of the Breton countryside, Châtelaudren was a topographical anomaly. The village was also a social anomaly, and, as we shall see, it elicited feelings of deep ambivalence in the population of the surrounding rural parishes. For a start, the inhabitants could not feed themselves since they controlled very little land. In 1797 only seven households out of 212

[8] G. Duby and A. Wallon (eds.), *Histoire de la France rurale* (4 vols., Paris, 1975–6), II, pp. 368–9.

[9] A. D. des Côtes-d'Armor, 2E Dépôt 19, 1L 583; [J.]Ogée, *Dictionnaire historique et géographique de la province de Bretagne* (2 vols., Mayenne, 1843 [reprint 1973]), I, p. 175; R.-H. Le Page, *Les Bleus du Châté: histoire des châtelaudrinais sous la Révolution* (Lorient, n.d. [1974]), p. 41.

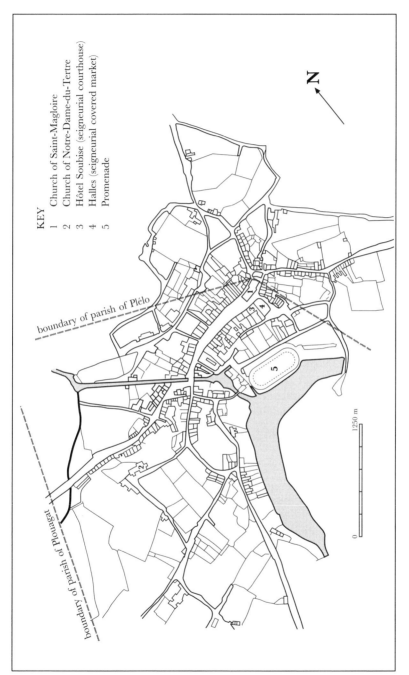

N

KEY
1 Church of Saint-Magloire
2 Church of Notre-Dame-du-Tertre
3 Hôtel Soubise (seigneurial courthouse)
4 Halles (seigneurial covered market)
5 Promenade

boundary of parish of Plélo

boundary of parish of Plouagat

0   1250 m

Map 4. Châtelaudren (based on the cadastre of 1837)

made a living from farming, although a further seventeen put themselves
out to hire in neighbouring parishes. The remainder, logically, relied on
the weekly grain market which, in tandem with the daily flow of goods
and travellers passing along the highway, generated the economic lifeblood
of the village. An occupational profile confirms this reality: alongside the
twenty-four heads of household involved in agriculture we find twenty-
three merchants, eighteen tavern- and innkeepers, twenty-nine craftworkers, a host of domestics, a nucleus of thirteen professional families – most of
which supplied services on behalf of the absentee seigneur – and, unusually,
two titled families 'living nobly'.

SAINT-ALBAN-SUR-LIMAGNOLE

Space was not a problem for the highlanders of Saint-Alban, and torrents of
water were not the natural hazard they lived most in fear of. This remote village located deep in the mountainous hinterland of the southern province
of Languedoc constituted something of a dead-end for travellers. Still some
distance from anything resembling a highway at the end of the *ancien
régime*, it had no market, no post office, nor any institution that might have
attracted attention or consideration. The nearest genuine town was Mende,
some forty kilometres to the south, but access to this subprovincial capital
involved a precipitous downhill journey after first traversing a 1,200-metre
plateau. Much nearer (thirteen kilometres) was Saint-Chély-d'Apcher, a
bourg scarcely different from Saint-Alban in terms of size or appearance. It
was situated on a road capable of carrying wheeled vehicles during the dry
season, however, and in 1790 would become the site of one of the new District administrations. A post office followed not long afterwards. The village
of Saint-Alban hugs the 950-metre contour and owes its existence (and
no doubt its modern name) to a shallow and fairly fertile valley (*limagne*)
that extends to the east. But most of the territory of the community or
parish – the two coincided – lay at higher altitudes (up to 1,400 metres)
stretched along the granite flanks of the Margeride mountain spine.

Space was not a problem because the agro-pastoral economy of the
Margeride has never been able to support a resident population of more
than about twenty-five per square kilometre.[10] Settlement dispersion has
always been the rule, and when the human habitat began to 'thicken' in the
early nineteenth century, it did so on a basis of hamlets not nucleated

[10] *La Margeride: la montagne, les hommes* (Paris, 1983), p. 118; see also A. Fel, 'Notes de géographie humaine sur la montagne de Margeride', in *Mélanges géographiques offerts à Philippe Arbos* (Clermont-Ferrand, 1953), p. 78.

Plate 4. The village of Saint-Alban, c. 1900

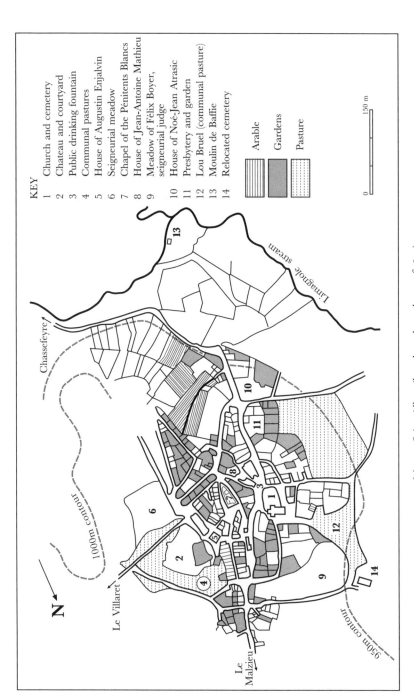

KEY

1 Church and cemetery
2 Chateau and courtyard
3 Public drinking fountain
4 Communal pastures
5 House of Augustin Enjalvin
6 Seigneurial meadow
7 Chapel of the Pénitents Blancs
8 House of Jean-Antoine Mathieu
9 Meadow of Félix Boyer,
   seigneurial judge
10 House of Noé-Jean Atrasic
11 Presbytery and garden
12 Lou Bruel (communal pasture)
13 Moulin de Baffie
14 Relocated cemetery

Arable

Gardens

Pasture

0   150 m

N

Le Villaret

1000m contour

Chassefeyre

Limagnole stream

950m contour

Le
Malzieu

Map 5. Saint-Alban (based on the cadastre of 1827)

villages. This is a type of habitat that we have not encountered hitherto, and it tended to throw up problems and responses to problems that simply never arose in villages, and between villages, encamped on the flat and neatly ordered lands of the north and east. Even by the standards of the Margeride, however, the 'community of inhabitants' of Saint-Alban controlled an exceptionally far-flung territory of some 7,244 hectares. So much so that the in-coming revolutionary administrators were willing to make Saint-Alban a 'canton' in its own right with the addition of just one, much smaller, locality. But 'control' and 'territory' are ambiguous terms in this particular context. The community/parish of Saint-Alban numbered about 2,000 souls in 1790, of whom around 800 lived in the village proper. The remainder resided in thirty hamlets for want of a better term, and some of these settlements were up to ten kilometres from the parish church. Although civil and ecclesiastical territory was supposedly indivisible (notwithstanding a decision by the bishop to allow the most distant settlements to construct a chapel-of-ease), each hamlet jealously guarded its own 'ecological territory', that is to say forest, water-courses and, above all, communal pastures.

In this part of the Gévaudan (subprovince of Languedoc) population densities were linked closely to the fortunes of the domestic woollen industry. Nearly every farm contained a loom for the manufacture of rough fabrics known as *serges* and *cadis*, as lease contracts bear witness; but this substantial rural industry was on the wane by the time the Revolution erupted. The high decades had been the 1750s and the 1760s, and there are clear indications that the population of the village, and probably also that of the outlying hamlets of Saint-Alban, entered a phase of decline after this period. Enumerators counted 403 households in the parish in 1766, but only 318 in 1788. Unfortunately there is no reliable way of calculating the distribution of the population, although occupational analysis suggests that the main losses occurred in Saint-Alban proper. If the estimate of 800 can be taken as roughly accurate, Saint-Alban appears to have vegetated in the 1790s and early 1800s (see figure 2). There may have been a population recovery in the parish at large from the time of the Empire, but the prefect of the Lozère on a visit of inspection in 1813 still found only around 800 inhabitants in the *bourg*. And in any case, the recovery was sharply curtailed by a damaging three-year cycle of harvest shortfalls beginning with hailstorms in the summer of 1815. When the overall population of the parish in 1820 – the end of our period – is compared with the total for 1790, the picture is close to one of stagnation.[11]

---

[11] Archives Nationales [hereafter A. N.], B^{a}51, F^{16}970, F^{20}212; A. D. de la Lozère, C 62, M 11853, 59V2, 2Z 1; *Almanach historique, politique et économique du département de la Lozère pour l'an IX*

The harvest shortfalls of the late Empire and early Restoration were so damaging precisely because the resources provided by cottage textile manufacture had dwindled away. In effect the village was reaffirming its agro-pastoral vocation, as a producer of cereals for domestic consumption in a marginal landscape. Although the high pastures were fit only for sheep, whether the flocks of local farmers or those of transhumant shepherds, neither altitude nor granite subsoil posed an insuperable obstacle to the cultivation of rye. The danger came rather from winter snow cover inadequate to protect sowings from frost, and also from summer hailstorms. Rye was the hallmark of 'petite culture', of course. Its presence is a reminder that we have travelled far beyond the northern and northeastern plains where agricultural practices more closely resembled those of England and the Low Countries than those of the rest of France. In Saint-Alban mule trains were still used for moving goods at the end of the *ancien régime*, horses were an unusual sight and were never used for farm work. Ploughing was undertaken by bullocks and even cows, which were quite incapable of the traction exerted by a four-, six- or eight-horse team working the heavy clays of Lorraine. On the other hand the thin boulder-strewn soils of the Margeride scarcely tolerated deep ploughing, and when an enlarged arable surface was required it could usually be obtained by employing slash-and-burn methods (*écobuage*).

In common with many southern villages, Saint-Alban was dominated by a bourgeois elite (approximately a dozen households) which lorded over the rest of the population when not engrossed in internecine quarrels. There were no nobles apart from the seigneur, who came to reside permanently in his chateau from 1789 onwards and who played a full part in the life of the community. The seigneurie or 'barony' of Saint-Alban exercised jurisdiction chiefly in the form of a right of *censive* applicable to the arable territory of fifty-two surrounding hamlets. Although surviving lease documents make mention of up to seven seigneurial farms, it is clear that these *censives* constituted the most valuable source of income (see p. 71). Collection was usually subcontracted to local bourgeois who also took turns staffing the seigneurial assize court. Before 1789 the bourgeoisie and the seigneurie cooperated to mutual advantage, therefore, although this did not prevent a rift from opening once the news of the 'abolition' of feudalism came through. Alongside this bourgeoisie should be ranked a more numerous *ménager* class, most of whom farmed their possessions in person. Although matching the notaries, attorneys, bailiffs and sundry writ-servers in terms

de la République (1800 et 1801 vieux style) (Mende, n.d.); B. Bardy, 'Les Tournées du préfet Gamot (suite)', *Revue du Gévaudan*, 1955, 63.

of economic muscle, they generally played second fiddle, either because they lacked the leisure and linguistic skills to play a public role, or because they resided outside the *bourg*. The rest of the population lived in more or less endemic hardship. Few, if any, households were entirely without access to land, it is true, and in this respect there is a contrast to be drawn with the small fry of plains villages such as Villepreux. However, a pocket-handkerchief of arable and the chance to put a cow or a few sheep on the common did not make for a living, particularly in an environment where opportunities for wage labour were severely limited. This is why the decline in the market for rough woollens was felt so keenly, and it is noticeable that householders recorded as 'weavers' in the tax rolls of the 1750s often reappear under the heading 'day labourers' some thirty years later. If work could not be found locally, the menfolk migrated from the village in search of it as soon as the autumn sowings had been completed.

ALLAN

Travellers heading south along the A7 motorway catch a glimpse of Allan as the carriageway deviates in order to skirt round Montélimar. Looking east they will notice the ruins of a fortified village embedded in a nearby escarpment. The fact that no modern line of communication approaches the village speaks volumes, for Allan is a place that has experienced a crisis of identity. The climax occurred in 1857 when it was decided to abandon the hilltop site and to relocate the village in the plain, closer to the then main road. In reality, though, this highly controversial decision of the municipal council had been impending since the 1820s; it was, moreover, just the final act in a long-running saga of identity lost and identity regained.

In 1789 Allan depended on the small town of Grignan some twenty kilometres to the southwest to all administrative and judicial intents and purposes. This, despite the fact that Montélimar, the economic hub of the district, lay only a short distance to the north. Why the anomaly? Because Allan, Grignan and twelve other localities formed part of a greater anomaly known as the 'Terres Adjacentes de Provence', that is to say a block of territory that looked to Aix, took orders from Aix and considered itself indistinguishable from the Provençal 'nation', even though it was entirely enclaved within the province of the Dauphiné. Ecologically speaking, it is true that Allan belonged more properly to Provence than to the Dauphiné, but the origins of the Terres Adjacentes do not lie in this quarter. Rather they can be found in political feuds dating back to the thirteenth century. Nevertheless, the Terres Adjacentes managed to cling on to substantial fiscal

Plate 5. The abandoned village (*castrum*) of Allan

privileges until near the end of the *ancien régime* (see pp. 79–80). As a result the process of unification of 1788–90, in which all villages participated to some degree, was for Allan more than usually tortuous. Barely had the villagers reasoned their withdrawal from the Provençal 'nation' in favour of a union with the Dauphiné, than a new identity freshly minted by the National Assembly swept away all provincial allegiances of whatever complexion or antiquity.

While the inhabitants of Allan lived in conditions of some confinement behind well-maintained curtain walls, they exerted control over a very considerable territory of some 2,871 hectares. This territory was undergoing a steady repopulation in the seventeenth and eighteenth centuries as considerations of comfort and access began to outweigh the imperative of defence. Indeed, the issue of accessibility (to cultivated land, to the church, to the road) would be the central plank in the argument of those who campaigned for relocation. In the early seventeenth century the vast majority of villagers still lived in the *castrum*, although the outlying seigneurial farms (*granges*) were showing signs of developing into miniature hamlets. A century later the habitat had thickened to include five hamlets as well as twenty-three so-called *granges*. By 1792 there seem to have been over forty-five inhabited places quite apart from the *castrum* and the hamlets, and by 1806 108. Since population totals did not increase to any significant degree across the period in question, it is difficult to avoid the conclusion that villagers had been voting with their feet for quite some time before the fateful decision of the municipal council. A recently undertaken archaeological survey of the 'vieux village', as it is now called, indicates that it once contained about 150 houses, but we know that only 125 were occupied in 1792, which suggests that at that date around 500 people lived in the *castrum* and some 300 in dispersed settlements down on the plain. Sustained population growth finally began to register during the Empire – here as elsewhere – and by 1835 only 300 out of a total head count of 1,124 continued to reside in the old village (see figure 2).[12]

To what use was this extensive and undercolonised territory put? Scrub woodland of a Provençal type (i.e. Mediterranean pines and evergreen oaks) is the constant factor in land-use statistics across our period. It covered approximately half of the area in question and served as a battleground where the community and the seigneur tested their respective rights. Since the jurisprudence of the Parlement of Aix disallowed *vaine pâture*, pasturage was always at a premium. Even today forest and scrub continues to occupy around half of the surface area of the commune. The lack of irrigation and seasonal drought impeded the development of natural grassland, let alone

[12] A. D. de la Drôme, L 204, 51V 66, 53V 1; Archives Communales [hereafter A. C.] d'Allan, RV 27; M. Delacroix, *Statistique du département de la Drôme* (Valence, 1835), pp. 420–1; *Paroisses et communes de France: Drôme* (Paris, 1981); H.-F. Orband, *Villages fortifiés de la Drôme: histoire d'Allan en Provence* (Taulignan, 1990), pp. 26, 76.

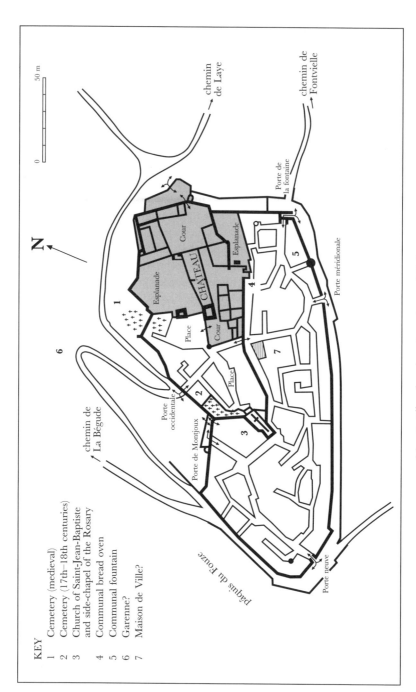

KEY

1 Cemetery (medieval)
2 Cemetery (17th–18th centuries)
3 Church of Saint-Jean-Baptiste
   and side-chapel of the Rosary
4 Communal bread oven
5 Communal fountain
6 Garenne?
7 Maison de Ville?

N

0   50 m

Esplanade

Cour

CHATEAU

Cour

Place

Esplanade

Place

Porte occidentale

Porte de Montjoux

Porte de
la fontaine

Porte méridionale

Porte neuve

chemin
de Laye

chemin de
Fontvielle

chemin de
La Bégude

Pâquis du Fouze

1

6

2

3

4

5

7

Map 6. Allan (based on the cadastre of 1811)

fodder crops. Indeed, even drinking water could be in short supply during the summer months. The local economy therefore relied on cereal agriculture, on vines and on the cultivation of mulberries whose leaves provided the sole source of nourishment for the silkworm. However, the balance between these activities altered markedly in the course of the eighteenth century. Rye was the principal subsistence crop since it coped with the dry conditions better than any other bread grain, but, while we can work out the quantities being harvested by the end of the *ancien régime*, the trend during the preceding decades remains far from clear. The question is relevant because all the signs point to a considerable expansion of the areas planted under vines during the course of the century. In volume terms wine production more than tripled between 1745 and 1789. As at Neuviller, therefore, it is likely that a process of land conversion was under way.

The economy of Allan remained better balanced than that of Neuviller, however, because it was more diversified. Even in 1789 the village could grow almost enough cereals to meet its subsistence needs, always assuming that the yield of the harvest was not exported from the community. Wine and silkworm cocoons performed the same function as domestic woollen maufacture in the Gévaudan, that is to say they generated the wherewithal to meet immediate cash needs such as debt repayments and quarterly tax bills. The villagers were not immune to short-term crisis, however. The hardship of 1788–9, they explained in their *cahier de doléances*, stemmed from a combination of stagnating wine prices and a reduction in the cocoon harvest following the destruction of the mulberry plantations by frost. In such conditions attention inevitably turned towards those who it was felt were extracting profit from the community without supplying anything in return, in this instance the seigneur. Although the pattern of land holding cannot be reconstructed in any detail, the *cahier* tells us that the absentee seigneur of Allan owned the six best farms in the territory, making her far and away the largest proprietor. In 1790 erstwhile seigneurial property bore 51 per cent of the total tax load of the community. Unlike the barony of Saint-Alban, however, the major and most reliable source of seigneurial income in Allan was the *réserve*, that is to say landed possessions put out to lease. Even so, harvest dues and rights were by no means negligible. The land area left over once seigneurial possessions have been subtracted was shared between some 252 resident households since there were no other institutional or absentee landowners of any substance. Eleven households (4 per cent) paid either no tax at all in 1792 or insufficient to qualify for the vote, which must surely mean that they were landless to all intents and purposes. Of the remainder, 96 per cent declared an income from land of under 100 *livres*, which suggests that we are dealing with a highly compact social structure.

The most arresting feature of the social make-up of Allan, however, was the absence of a bourgeoisie of skilled professionals. Once upon a time the village had been replete with resident lawyers, attorneys and businessmen, or so the *cahier* asserted. By 1789, though, there remained just a couple of priests, a barber-surgeon, one substantial merchant and a small number of self-sufficient peasant farmers (*ménagers*) who were a cut above the rest. This absence of a mediating class of legally trained professionals hampered the villagers' dealings with established sources of authority. It prevented the seigneurie from 'taking root' in the community inasmuch as there existed no locally based elite with a vested interest in its preservation, and it may also help us to understand how the villagers could move swiftly from a posture of submission to one of outright revolt. The lack of resident expertise also resulted in some mismanagement of community affairs and a tendency towards overreliance on outside 'intercessors'. The only other point worth noting at this stage is that the village was divided by religion. Notwithstanding the Revocation of the Edict of Nantes in 1685, approximately 15 per cent of the population continued to adhere to the Reformed faith and contrived to practise their religion by one means or another. In this respect Allan stands apart from the other villages on which our study is based. Yet as we shall see, the religious divide did not make a major difference to the political apprehensions of the bulk of the population.

ROQUELAURE

Roquelaure, the ancestral seat of the dukes of that name, was the most thoroughly agricultural of our six villages. It lies seventy-eight kilometres to the west of Toulouse, the regional capital of the far southwest, and nine kilometres north of the episcopal town of Auch, amid the low hills flanking the river Gers. We are dealing with a Gascon village, therefore, and one in which Gascon was the language used for everyday intercourse during the period covered by this study. The village occupies a hilltop position and in 1789 was fortified, although not on the scale of Allan. Most of the dwellings were aligned along a slender finger of relatively level ground adjacent to the church and the chateau. While the crypt of the church still housed the tombs of the dukes, the feudal chateau no longer served a residential purpose. When visiting their estates, the seigneurs of the eighteenth century preferred to lodge in a more recently constructed chateau situated a short distance to the northeast. A small *faubourg* extended the perimeter of the

Plate 6. The modern village of Roquelaure

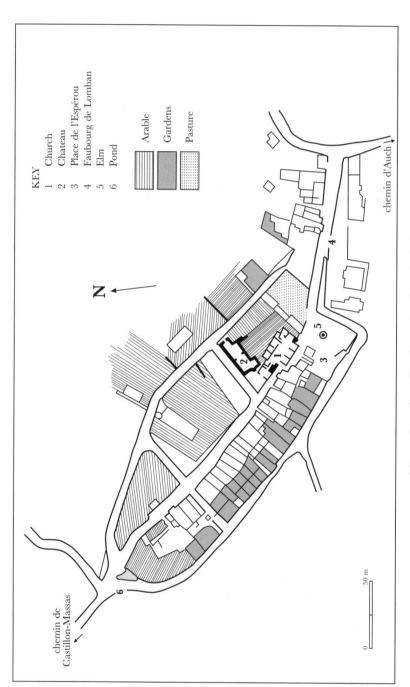

KEY

1 Church
2 Chateau
3 Place de l'Espérou
4 Faubourg de Lomban
5 Elm
6 Pond

Arable
Gardens
Pasture

N

chemin de
Castillon-Massas

chemin d'Auch

0   50 m

Map 7. Roquelaure (based on a plan drawn in 1855)

village in a westerly direction, but a traveller arriving from Auch would have observed a countryside dotted with farmsteads long before he caught sight of the village proper. These farmsteads, known as *métairies*, were a typical feature of the landscape of the Haut-Armagnac. In origin they resembled the seigneurial *granges* of Provence, except that they were under sharecrop tenancy and were highly visible one to another. So, while the 1,825 hectare territory of the community of Roquelaure exhibited unmistakable signs of habitat dispersion, we are scarcely dealing with a *bocage* landscape. The undulating ploughland of the *métairies* was demarcated by ditches, hedges and occasional stands of timber.

The proportion of the population actually residing in the village is not easy to determine in the absence of detailed census data. In 1760 an un-named official of the Intendance in Auch declared scornfully that the village 'amounts to little more than fifteen houses most of which are abandoned and in ruin', but this is clearly a partisan judgement that needs to be read in a different context (see pp. 75–6). Nevertheless, it would be surprising if the level of concentration exceeded 40 per cent, in view of the number of *métairies* and the fact that at least five of them had 'thickened' into substantial hamlets in the course of the eighteenth century. If the parish numbered 800 inhabitants (i.e. 180 households) in 1789, a maximum of about 300 residing in the village proper seems about right. On the other hand we do know that Roquelaure shared in the economic and demographic buoyancy of the *généralité* of Auch during the third quarter of the century.[13] Between 1741 and the end of the *ancien régime*, the population of the parish rose by 30 per cent (see figure 2). Most of this increase must have occurred in the 1760s and early 1770s, though, during the period of high grain prices and major improvements to the road infrastructure. The 1780s were a stagnant decade by comparison, and the population of the village and of its surrounding settlements would not start to edge upwards again until the revolutionary climacteric had passed.[14]

With no common land to speak of, and little forest, the territory of the village was substantially given over to arable cultivation. Nearly all farmers planted wheat in preference to any other cereal since roughly half the arable surface passed muster as being of 'good' quality, and only a quarter as 'substandard'. And wheat, as landowners were all too aware, was a cash crop that could easily be marketed thanks to the nearby 'route d'Espagne', that is to say the highway running from Auch to Agen, the Garonne and places

[13] Morineau, *Pour une histoire économique vraie*, p. 125.
[14] A. N., NN 96/2; A. D. du Gers, C 22, 6M 33, 6M 977, 3P 42; G. Saint-Martin, *L'Histoire, la vie: Roquelaure près d'Auch, village de Gascogne* (Miélan, n.d. [1983]), p. 241.

beyond. In 1804, therefore, we find wheat accounting for 92 per cent of the annual cereal harvest. Unlike Saint-Alban or Allan, rye scarcely registered in popular consciousness. Wheat was not the only production, however, even if it accounted for two-thirds of the total by value. The community produced some wine and also hay from meadows bordering the Gers and the Talouch stream in quantities that exceeded local consumption needs. Cottage industry, on the other hand, seems to have been negligible both in Roquelaure and in neighbouring communities, which serves to underline the point that we are dealing with a solidly agricultural village situated in a district where the whole economy turned on ground rent. Arthur Young grasped as much on his arrival in Auch in August 1787: 'the town is almost without manufactures or commerce, and is supported chiefly by the rents of the country'.[15]

The easy proximity of Roquelaure to the ecclesiastical capital of Auch explains a lot about life and labour in the village both before and during the Revolution. For a start, there were no fewer than seventeen *forains* (nonresident landowners) extracting rent, four of whom were of noble birth and most of whom lived in Auch. Land classified as 'noble' (since we are in a region of *taille réelle*) totalled about 7 per cent of the territory of the village, and in 1789 most of it belonged to the seigneur (also noble and ordinarily resident in Toulouse).[16] The seigneur owned 'commoner' land as well, however, in the shape of seven sharecrop farms (*métairies)*. Who owned what remained is unclear, not least because it is difficult to disentangle – in quantitative terms – the holdings of the other *forains* from those of the residents. But one fact does seem reasonably well established: the bulk of the land was partitioned into *métairies*; before the Revolution there were relatively few plots and parcels left over for artisans and agricultural labourers.

Heavy surplus extraction via the mechanism of rent is therefore the salient characteristic of this locality. In none of the other villages was sharecropping much in evidence. Cash tenancy had long prevailed on the plain of Allan, whereas the highland farmers of Saint-Alban tended to settle their six-year leases in kind for the most part (cereals, cheese, cloth). It is true that some archaic forms of land tenure were practised in the neighbourhood of Châtelaudren (see p. 96), but in Neuviller and Villepreux sharecropping was completely unknown. Moreover, in none of the other localities were villagers required to pay the ecclesiastical tithe at a rate in excess of 10 per cent. On the eve of the Revolution a movement of resistance (see pp. 114–15) secured a reduction in the tithe of Roquelaure from 12.5 per cent

---

[15] A. Young, *Travels in France during the Years 1787, 1788 and 1789*, ed. M. Betham-Edwards (London, 1976), p. 54.
[16] A. D. du Gers, C 76.

to 10 per cent, but the villagers of Allan gave up only 3.3 per cent of their harvest and those of Saint-Alban 6.7 per cent. In Neuviller and Villepreux the 'take' was higher (9.1 per cent and 8 per cent respectively). Sharecropping and tithe farming, then, were omnipresent features of collective life in the village of Roquelaure. Cropper households constituted very nearly one-third of the parish in 1836, a proportion that is unlikely to have altered very much across the revolutionary watershed and that corresponds to the norm for the department. If farm servants are included in the reckoning, it seems safe to assume that the *métairies* occupied roughly half of the population. The tithe farmers, or proctors, were mostly drawn from the local bourgeoisie (about the intermediate group, the artisans, we know very little). In this respect the analogy of Saint-Alban is more relevant than that of Allan, for in 1789 it is possible to identify about fifteen resident 'demi-bourgeois', all heavily engaged in maintaining the power structures of the *ancien régime*. Many combined the familiar collecting functions (tax, tithe, rent, dues, etc.) with employment in the seigneurial court, and they took it in turns to represent the community as *sindic, consul* or *jurat*.

Can six villages drawn from a potential choice of around 40,000 provide conclusive answers to the big questions that have preoccupied historians of the early modern countryside in the age of the French Revolution? Plainly not: all we can hope to do is to capture a range of experiences. But the selection of our case studies is by no means eccentric (as should be evident by now); nor is it in any fundamental sense 'unrepresentative'. Our villages span the landscapes of the *ancien régime* and embrace, in large measure, its cultural and institutional diversity. It is to be hoped that they will serve as a prism through which we will be able to view the behaviour of a generation of French men and women as they came to terms with the collapse of one socio-juridical order and participated in the effort to put another in its place. With a maximum size of one thousand inhabitants, all six villages satisfy the requirements for what ethnographers call 'face-to-face' societies, which is surely appropriate since rural France has long been characterised by short-range social contact and mobility. Even today three-quarters of *communes* – the linear descendants of our villages – contain fewer than 500 inhabitants. In such localities individuals were bonded together in multiple and overlapping ways: they were neighbours and kinsmen, they borrowed agricultural tools, lent plough-teams, grain, money, and so on. In short they knew each other, and each other's business. The very complexity of these relationships imparted a special character to the political life of the village, and we shall need to keep in mind that beneath the official politics of the *procès-verbal* there existed a politics of informality and orality rooted in space and sound, custom and practice. Face-to-face societies were not of necessity consensual, however; and in one instance, as we shall see, it would be more exact to think in terms of a 'back-to-back' society, such was the degree of fear and distrust.

Political choices, whether collective or individual, consensual or conflictual, would be arrived at by many different routes, then. No single model or template is likely to accommodate what we shall find. Nevertheless, there were certain conditioning factors with a wider purchase and one of these was distance. Contrary to the bundle of images associated with the notion of 'la France profonde', the countryside was neither remote, nor inaccessible, nor intrinsically refractory. Indeed, the village had never been more accessible than on the eve of the Revolution. The number of post offices more than doubled during the course of the eighteenth century. By 1789 there were 1,320 and the map of their distribution reveals no obvious gaps in the network. The efforts of successive revolutionary legislatures would add another 150 or so, with the result that by 1795 the maximum time that it took to transmit a letter from Paris to any other part of the country was eleven days. Moreover, travelling times had been dramatically reduced during the final decades of the *ancien régime*. In 1765 a fast coach took thirteen days to cover the 583 kilometres between Paris and Bordeaux, and fifteen days to reach Toulouse (709 kilometres). By 1780 these journey times had been reduced to five and eight days respectively. On good roads, in fact, a man in a hurry (i.e. on horseback) could cover over 100 kilometres a day: the news of the taking of the Bastille somehow managed to reach Bordeaux within forty-six hours, while the citizens of Toulouse were apprised of their king's flight within three days of the news breaking in Paris.

On the other hand not all roads were equally good, not all villages were linked to post roads, and the news did not always come from the direction of Paris. The villagers of Neuviller seem to have heard about the stopping of the king at Varennes before they learned of his flight from Paris. Their confusion can only be guessed at. News also travelled at different speeds depending on its urgency, relevance and, not least, the linguistic idiom in which it was expressed. Located some 370 kilometres from the capital, Neuviller usually waited upon Nancy in order to learn of events of nationwide importance; and since the province of Lorraine boasted one of the best maintained road networks in the kingdom (see pp. 80–1), this could mean a time delay of as little as three days. Châtelaudren was also extremely well connected. Throughout the Revolution the villagers revealed themselves to be consistently and accurately informed about parliamentary debates, notwithstanding the 473 kilometres separating them from Paris. Of course receptivity must count for something, too. The Châtelaudrinais were patriots almost to a man; they *wanted* to know what was going on and made it their business to find out. That said, post coaches could deliver the latest news to their doorstep in about three and a half days.

Distance posed a greater problem in the south of the country, under-standably enough, as did terrain. The dissemination of news laterally from nodal points on the arterial post roads worked less effectively. As a result villages were often by-passed and in consequence forced to rely on round-about routes for access to information. For instance, Paris news might reach Auch and its surrounding villages via Toulouse; thus Roquelaure at 790 kilometres from the capital might wait for up to eight days before being put in the picture. The same applies to Allan (616 kilometres). Usually the Paris mail coach travelling down the Rhône valley reached the 'auberge du Pélican' – the nearest relay station – in about six days, but the established link between the Terres Adjacentes and the city of Aix sometimes brought the news in from the south (i.e. via Salon and Grignan) instead. And depending on the season, transhumant shepherds could pass on information far more quickly than any post chaise. Allan was, after all, completely inaccessible to wheeled transportation.

Of the localities explored in this study Saint-Alban alone is likely to have faced a significant problem when trying to keep in touch, and several reasons can be identified. For a start, geography and climate tended to isolate the whole of the Gévaudan from the main axes of north–south com-munication. By the end of the *ancien régime* coaches could, with difficulty, cover the 570 kilometres separating Saint-Chély-d'Apcher from Paris in eight days, but that was in the dry season. In the winter, journey times could double; moreover, communication southwards was harder still because the post roads of the Midi and those of the Auvergne did not connect. Anyone wishing to travel from Mende to Narbonne by wheeled transport in winter (a distance of 120 kilometres as the crow flies) was obliged to pass via Nîmes, and the journey demanded at least ten days. Saint-Alban lay beyond both Saint-Chély and Mende, of course. But in this instance the problems associated with information flow were exacerbated by habitat. Once despatches had been unloaded from the mail coach, they would be distributed by messenger service to nearby villages. Parish priests and/or mayors then took over the task of onward transmission and, in normal circumstances, they held on to information until it could be broadcast orally at either the Sunday Mass or perhaps the *décadi* assembly. The inhabitants of the outlying hamlets tended, therefore, to receive the news at fixed intervals and perhaps a week or so later than the inhabitants of the *bourg*. Or to put the problem another way, in a thinly populated habitat it could take as long for news to travel ten kilometres by word of mouth as it did for news to travel 500 kilometres by mail coach. Only at Villepreux (Versailles ten kilometres, Paris thirty kilometres) were the speeds of transmission roughly comparable (four to eight hours).

It helped, of course, if country dwellers could understand what they were being told, or invited to read. Language fluency and literacy must therefore be ranked among the factors conditioning behaviour in the village. At Roquelaure (or 'Roquolaouro' in the local idiom) the parish priest habitually spoke Gascon when preaching to, or catechising, the young. He discontinued the practice in 1776, however, perhaps in response to ecclesiastical orders, and as a result a nodding acquaintance with the French tongue seems to have developed among a proportion of the villagers. Understanding complex ideas expressed in French remained an unmanageable proposition for the majority of the population, though, and the issue of language finally came to a head in a session of the local Jacobin club held on 20 Nivôse II/9 January 1794. Monolingual Gascon speakers pushed for acceptance of a motion that the Society's proceedings be conducted henceforth in the native idiom. But they were resisted by the mayor, a member of the bilingual bourgeois elite, who pointed out that the armies of the Republic spoke French and that the manoeuvres of the National Guard were also carried out in that tongue. Cowed by this intervention, the clubists settled for a solution that, one suspects, was distinctly second best. Proceedings would continue in French, but with the mayor providing a summary in Gascon of all major items of legislation, of Departmental circulars, and of instructions from the *représentants-en-mission* in case anyone should presume to claim that they did not understand what was going on. As the minutes put it, 'pour que personne n'en prétende cauze d'ignorance il en faira le rézumé en Gascon'.[17]

This anecdote both alerts us to the language problem and hints at some of its implications for village political culture. Similar scenes may well have been played out in Saint-Alban and in Allan; and in the neighbourhood of Châtelaudren, we know, the courts kept interpreters at the ready. Even in Lorraine the linguistic factor should not be discounted. The schoolmasters of Roville and Laneuveville would both report the rapid decline of the archaic form of the French language widely spoken in Lorraine, but their comments date from 1888. Only in Villepreux is it safe to assume that the documents available to us capture the authentic tones of the 'peasant voice', albeit spasmodically. As map 8 indicates, spoken French was still a minority

---

[17] A. D. du Gers, L 699*.

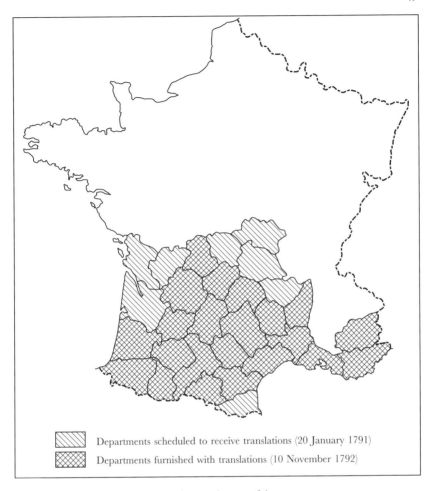

Departments scheduled to receive translations (20 January 1791)

Departments furnished with translations (10 November 1792)

Map 8. Vernacular translations of decrees, 1791–2

language in large areas of the countryside in 1789, but in Villepreux, at least, it was the only language spoken. The problem of transmission was not complicated by linguistic dissonance between well-to-do and ordinary villagers. Only when it was pointed out that linguistic particularism might give rise to other, more noxious, forms of particularism, did the revolutionaries pause to consider the question. As a result steps were taken to make translations of the more important decrees available in local idioms throughout much of the southwest and south of the country. In Auch, for example, the Departmental authorities were supported in their efforts to

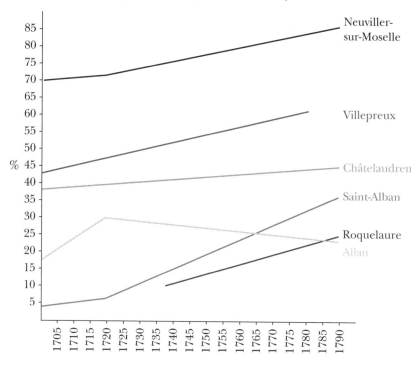

Figure 3a. Functional literacy (males) in case-study villages

communicate with sharecroppers through the medium of Gascon. Yet the initiative was misplaced in several respects. Apart from anything else, there was little evidence that non-French vernacular tongues sustained a mentality of separatism that might pose a threat to the interests of the Republic One and Indivisible. The inhabitants of Roquelaure were no less patriotic than those of Villepreux because they habitually spoke Gascon. And if the highlanders of Saint-Alban never evinced more than lukewarm attachment to the Revolution, linguistic isolation played only a minor and non-essential role in the equation, as we shall see. Language was not a barrier in truth: it was a filter.

The problem, if problem there was, lay rather at one remove. A proclamation drafted in Gascon or in Occitan and nailed to the church door was no more accessible than one printed in French to a population that was unable to read. Literacy can be measured in many different ways and in the eighteenth and early nineteenth centuries it was not usual for the skills of reading and writing to be acquired in tandem. Moreover, those among the general population who acquired such skills tended to acquire them

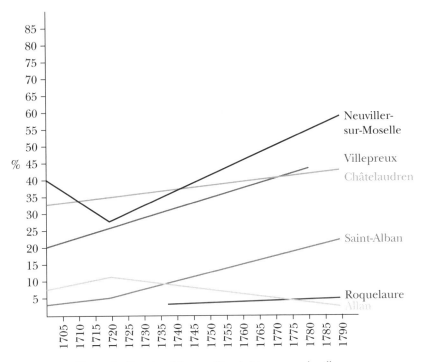

Figure 3b. Functional literacy (females) in case-study villages

incompletely. Reading might be restricted to certain 'set texts' (a missal, a bible, a notarial deed), and writing to the ability to trace a signature for the purpose of authenticating legal documents. Defining and then measuring literacy is therefore a matter for some discussion among historians, but even if we confine our approach to a simple count of the frequency with which marriage partners signed the parish register, it is evident that a differential geography of functional literacy existed at the end of the *ancien régime*. Broadly speaking, the Revolution erupted in a society that can be divided by a diagonal drawn from Saint-Malo situated on the Channel coast to Geneva. To the north and east of this fictional frontier more than half of adult males could read (something) and write (something), whereas to the south and west more than two-thirds could do neither.

How do our villages compare in this respect? Parish registers for all six have survived, although with gaps and other shortcomings. On the whole they confirm the overall picture inasmuch as they reveal a culture of illiteracy pervading the south, southwest and, to a lesser extent, the west (see figures 3a and 3b). By the end of the *ancien régime* nearly all of the menfolk of Neuviller whose marriage bans were published in the parish responded positively when invited to sign the register, whereas nearly 63 per cent of male marriage partners left no trace whatsoever in the parish registers of Saint-Alban.[18] There is some evidence to suggest that this latter figure might be adjusted downwards in order to allow for clerical error and negligence. The parish registers of the Gévaudan are notoriously defective and a spot check of marriage contracts recorded before notaries yields a better harvest of signatures. Nonetheless, in Allan the frequency of signatures is also low, and here the *curé* performed his duties as recording officer far more conscientiously. The data compiled for Roquelaure (75 per cent of male marriage partners unable to sign)[19] point in the same direction: a sharply contrasting geography of illiteracy as between the south and the north, and one that would not significantly alter before the second half of the nineteenth century. Clearly the traits of this particular landscape were deeply embedded; in the absence of state intervention to provide primary schools – something that the revolutionaries talked about incessantly but failed on the whole to deliver – it simply endured. Although the levels of functional literacy improved in all six villages between 1700 and 1789, the pattern remained the same. The same is true of female literacy: in Allan, Roquelaure and Saint-Alban it was negligible, but between a third and two-thirds of the brides of Villepreux, Neuviller and Châtelaudren managed to craft their signatures on the eve of the Revolution.

What weight should we attach to literacy as a conditioning factor in the final analysis? For historians engaged upon the study of large-scale social and cultural processes, the spread of literacy offers a tempting explanatory model. According to the authors of the influential *Histoire de la France rurale*, the substantial trend towards increasing village literacy in the eighteenth century may well have sapped the *ancien régime* from within and brought to maturity an embryonic political consciousness.[20] A plausible generalisation no doubt, but micro-historians have to work to a narrower and more demanding remit. Among other things, we must remember that the measurement of literacy at the level of the village rests on a methodological weakness. Does a signature, often crudely constructed, denote access to a wider written culture? Even if it does, the evidence gathered for our six villages scarcely amounts to a dramatic literacy breakthrough. Those localities already 'literate' at the start of the eighteenth century remained

---

[18] A. D. de Meurthe-et-Moselle, AC 398 1; A. D. de la Lozère, E Dépôt Saint-Alban: 132 (GG1), E Dépôt Saint-Alban: 132 (GG7).
[19] A. D. du Gers, 5E 552.
[20] See Duby and Wallon (eds.), *Histoire de la France rurale*, II, p. 534.

so at its end, whereas the oral and predominantly patois-speaking environment characteristic of southern villages seems to have retained its cohesion
thanks to the mediating abilities of bilingual elites. In any case it would
be unwise to draw too close a parallel between literacy and politicisation.
Villagers managed to keep themselves informed whether they lived eighty
or 800 kilometres from Paris, whether they could or could not read notices pinned onto the church door. Their political 'maturity' seems to have
developed less by a process of steady cultural osmosis than by leaps and
bounds, most notably during the crisis of 1788–9.

CHAPTER 2

The structures of village life towards the end of the ancien régime

If village life really had become moribund by the end of the *ancien régime*, as Alexis de Tocqueville argued,[1] it becomes quite difficult to explain the collective vigour and spontaneity which ordinary French people displayed for much of the revolutionary decade. No doubt he would have recognised the problem had the second volume of his famous study ever taken on permanent shape. Indeed, the failure to complete the work may amount to a tacit acknowledgement of the frailties embedded in the original thesis. What is this thesis? As far as the village is concerned, Tocqueville makes five bold assertions which lead him to the general conclusion that state centralisation had become all-embracing and stifling. First, he suggests that whilst villagers had once possessed representative institutions, these amounted to little more than a hollow shell by the time of the Revolution. Second, he argues that local administrative superstructures had decayed to the point where most villagers possessed no more than a *sindic* and a tax collector. Third, he claims that titular seigneurs had withdrawn from the management of the village completely, although they still had the capacity to impede the smooth running of parish life by virtue of their privileged status. Fourth, he depicts the eighteenth-century village as depleted of its natural leaders, the rural bourgeoisie having decamped to the towns. Nevertheless, resident peasant households – for all their incapacity – remained pathetically grateful even for the simulacrum of local self-government that had survived. This is his fifth point.

The present chapter will paint a picture of village life that departs significantly from the one drawn above. While Tocqueville's general thesis can be endorsed, with qualifications, his detailed assertions do not always withstand close scrutiny. In the light of evidence assembled here, they appear open to question on grounds of accuracy. And even where accurate in detail, Tocqueville's strictures often fail to take the larger picture into

[1] A. de Tocqueville, *L'Ancien Régime*, ed. G. W. Headlam (Oxford, 1969), pp. 56–60.

48

account, since he prefers to exaggerate for rhetorical effect. As for his overall argument, the difficulty is one of presentation rather than approach. Writing from retirement and with an undisguised political agenda, Tocqueville is inclined to view the process of state centralisation in excessively linear terms. He makes insufficient allowance for the very considerable respect for local privileges and freedoms that continued to animate the government machine at the end of the *ancien régime*, even as it grappled with problems that seemed to demand a further increment of centralisation if they were to be solved.

INSTITUTIONAL DIVERSITY

It is broadly true that village life was less structured – in the institutional sense – in northern France than in the south of the country at the end of the *ancien régime*. That Tocqueville, whose archival researches were confined mainly to the region around Tours and Orléans, should have reached the conclusions he did is therefore not altogether surprising. Albert Babeau, another pioneer historian of the village, who drew his information from the countryside to the east and southeast of Paris, reached rather similar conclusions.[2] More recent research confirms this picture. In the Ile-de-France the corporate life of the pre-revolutionary village appears to have been rudimentary in the extreme. A *sindic* and a tax collector (both usually appointed from above) maintained basic services, and formal deliberative assemblies, whether of all households or simply of the well-to-do, were infrequent occurrences. In many villages corporate life – in its civil dimension – probably amounted to little more than an annual meeting to endorse the tax roll for the year ahead. At Chevreuse village assemblies took place three or four times a year, but at Villepreux, as we shall see, it is difficult to be certain that even one annual meeting took place prior to 1787. In this respect Tocqueville's depiction of the village carries some weight, and there are grounds for supposing that his judgement of decay may not fall far short of the mark either. Serge Bianchi, the historian with the most comprehensive knowledge of village life around Paris in the eighteenth century, detects signs of a breakdown in the procedures for the appointment of *sindics*.[3] Slightly further afield, in Normandy and also in the Artois, a similar picture emerges: infrequent, sparsely attended village assemblies, although the trend

[2] A. Babeau, *Le Village sous l'Ancien Régime* (Paris, 1915).
[3] S. Bianchi, 'L'Election des premiers maires (1790) en milieu rural dans le sud de l'Ile-de-France: sources, résultats, interprétation', in R. Dupuy (ed.), *Pouvoir local et Révolution, 1780–1850: la frontière intérieure* (Rennes, 1995), pp. 154–5.

and the forces in play were not necessarily the same. In the Artois it was seigneurialism that was throttling village self-government, not royal power.

The frequency of meetings or the number and complexity of administrative roles is not, of course, an infallible measure of collective vitality. In a well-nucleated environment such as the Ile-de-France it would be paradoxical to argue that because administrative structures were rudimentary there was no such thing as village sociability, or group decision-taking. The disciplines of open-field cereal agriculture (the rotation of crops, the policing and enforcement of common rights) alone would have generated a collective consciousness. And we shall also need to make allowance for the representational functions of the church and its parish-level institutions, not to mention those of the seigneurie. Tocqueville attaches significance to neither, such is his determination to tell an uncomplicated story of irresistible centralisation. But even in the part of northern France that best exemplifies his thesis, we cannot afford to leave these institutions out of account. Moreover, we shall need to bear in mind the possibility that 'community' is a cultural value independent of formal structures. In which case the relative 'underdevelopment' of northern villages will count for little when we come to explore their collective behaviour during the Revolution.

Institutional underdevelopment was not a characteristic of all northern villages in any case. This oft-repeated generalisation is in fact rather misleading and useful only insofar as it draws attention to the very different patterns of development shaping the village in the south of the country. In common with those of the Ile-de-France and Normandy, the villages of Picardy, Champagne, Lorraine and the Berry relied on a single *sindic* to handle matters of collective concern. The capacity of such individuals to play a representational role was hindered by the fact that they were not legally empowered. On the rare occasions when villagers gathered in order to deliberate, their decisions remained strictly unenforceable unless endorsed by a notary, an officer of the seigneurial seat of justice, or by the intendant. This state of affairs did not necessarily make for greater royal control as Tocqueville supposed, however. For there was a sense in which central government needed village institutions, and never more so than in the second half of the eighteenth century with the advent of interventionist, administrative monarchy.[4] What it did not need, or needed less, were institutions whose *raison d'être* lay elsewhere, or whose authority was sanctioned from below. In Lorraine and Champagne seigneurial control of such

---

[4] For this development, see P. M. Jones, *Reform and Revolution in France: The Politics of Transition, 1774–1791* (Cambridge, 1995).

institutions of village life as existed posed the principal threat, and in 1776 the government promulgated an edict curbing the power of seigneurial judges in the latter province. In Burgundy, too, the intendants chose to nurture the collective life of the village in an effort to combat the interfering habits of local seigneurs. Loss of control to forces *within* the village presented much less of a problem. Or at least, it only became a problem when the whole basis on which administrative *tutelle* had hitherto rested was overturned, momentarily, in 1764 (see pp. 58–9).

The clean lines of the picture drawn by Tocqueville, then, are already becoming a little blurred. Let us add a further layer of complication. In the east, and specifically in Alsace, village communities were not in decline at all. In fact the picture painted by Jean-Pierre Boehler is one of brimming self-confidence and organisational energy, and it leads him to question whether the stark north–south divide has not been overdrawn.[5] The rural communities of late eighteenth-century Alsace more closely resembled the semi-urbanised villages of the Mediterranean Midi than they did their counterparts in northern France, he argues. This may be an exaggeration or perhaps an unhelpful comparison, but the fact remains that Alsatian villagers had developed mechanisms for budgeting, for the management of community assets and for the regulation of day-to-day life. How had these mechanisms evolved? As collective acts of resistance to seigneurialism, we are told. So, it seems that we shall need to allow that village communities could express themselves both through their seigneurs and against their seigneurs, and moreover that government power strategies took careful account of local and regional circumstance. Where seigneurialism posed the principal barrier to administrative *tutelle*, it was important to muster all of the resources of the village in a posture of resistance, but where seigneurial authority was already on the wane the agents of the monarchy could afford to concentrate on their second objective which was to restructure the rural community into a pliable and biddable oligarchy. Yet such policies could not always be pursued transparently. The late *ancien-régime* monarchy remained publicly committed to the 'society of orders' and to privilege. Each act of royal interventionism in the village necessarily involved a redistribution of power, and if seigneurs complained loudly enough they could usually persuade ministers to compromise.

The biggest challenge to a structural analysis of the village rooted in a north–south polarity, however, is Brittany. Here rural communities had

---

[5] See J.-M. Boehler, *Une Société rurale en milieu rhénan: la paysannerie de la plaine d'Alsace, 1648–1789* (3 vols., Strasbourg, 1994), II, pp. 1295–303; 1991–2.

evolved institutional superstructures every bit as sophisticated as those to be found in Provence in the opposite corner of the kingdom. Several common denominators help to explain how this situation had come about, although we should not overlook the palpable differences between the two provinces either. For a start, both Brittany and Provence were *pays d'états* whose annexation to the kingdom of France in the late fifteenth century took place on terms designed to preserve their ancient freedoms and liberties. In neither province did the royal intendants enjoy untrammelled power, therefore. Indeed, it would be truer to say that they shared power with pre-existing provincial institutions. Moreover, in both provinces the *parlements* took a close and enduring interest in the policing – that is to say the regulation – of village life. From the late seventeenth century onwards, a succession of *arrêtés* effectively fashioned a corporate or institutional identity for the Breton village. The *assemblée générale* was to comprise twelve representatives (*délibérants*) of the parish who were subject to annual renewal, in addition to the seigneurial judge, the parish incumbent and a *sindic*. All deliberations were to be recorded in a register maintained for the purpose and signed by those present, insofar as they were able. The *général* appointed officials to specific tasks (churchwarden, beadle, treasurer, tax assessor, etc.), and the written record of its debates and decisions was kept locked away in a chest during the interval between meetings.

Even if these arrangements were not always adhered to, the level of incorporation far exceeded anything we have observed elsewhere. And the *sindic* usually cut a poor figure in the august company of the *général*; so much so that the intendant was able to exercise very little control over Breton village communities. In fact Breton villages enjoyed considerable room for manoeuvre at the end of the *ancien régime*, always provided that they respected the procedural requirements of the Parlement of Rennes. The Provincial Estates held royal power at bay and seigneurs, or their agents, often took only intermittent interest in the activities of the *généraux*. Tocqueville's arresting image of villages awaiting permission from Paris before carrying out repairs to the church roof does not make much sense in Brittany. This degree of organisational sophistication is all the more striking inasmuch as it owed nothing to habitat. Unlike lowland Provence where the human environment helped to foster habits of association, Breton country dwellers organised in defiance of an environment that appeared designed to keep them apart. How was the feat achieved? By structuring village life on the template of the parish. Almost uniquely, the Breton *général* combined civil and ecclesiastical functions in a seamless whole – a concentration of responsibilities symbolised by the *ex officio* presence of the parish priest in the *général*. Not only did the rector participate fully in the secular life of the community, the jurisprudence of the Parlement of Rennes made him a key-holder (along with the seigneur's agent and the senior churchwarden) to the trunk where the register of deliberations was kept. Only in the far southwest of the kingdom, in the neighbourhood of Bigorre, is it possible to find a comparable fusing of civil and ecclesiastical structures.

Tocqueville's generalisations break down almost completely when we turn our attention to the south of the country. In the eighteenth century it would have been possible to draw a meandering line extending from Bordeaux to Grenoble that marked out the regions of well-endowed villages from the rest. Such a line would have traversed the Bordelais and the Massif Central and skirted to the north of the Dauphiné. The legacy of Roman or written law is usually cited as the reason why southern villages had evolved sophisticated institutional structures, but it is also necessary to bear in mind the inadvertent consequences of different tax regimes. Where the *taille* was *réelle*, that is to say assessed on land, the need to measure and to record land holdings provided a powerful incentive to develop permanent institutions capable of carrying out this task. For instance, all such villages possessed primitive land registers or *cadastres*, and they had to be kept up to date if they were to serve any useful function. On the other hand, in villages where presumed wealth served as the criterion for tax distribution (*taille personnelle*), the fiscal incentive to incorporation was lacking. The point can be illustrated by taking the *généralité* of Bordeaux, which embraced *élections* subject to both tax regimes. In the *taille réelle* areas all of the villages tended to possess a municipal superstructure of some description, according to a contemporary report, whereas in the areas of *taille personnelle* only the towns could boast such structures: 'dans toutes les autres paroisses... ni maire, ni consul, ni jurat, ni hôtel de ville ou maison commune; il n'y a que des simples collecteurs pour leurs tailles et autres impositions'.[6]

What did these municipal structures amount to? In Provence, Languedoc, Gascony and most of Guyenne even modest-sized villages boasted officials in whom was confided a power of management. Known variously as *consuls* or *jurats* in a deliberative evocation of the civic heritage of ancient Rome, such officers frequently delegated some of their responsibilities, thereby creating a second tier of agents which would certainly have included a clerk and a tax collector, and quite possibly individuals with more specialised functions, too. Thus a well-endowed village in Provence

---

[6] Cited in A. Zink, *Clochers et troupeaux: les communautés rurales des Landes et du Sud-Ouest avant la Révolution* (Bordeaux, 1997), p. 368.

might possess a 'management team' of up to four *consuls*, a clerk, a tax collector (*trésorier*), several inspectors of accounts (*auditeurs*) and an officer of police, not to mention sundry subaltern employees to run errands, wind the clock, and open and close the gates at dawn and dusk: to all intents and purposes a municipal 'council' that would not have disgraced a medium-sized town in the north of the kingdom. Most important, the *consuls* or *jurats* were legally empowered representatives of their communities, which greatly simplified the question of *tutelle*. In the south the government always knew whom it was dealing with, even if the *consuls* preferred to shelter behind the *parlements* and the tax courts (*cours des aides*) of Montpellier and Montauban on occasion. In the north of the country, by contrast, the village remained a frustratingly opaque entity and the intendants sometimes chose to send their communications to the parish priest rather than to an illiterate or semi-literate *sindic*. When the hour struck for the rebuilding of local government, reformers would draw their inspiration from the traditions of the south, not those of the north.

If the *consuls* were, in the fullest sense, the representatives of their communities, the next question to arise is that of their appointment. In theory they were liable to annual renewal in common with the *délibérants* of the Breton *général*, but on the sanction of whom? Truly democratic election seems to have lapsed nearly everywhere by the end of the *ancien régime*, and in this respect Alexis de Tocqueville's observations appear well founded. Nevertheless, we are bound to question whether his 'mythic past' of fully representative village institutions ever existed in reality. General assemblies of all household heads still took place from time to time during the second half of the eighteenth century, but it is rare to find them entrusted with the job of choosing the *consuls*. That task had generally devolved on the *sanior pars*, that is to say a more socially exclusive body usually referred to as the *conseil politique*. Within this context it is possible to discern something resembling a modern electoral arena, but only in Provence where villagers had managed to restrict seigneurial involvement in local government to a token presence. Elsewhere in the south *consuls* and *jurats* were selected, as we shall see, by a process combining co-option, presentation and election.

Let us consider now how our six case-study villages fit into this broad outline. The first distinction that needs to be drawn is between Neuviller and Villepreux and the rest. Even allowing for the probable destruction of certain documentary sources, it is undeniable that these two villages functioned with minimal recourse to formal structures. In Lorraine, the seigneurie provided the frame for village life to all intents and purposes, a situation that would not alter until 1788 when the Calonne–Brienne local government reform was introduced to the province (see pp. 88–9). Thus the villagers of Neuviller gathered once a year in a meeting known as the *plaid*. The presence of all inhabitants was *de rigueur* since this was an assembly of vassals convened primarily in order to reaffirm the rights of the seigneur and to appoint 'his' officers, the *maire*, the *sergent*, the *juge*, and so on. It is possible that the village schoolmaster, the common shepherds and even the *sindic* were chosen on this occasion as well, but since no records of the *plaids annaux* have survived it is difficult to know for certain. It is clear that meetings outside the framework of the seigneurie were possible, for the inhabitants assembled in December 1768 in order to discuss the merits of reorganising their agricultural territory (see pp. 238–9). Yet even this meeting was called at the behest of the seigneur, and we know of no other before 1768.

If the 'civil society' of the village of Neuviller seems rather indistinct, that of Villepreux is even more opaque. The combination of a non-resident seigneur (the king), passive seigneurial personnel and the complete absence of a corporate tradition in the Ile-de-France (even the adjacent city of Versailles functioned without a municipality until 1787) leaves a void. Reasoning by analogy, however, it is likely that the inhabitants of Villepreux *did* assemble, after Mass on Sundays, but not at regular intervals. The tasks of such meetings would have been to propose the name of a literate individual for *sindic*, to arrange for the collection of taxes and to discuss the reclassification of land holdings necessitated by the *taille* reform of intendant Bertier de Sauvigny.[7] To judge from the local adage 'dix habitants font un peuple', it is likely that the village was governed by an oligarchy of tenant farmers and professionals.

For reasons that should by now be clear, we are much better informed about the mechanisms of collective life in the remaining villages during the years before the Revolution. Only Saint-Alban gives cause for concern inasmuch as the deliberations of its *consuls* were lost when the *mairie* caught fire in 1914. Let us proceed thematically, therefore, beginning with the institution of the *assemblée générale*. As Tocqueville surmised, albeit on slender evidence, village political life exhibited a distinctly censitary character by the end of the *ancien régime*. The *général* of Châtelaudren was supposed to comprise the generality of the households of the parish (almost nowhere before 1789 did individuals represent themselves), but in fact it did not. Between 1757 and 1787 membership tended to oscillate between fifteen

---

[7] M. Touzery, *L'Invention de l'impôt sur le revenu: la taille tarifée, 1715–1789* (Paris, 1994). Also M. Touzery, *Dictionnaire des paroisses fiscales de la généralité de Paris d'après le cadastre de Bertier de Sauvigny, 1776–1791* (Caen, 1995), p. 399.

and seventeen (the parish contained roughly 220 households). During the same period not a single meeting of a wider representational character took place, although this would change – in common with other villages – as rural France entered the phase of the Pre-Revolution (see pp. 88–94). At Saint-Alban the status of the *assemblée générale* is impossible to resolve satisfactorily, but in this far-flung parish it would be extraordinary indeed if effective political power had not lain in the hands of the *bourg* oligarchy. As for Roquelaure, there is evidence here to suggest a more tenacious practice of general assemblies. Gascony was a region that resisted the trend towards an oligarchisation of the rural community, as Maurice Bordes has pointed out,[8] and wider assemblies took place in Roquelaure on seven occasions between 1766 and 1787. Significantly, they tended to occur when the village elite broke ranks, an event that was not uncommon for reasons that will be explored later on in this chapter. Oligarchisation was never as well advanced in Roquelaure as it was in Châtelaudren in any case. Ordinary meetings of the *conseil politique* routinely involved twenty or more participants, and the deliberations of general assemblies often carried fifty or even sixty signatures.

The unusual situation of Allan, a Provençal village located outside the infrastructure of the Procureurs du Pays, is of particular interest in this connection. Generally speaking, public life in Provençal villages was both highly organised and highly concentrated; only in the hill villages of the subalpine interior did the mantle of political power extend to cover the totality of households on the eve of the Revolution. Although a 'village perché', Allan was not a remote hill village and its institutional history illustrates a slow transition from relative democracy to semi-oligarchy. In the early seventeenth century the general assembly of households had routinely appointed the *consul*s, albeit under the supervision of the seigneur, but this practice was disrupted by the venal office creations of the reigns of Louis XIV and Louis XV (see pp. 75–8) and gradually lapsed thereafter. Between 1769 and 1787 an *assemblée générale* appears to have convened on only three occasions, although a gap in the records makes the count rather uncertain. On the other hand, power concentration never proceeded to the degree characteristic of lowland Provençal villages. The *conseil politique*, which largely replaced the general assembly of households, remained a fairly large and undifferentiated body. In 1774 it comprised three agents of the seigneur,

[8] See M. Bordes, 'Consulats et municipalités en Gascogne à la fin de l'Ancien Régime', in *Recueil de mémoires et travaux publié par la Société d'Histoire du Droit et des Institutions des anciens pays de droit écrit* (Montpellier, 1974), pp. 67–82; see also the remarks of G. Fournier, *Démocratie et vie municipale en Languedoc du milieu du XVIIIᵉ siècle au début du XIXᵉ siècle* (2 vols., Toulouse, 1994), I, pp. 365–9.

two *consuls* and a scribe, four aldermen (*conseillers*) and eleven miscellaneous 'notables, manans et habitans',[9] that is to say approximately 12 per cent of resident households.

The tendency towards concentration is well attested, then. Only in Roquelaure might we hypothesise that the Calonne–Brienne attempt to institutionalise oligarchy in the shape of the 1787–8 local government re- form engendered a brusque alteration in the trajectory of local political life. But does this mean that village freedoms were in decay as the Revolution approached? Not really. The restructuring of the rural community, whether from below or above, had a streamlining effect. It galvanised local elites, enlisting their energy and resources in the defence of ostensibly commu- nity interests. More particularly, it facilitated the emergence of the village bourgeois as a political force. This process can be explored more closely if we turn to look next at the role and activities of the *conseil politique*.

The village of Neuviller had no institutions that it could truly call its own, as has been established. The future leaders of the community can therefore be identified only retrospectively. Nevertheless, it is clear that the organism of the seigneurie provided an excellent training ground. Pierre Dieudonné, the man who would crystallise and channel the awakening political consciousness of the inhabitants, learned his trade in the seigneurial court where he was the clerk (*greffier*) who took down the minutes. Whether Dieudonné's own *prise de conscience* predated the events of 1787–8 is a question to which there can be no answer, however. Again, in the case of Villepreux, we can make an educated guess as to the balance of power at the end of the *ancien régime* on the basis of what came after. Here, it is likely that a handful of big tenant farmers and well-to-do merchants represented the village, informally if not formally. Their power and self-confidence was rooted in the control of economic resources. It owed little, if anything, to the seigneurie.

The *général* of Châtelaudren was edging away from seigneurial control in the second half of the eighteenth century. Its two *ex officio* members, Gilles Le Corvaisier the rector and Jean-Louis Rivot, the *receveur-général* of the seigneurie, attended nearly every session and for the most part co- operated without any obvious signs of tension. As the principal seat of the Comté de Goello, the economic life of the village partly depended on the business attracted by sessions of the seigneurial courts. Nevertheless, there were sources of tension, and in 1787 the *général* decided to switch its meet- ings from the courthouse to the vestry. Le Corvaisier profited from the

[9] A. C. d'Allan, BB 3–4.

move to take over the presidency, although this placed the assembly in an irregular situation and laid its deliberations open to procedural challenge. The precise configuration of power in Saint-Alban is more difficult to determine. Ostensibly, a *conseil politique* comprising three consuls, a clerk and twelve *conseillers* had managed the affairs of the community since 1744, if not earlier. A record of only one of the meetings survives, however, from which we learn that the 'seigneur haut justicier' retained the right to preside over the sessions. In practice, this function was exercised by his local lieutenant on a par with Châtelaudren. But in Saint-Alban there is no sign of formal clerical involvement in the administrative life of the community. Quite the contrary, for Alexandre Béraud, the Saint-Sulpice-trained parish incumbent, regarded secular affairs with considerable disdain. In fact he was at loggerheads with the *consuls* on the eve of the Revolution.

Who appointed the *consuls* of Saint-Alban? Not the seigneur, it appears. They were 'nominated', that is to say the names of candidates were presented by the outgoing officers to a wider assembly ('conseil renforcé'), and this body made the final choice. In view of the deep antagonisms that would subsequently punctuate the life of this village, it is interesting to note that the *consuls* were ranked according to social and geographical origin. The first *consul* was always chosen from among the qualified legal and professional bourgeoisie, the second from among the unqualified *hommes de plume* and the mercantile families, while the third post was earmarked for the representative of the outlying hamlets (usually a well-to-do farmer). Unsuccessful candidates and also outgoing *consuls* tended to be recruited as *conseillers*. Effective power tended to be concentrated in the hands of the first *consul*, who was always a resident of the *bourg*, and the individual who held that office most frequently before the Revolution was the notary Noé-Jean Atrasic.

Unlike their counterparts in Saint-Alban, the leading families of Roquelaure had not managed to wrest control of the process for selecting the consuls from the seigneur by the time the Revolution broke. Here, four *consuls* were chosen from a slate of eight candidates, either by the seigneur in person or by his nominee, the *procureur fiscal*. Two developments that will require fuller discussion later on had served to undermine this custom, however, although not necessarily in the way the inhabitants would have preferred. Municipal office holding, here as elsewhere, had had the effect of jeopardising the rights of nomination of both communities and seigneurs, and the Laverdy reform interrupted established patterns of presentation and representation for a brief period in the 1760s as well. After the exit of Laverdy from the Contrôle Général and the abrogation of his edicts, the community reluctantly reverted to ancient practice – symbolised by the adoption once more of the chateau as the venue for meetings. The arrival on the scene of a more easy-going seigneur did enable the *conseil* to recover some political ground: in 1774 it adopted the practice of signalling the four names on the slate of eight that were its preferred choices for the consulate. But then the seigneurie changed hands again, and this advantage was lost.

During the years immediately preceding the Revolution the social purchase of Allan's *conseil politique* perceptibly narrowed, a development probably linked to deteriorating relations with the seigneur. A court case begun in 1785 and not finally settled until 1818 (see pp. 174–6) placed loyalties under close scrutiny, and the *consuls* seem to have concluded that the wider assembly format was too great a hostage to fortune inasmuch as it offered scope for pro-seigneurial intrigue. The community had long controlled the appointment of its officers, of course, but here, too, some streamlining seems to have taken place. When, each January, the moment for office renewal came around, the *consuls* simply co-opted their replacements. Nevertheless, the court case threw into sharp relief the structural problem facing nearly all villages when contemplating litigation against the rich and the powerful. Assembly deliberations – where they were possible at all – had to take place in the presence of the seigneurial judge. When the *consuls* of Allan remonstrated at this state of affairs, they were advised that the jurisprudence of the Parlement of Aix would allow them to bring in a notary from the nearby town of Montélimar in order to authenticate their deliberations. This they did, but it was a solution that presupposed a degree of political maturity as well as a favourable institutional context. For most villagers it was not an option.

Seigneurs, or more likely their agents, then, possessed a power to influence the agendas of daily life at the end of the *ancien régime* that should not be underestimated. Indeed, in many parts of the kingdom theirs was the power to decide whether there was *any* corporate life at the level of the village. At Neuviller and perhaps at Villepreux the seigneur determined whether the villagers should meet collectively, and, if so, when. The intendants also possessed such powers, of course, but used them sparingly and for narrowly administrative purposes. The point that needs to be emphasised is that villagers possessed no generalised right to summon *one another* to formal meetings before 1787. Where a right of assembly had developed, it had done so by virtue of local privileges and immunities. On the other hand, where the practice of regular assembly was admitted, it facilitated a rapid efflorescence of collective life. Regular assembly was an established feature of four out of our six villages, and in three of them it is possible to reconstruct the ecology of this collective life in some detail.

At Châtelaudren regular assembly was not only admitted, it was mandatory. The *général* met on average 7.4 times a year between 1757 and 1787.[10] So deeply embedded were the habits and practices of assembly that it would meet even when there was no business to transact (as on 1 December 1771), and would adjourn if inquorate (fewer than the requisite twelve *délibérants* present). Such diligence was not unusual, as Christian Kermoal and other regional historians have demonstrated.[11] The Breton *général* provided discreet training for a whole generation of peasant activists who would come into their own in 1788 and 1789. The inhabitants of Roquelaure were no less attached to the practice of assembly, as we have seen. Between 1766 and 1787 the *consuls* called an average of seven meetings a year, meetings often attended by large numbers of *jurats*, that is to say principal householders.[12] Earlier in the century, when the sale of municipal offices caused an outcry, the inhabitants had even organised parallel meetings. The formal framework of collective life was also well developed in the village of Allan. On average the *consuls* summoned the *conseil politique* 6.6 times a year between 1769 and 1787.[13] Averages tell only part of the story, of course, as figure 4 makes clear. Not until 1787 would legislation establish a calendar for parish assemblies (meetings to be held every Sunday after the church service), and even then it was mostly honoured in the breach. Instead, villagers would generally meet when there was business to transact, although seasonal patterns of agricultural activity often intruded and caused business to be held over. The *consuls* of Allan preferred to call their meetings in the agricultural dead season (January, February and March) and systematically avoided the period of the wine harvest. Only in Châtelaudren does it appear that something approaching an administrative 'routine' was adhered to – more evidence of the structural sophistication of Breton parish life at the end of the *ancien régime*.

For what purposes did country dwellers gather in deliberative assemblies? Certain tasks were common to all of the villages whose collective life we have managed to piece together. Leadership roles had to be reallocated

[10] A. D. des Côtes-d'Armor, 20G 42.
[11] C. Kermoal, 'L'Apprentissage administratif et politique des paysans à travers le fonctionnement des généraux de deux paroisses trégorroises: Ploubezre et Bourbriac', in R. Dupuy (ed.), *Pouvoir local et Révolution*, pp. 93–112; G. Minois, 'Le Rôle politique des recteurs de campagne en Basse-Bretagne, 1750–1790,' *Annales de Bretagne et des pays de l'Ouest*, 89 (1982), 153–64; see also *Les Bretons délibèrent: répertoire des registres de délibérations paroissiales et municipales, 1780–1800, et des cahiers de doléances, 1789* (St-Brieuc, Quimper, Rennes and Vannes, 1990).
[12] A. D. du Gers, E Supplément 1010[1–3].   [13] A. C. d'Allan, BB 3–4.

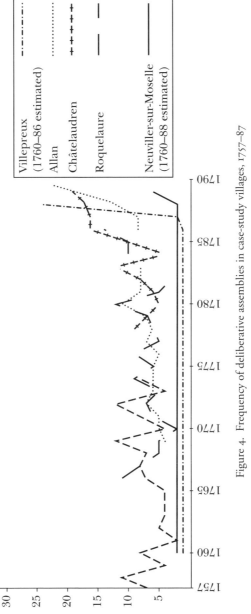

Figure 4. Frequency of deliberative assemblies in case-study villages, 1757–87

Legend:

Villepreux
(1760–86 estimated)

Allan

Châtelaudren

Roquelaure

Neuviller-sur-Moselle
(1760–88 estimated)

from time to time, or sanctioned afresh; tax collectors had to be appointed and the *mande* (tax quota) allocated between the households; collectively owned property required policing; decisions regarding debts and loans had to be taken; running repairs to the physical fabric of the village (walls, roads, pathways, drinking fountains, water troughs, church bells, etc.) had to be carried out. Last but not least, budgets had to be drawn up and presented for scrutiny. It is a tribute to the seventeenth-century architects of monarchical absolutism that matters relating to (direct) taxation occupied most village assemblies most of the time. At Châtelaudren the annual appointment of *égailleurs* (assessors) and decisions concerning the *tailles et fouages* and the *capitation* taxes dwarfed all other types of business transacted by the *général*. Significantly, the renewal of *fabriciens* (churchwardens) and the management of the two churches in the village, together with their respective endowments, came next. In Allan, too, there seems to have been some overlap of civil and ecclesiastical functions, with the *consuls* taking on responsibility for the administration of an important legacy in favour of the poor. Nevertheless, a thematic analysis of the deliberations of the *conseil politique* indicates that the subject of taxes was raised and discussed at no fewer than 42 per cent of meetings.[14]

Other activities tended to be more specific. For instance, labour service on the roads was a burden shouldered by the villagers of Neuviller, Villepreux, Châtelaudren and Roquelaure from the mid-eighteenth century. It necessitated frequent meetings and occasioned not a little recrimination (see pp. 80–2). In Languedoc and Provence, however, the Provincial Estates had made alternative arrangements for road repair with the result that the *corvée* was not an issue for discussion either in Saint-Alban or in Allan. At Saint-Alban it is likely that the *conseil politique* devoted much more time and energy to the management of the extensive common pastures of their highland parish, some of which were leased each year to transhumant shepherds. In the hill village of Châteauneuf-Randon just a few kilometres to the east, where a similar rural economy prevailed, twenty-one of the thirty-nine deliberations recorded between 1754 and 1788 concerned the policing of the commons.[15] Management of communal property also preoccupied the villagers of Allan, although here it would be more apt to attach the label 'court cases' to this type of business. Litigation was a major activity in all of the villages in any case, whether directed against seigneurs, tithe proctors, absentee land holders (*forains*, *horsains*), or simply neighbouring parishes.

[14] *Ibid*.
[15] R.-J. Bernard, 'Les Communautés rurales en Gévaudan sous l'ancien régime', *Revue du Gévaudan, des Causses et des Cévennes*, new series, 17 (1971), 110–65.

By the second half of the eighteenth century, *assemblées générales* seem only to have convened when there was exceptional or urgent business to transact. A wider assembly of this nature was held at Roquelaure in 1773 when the *consuls* presented for endorsement a new *compoix cabaliste* which linked stock ownership to property holdings in an effort to curtail anarchic grazing in fields and hedgerows. Six years later another *assemblée générale* was triggered when the seigneur published a *dénombrement* which did not correspond with the villagers' perception of their obligations. In 1786 the issue was one of resistance to the tithe. Implicit in many of these wider, or 'reinforced', assemblies was the prospect of self-taxation in order to raise funds over and above those already budgeted for. This inevitably presupposed a larger attendance than usual, if only because the intendants and the Provincial Estates insisted on the participation of major taxpayers, resident or non-resident, whenever initiatives that might erode the fiscal capacity of the rural community were in contemplation. The revolutionary and Napoleonic authorities would behave no differently.

In view of the repeated restructuring that villages would undergo from 1787, or thereabouts, it is interesting to note that politics (understood for the time being as external ideological stimuli) scarcely ever registered. Before 1787 villagers assembled in order to debate concrete issues that were – in the most literal sense – close to home. The engagement with abstractions ('privilege', 'regeneration', 'constitution', 'nation', 'republic', etc.) lay in the future. Occasionally assemblies took note that 'France' had gone to war, or that peace had been concluded, but the decision of the *conseil politique* of Allan to convene on 7 June 1774 in order to swear an oath of loyalty to the new monarch, Louis XVI, is very unusual.[16]

SEIGNEURIAL PRESENCE

Enough has been said to indicate that seigneurs, if rarely physical participants in community deliberations, certainly retained an institutional presence. Tocqueville suggests that seigneurs had evacuated the local power arena by the end of the *ancien régime*, but our study provides little evidence that can be used to support this claim. On the contrary, the arresting fact that emerges is the continuing relevance to village life of seigneurialism in all six localities. Not only did the seigneurie continue to function as a regulatory institution, but in several instances the titular seigneurs were personalities in their own right (see the conclusion). As such they possessed

[16] A. C. d'Allan, BB 3–4.

the power to alter the trajectory of village life in the decades before the Revolution and used that power without scruple, whether at the mundane level of self-enrichment or in pursuit of grandiose schemes of reform and social regeneration. Eighteenth-century villagers routinely complained about the unbridled activities of seigneurial officers and agents, but they were also acutely aware of the drawbacks attaching to the resident or semi-resident seigneur who constantly intervened in the life of the community. Insofar as a choice was possible, they preferred to have the king rather than a private individual as their seigneur. Administration by a steward of the Royal Domain was generally less onerous economically (although this would change with the appointment of Jacques Necker to the Contrôle Général in 1781), and also less likely to generate division and partisan behaviour among resident households.

Only the villagers of Villepreux enjoyed the sustained protection of the monarch, however. In 1776 the Francini family passed on the 'terre et seigneurie' of Villepreux to the Royal Domain of Versailles. A logical solution, since half of the territory of the village was already enclosed within the Grand Parc, and the Francinis had long ceased to show any interest in their vassals. In Neuviller, by contrast, the imprint of ambitious, even unbridled, seigneurial authority was everywhere visible. A long-time possession of the Princes de Salm-Salm, the village was acquired in 1749 by Stanislas I, King of Poland and Duke of Lorraine. Two years later Stanislas bestowed the seigneurie on his chancellor, Antoine-Martin Chaumont de La Galaizière, having first erected it into a *prévôté-bailliagère*. La Galaizière and subsequently his son Antoine, who would succeed him in the post of intendant of Lorraine, set about remodelling the old feudal chateau into a country seat to emulate the residence of the king and the Court at Lunéville. A park was laid out, an experimental farm set up, a seigneurial side-chapel added to the parish church, and the boundaries of the seigneurie extended to embrace the adjacent village of Roville together with the greater part of the marquisate of Bayon. Much of the rebuilding was undertaken using *corvée* labour (see pp. 80–1). By 1768 the La Galaizières were ready to embark upon their most ambitious project of all – a complete recasting of the agricultural landscape which was intended to serve as a model for a general land-reform measure applicable to the whole of the kingdom. This last initiative, as we shall see, sowed deep divisions in the two communities, and would set the terms of political debate for a generation and more.

The inhabitants of Neuviller and Roville had good reason to rue the day when a powerful figure at the court of Lorraine decided to take up residence among them, and to make them reluctant accessories to an experiment in practical agronomy and self-aggrandisement. As they were to put it later, their 'consent' to the exercise was obtained at a time when 'everything was permitted'[17] to seigneurs (see pp. 119–20). A similar future seemed to beckon for the villagers of Roquelaure when, in 1750, the Marquis de Mirabeau acquired the seigneurie, sight unseen, for 450,000 *livres*. The main motive for the purchase may have been the dukedom that went with it, but Mirabeau was none other than 'l'ami des hommes', the physiocrat propagandist and disciple of Quesnay. Accordingly, he wasted no time in applying his theories on the ground. Both the judicial and the policing powers of the seigneurie were redefined. Local agents were instructed that justice should not be put up for sale and were reminded of the reciprocities of seigneurial power, notably with regard to foundlings. However, Mirabeau was a dreamer whose aptitude for practical reform was negligible, a point that he readily conceded. He lacked the capacity for the kind of sustained effort required in order to turn visions into reality. An infrequent visitor to Roquelaure, he soon lost interest. In 1758 the seigneurie passed into the hands of the king following a recommendation from the intendant that the chateau of Le Rieutort would make a suitable location for a cavalry stud. The stud farm failed, however, and on 18 September 1771 the villagers awoke to the news that their new seigneur was a certain Colonel Dubarry. Dubarry acquired the seigneurie as part of a deal designed to provide the Comtesse Dubarry, formerly Jeanne Bécu and now the royal mistress, with a cloak of respectability. Not surprisingly, perhaps, he turned out to be an easy-going seigneur and the villagers grew to know and like him. While both his 'wife' and older brother fell victim to the Revolution, Guillaume Dubarry lived out his days in retirement near Toulouse. Dubarry was not the last seigneur of Roquelaure, however, for in 1781 the title and the lands passed by deed of sale to a Toulouse *parlementaire* family, the Reversac de Celès de Marsac.

During the second half of the eighteenth century the seigneurie of Roquelaure thus changed hands four times – an indication of the vigorous market for land and its perquisites in the vicinity of Toulouse. Elsewhere seigneurialism exhibited a more stable profile. Charles de Rohan, otherwise known as the Prince de Soubise, held the seigneurie of Châtelaudren from 1746 until his death in 1787 when it passed to his grandson Louis de Condé. Peer and marshal of France, he rarely visited his estates in Brittany, and the Comté de Goello was administered from Châtelaudren by Jean-Louis Rivot, the *receveur-général*, to all practical purposes. At Saint-Alban a family

---

[17] A. D. de Meurthe-et-Moselle, N[on] C[oté] G3 94/1/1, 27 September 1809.

of ancient noble lineage, the Molette de Morangiès, had held court since the middle of the seventeenth century. They were a dynasty of soldiers who resided infrequently, but in 1741 Pierre-Charles de Molette obtained the elevation of the ancestral seat to the status of a barony with a right of admission to the Estates of Languedoc. His three sons all occupied the chateau of Saint-Alban, at different times, from 1779 onwards, and they all played a part in the public life of the province both before and during the Revolution. Jean-François-Charles, the eldest (known as the Comte de Morangiès) was a notorious spendthrift and reprobate whose exploits were a regular topic of conversation among his contemporaries. In 1771 he contrived to borrow a large sum of money only to deny subsequently that he had ever received payment. The case became a *cause célèbre* involving Voltaire and d'Alembert,[18] and although both the Parlement of Paris and the Conseil du Roi eventually exonerated the count, he became a fugitive assailed by creditors and by allegations of bigamy. In 1789 he returned to the chateau of Saint-Alban broken and penniless. The two younger brothers, Jean-Annet (known as the Baron de Morangiès) and Jean-Adam (the Chevalier de Morangiès), numbered prominently among his detractors. Both would play a role during the Revolution in and around Saint-Alban, and the ill-feeling between the younger siblings and their reckless older brother turned to violence on more than one occasion.

François-Lucrétius-Henri de La Tour-du-Pin-Montauban, seigneur of Allan, was an altogether less colourful character. Scion of a family of Court nobles with extensive possessions in the Dauphiné, his link with Allan was tenuous inasmuch as the 'terre' formed part of the dowry of Françoise-Hippolyte Lériget de La Faye whom he married in 1758. The couple cultivated links with the *philosophes* and travelled constantly. They do not appear to have visited their Allan estates very frequently. In any case, the Comte de La Tour-du-Pin-Montauban disappeared abroad several years prior to the Revolution and would die without issue in 1806. Since the Comtesse had kept her property separate from that of her husband, she therefore remained the effective seigneur of Allan. And she was the redoutable woman against whom the villagers waged an epic struggle that was still unresolved at the time of her death in 1814.

Seigneurial 'presence' at village level registered in two main ways. In five out of the six localities on which this study is based, the seigneur was far and away the largest owner of land. Moreover, each possessed additional lucrative rights and privileges by virtue of his or her juridical status. On

---

[18] See J. Renwick, *Voltaire et Morangiès, 1772–1773, ou Les Lumières l'ont échappé belle* (Oxford, 1982).

Table 2. *The economic impact of seigneurialism towards the end of the ancien régime*

Village	Estimate of seigneurial *réserve* as % of total village territory	Estimate of seigneurial income from land rents (annual, in *livres*)	Estimate of seigneurial income from feudal prerogatives: dues, tolls, monopolies, justice (annual, in *livres*)	Estimate of total seigneurial income from village (annual, in *livres*)	Total direct taxation (in *livres*) from village (for comparison)
Allan	50[a]	5,955[#]	5,103[#]	11,058[#]	3,672[#b]
Châtelaudren	0	0	2,600[#]	2,600[#]	2,644[#c]
Neuviller-sur-Moselle	53	?	1,000[#]	?	6,730[#d]
Roquelaure	20	?	1,200[#]	?	3,132[#e]
Saint-Alban	?	13,106[#]	12,000[#]	25,106[#]	12,241[#f]
Villepreux	52	10,627[#]	2,000[#]	12,627[#]	9,649[#g]

Notes
[a] Figure includes disputed forests
[b] *Don gratuit [taille]* + *vingtièmes* + *accessoires* for 1790
[c] *Capitation* + *fouages* + *vingtièmes* for 1790 [*contribution foncière* assessment in 1791 = 4,871[#]]
[d] *Taille* + *vingtièmes* + *accessoires* for 1790
[e] *Taille* + *vingtièmes* + *accessoires* for 1784
[f] *Taille* + *vingtièmes* + *accessoires* for 1785
[g] *Taille* + *capitation* + *accessoires* for 1790

grounds of economic weight alone, therefore, the argument for treating seigneurialism as one of the major connecting threads of village life is diffi-cult to resist. Whether or not the titular seigneur was physically present in the community, villagers came into near daily contact with the representa-tions of his power: when bringing corn to the mill and dough to the bread oven, when paying rent or dues, when seeking work, when transporting goods to market, and when queuing for Holy Communion in church on Sundays. Table 2 sets out, as succinctly as possible, this economic reality in each of the six villages. An explanation of the data, together with a com-mentary, is provided in the following paragraphs. It is important to bear in mind, however, that these findings do not lend themselves to easy gener-alisation. Seigneurs were not, *ipso facto*, major landowners in the localities over which they exercised jurisdiction; nor should the coherence of the seigneurial regime as we have uncovered it be taken for granted. In many parishes the link between lordship, land and rights had succumbed by the end of the *ancien régime*, resulting in a picture of considerable disarray.

   The dominant position of 'la Dame d'Allan' has already been alluded to in chapter 1. In this far-flung and partly wooded community the seigneurial *réserve* embraced most of the irrigated arable and a good proportion of the vineyards. It was divided into six *granges* or farms and put out to tenants on cash rentals. By the end of the *ancien régime* the farms alone were bringing in 5,200 *livres* each year. This property was all the more valuable in that it was classed as 'bien noble' and thereby exempt from the *taille*. Or so the seigneur claimed; the villagers begged to differ. In addition, the seigneur's administrator, Pierre de Villacroze, collected payments totalling around 5,000 *livres* each year in respect of feudal rights, privileges and monopolies. Two banal mills brought in 1,173 *livres*, the lease on the banal bread oven 330 *livres*, property transfers attracted an *ad valorem* tax of 6 per cent, and all grain grown in the community was liable to a *tasque* or harvest due of one twenty-fifth.[19] As for the scrub woodland that covered about half of the territory of the village, the seigneur claimed most of this area, too. Indeed, it was a move to restrict access to the forest that, in 1785, triggered the first in the series of court cases that put villagers and their (ex)-seigneur at loggerheads for over thirty years.

   At Châtelaudren the main weight of the seigneurial regime tended to be deflected onto the population of adjacent rural parishes. The village possessed no agricultural territory to speak of, and therefore sidestepped the

---

[19] A. D. de la Drôme, L321; B. M. de Grenoble, Notes sur la commune d'Allan avant et pendant la Révolution, J. Michel to Monsieur l'Inspecteur d'Académie, Allan, 29 August 1887. A. Lacroix, *L'Arrondissement de Montélimar: géographie, histoire, statistique* (Valence, 1868), pp. 77–139.

burden of harvest dues. Instead the seigneur sought to tap the commercial and industrial wealth of the village by means of hefty charges for the use of his grain mills powered by the waters of the pool and of fulling mills along the banks of the Leff. Or at least he leased out these monopolies at rates that forced the millers to recoup their investment as best they could. Lesser seigneurs followed suit: the lease price of a banal bread oven owned by the Le Gac family rose from 60 *livres* per annum in 1678 to 1,500 *livres* by 1774. With Suzanne Erhel, the tenant, taking between one-fifth and one-sixth of the dough as her *droit de cuisson*, the *général* finally lost patience and took both tenant and proprietor to court with the demand that baking fees be converted into a monetary payment. The administration of justice seems to have been the other major source of income of the seigneur of Châtelaudren. Each week several jurisdictions held their assizes in the Hôtel de Soubise, the impressive stone courthouse that still stands next to the parish church. With plenty of legal work and rich pickings, offices could be sold at a premium. That of *sénéchal* sold for 6,400 *livres*, while the post of *procureur fiscal* (investigating magistrate) in the *châtellenie* of Châtelaudren changed hands for 2,000 *livres*.

When, in 1760, Antoine-Martin Chaumont de La Galaizière ceded his possessions in Neuviller, Roville and Bayon to his son Antoine in return for 500,000 *livres* he was already the largest landowner in these parishes. Only the colossal wealth of the Prince de Beauvau in nearby Haroué put him in the shade. La Galaizière *fils* exploited the *remembrement* operation in order to increase as well as to concentrate the family's land holdings, with the result that by 1771 he owned approximately half (235 hectares) of the territory of Neuviller, and somewhat less than half (around 190 hectares) of that of Roville where a similar reorganisation of the agricultural landscape had taken place. Nothing in the surviving family papers enables us to estimate the yield of the Neuviller estates, unfortunately, but it would have far exceeded the income generated from La Galaizière's feudal prerogatives. General harvest dues (*champarts*) and property transfer fees (*lods et ventes*) were rare in Lorraine, although monopoly rights (*banalités*) were still vigorously enforced in the eighteenth century. An examination of Antoine Chaumont de La Galaizière's entitlements suggests that they fell into what we might term the 'vexatious' category. New entrants to the village had to pay a fine of 15 *livres*;[20] the inhabitants were liable to a collective seigneurial *taille* and a *cens* worth about 300 *livres*; they could be requisitioned for

---

[20] The 'livre de Lorraine' was employed in routine financial transactions until as late as 1792; it was worth approximately 75.5 per cent of the value of the 'livre de France', i.e. 1 *livre de Lorraine* = 15 *sous* 6 *deniers tournois*.

corvées (errand running, haymaking, etc.); and they each paid a small annual tax in lieu of *banalité de moulin*. The common bread oven belonged to the priory of Flavigny rather than the titular seigneur. Nevertheless, the villagers had bought out the obligation to use it in return for a per capita payment of 28 *sous* each year. Only the seigneurial winepress monopoly still remained intact in 1789; and to judge from the community's *cahier de doléances* it was bitterly resented.

Although the last seigneur of Roquelaure scarcely ranked alongside La Galaizière *fils* he outshone all of his neighbours for all that. His son, Prosper Reversac Marsac, would declare a list of possessions in the commune totalling 320 hectares when the so-called Napoleonic *cadastre* was compiled between 1819 and 1823. This holding amounted to a little over 17 per cent of the territory of Roquelaure and was five times bigger than that of the second largest owner of land.[21] Before the Revolution it may have been larger still. We know that Madame Reversac de Celès de Marsac had been forced to sell off land following the sentencing of her husband by the Revolutionary Tribunal and his subsequent execution. The sources relating to land holdings in the community of Roquelaure during the 1770s and 1780s are rather fragmentary, however, and it is impossible to be sure about the size of the seigneurial *réserve*. The only certain fact is that it was divided up into seven *métairies* that employed a total of twenty-two plough-teams. Using the standard multiplier in the district, this would indicate a holding of about 220 hectares (of arable). An alternative possibility, of course, is that Reversac Marsac *fils* significantly expanded the old seigneurial domain during the Empire and early Restoration; but this, too, is difficult to verify. Either way, though, the seigneurie of Roquelaure was unquestionably the economic hub of the village.

As in the case of Neuviller, it is not possible to analyse in detail the composition of seigneurial revenue. Sharecrop rents, like the tithe, were paid in kind (a proportion of the harvest plus the annual increase in livestock), whereas the perquisites of lordship were expressed either in monetary terms or as services that the inhabitants were required to perform. Thus a residual harvest due (*agrier*) of one-eleventh, which in any case applied to only a few plots of ploughland, had been commuted into a cash payment of 200 *livres*, and *lods et ventes* were reckoned at 12 *livres*. The seigneur also collected 2 *sols* 8 *deniers* on every *concade* (1.53 hectares) of commoner land that would have yielded about 137 *livres*. More lucrative, without a doubt, were his monopolies (two flour mills and a forge) and the right to collect tolls on carts and pack animals traversing the seigneurie,

---

[21] A. D. du Gers, 3P 1386.

and on fat stock making its way to market.[22] These levies would have hit the peasant carters of the Pyrenees, in particular, who each autumn converged on Roquelaure and surrounding villages in order to fill casks with wine. The seigneurs of Roquelaure were also attentive to the symbolic dimension of their power. In 1744 they obtained the visa of the Parlement of Toulouse for a comprehensive reaffirmation of their rights of precedence – in church, in processions to and from the church, and in all civil assemblies.

On the eve of the Revolution the barony of Saint-Alban comprised six or seven farms and a right of *censive* applicable to forty-three localities throughout the parish. All of the farms were put out to lease, and the biggest of them (known as the 'domaine de Saint-Alban') was yielding about 3,300 *livres* in cash, or cash equivalent, in 1781. Unlike Neuviller or Roquelaure, though, the main source of seigneurial power here was not rent, but feudal dues. The *censives* were expressed in fixed quantities of grain, which ensured that each year the Molette de Morangiès brothers extracted about 545 *setiers* of rye, 29 *setiers* of wheat and 130 *setiers* of oats from the surrounding countryside.[23] Depending on the harvest conjuncture, therefore, these assets might be worth anything between 7,500 and 14,000 *livres*. If stockpiled they could be worth even more: in March 1778 hungry peasants from neighbouring villages complained that the seigneurial granary in Saint-Alban contained 2,000 *setiers* – enough to meet the immediate subsistence needs of the population of the *bourg* some ten times over. Compared with this harvest impost, the other prerogatives of the barony were mere trifles: a cash *censive* worth 217 *livres*, a toll leased for 100 *livres*, *lods et ventes* at 6 per cent, varying quantities of butter, cheese and wax, twenty-four sheep and seventy-three fat hens (*gélines*).

When the seigneurie of Villepreux entered the royal domain in 1776, it was valued at 305,694 *livres* of which the rights and perquisites were reckoned to be worth some 40,010 *livres*.[24] Expressed in (gross) income terms, therefore, the king was extracting not less than 12,627 *livres* each year from the village on the eve of the Revolution and about 18 per cent of this income stream derived from the exercise of his seigneurial prerogatives. Figures such as these leave little doubt about the commanding presence of the monarch in Villepreux. Yet it was an impersonal presence inasmuch as the estates acquired in 1776 belonged not to the king directly but to the Civil List. Unlike the duchy of Roquelaure which had never formed

---

[22] A. D. du Gers, E 1252, Dénombrement, 1772.
[23] A. D. de la Lozère, 4J 75, Tableau général de la censive dûe à la terre et seigneurie de Saint-Alban.
[24] See H. Lemoine, 'Notes historiques sur Villepreux (Seine-et-Oise)', *Revue de l'histoire de Versailles et de Seine-et-Oise*, 30 (1931), 85–6.

part of the Royal Domain, the seigneurie of Villepreux – once purchased – could not be sold on. At least that was the theory prior to 1789. Be that as it may, the fact remains that over half (52 per cent) of the territory of Villepreux was held by the monarch on the eve of the Revolution. Whilst forest and game covers enclosed within the Grand Parc occupied about 129 hectares, the bulk of the royal holding (399 hectares) consisted of rich arable land that was leased out to four 'gros fermiers'. The farms of Les Bordes (58 hectares) and Le Val-Joyeux were the only sizeable properties not in royal possession. The ordinary inhabitants of Villepreux, as has already been noted, controlled only a tiny percentage of the soil surface and matters were no different in the adjacent hamlet of Rennemoulin.

Although the king played no direct part in the life of the village, except when in pursuit of game, his seigneurial rights and perquisites were not inconsiderable. The most lucrative, according to the deed of sale, were 'cens et rentes seigneuriales', although there is no trace of a significant harvest due in the village. Nevertheless, the Domain each year collected about 1,000 *livres* from this source. *Lods et ventes* also yielded a healthy revenue (594 *livres*), in keeping with the buoyant land market around Paris and Versailles in the decades before the Revolution. The provision of seigneurial legal and judicial services brought in a tidy sum, too. By contrast the major revenue earners that we have identified elsewhere – monopolies and tolls – were all in decline. Fair and marketplace fees generated about 90 *livres* in 1776, but trade routes had already circumvented Villepreux and by 1789 the market was virtually extinct. As for mill and winepress monopolies, the exclusive rights of the seigneur had lapsed in the early eighteenth century. The two mills in the village were privately owned, and vine cultivation had in any case yielded to cereal monoculture by the time of the Revolution. The banal bread oven, so often a flashpoint in other villages, was not even a dim memory in the minds of Villepreussiens.

Nowhere, not even in Villepreux, could it be argued that seigneurialism had become an institution extraneous to village life, then. Whether by virtue of his right of administrative *tutelle*, or his capacity to apply economic pressure, the seigneur remained an important player in the local power arena. But attempts to measure and to quantify the concrete aspects of the institution succeed, if they succeed at all, only in producing an outsider's view. They tell us little about how the seigneurie was perceived from within. To get to the heart of the relationship between seigneur and villager we need to adopt a more imaginative approach to the evidence, and also to generalise.

On the strength of our six case studies it would be wrong to conclude in favour of a posture of endemic distrust between seigneurs and rural communities. Villagers wanted to get on with their seigneurs and they both understood and valued the principle of reciprocity to which John Markoff and other rural historians have drawn attention.[25] But when the transactional underpinnings of seigneurial authority crumbled, or were exposed as fraudulent, tension could easily develop. Even so, tensions were not bound to lead to endemic distrust or resistance. Villagers might grumble about mill monopolies or the *banvin* while continuing to attach importance to the availability of near-to-hand seigneurial justice. If this study can be used as any kind of guide, the reputation of seigneurial courts as dispensers of arbitrary justice is in any case not entirely merited. As for whole-hearted resistance, it was difficult to organise for the reason that village elites spent a good deal of their time actually servicing the seigneurie. A posture of outright resistance required them to change sides, and while this did occasionally happen before 1787, it was a rare occurrence, and more rarely still did it signal a full-scale *prise de conscience*. Historians have rightly noted the facility that villagers developed for taking their seigneurs to court in the second half of the eighteenth century, but it is doubtful whether this should be construed as the opening salvo of the Pre-Revolution. More likely we are dealing with a widespread perception that the sovereign courts could now be enlisted to help enforce the transactional nature of seigneurial power.

The first hint that the principle of reciprocity could no longer be relied upon in Châtelaudren materialised in the aftermath of the flood of 18–19 August 1773 that swept a large number of villagers to their deaths. Despite urgent calls for help from village worthies, the absentee Prince de Rohan-Soubise displayed extreme tardiness in allocating funds for the rebuilding of the dam necessary to retain the waters of his pool. As a result another inundation occurred on the night of 11–12 November in that same year. Consequently the *général* reacted with brusque impatience when the dispute over the bread oven, which all the inhabitants were constrained to use, blew up a few months later. Admittedly it involved a different and lesser seigneur, but the *général* seems to have concluded that they were all the same. To be sure the 'seigneur de Ruvéré' had helped to rescue people at the time of the first flood, but this was no more than an act of common humanity, argued the barrister for the community. And in any case it was Louis Le Gac de Ruvéré's profiteering lease increase on the morrow of the flood that had started the commotion in the first place.[26]

[25] For the argument, see J. Markoff, *The Abolition of Feudalism: Peasants, Lords and Legislators in the French Revolution* (University Park, Pa., 1996), pp. 18–19 and notes.

[26] A. D. des Côtes-d'Armor, 20G 42; Le Page, *Les Bleus du Châté*, pp. 81–4.

While the *général* of Châtelaudren was pursuing its case against the owner of the banal bread oven, the inhabitants of Roquelaure were congratulating themselves on the turn of fortune that had brought the Comte Dubarry to their village. The new seigneur acceded to every request for assistance with road repairs and willingly mobilised his croppers and draught animals to help with the transportation of raw materials. In 1773 he ordered the building of a raised causeway to the Moulin Neuf mill, insisting that he would pay for its upkeep as well as all construction costs. The *consuls* were charmed, and it was therefore with considerable embarrassment that they felt obliged, several years later, to point out some discrepancies in Dubarry's listing (*dénombrement*) of his rights. In a deliberation dated 3 May 1779 the *conseil* insisted that it had no wish to challenge anything possessing 'la moindre vraisemblance de légitimité', while acknowledging that it might find itself facing 'la durre nessesité de faire valoir ses droits'[27] before the Parlement of Toulouse. This shifting from one footing to another probably best captures relations between rural communities and their seigneurs. Even the villagers of Allan, who frequently sparred with their overlord, and who moved close to a posture of outright resistance in 1785, retained a faith in seigneurial interventionism for certain purposes. Irretrievably divided on the issue of whether to equip the village with a pendulum clock, they contemplated asking the Comte de La Tour-du-Pin-Montauban to mediate in 1781. The trouble with resistance was that it threw everything into jeopardy. In November 1789 the *consuls* of Allan tried, unsuccessfully, to secure the arrest of a local ne'er-do-well who had been condemned to the galleys several years earlier by the Parlement of Aix. Ever since the start of their court case with the seigneur, they noted ruefully, day-to-day law enforcement had completely broken down.

THE NORMATIVE ROLE OF MONARCHY

Seigneurs were integral to the fabric of village life, then. Moreover, they retained a capacity for involvement in the administrative affairs of rural communities that should not be underestimated. Indeed, there is evidence to suggest that their authority in this area persisted precisely because it commanded popular support. But if public opinion – in the modern sense of the term – did not declaim against seigneurialism, at least not before 1787, who did? The biggest challenge, in fact, came from the monarchy, which was trying to get a grip on the issue of structural reform in the second half of

[27] A. D. du Gers, E Supplément 1010².

the eighteenth century. When we come to track this reform impulse at the local level, however, we find a picture lacking in coherence, and for two main reasons. First, ministers were either unable or unwilling to pursue a policy of institutional refurbishment consistently, with the result that reform was frequently deflected by competing agendas for action; and second, the institutions of state did not speak with one voice. While intendants might wish to unpick the threads of seigneurialism in order to weave the village ever more firmly into the command structure of central government, the Provincial Estates, the *parlements* and the other sovereign courts envisaged an aggrandisement of their *own* powers at the expense of seigneurialism, not the creation of a streamlined form of Bourbon absolutism.

We can explore these pressures and cross-currents more closely by taking the case of Roquelaure, a village that experienced the whole gamut of reform initiatives between 1750 and 1787. Even before the arrival of the Marquis de Mirabeau on the scene, the administrative routines of the community had been upset by the creation and sale of venal municipal offices. Office holding would bedevil all attempts at institutional reform in the second half of the eighteenth century, in the sense that improvement in the working of the government machine required its abolition while the Great Power ambitions of the Bourbons rested in part on the income-flow that it generated. This is well known, of course; what is less commonly appreciated is that the conflicting priorities of government caused turbulence even at the level of the village. The edict of 1733 creating a further batch of venal municipal offices attracted few takers in Roquelaure, and the government responded with an embargo on consular 'elections' until such time as the offices were taken up. This ban remained in force for ten years, and throughout that period the *consuls* chosen in 1741 remained in post. In 1750 ministers changed tack, however, and resolved to parcel up all unsold offices and convert them into a supplementary tax. In the *généralité* of Auch about one million *livres* were added to the region's tax burden and the 'debt' registered against the village of Roquelaure amounted to 525 *livres* redeemable over ten years.

But at least the royal ban on renewals had been lifted. In 1751 the villagers proceeded to 'elect' their officers, persuaded that they had, in effect, 'bought' the right to do so. However, this interpretation required them to 'forget' that the prerogative of appointment still resided, properly speaking, with the seigneur even though it had been set aside for nearly ten years. In 1752 the *jurats* renewed the *consuls* again and at this point Mirabeau, who had acquired the seigneurie two years earlier, intervened to complain that his powers of supervision were being eroded. In practice the episode had produced a 'no win' situation, unless temporary fiscal relief can be counted a gain. The incoming intendant of Auch, Megret d'Etigny, resolutely opposed anything smacking of democratic election, whether at town or village level; on the other hand, the sale of offices alienated a portion of public authority to private individuals and diminished his powers of *tutelle*. The seigneur likewise regarded municipal office holding and for that matter any other initiative tending to alter the administrative status quo with deep suspicion. As for the villagers, or perhaps we would do better to say those who spoke on their behalf, they felt aggrieved that their bid for municipal autonomy had come to nothing. In the 1750s the practice of presenting a slate of eight candidates to the seigneur was resumed once more, as was the ceremony of oath taking by the successful candidates before the seigneurial judge.

In the 1760s the whole scenario was enacted afresh, albeit with a new leading player – Controller General Laverdy. Despite the forced purchase of 1750, further batches of municipal offices were offered for sale by the Crown, and on 31 December 1760 the intendant notified the *consuls* of Roquelaure that Antoine Bergelasse had been appointed over their heads to the office of mayor.[28] The timing was unfortunate to say the least, in that the putative *consuls* for 1761 had just been chosen and had been sworn in by the seigneurial judge only three days earlier. But Bergelasse, a wool-carder, had paid 600 *livres* for his post, and, as the new executive officer of the village, insisted that the *consuls* surrender to him the tax *mande*. Among other repercussions, this 'coup' – for that was how it was perceived – mobilised the *assemblée générale*, which constituted an active ingredient of collective life in Roquelaure as we have noted. Imagine the satisfaction, therefore, when Controller General Laverdy announced a clean-sweep reform of local government in 1764. Not only was the venal office of mayor abolished forthwith, but Laverdy's edicts also signalled a sharp reduction in the supervisory powers of intendants and seigneurs.[29] On the face of it, the reform sounded the death-knell of self-serving and self-selecting oligarchies and encouraged villages such as Roquelaure in the expectation that they would shortly be equipped with truly elective municipal councils.

The first folio of the earliest extant register of deliberations of the *conseil politique* of Roquelaure is dated 2 March 1766. It enshrines a personal letter from Laverdy despatched on 29 January endorsing the steps taken by the village elders in order to implement his edicts. Another followed a fortnight

---

[28] A. D. du Gers, E 1215, Pomès to Monseigneur le contrôleur général [n.d.].

[29] See M. Bordes, *La Réforme municipale du contrôleur-général Laverdy et son application, 1764–1771* (Toulouse, 1968).

later, and from these and surviving deliberations we can piece together what had been going on.[30] The obstacle of office holding had been overcome as the villagers moved to elect a municipal body comprising *échevins* and *conseillers* in accordance with the legislation. The challenge of seigneurial oversight or 'interference' had proved more troublesome, however, in part no doubt because the Parlement of Toulouse had come to the assistance of seigneurs with an amendment to the edicts. In an *arrêt* of 16 July 1765 the Parlement reserved to seigneurs the right to confirm the new *élus* in office in localities where they had possessed this right previously.[31] Nevertheless, the *conseil* of Roquelaure asked the judge to leave the meeting whenever it wished to discuss the contents of Laverdy's letters, or matters touching upon relations between the community and the seigneurie.

It is probably significant that the written record of municipal life in Roquelaure should begin where it does, for the Laverdy edicts laid the foundations of alternative power structures in small towns and *bourgs* in several parts of the kingdom. And lest we forget, they were an initiative of central government: a further indication, therefore, that Tocqueville's schematic portrayal of the suffocating force of centralisation fails to do justice to the complexity of the *ancien-régime* state. Only in Roquelaure is it likely that the reform set municipal life on a new trajectory, however. The Parlement of Brittany never registered the edicts, thereby ensuring that we find no trace of the initiative in Châtelaudren; and in Languedoc the government retreated from some of the main provisions of the reform in order to secure compliance. The Molette de Morangiès of Saint-Alban procured a printed copy of the more dilute regulations for Languedoc, and to judge from their underlinings they were chiefly concerned by the stipulation that municipal elections be conducted on the basis of a ballot ('voie de scrutin').[32] Only in Allan do we find a situation in some ways similar to that prevailing in Roquelaure, although it should be said at the outset that the Laverdy edicts were not actually enforced here either. In Provence the Procureurs du Pays fought a long battle with the monarchy over venal office holding; they argued that the sale of posts such as mayor or *consul* was contrary to the 'constitution' of the province, according to which such dignities were bestowed on the basis of public trust. Whenever the protests of the Parlement of Aix proved insufficient, the representatives of the province endeavoured to buy the new creations out. The net result of this strategy was a heavy debt overhead. By 1772 they had borrowed

[30] A. D. du Gers, E Supplément 1010¹.   [31] *Ibid.*, 2 March 1766.
[32] A. D. de la Lozère, 16J 1, Edit du roi donné à Versailles au mois de mai 1766 contenant règlement pour l'administration des Villes et Communautés de la Province de Languedoc.

amounts totalling 12.5 million *livres*, which sum, distributed on a *pro rata* basis, left the villagers of Allan facing a debt burden of 3,694 *livres*.[33]

When Laverdy fell from power in 1768 everything changed. The brief experiment in elective local government, which had also served to redirect the administrative supervision of rural communities via the courts (Laverdy was an ex-*parlementaire*) rather than the intendants, came to an end. His successor at the Contrôle Général, Terray, was not interested in municipal reform and reinstated the sale of offices. The Procureurs du Pays and the Parlement of Aix responded with such a barrage that they eventually won an exemption for Provence from this fresh round of office creations. As a result Allan's debt did not increase in the years before the Revolution and the villagers, or rather a small number of better-off households, retained control over the appointment of the *consuls*. But in Roquelaure the disgrace of Laverdy delivered a blow to burgeoning municipal pride. The village was again threatened with office creations, and on 3 September 1772 the *consul*-candidates were summoned to the chateau ('les officiers municipaux ayant été supprimés')[34] so that the seigneur could exercise his right of nomination.

In the context of the eighteenth century the question as to who held the whip hand over rural communities mattered to central government mainly for reasons of taxation. Revenue extraction and road building or maintaining were the two great monuments to Bourbon absolutism in the countryside, and both presupposed a high degree of supervision. Yet the exercise of power in these areas was far from straightforward. Rural communities enjoyed the right to appoint their own tax collectors and they enjoyed a fair degree of autonomy in the matter of assessment. (Neither freedom, it should be said, would long outlive the Revolution.) The intendants, as relatively recent arrivals on the scene, were obliged to share the power of fiscal oversight with older and more prestigious institutions of state; meanwhile the day-to-day expedients of a revenue-hungry government could easily cut across attempts to maintain an efficient tax administration. One of the objections raised against the venal mayorship of Bergelasse at Roquelaure in 1761 was that it would not be prudent to entrust such an individual with a tax roll worth 9,000 *livres*.

At Châtelaudren we rarely hear from the intendant. Tax instructions came from the Estates of Brittany and when, in 1786, the *général* decided to raise a loan in order to meet the needs of the poor it sought the endorsement of the Parlement. By contrast the intendant exercised extensive jurisdiction

---

[33] A. D. des Bouches-du-Rhône, C 2577; also G.-H. de Coriolis, *Traité sur l'administration du comté de Provence* (3 vols., Aix-en-Provence, 1786–8), III, pp. 193–217.

[34] A. D. du Gers, E Supplément 1010[1].

over the tax affairs of the community of Roquelaure, but even this was not total, for the Cour des Aides of Montauban retained the right to scrutinise village accounts. In Languedoc and Provence the intendants took few, if any, decisions independently of the *sindics* of the Estates, with the result that relations between the inhabitants of Saint-Alban and the chief agent of central government were quite different from those prevailing in, say, Villepreux. Here, intendant Bertier's *taille* reform had more or less removed from the hands of the village collector the drawing up of the tax roll. After 1773 the task was carried out by tax professionals (*commissaires aux impositions*).

Allan was the exception to all of these permutations, however. Although the village formed part of Provence, it lay outside the protective fiscal cocoon woven by the old Estates and their successor institutions, in the sense that its tax load was allocated by the intendant alone (through the intermediary of the subdelegate of Grignan). On the other hand, the intendant was Charles-Jean-Baptiste Des Gallois de La Tour – a man who identified strongly with a province in which he had served for over forty years by the time the Revolution broke out. The result: a fiscal history that speaks volumes about the pressures facing ministers who decided to grip the nettle of reform. The Terres Adjacentes of which Allan formed a part paid the *taille* in the form of a global figure or *don gratuit* of 70,000 *livres*, which each year the monarch abated by one-third – supposedly in recognition of various misfortunes that had befallen the district. Allan's share of the revised sum was about 1,052 *livres*, and between 1750 and 1779 this figure scarcely altered. Terray was the first minister to question this cosy arrangement and to try to change it. He swiftly encountered a barrage of protest from vested interests, however, pointing out that some of the privileges of the Terres Adjacentes dated back to 1291 and had been confirmed afresh as recently as 1761. He gave up, or perhaps fell from power before any remedy could be found. Nevertheless, the anomaly clearly irked ministers, and not least because the towns and villages of the Terres Adjacentes continued to petition for special-factor rebates over and above that already accorded. In 1779 councillors returned to the issue and ruled that while the king would always lend a sympathetic ear to real cases of need or distress, the automatic rebate should be phased out. The intendant was advised of this decision, to take effect from 1780, but he 'forgot' to do anything about it and submitted the standard paperwork with rebates taken into account as usual. France was now at war, however, and Necker, on whom the task of making economies devolved, was in no mood to compromise. His advisers pointed out that all the communities of the Terres Adjacentes could not be suffering each year from the same misfortunes: ergo, a flat-rate rebate was unjustified. Over three years the rebate was phased out and intendant La Tour dutifully raised the *taille* assessment for the village of Allan from 1,118 to 1,755 *livres*.[35]

The taxing function of the monarchy was generally accepted in the eighteenth century. Villagers did not rise in revolt when a new *vingtième* was added or an old one extended. Instead, the sense of injustice, if indeed there was one, was deflected towards exemptions (of persons in the north, of land as well as persons in the south). Ever since the 1760s the villagers of Allan had grumbled among themselves that the seigneur's farms included commoner land that should by rights be listed on the *taille* roll. After 1779 these grumbles would become louder. By contrast labour service on the roads was less readily accepted as a prerogative of the Crown, in part because it was a new imposition with a pedigree stretching back no further than 1738, in part because it gave rise to systemic abuse, and also no doubt because it was reminiscent of personal servitude in an age that was growing steadily more sensitive to the issue. The inadequacies of the jurisprudence governing the implementation of the *corvée* made abuse, if not inherent, at least highly likely, for they left the intendants a large margin for manoeuvre. And as we shall see, those regions where the powers of the intendants were curbed, or counterbalanced, by the existence of parallel institutions tended to fare rather better. Indeed, the villagers of Allan and Saint-Alban had no direct experience of the *corvée* whatsoever.

In 1759, or thereabouts, an anonymous and undated denunciation observed that a right-angled bend ('un coude considérable')[36] in the Charmes–Flavigny road as it entered the village of Neuviller had been created so as to ensure that the carriageway did not cut through the property of seigneur Chaumont de La Galaizière. As a result the road passed too close to the river Moselle and was liable to flooding. The writer then went on to recount a history of abuse of the *corvée* that would appear exaggerated if it could not be corroborated from other sources. As both chancellor to Stanislas I and representative of the king of France, Antoine-Martin Chaumont de La Galaizière was all-powerful in Lorraine in consequence of the marriage of Louis XV to Marie Leszczynska as we know. He pressed forward public works projects throughout the province with almost total disregard for the consequential effects on the rural population and on agriculture. Two of these building sites became notorious: that of the 'Ponts de Toul', where thousands laboured for seventeen years in order to level the

[35] A. N., H1258.
[36] A. D. de Meurthe-et-Moselle, 1F 317, Mémoire sur lequel on peut compter, les faits y détaillés n'étant tirés que du local.

main Nancy–Toul highway in its passage through the forest of La Haye, and that known as the 'Route de Nancy à Charmes', whose sole purpose, contemporaries claimed, was to link up the properties purchased by La Galaizière *père* in and around Neuviller. Between 1756 and 1759 the inhabitants of some 200 villages were conscripted to work on the latter project, which included the demolition of the old chateau of Neuviller, the clearing of the site for the new, and construction of the walls of a park. Villagers were forced to march at short notice with no opportunity to collect food for themselves or fodder for their draught animals. Those living beyond the Moselle had to pay in order to cross the river (one of the three ferries was owned by the seigneur), and there were fatalities and stock losses when those unable to pay chose to brave the waters. Over a thousand *corvéables* were employed on the Neuviller site for between three and six weeks each year, but this was no more than a microcosm of what was taking place throughout the province. Even as late as 1777, by which time Antoine Chaumont de La Galaizière *fils* had taken steps to eradicate the worst abuses in the 'slave system' perfected by his father, approximately one-eighth of the population of the province (110,000 *corvéables*) were being put to work on the roads each year. In 1760, for the first time in three and a half years, there was no forced construction work taking place in and around the chateau of Neuviller. But by that time the damage to the rural population, both material and psychological, had been done. Moreover, the Parlement of Nancy had gathered a substantial dossier of evidence about the activities of La Galaizière *père* that it transmitted to the Controller General in Paris.[37]

In conditions such as these, the question of exemptions scarcely arose. If villages failed to turn up for their work detail, La Galaizière *père* simply imposed collective fines. His counterpart in Gascony handled matters rather differently, however. D'Etigny, too, was fired with the ambition to open up his province by means of roads, but not at any cost. The inhabitants of Roquelaure were never conscripted for more than ten days a year, and in normal circumstances for not more than six. The intendant of Auch would tolerate no favouritism, either. Among commoners, only sharecroppers cultivating noble land were deemed exempt together with their draught animals. All others were required to contribute, whether or not the proprietor was a *privilégié*. This issue caused problems, however, for while the intendant might be clear in his own mind where the obligation of the *corvée* began and ended, his subdelegates were more vulnerable

---

[37] See P. Boyé, *Les Travaux publics et le régime des corvées en Lorraine au XVIIIe siècle* (Paris and Nancy, 1900), pp. 54–5.

to pressure exerted by local bigwigs. In the mid-1760s, at a time when the village of Roquelaure was feeling its way towards civic independence, the *consuls-échevins* complained that the number of draught animals owned by the seigneurie had been deliberately underestimated. In the 1770s and 1780s the difficulty lay rather with the *forains*, that is to say the non-resident landowners who were reluctant to allow their croppers to be requisitioned. The problem of exemptions also threatened to divide the inhabitants of Châtelaudren. They needed no reminding of the importance of the *corvée*, for the busiest highway in Brittany passed down their main street. The village contained a disproportionate number of officials and office holders, however, some of whom enjoyed exemptions of a questionable nature. On 12 May 1782 the *général* wondered aloud whether it was fair that the postmaster should escape the *corvée* when he also possessed wagons and horses linked to a flourishing food retailing business.[38] But at least there was nothing arbitrary about the work detail to be performed by the village, for in Brittany the *corvée* was administered not by the intendant but by the Provincial Estates.

When the *corvée* became intolerable to villagers, for whatever reason, the solution that beckoned was commutation, that is to say conversion into a cash lump sum that was simply added to the tax rolls. This is what happened in Languedoc and Provence, and support for a general measure of commutation gradually built up within the Contrôle Général in the 1770s. But commutation provided no instant answer to the problem of exemptions since it begged the question: who was liable to pay the replacement tax? The villagers of Roquelaure discussed the issue in 1784 and in the final analysis resolved that they would rather continue performing labour service. Likewise those of Neuviller and surrounding villages, despite all the hardship they had suffered in the 1750s. Following Controller General Turgot's ill-starred attempt at abolition, only 240 Lorraine villages out of a total of around 1,700 opted to keep the monetary payment in place of the *corvée*. Villepreux alone among the villages in this study seems to have favoured commutation, although it is not clear whether this was before or after the edict of June 1787 that finally brought the *corvée* to an end. The cost amounted to 520 *livres*, that is to say a 13 per cent increase in the community's tax burden, or 2 *livres* 10 *sols* extra per household.[39]

Who, then, were the natural leaders of the village during these final decades of the old monarchy? It is not an easy question to answer, unless of course we take Tocqueville's line that such individuals no longer existed.

[38] A. D. des Côtes-d'Armor, 20G 42.   [39] A. N., Z1G 461.

Enough has been said, however, to indicate that this view is not sustainable. An obvious candidate would be the parish priest – a literate and omnipresent fixture in every village until the Dechristianisation impulse of 1793–4 (see pp. 210–13). But institutions that function smoothly tend to leave few traces, which helps to explain why the parochial dimension of village life has not featured prominently in our analysis thus far. Only in Châtelaudren did a formal relationship exist between priest and civil community. In Saint-Alban the long-serving incumbent, Béraud, had a poor opinion of village assemblies, 'qui ne sont jamais que cabales ténèbres, tyrannies,'[40] as he would put it in a long *mémoire* submitted in 1789. It *is* significant, however, that *curé* Dompnier should emerge to play an administrative role in Roquelaure during the period of the Laverdy reform. For this was the model that ministers wanted to encourage. Indeed, Controller General Turgot had envisaged a formal role for clergy in village assemblies, and the Calonne–Brienne reform of 1787–8 (see pp. 88–90) would contain a provision to that effect.

Yet priests carried around with them considerable baggage which might undermine any claim to natural authority. For a start, they could not entirely escape the opprobrium of the tithe, even where its proceeds were siphoned off into the pockets of bishops, chapterhouses and lay individuals. At Roquelaure a swingeing 12.5 per cent impost on gross harvest yield fuelled resentment against all forms of ecclesiastical authority in the 1780s. Moreover, village-based clergy could be substantial secular figures. According to the *capitation* rolls of Saint-Alban, Béraud had five domestics and employed three ploughmen to farm a small estate that he owned. As for Joseph-Etienne Seignelay, *curé* of Neuviller, he was beholden to the seigneurie, as events in 1790 would demonstrate (see pp. 110–13). In any case, he was not the most important ecclesiastic in the village; that position belonged to the prior who was none other than the brother of Antoine Chaumont de La Galaizière. What all of this suggests is that rural communities tended to display ambivalent attitudes towards their priests. Whether these individuals could call upon a fund of moral or spiritual authority that outweighed the jealousies and resentments they also attracted remains largely imponderable, therefore. Not until the crisis triggered by the clerical oath, in 1791, will we really learn what country dwellers thought about their priests.

In reality the natural leaders of the village on the eve of the Revolution are likely to have been those wielding economic power: that is to say the

---

[40] A. N., B^a 51, *bailliag*e of Gévaudan.

microscopic legal bourgeoisies of Châtelaudren, Roquelaure and Saint-Alban, the *ménagers* of Allan, the *laboureurs* of Neuviller and the 'gros fermiers' of Villepreux. Is this a paradox? Not necessarily. The *ancien-régime* village, as we have described it, was a place of institutional overlaps, a place with no unambiguous political alignments, a place where collective postures interacted in a manner that the historian is at pains to explain, if deeply meaningful to participants. Deference towards those who controlled the resources of the village was a reality, but it does not follow that this deference was forced or unconditional. Neither should we forget that power, understood now as a resource, could take on many different forms. Moreover, those who were to prove adept at construing this resource in its new post-1787 forms were already waiting in the wings.

CHAPTER 3

Agendas for change: 1787–1790

'If only the king knew,' sighed country dwellers as they strove to overcome the hurdles of day-to-day life. At least, this is the remark recorded by Auget de Montyon – one-time intendant and enlightened councillor of state to Louis XVI – in jottings intended to become a study of the 'science of administration'.[1] But of course the king does know, he replied to himself, and it is a vulgar error to suppose otherwise. For as long as the ordinary inhabitants of town and country continued to believe that the System could not change, only the relative position of individuals within it, the fiction of absolute monarchy faced no serious challenge from below. The present chapter is intended to show how this fiction became dangerously exposed at the level of the village. The aim is to explore the conceptual underpinnings of established authority in the hope of providing an answer to the question: 'How did the sense of a definitive break with the past come about?'

Although the notion of 'agendas' sounds rather modern and formal, it will enable us to highlight the contingent and interactive quality of popular grievances and ambitions. The compilation of the *cahiers de doléances* in nearly every rural parish served to fix those grievances and necessarily fixes the historian's attention. But popular aspirations for reform did not appear from nowhere in the late winter of 1789; nor did they remain unchanged thereafter. *Cahier* drafting was an important moment in an on-going process that began when Controller General Calonne summoned an Assembly of Notables to consider a range of far-reaching alterations to the fabric of monarchy, and only ended with the successful installation of replacement institutions of local government some three years later. During these years the familiar *ancien régime* died in the minds of villagers, and gradually – perhaps more gradually than is usually allowed – something new took its place. This process, in which the convening of parish assemblies in order to formulate and focus opinion in readiness for the Estates General is merely

---

[1] Archives de l'Assistance Publique, Fonds Montyon, carton 5: Droit constitutionnel.

the best understood and best documented episode, generated multiple, even competing, agendas. Differences of priority and emphasis between villages developed, while individual village communities opted to modify their agendas for change as new and hitherto 'unthinkable' opportunities beckoned. It is even possible to detect the emergence of regional agendas to which a number of villages subscribed, the more so as an interactive mode of political expression came to replace the paternalism of Bourbon administrative monarchy.

'Agendas', then, is a loose term. It embraces both the identification of deficiencies rooted in the structures of the old regime and the identification of possibilities inherent in the embryonic structures of the new. A deficiency identified became a grievance, particularly once remedies appeared to lie close to hand, whereas the possibilities of the first full year of Revolution mostly took on the appearance of golden opportunities. Village grievances are not easy to generalise, as we shall see, but two themes in particular stand out: restitution and reciprocity: of feudal dues overpaid (the case of Saint-Alban), or taxes underpaid (the villagers of both Allan and Roquelaure asserted that their seigneur had systematically avoided paying tax on 'biens roturiers'). As for reciprocity, the case of Châtelaudren and the repercussions of the flood have already been mentioned, but the sense of deep hurt at the breakdown of reciprocity can be detected in Allan, too. Here, the seigneur was entitled to remove wood from the communal forest with which to fire his bread oven. In return he provided a free distribution of a *quintal* of loaves to the poor. Until 1753 that is, after which date the handouts ceased even though wood cutting continued.

Yet long-nurtured grievances could easily yield ground to more opportunistic considerations. In the summer of 1789 the villagers of Allan simply sidestepped the issue of wood cutting by taking their dough elsewhere, thereby condemning the banal bread oven to rapid oblivion. A new regime was in the making. From that autumn opportunities inviting a redefinition of agendas flowed thick and fast. The National Assembly dangled the prospect of fiscal harmonisation with a widely reported, and much misunderstood, law entitling rural communities to collect 'back tax' from nobles and other privileged persons for the final six months of 1789. The placing of ecclesiastical property at the disposal of the Nation raised the tempting scenario of villagers bidding collectively for *biens nationaux*, while the Municipal Law of December 1789 unveiled a vista of administrative autonomy in which even the smallest localities could expect to break free from seigneurial and monarchical *tutelle*. As the territorial reconfiguration of the kingdom took on permanent shape in the early months of 1790, villages even discovered that they could enter bids for recognition as seats of cantons, or perhaps districts. Neuviller, Roquelaure and Châtelaudren all secured cantonal status but Allan and Villepreux were thwarted, while Saint-Alban had to settle for a canton and a resident *juge de paix* after being beaten into third place by better-placed rivals for the dignity of a District administration.

Fresh agendas were also constructed out of the manifold shortcomings of the National Assembly's legislation. The uneasy compromise over the clerical tithe is a case in point. Scheduled for immediate abolition following the events of August 1789, the deputies subsequently repented their act of generosity and cast around for a method of compensation. A compromise solution that reinstated the tithe for one more year as a preliminary to abolishing it outright pleased no one, least of all the sharecroppers of Roquelaure for whom it remained the pre-eminent issue of the early years of the Revolution. It is clear that the promulgation of the redemption legislation applicable to non-extinguished feudal dues in the spring of 1790 had a galvanising effect on village agendas, too. In Saint-Alban the growing suspicion that their seigneurs had for years been collecting lucrative harvest dues at an unjustified rate produced first a demand for restitution and then a mood of refusal to make any payment whatsoever. In Villepreux, whose farmland – it will be remembered – was partially enclosed within the Grand Parc of Versailles, hunting was the most visible issue. Virtually all of the villages making up the *bailliage* of Versailles alluded to the problem posed by game in their *cahiers*, albeit more in sorrow than in anger. Consequently there was an overwhelming feeling of satisfaction when the news of the abolition of exclusive hunting rights came through; only a month prior to 4 August three poachers had been hanged in the village. Imagine the sense of outrage, therefore, when it transpired that the personal *plaisirs* (hunting reserves) of the king were exempted from this most tangible of freedoms.

Agendas evolved, then. Between the summer of 1787 when Calonne's package of reforms first began to take effect at the local level and May–June 1790 when the summoning of the cantonal primary assemblies afforded villagers a public platform from which to express their hopes and fears, the sense of what was possible altered profoundly. But if agendas altered over time, they also evinced a tendency towards social reconfiguration. This is another way of saying that agendas were not, of necessity, whole village constructs. To judge from police reports the rich no less than the poor were incensed by the continuing ban on hunting within the royal game parks. But the problem of game had been solved by the end of the first full year of Revolution (see p. 100). And at this point an arguably 'truer' representation of the ambitions of the land-hungry villagers of Villepreux emerged in the shape of a campaign to curtail land engrossment. So, agendas could be camouflaged. They could also be gratuitous. Once the calling of an Estates General had been announced, many rural clergy hastened to draft unofficial *cahiers* supposedly giving 'voice' to the concerns of their parishioners. The *abbé* Béraud, incumbent of Saint-Alban, is a case in point. In May 1789 he penned a twenty-three-page programme of reforms, most of which the villagers would not have recognised. On the other hand some agendas were plainly constructed with the help of outside 'intercessors'. The inhabitants of Allan relied heavily on the advice of Pierre Henri Legrand, a senior official in the taxation bureau of the intendancy of Aix, who appears to have had kith and kin in the village. From 1785 until the summer of 1790, when the transfer of power to the new local government bodies was finally consummated, he acted as their mentor – helping them to put their thoughts into words. He aided and abetted their efforts to plead against their seigneur, and did not hesitate to make cautionary noises when ambitions started to run ahead of political possibilities – as, for example, in January 1790, when he counselled that it would not be prudent to stop paying the *tasque* since the recent court case had demonstrated that this was the one feudal prerogative for which the seigneur possessed an unambiguous title.

MUNICIPAL ASSEMBLIES

The first intimations at the village level that Bourbon administrative monarchy had entered a critical phase in its development came hard on the heels of Calonne's Provincial Assemblies reform. Loménie de Brienne, who ousted Calonne from the Contrôle Général in May 1787, nudged the reform in a liberal-minded direction with a scheme to replace the confusing diversity of local power structures with elective municipal assemblies. These assemblies would – in the fullness of time – give birth to an integrated system of representative government, or so the policy makers argued. In a village such as Villepreux with no discernible corporate existence prior to 1787, the reform marked a dramatic break with the practice of absolutism. On Sunday 12 August 1787, after Vespers, the congregation was invited to stay behind and choose a six-man municipal assembly whose responsibilities were to extend to the apportionment of taxes in partnership with the existing authorities. At a stroke Tocquevillian centralisation had been put into reverse and a rudimentary structure established which would prove capable of sustaining a form of collective political life. The first municipal register of Villepreux reads as a continuous record of deliberations running from

12 August 1787 through to 12 September 1791.[2] Likewise the deliberations of the neighbouring hamlet of Rennemoulin, which also commence in the summer of 1787.

Elsewhere, however, we do not get the same clear sense of an administrative break with the past. For a start, the Calonne–Brienne experiment with quasi-representative local government institutions was never applied to the *pays d'états*, and therefore made no impact upon the villages of Allan, Châtelaudren and Saint-Alban. And where it was applied, the reform could rarely be implemented in conditions of near political vacuum such as those prevailing on the outskirts of Paris and Versailles. In Lorraine there was a delay of almost a year before the municipal component of the reform took effect. Nevertheless, the villagers of Neuviller were invited to choose a municipal assembly in the early summer of 1788. Here, though, the challenge lay in establishing municipal independence *vis-à-vis* the seigneurie and it was not surmounted. Significantly, no record of the municipal assembly's deliberations has survived, and we know from later evidence (see pp. 110–11) that the body was quickly packed by agents and cronies of the seigneur. By contrast and for reasons that are not entirely clear, the adjacent village of Roville, which was no less subject to the will of Antoine Chaumont de La Galaizière, managed to prevent its municipal assembly from becoming a tool of the seigneurie. The critical ingredient seems to have been the attitude of the parish priest. In Neuviller Joseph-Etienne Seignelay worked hand in glove with the La Galaizière, whereas *curé* Dumaire who presided over the municipal assembly of Roville was all too conscious of the longrunning court case between the villagers and their seigneur (see p. 244) and trod a more independent path. What of Roquelaure? In this Gascon village with a home-grown municipal superstructure and solid grounds for a distrustful attitude towards outside interventionism, the reform caused confusion. Bertrand de Boucheporn, the intendant of Auch, sent out a circular requiring all non-urban parishes to elect municipal assemblies on 14 October 1787 and the villagers of Roquelaure duly complied. Yet it is clear that they felt uneasy with a reform that appeared to be setting up a dual power regime. From the autumn of 1787, the deliberations of the *conseil politique* become disjointed as though no one was sure any longer of the source from which power emanated, and who was to hold it. Was it the *consuls* – nominally still appointed by the seigneur – or an undifferentiated body of taxpayers? In fact the community rallied round its *consuls* who,

---

[2] A. C. de Villepreux, D1; for Rennemoulin, see E. Tambour, *Les Registres municipaux de Rennemoulin* (Paris, n.d. [1903]).

from November 1788, took the precautionary step of relabelling themselves the 'municipality' of Roquelaure.

Although the meeting to set up Villepreux's first municipal body was held straight after Evensong, only fourteen heads of household stayed behind. Or, more probably, only a handful of adult males were deemed fit and proper persons to deliberate on such a weighty matter. This serves to remind us that neither in effect nor in intent was the reform a democratic exercise. Its significance lay elsewhere. By implementing the reform Brienne announced a new approach to the 'science of administration' predicated on a reduction in *tutelle*. He also, and perhaps inadvertently, initiated a process of politicisation at the grass roots. Assemblies implied participation, discussion and even consent. Not as an occasional exercise called into being by a cash-strapped government, but as a regular, on-going activity. The enabling legislation stipulated that members of municipal assemblies were to gather weekly, without prior notification, and irrespective of whether there was any business to transact. They were also to keep a proper record of their meetings in a bound register or minute book. In those parts of the kingdom where the reform was actually enacted it therefore marked the inception of a political routine. It also marked the first concerted attempt by government ministers to shape a fiscal concept of citizenship. The fourteen Villepreussiens who had stayed behind after the Sunday service were all big taxpayers assessed for at least 10 *livres*, and they voted (out loud) for six even bigger taxpayers (minimum requirement for eligibility 30 *livres*). To be sure, ministers did not cut adrift from the 'society of orders' altogether – seigneurs and parish priests entered the municipal assemblies in an *ex officio* capacity – but the writing was on the wall.

Thanks to the municipal assemblies reform, then, we can take the first in a series of snapshots of those late *ancien-régime* elites that would jockey for position as established power structures started to weaken following the announcement of an Estates General for 1789. In Villepreux only fourteen (7 per cent) out of around two hundred resident households were involved in choosing the municipal assembly, as we know. But in view of the threshold tax qualification this proportion is scarcely relevant. In practice about 37 per cent of those actually entitled to participate did so. They elected three of their own number (the miller and two wholesale victuallers engaged in the lucrative provisioning trade with the Palace of Versailles), two middling farmers and the second biggest tenant farmer in the village. To all intents and purposes, therefore, they conferred political recognition on those who already controlled the economy of the village. Only the (elected) *sindic*, Etienne Mongrolle, did not belong to this magic circle. He was a

barber-surgeon whose tax assessment barely reached the minimum threshold; the others paid an average of 234 *livres* each (almost three times the
annual earnings of an agricultural labourer). Owing to the loss or, more
likely, the destruction of both the minute book and the tax roll, it is impossible to be as specific about the situation in Neuviller. However, the creation
of the municipal assembly is not likely to have disturbed the balance of
power in the village. It would take an event of the magnitude of the Revolution to shake the position that La Galaizière *fils* had secured for himself
following the land distribution of 1770–1. Apart from the *curé*, the dominant figure in the municipal assembly was Antoine Prost, the seigneurial
maire and, in 1789, the holder of the contract for the collection of feudal
dues. At Roquelaure, the coterie of bourgeois families who had traditionally
rotated consular offices among themselves initially reacted with dismay, as
previously noted. We can only guess at the manoeuvring that must have
been going on across the summer and autumn of 1787. At any event, the
first *consul*, Joseph-Marie Barrué, managed to get himself elected as *sindic*
in a move that, if permissible, was scarcely in the spirit of the reform. That
done, and with a strategic name change, the familiar figures at the helm
of the village managed to ride out the turbulence caused by Calonne and
Brienne's initiatives. No doubt they were helped in this by the return to
power of Jacques Necker in September 1788, for Necker was known to hold
the view that the municipal assemblies experiment should never have been
applied to the southwest, where villages generally possessed consular institutions. Had the creation of municipal assemblies quickened the pace of
political thinking at the grass roots? Almost certainly, although it is difficult
to provide clinching evidence. The villagers of Neuviller and Roquelaure
anxiously discussed the future of the *corvée* once news reached them of
the Royal Declaration of June 1787 that required the conversion of this
labour obligation into a monetary payment. Those of Villepreux used the
new organ to declaim against an allegedly unfair tax assessment that took
no account of the damage caused by game. Only in Roville, the village
adjoining Neuviller, did the inhabitants use the opportunity afforded by
the reform to raise the question of seigneurialism, but here a court case had
already sharpened perceptions, as we shall see in chapter 7.

   In the *pays d'états*, where the three villages not mentioned so far were
situated, the process of agenda formation was driven by a different issue
altogether: the regional campaigns to reshape or in some instances resus-
citate the Provincial Estates. The excitement over municipal assemblies
during the autumn and winter of 1787 passed the *général* of Châtelaudren
by. Likewise Lamoignon's reform of the judiciary and subsequent exiling of

the Parlement of Rennes, although there is a suspicion that the legal bourgeoisie of Châtelaudren were hoping to benefit from the dismemberment
of the appeal court's jurisdiction. The cavalier treatment of the various dep-
utations despatched to Versailles by the embattled magistrates did produce
a reaction in the village, however, and it is also likely that the news emanating from Vizille in the Dauphiné was fermenting in men's minds. At
any event, the arrival in Châtelaudren on 28 September 1788 of the Comte
de Coëttando, a member of the joint delegation that had finally obtained
the ear of the king, became an occasion for massive rejoicing. But at this
juncture the agenda of Châtelaudren's educated inhabitants did not extend
beyond the horizons of the province. The *général* had a heartfelt grievance
rooted in its non-urban status, which disqualified it from deputing to the
Provincial Estates, as we know, and it was just beginning to have thoughts
about reform on a broader front. Those thoughts were brought into sharper
focus in the course of that autumn in response to the anti-noble campaign
waged by the bourgeoisie of the big cities of Brittany. On 2 December
1788 the *général* received an urgent communication from the mayor of the
neighbouring town of Saint-Brieuc, and even though it was not a Sunday
they sent a drummer round the village to call the inhabitants to an extraordinary meeting. The packet contained the news that an Estates General
would shortly be summoned, and also a printed resolution in which the
bourgeoisie of Saint-Brieuc set out a number of demands for the reform
of the Breton Estates, which were scheduled to convene at the end of the
month.

Under this stimulus the political education of the Châtelaudrinais
ripened within a matter of days. At its meeting on 14 December the *général*
added to the long-standing remonstrance about representation the request
that the Provincial Estates address the question of *capitation* tax inequalities
between the second and third estates, arrange for the restitution of overpaid
fouage tax, and proceed to the abolition of the *corvée* on the understanding
that it would be replaced by a monetary imposition levied on all three orders. For good measure they also called for the permanent rebuilding of two
stone bridges that had been carried away by the flood of 1773. Most of the
evidence, then, suggests that the Châtelaudrinais had allowed themselves to
be enlisted behind an agenda peddled by the bourgeois elites of the cities.
Indeed, it is clear that they were flattered to be solicited first by Saint-Brieuc,
the local town, and then by the distant metropolis of Nantes. Nevertheless,
there were some latent tensions of an anti-seigneurial character, as we know.
The year had begun with a quarrel over precedence between the rector and
the officers of the seigneurie. The campaign to restructure the Estates could

only inflame these tensions, but the campaign and the politicisation that accompanied it remained regional in focus. Not until March 1789, in the face of continuing noble intransigence, do we find a clear recognition that the solution to third-estate grievances lay outside the province.

Unlike Châtelaudren, whose post road brought early news of every twist and turn in the debates of the Pre-Revolution, the *bourg* of Saint-Alban only picked up reports of events being transacted in Montpellier and Toulouse, hundreds of kilometres to the south and southwest, in a dilute and hearsay form. Nevertheless, it is probable that initial agendas were framed in the context of provincial 'regeneration' here as well. For all their reputation for enlightened administration, the Estates of Languedoc were scarcely exempt from reproach on grounds of composition. Although the third estate was generously represented by comparison with the Breton Estates, proceedings still tended to be dominated by the upper clergy. There existed, moreover, a well-founded suspicion that the administrator-clerics of Montpellier were more interested in beautifying the cities of the plain than in spending money on more humdrum public works projects in the mountainous hinterland of the province. This was the criticism that *abbé* Béraud picked up. What his parishioners wanted were sturdy stone bridges, not esplanades and tree-lined squares, he argued, before concluding with a plea for the subprovince of the Gévaudan to be detached from Languedoc. Unfortunately there is no way of knowing how far the population of Saint-Alban shared this analysis. In the absence of the deliberations of the *conseil politique* even the fractious and quarrelsome bourgeoisie of the *bourg* remain tongue-tied. But perhaps this silence conveys a deeper message: in a region where public opinion at the end of 1788 was totally absorbed by the struggle between the nobility and the clergy for supremacy, there *was* no independent third-estate voice.

Allan was suspended in limbo between two provinces, each of which played a leading role in setting agendas for change on the eve of the Revolution. Surrounded on all sides by the territory of the Dauphiné, the villagers could not have been unaware of, or uninfluenced by, events taking place in Grenoble, Vizille and Romans during the summer and autumn of 1788. That said, however, they were also profoundly conscious of belonging to a Provençal 'nation', even though magistrates and administrators in Aix were apt to forget that the Terres Adjacentes existed. The third factor shaping villagers' apprehensions as the kingdom slipped into crisis was the bitterly fought court case already alluded to. It had arisen in 1785 following a decision by the seigneur's steward to impose a curtailment of grazing rights (*cantonnement*) in two forests that the community regarded as vital economic assets. This case intersected and interacted with events at both the national and the regional level, and it provides us with the best view yet of how villagers evolved political agendas and adjusted them in response to circumstances. The case went to appeal before the Parlement of Aix and was scheduled for a hearing in late 1787, at which point the seigneur's counsel was despatched to Paris on more important business as part of a delegation calling for the reform of the 'constitution' of the province. Hearings were again halted in May 1788 when the Parlement was exiled following the enforced registration of the Lamoignon edicts. Joseph Laurans, whom the *consuls* had sent to Aix in order to press forward their suit, hung on until the middle of the month and then returned home to regale his fellow villagers with an account of the larger spectacle now being played out. Laurans was back waiting in the antechamber of the Parlement the following year having been tipped off to expect the verdict on 28 July. On this occasion, however, judicial proceedings were disrupted by the descent on Aix of 4,000 Marseillais peace marchers. An excited Laurans penned a graphic narrative of the day's events.

While Allan's small drama was being played out, educated minds were pondering the implications of the government's decision to allow the reconvening of the Estates of Provence (in abeyance since 1639). The enfeoffed nobles who largely dominated the sessions appeared willing to compromise on the question of representation, but they firmly rejected any suggestion that 'biens nobles' should be taxed on a par with commoner property. For the inhabitants of Allan this was a key issue, not least because they strongly suspected their seigneur of arbitrarily ennobling (i.e. exempting from tax) the commoner land that she had acquired. Even as they fought to retain scrub grazing for their sheep flocks, a secondary agenda was in the making. The Dauphiné nobles, it is true, showed no greater inclination to make this concession in the summer of 1788. The turning-point would occur towards the end of that year. Once the Romans assembly had signalled its willingness to consider the relinquishment of tax exemptions, a wave of noble renunciations followed in rapid succession. This gave the elders of the village of Allan the courage to put into words and, more important, to put down on paper their grievances on the subject of taxes.

DECODING THE *CAHIERS DE DOLÉANCES*

For most rural communities the business of compiling *cahiers de doléances* took place in the late winter of 1788–9. Whatever the strengths or weaknesses of these documents, therefore, we can only expect them to reveal to us what was coursing through men's minds in March or perhaps April of that year. The *cahiers* of Roquelaure, Saint-Alban and Neuviller (together with the adjacent settlements of Roville and Laneuveville) were all compiled towards the middle of March; that of Allan was signed on 24 March after a marathon session, and that of Villepreux (together with Rennemoulin) in the early part of April. Unfortunately, however, the *cahiers* of Roquelaure and Saint-Alban have not survived, while a '*cahier*-like' document exists for Châtelaudren, but dates from the very end of 1788. In nearly every case, though, it is possible to identify the context in which these documents were drawn up, and it becomes immediately apparent that we are no longer dealing solely with established village elites well accustomed to expressing their opinions. At least sixty-three parishioners (31 per cent of households) were present at the socially diverse meeting which endorsed the *cahier* of Roquelaure, and a similar number (54 per cent of households) signed the *cahier* of Neuviller. Between two and three dozen individuals appear to have been present for the operations in Allan, Châtelaudren and Villepreux.

It is true, of course, that the meetings nearly always took place under the chairmanship of a seigneurial judge, or of a public official, which usually amounted to the same thing. This has prompted some historians to conclude that the *cahiers de doléances* should be treated as circumspect understatements of peasant concerns,[3] and it is certainly disconcerting to learn that the list of grievances of Roquelaure was simply produced for those present to sign. But the *cahiers* probably contained as much exaggeration as understatement: that of Villepreux greatly exaggerated the economic difficulties faced by the locality, and there is a strong suspicion that the villagers of Allan did likewise. For this reason, and others, it would be unwise to try to extract more from the *cahiers* than they are capable of providing. Serge Bianchi, whose in-depth investigation of village life in the Ile-de-France is the closest equivalent to the present study, believes it possible to compare *cahiers* and thereby to disclose collective village temperaments with predictive value for behaviour later on in the Revolution,[4] but this may be to look for meaning where there is none to find. The *cahiers de doléances* are best understood as blurred snapshots of a fleeting moment and not as fixed statements, whether endorsing the status quo or looking towards a programme of change.

---

[3] Lefebvre, *Les Paysans du Nord*, p. 344; see also the discussion in G. Shapiro and J. Markoff, *Revolutionary Demands: A Content Analysis of the Cahiers de Doléances of 1789* (Stanford, Calif., 1998), pp. 150–8 and notes; also Markoff, *The Abolition of Feudalism*, pp. 25–9 and notes.

[4] S. Bianchi and M. Chancelier, *Draveil et Montgeron, deux villages en Révolution* (Le Mée-sur-Seine, 1989), pp. 5, 71, 106–22.

Nevertheless, they do help us to know what was uppermost in country dwellers' minds at a point when the arena for political debate was about to be massively enlarged. The *cahier* of Roquelaure, had it survived, would almost certainly have given voice to resentments about the tithe. This was an issue on which croppers and the local bourgeois (the most likely authors of the *cahier*) held broadly convergent opinions, at least until the early months of 1790. Most of the seventy-six extant *cahiers* of the future department of the Gers had something to say about the tithe – unsurprisingly since the diocese of Auch had been riven from the mid-1770s by well-organised tithe 'strikes'.[5] Increasingly confident of judicial support from the Parlement of Toulouse, village communities questioned the swingeing assessment rates on the main bread-making cereals; they complained about the loss of straw which then had to be bought back from the tithe proctors at extortionate prices; they argued that it was unfair to tax seed-corn, and demanded that hay, wool, newborn lambs, beans and other 'new' crops be exempted altogether. How can we be confident that the tithe was Roquelaure's principal grievance? Because the villagers fought two court cases in the 1780s: to secure a reduction in the price of straw, and relief from a rate of 1:8 on cereals. Significantly, though, no one was calling for the outright abolition of the tithe at this stage, whether in Roquelaure or any other parish.

By contrast, the *cahier* of Châtelaudren showed no interest in agrarian matters whatsoever. The village had little agricultural territory, as previously noted, and could afford to regard issues such as the tithe, seigneurial harvest dues or collective rights over stubble and meadow with almost complete detachment. Surrounding parishes (notably Plélo and Plouagat) lay within the zone of seigneurial tenure known as *domaine congéable* (see pp. 251–2), but the only experience that Châtelaudrinais had of this highly contentious mode of land tenure occurred when defaulting tenants were hauled before its seigneurial courts. Instead, they continued to be driven by what we might loosely term 'urban' considerations: the iniquities of labour service on their arterial highway, the free quartering of migrating troops on local households, and, above all, the dogged refusal of the Breton nobility to agree to fiscal equality. Villepreux, too, complained about roads, but in this instance they attributed many of their woes to the loss of the main artery that now passed via Saint-Nom and had sucked the economic life-blood from their marketplace. For the rest, game provided the usual refrain;

[5] G. Sourbadère, 'Quelques aspects de l'oeuvre de l'intendant d'Etigny à travers les cahiers de doléances gersois', *Bulletin de la Société archéologique et historique du Gers*, 1996, no. 3, 361–4; also A. Tarbouriech, *Les Cahiers du clergé et du Tiers Etat de la Sénéchaussée d'Auch en 1789* (Nîmes, 1992), pp. 25–30.

although the *gardes-chasses* whose job it was to police the royal game covers were now condemned in more forthright terms.

Would that we knew what kind of *cahier de doléances* the villagers of Saint-Alban submitted, but in this locality it is all but impossible to get a sense of the movement of opinion before the summer of 1789. Not so Allan, where the principal inhabitants spent several days on the task of compilation. We can be certain of this because the village archives contain a payment receipt for the substantial quantity of firewood that was burned during the deliberations.[6] The result was a fourteen-page document of rare quality: lavish in detail and highly informative. It begins with a somewhat melodramatic statement of long-term decline and, more plausibly, of short-term economic distress before moving on to the subject of taxation. Fairly mild strictures about assessment follow, drafted no doubt in the knowledge that the Terres Adjacentes had, until 1780, enjoyed a generous rebate on their *don gratuit*. At the regional and the national level the village elders plainly felt themselves to be on safer ground, however, for they uttered an unambiguous demand that all three orders of the realm should pay tax in proportion to their resources. Clearly the campaign against fiscal privilege waged by the lawyer Pascalis and the bourgeoisie of Aix over the previous eighteen months had done its work.[7] To this demand was added a specific requirement that all noble and ecclesiastical property holdings be recorded in the tax register or *cadastre* – a coded reference to one of the many points at issue between the villagers and their seigneur. The remainder of the *cahier* is in fact a long and detailed depiction of the role played by the seigneurie in the economic life of the community. It reads more like a well-rehearsed legal brief than a statement of barely suppressed moral indignation, which is scarcely surprising in the circumstances. The time for emotional release would come in the summer.

The *cahier de doléances* of the 'bourg de Chaumont-sur-Mozelle', as the village of Neuviller had been known since 1776, was compiled in the presence of the seigneur's *bailli*, Nicolas Lambert. It is a good example of the way oppressive seigneurial *tutelle* could actually become counterproductive in the conditions unfolding during the late winter and spring of 1789. Close examination reveals that the *cahier* passed through at least three drafting hands before being approved, and, in view of the large number of signatures appended, it seems very likely that the document was negotiated in open assembly. The initial mild and non-specific statement may well have

[6] A. C. d'Allan, CC 56, receipt dated 25 November 1789.
[7] See J. Egret, 'La Pré-Révolution en Provence, 1787–1789', *Annales historiques de la Révolution française*, April–June 1954, 100.

been culled from one of the 'model' *cahiers* doing the rounds in the district of Vézelise early in March. It called for the restoration of the Provincial Estates of Lorraine, universal taxation, a reduction in the price of salt, and so on. Only on the subject of winepress monopolies (*banalités*) did it touch a raw nerve. This preliminary and largely uncontentious *cahier* was over-written, however: a clause drafted in a different hand was interpolated to demand 'la suppression des intendans'[8] (La Galaizière *fils* was the intendant of Alsace having previously held this commission in Lorraine), and several more highly specific clauses were added. The villagers wanted to see the 1770–1 land redistribution (La Galaizière's pride and joy) overturned; they called for the removal of all restraints on grazing by the common herd; an end to seigneurial errand-running; and the freedom to continue performing the *corvée* in kind if they so desired. Then, once the document had been signed, two further clauses were added in a third hand.

   All of these additions and insertions are more radical and pointed than the demands contained within the original draft, and they demonstrate how previously camouflaged agendas could come into the open. The document also helps us to understand the movement of ideas, for the additions include positive assessments of the role of the municipal assembly of Neuviller. Clearly, an institution that looked incorrigibly beholden to seigneurial power in the bountiful civic atmosphere of the spring of 1790 was not so despised in the more limited conditions for expression of 1788–9. Neuviller's *cahier* became, in turn, the inspiration for the *cahiers* of four neighbouring parishes, and in the process matters still referred to allusively in the master document became more explicit. For instance, the impediment to free grazing of stock was firmly identified by the villagers of Laneuveville as being the 1768 Edict of Enclosure, and those of Roville were at pains to make the same connection. The edict had been procured by La Galaizière *fils* as a preliminary to his pilot scheme for land reform (pp. 237–8), but it violated the terms of the Custom of Lorraine and was resisted by the Parlement of Nancy. In March 1789 vast numbers of Lorraine parishes protested the measure and the trend towards agrarian individualism that it had unleashed. This, at heart, was the central grievance of the landless and nearly landless poor of Neuviller and Roville. Like enclosure operations everywhere, the edict threatened to accentuate the polarisation of the rural community and make them the victims. The *cahiers* of Neuviller,

[8] See C. Etienne, *Cahiers de doléances des bailliages des généralités de Nancy*, III: *Cahiers du bailliage de Vézelise* (Paris, 1930), pp. 56–61. The original of the *cahier* can be found in A. D. de Meurthe-et-Moselle, E Supplément 3121–30.

Roville and Laneuveville bring out into the open nearly twenty years of grumbling about the issue.

After a week of mounting tension, the inhabitants of Allan burst into the chateau on 29 July 1789. Someone claimed to have spotted the seigneur's steward peering from an upstairs window. Five days later the news of a stunning victory in the courts reached the village. What had begun as a defensive reflex following reports of 'brigands' approaching from the direction of Valence and Montélimar ended up as a festive occupation. On the same day – 29 July – the urgent tolling of the church bell called the inhabitants of Villepreux to an assembly presided over by their municipal officers at which it was decided to create a militia. A nearly identical meeting took place in Châtelaudren five days later, and with the same purpose in mind. In the south and the southwest, meanwhile, confused accounts of armed fire-raisers penetrated as far as Saint-Alban on 1 August and Roquelaure two days later. Agendas which had been formulated with caution, even circumspection, only a few months earlier, now took on a more compelling aspect. They also started to shift as villagers sensed that established power was in retreat and new opportunities were opening up.

Four days after the invasion of the chateau, the *consuls* of Allan informed Legrand, their intercessor, that payment of both the tithe and the *tasque* would be withheld for the time being: 'Nottès que chaque hab[itan]t tiendra compte de ce qu'il aura perçu, et chaq'un s'offre a payer s'il doit, en son tems, ayant parfaite connoissance de cause.'[9] Since the verdict in the case before the Parlement was not yet known and the deputies in Versailles had yet to settle on a plan of action, this decision could only have been taken in response to other stimuli – the news of the fall of the Bastille, the 'brigand' emergency (otherwise known as the Great Fear), and perhaps also the electrifying account of the march on Aix by the Marseillais. But within a matter of weeks the villagers were interacting with the decrees of the National Assembly, and this is the pattern we observe in all of the localities. On 23 September – at one of the busiest and most anxious times of the agricultural year – the *conseil politique* met to record formally that *they* now possessed the power of police following a decree of the National Assembly. With evident satisfaction they also noted that their deliberations no longer required the legal endorsement of a representative of the seigneur.

[9] A. C. d'Allan, AA 9.

Ownership of the power of police was an important matter. The transfer had begun, in a *de facto* fashion, with the creation of militias, usually in response to the 'brigand' emergency of late July/early August. But the first wave of abolitionist legislation emanating from the National Assembly pandered inevitably to the growth of an anarchic sense of freedom. 'I have been pestered with all the mob of the country shooting,' wrote Arthur Young on 30 August as he crossed the delta of the Rhône, adding 'one would think that every rusty gun in Provence is at work, killing all sorts of birds'.[10] The sound of gunshots even awoke the king as villagers in and around the Grand Parc seized on the right to hunt. In Villepreux and Rennemoulin the Assembly's concession on hunting was far from purely symbolic. The profusion of pigeons, game birds, rabbits and deer did measurable damage to crops on a regular, annual basis. The idea that farmers cultivating land within the Parc should desist while everyone else was setting traps and loosing off firearms was therefore doubly galling. If the ban held until the winter it was mainly because the new impromptu authorities resolved to police it as an act of political loyalty to the National Assembly. The ultra-royalist National Guard of Versailles was especially active in this regard, but that of Villepreux also courted much unpopularity. Even members of the village's proprietorial elite were torn between the desire to obey the law and the desire to have some sport and at the same time rid the parish of game. Henri-Anne Mecquenem d'Artaize, colonel in the Villepreux militia, was reprimanded for illicit hunting. It was pretty clear, therefore, that the exclusion of the 'plaisirs personnels du Roi'[11] from one of the most potent freedoms to be declared on the night of 4 August 1789 would not hold for a second year running. As soon as the crops began to appear above ground in the spring of 1790 pressure mounted, and the newly elected municipality of Villepreux had little choice but to try to enforce the ban. Once the new District administration of Versailles took office in August, however, the wind began to change. There now existed a properly constituted body that could call the National Guard of Versailles to account. Sensing that a change of policy was in the air, the affected villages organised a collective trespass. Thousands of poachers descended on the Parc and destroyed game *en masse*. At Rennemoulin, by September 1790, a whole venison carcass could be had for 50 *sous*. Although blatantly illegal, the trespass solved the game problem. As for the National Assembly, it decided to look the other way.

The licence to hunt, in conditions of virtual impunity, would also help to rekindle smouldering agrarian conflicts. In Saint-Alban and Neuviller,

---

[10] Young, *Travels in France*, p. 256.   [11] Tambour, *Les Registres municipaux de Rennemoulin*, p. 63.

where custom and practice upheld a whole edifice of collective rights, villagers went on the offensive against those who supposed that they were entitled to withdraw their animals from the common herd. In both instances the point at issue was not so much the pasturing arrangements for home-reared animals as the temptation to 'buy in' additional stock which then overloaded commons, meadows and stubble. The community of Saint-Alban possessed vast common pastures, known as 'montagnes', which the *consuls* preferred to lease to lowland shepherds bringing up transhumant flocks; but they had not been able to prevent individuals in possession of common right from doing private deals (see p. 261). In the conditions prevailing from the summer of 1789 (temporary dislocation of power, politicised tensions between rich and poor, etc.), both communities and individual members of those communities behaved as though their rights had been enhanced. Yet at the same time they looked anxiously to the National Assembly for confirmation of those putative rights. In Neuviller and also in Laneuveville many of the poorer inhabitants were expecting to hear the news of the abolition of *troupeau à part*, but the deputies preferred to avoid making any categoric statement on the issue.

It is clear that a vivid popular memory of the old pre-1770–1 landscape had survived at Neuviller and that all agrarian discontents, whether the *triage* of the commons, enclosures, or *troupeau à part*, were linked to its demise. Villagers still identified with that portion of their territory where the commons had once been located and where the seigneur had subsequently planted poplar trees. At Saint-Alban, too, the despotic manner in which Noé-Jean Atrasic, the first *consul* and future revolutionary careerist, had encroached upon the commons of the hamlet of Les Faux was firmly embedded in the popular memory. In 1793 he, too, would be held to account for his actions. Elsewhere there were fewer resentments to rake over for the reason that the institutions of common right lacked substance both in practice and in law. Landowners had long enjoyed the right to enclose in Brittany, with the result that their behaviour in this regard was rarely contested. In Gascony, too, local practice seems to have amounted to a tolerance of gleaning, but that was all. Common rights also passed largely unrecognised in Provence. If the villagers of Allan had allowed their seigneur to close access to his forests, their sheep flocks would have been placed in grave jeopardy, for *vaine pâture* was disallowed on arable surfaces, meadows and of course among the vines. Only in Villepreux do we find echoes of the kinds of disputes that bedevilled village life in Saint-Alban and Neuviller (see pp. 236–7).

The inhabitants of Roquelaure were watching the National Assembly in expectation of confirmatory news about the abolition of the tithe at this juncture, as we know. Those of Châtelaudren, by contrast, were more concerned about another issue: the remodelling of the kingdom's judicial system. While the decisions taken on the night of 4 August presented opportunities galore, they also spelled danger for the numerous small localities whose livelihood was linked indissolubly to the existence of seigneurial institutions. What if the seigneurial jurisdiction of the Comté de Goello were abolished? What would take the place of the assize courts whose clients helped sustain the economy of the village? Would anything take their place? As the local implications of otherwise well received reforms began to sink in, the *général* of Châtelaudren grew alarmed. Imagining that seigneurial justice would cease *at any moment*, they held an emergency session on 16 August 1789 in order to discuss what to do, 'les justices seigneuriales étant supprimées dans tout le Royaume'.[12] In fact the assize courts would continue to handle cases until the new Justices of the Peace were put in place towards the end of 1790. Nevertheless, the quest for a replacement court shot to the top of the agenda, and would engage the energies of every member of Châtelaudren's bourgeois elite for the next twelve months or so. Self-preservation no doubt counted for a good deal in their campaign for 'un siège royal',[13] but their anxieties for the future were not misplaced. Châtelaudren had difficulty securing even the seat of a Justice of the Peace (see pp. 177–8), and in January 1792 the municipality sought a tax reduction on grounds of commercial decline ('depuis la suppression de la juridiction de Châtelaudren ce qui a rendu cette ville beaucoup moins fréquentée soit pour les marchés ou autrement').[14] The weekly markets were Châtelaudren's Achilles' heel, for they had been synchronised with the sessions of the courts. Saint-Alban also lost a busy baronial court as a result of the change in the regime and secured only a Justice of the Peace in return. Yet with no market and little in the way of an entrepôt role, the village did not experience the same degree of economic dislocation.

One area in which all six groups of villagers seconded the efforts of the National Assembly with enthusiasm, even gusto, was tax collection – specifically the recovery of taxes from clerics, nobles and individuals in

---

[12] A. D. des Côtes-d'Armor, 20G 42.
[13] *Ibid*. In the aftermath of Lamoignon's judicial reform (May 1788) Bertrand de Molleville, the last intendant of Brittany, recommended Châtelaudren as one of the sites for ten new prevotal courts. It remains unclear, however, whether the bourgeoisie of Châtelaudren were aware of the proposal.
[14] A. C. de Châtelaudren, Municipalité, délibérations du Conseil municipal, 9 février 1790–13, Nivôse II.

possession of exemptions of one sort or another. When the inhabitants of surrounding villages gathered in Allan for the St Clement's Day fair (23 November 1789) there was much ill-informed discussion of a decree which supposedly brought former *privilégiés* within the tax net. The *consuls* applied urgently to the subdelegate of Grignan for clarification, but to little effect. In fact the National Assembly had voted an interim measure instructing those hitherto exempt, or partially exempt, from taxation to pay a *pro rata* contribution for the last six months of 1789 on 25 September. Village tax collectors were required to draw up supplementary rolls for this purpose, and generally lost no time in doing so. The definitive text of the law reached Châtelaudren on 27 December and prompted immediate action, but the villages around Versailles had acted to implement this most congenial of reforms as early as the middle of November. In the south and southwest where the *taille* tax was *réelle*, that is to say assessed on commoner land, the ownership of which was recorded in registers known as *cadastres*, the process of implementation was necessarily longer and more contentious, however. Both Allan and Roquelaure had outstanding grievances relating to alleged fiscal impropriety by their seigneurs, as we know. The law therefore provided an opportunity to settle accounts and to put an end to interminable conflicts over the status of land. At Roquelaure the *consuls*, and their successors the municipal officers, were thus able to bring within the tax net twenty previously untaxed houses in the village, together with their gardens; the chateau and farm of Le Rieutort (allegedly established on commoner land in the early seventeenth century); and of course the extensive holdings of the seigneur that had always been reputed 'noble'. These adjustments to the *cadastre* boosted the fiscal capacity of the commune by '90 *livres livrantes*' (approximately 15 per cent). In Allan a similar inquisition finally began towards the end of February 1790 and would uncover more than eighty-six items of property that were now subject to tax. Their inclusion in the *cadastre* seems to have augmented the roll by 1,056 *florins* (around 28 per cent). The seigneur's agent settled her liabilities for the last six months of 1789 and the whole of 1790 with a one-off payment of 1,200 *livres*.

The sense of satisfaction that these steps towards fiscal equalisation produced was fleeting, however. Fleeting because there existed at the local level a widespread misconception that the additional monies thereby raised somehow belonged to the village concerned and could be applied to whatever purpose it saw fit. Some villagers clearly anticipated a rebate on their 1789 tax liabilities (often still outstanding) *pro rata* to the sums raised from the hitherto 'privileged'. A larger number assumed, at the very least, that the rolls for 1790 would be reduced in proportion. The newly installed municipal officers of Châtelaudren had to be put right on this score. Even the elders of Allan were confused, hoping (or perhaps affecting to hope) that the windfall revenue arising from the encadastration of seigneurial possessions could be put towards the extinction of their debts. But in the early months of 1790 they received a circular letter from the Commissaires des Communes de Provence in Aix expressing surprise and annoyance that some towns and villages were using the tax on the 'privileged' to make patriotic donations: 'le produit de la Contribution des ci-devant privilégiés, n'est pas la propriété particulière des Communes, dans le territoire desquelles les biens jadis exempts sont situés. Ce produit appartient aux Communes de Provence en général, c'est-à-dire, au Corps du Pays.'[15] These disappointments would fuse with the much bigger sense of disappointment that would greet the new fiscal regime in 1792 when it was discovered that 'visible' taxation had not decreased at all.

EXPANDING HORIZONS

The less than welcome intervention in the tax debate of the official commissioners of Provence serves to remind us that the process of breaking away from the past needs to be explored at the regional as well as the local level. On the evidence of the *cahiers de doléances*, such as it is, most of our villagers seem to have envisaged the future shape of the kingdom as a confederation of Provincial Estates presided over by an Estates General, with perhaps a tier of municipal assemblies at the base. Indeed, this is how Necker appears to have envisaged the reformed kingdom to judge from his opening speech before the Estates General. The reflexes of the villagers of Allan were certainly 'Provençal' at this juncture. Despite all the inconvenience, they accepted that Aix was, and would remain, the hub of their political universe and they uncomplainingly despatched the deputies bearing their *cahier* to the *sénéchaussée* assembly of Arles which was even further away. The Assemblée Générale des Communes de Provence, meanwhile, set up a three-man commission whose remit left no room for doubt ('préparer les bases et les détails de la régénération de la Constitution Provençale').[16] This body blithely pursued a Provençal 'solution' to the kingdom's woes despite mounting evidence that the terms of the debate were shifting. With spectacularly bad timing, it put in the post to Versailles on 15 July 1789

[15] A. D. de la Drôme, L1151 Printed circular from the *Commissaires des Communes de Provence*. Aix, 26 January 1790.
[16] A. D. de la Drôme, L 1151, printed circular entitled 'Compte-Rendu par la Commission des Communes de Provence. Aix, le [blank] juin 1790'.

a proposal for a new constitution which retained Provence as a 'Nation distincte et indépendante'.[17] When, then, did the inhabitants of Allan start to think in other than Provençal terms? Not before the autumn, it would seem. On hearing reports of the events of 4 August, the *conseil politique* simply passed a resolution urging that 'l'union sera entre tous les voisins tant de Provence que de Dauphiné'.[18]

The *cahier* of Neuviller makes a trite gesture in favour of Provincial Estates, as we have seen. It is impossible to deduce anything from such a remark, except perhaps that the illustrious history of the duchy of Lorraine no longer counted for very much. With Stanislas I long since departed from the scene, the only independence that Lorraine retained still in 1789 was a separate customs regime. To judge from later evidence the birth of an undifferentiated Nation did not occasion much turmoil in the minds of country dwellers, although the privileged towns of Nancy and Metz would require some cajoling. The same may be said of Roquelaure. The bourgeoisie of Auch may have harboured a hope that the Provincial Assembly set up in their midst in 1787 would transmute into the Provincial Estates of Gascony, but such ambitions had no purchase at village level. In Saint-Alban opinion was, if anything, antagonistic towards the Estates of Languedoc, always assuming that we can trust the testimony of the parish priest. As for Villepreux, the Court and the nearby capital had shaped its horizons for centuries. Of all the villages Villepreux was the most integrated politically, rarely if ever falling out of step with events in Versailles or Paris. In 1789 and 1790 the inhabitants looked for guidance to the *élection* assembly of Saint-Germain-en-Laye, which had come into being under the auspices of the Calonne–Brienne local government reform. With the brutal death of intendant Bertier in the aftermath of the seizure of the Bastille, this was the only administrative institution left functioning in the district. Only the case of Châtelaudren bears comparison with the position of Allan, in the sense that both sets of villagers had to rationalise a course of action that led away from a provincial identity to which they had been deeply attached. But the process of psychological distancing from an established source of regional power started earlier in Châtelaudren and was accomplished more swiftly, thanks largely to the behaviour of the Breton nobility. And besides, the decisions taken by the deputies on the night of 4 August left little room for doubt as to where Châtelaudren's future lay.

Only towards the very end of 1789 did that clarity of vision start to develop in the minds of the *consuls* of Allan. On 12 December they received an

---

[17] *Ibid.*   [18] A. C. d'Allan, BB 3–4, 16 August 1789.

invitation from Montélimar, their large Dauphiné neighbour, to participate in a 'federation' of National Guardsmen (see p. 150), and a few days later the *consuls* of Grignan received an important letter from Paris which we can assume was copied for onward transmission to all the villages of the Terres Adjacentes. Penned by Durand de Maillane, the third-estate deputy for the *sénéchaussée* of Arles, the letter gave warning that the Committee of the Constitution would find it very difficult to include the Terres Adjacentes in a future 'departmentalisation' of the old province of Provence owing to the large wedge of papal territory that lay between Grignan and Arles (Avignon and the Comtat Venaissin would not be annexed to France until September 1791). At this point, and only at this point, did it dawn on villagers that the 'regeneration' of the kingdom would necessitate a realignment of provincial loyalties and, moreover, that the only realistic option was to seek inclusion in a 'department of the lower Dauphiné'.[19] Allan's *consuls* tried to avoid taking a decision, hoping that the National Assembly would take one for them. But on 28 March 1790 the municipal officers in whose hands the future of the village now lay deliberated, hesitantly, to join the new territorial entity 'known by the name of the department of the Drôme'.[20]

Territorial reorganisation was something that had been included in few, if any, village agendas. Certainly none of the villages surveyed in this study had any inkling that it was going to happen before 4 August. Once the reorganisation started to acquire political momentum (between October 1789 and March 1790), however, village elites naturally did their utmost to nudge the process in the direction best suited to their interests. Every locality sought recognition under the regime now taking shape, and to some extent every locality *was* recognised. This was one of the purposes of the Municipal Law promulgated on 14 December 1789. It applied a version of the municipal assemblies reform – altered somewhat to take account of the abolition of privilege – to every town and village in the kingdom. But much more was at stake. Châtelaudren, as we know, considered it a matter of life or death to secure one of the new courts; either a District civil court or a Justice of the Peace. With the sizeable localities of Saint-Brieuc and Guingamp nearby, the first objective never looked feasible, but even the second proved far from assured. The National Assembly resolved that Justices of the Peace would be established ordinarily in the seats of the cantons, which meant that Châtelaudren had first to compete with the large rural parish of Plélo for cantonal status. Throughout March and April 1790 each locality jockeyed

[19] A. C. d'Allan, RV 2, Délibérations municipales, 21 March 1790.
[20] *Ibid.*, Délibérations municipales, 28 March 1790.

for position, making *ad hoc* alliances with lesser parishes and *trêves*, and petitioning furiously. The struggle was bitterly fought and would durably influence the political evolution of the two villages. For while Châtelaudren became ostentatiously patriotic Plélo descended into disaffected royalism. Châtelaudren finally secured the cantonal seat, but in November it would lose the election for the Justice of the Peace to the candidate of the rival parish.

In Villepreux roles were reversed. The village was passed over for the dignity of *chef-lieu de canton* in favour of the more urbanised locality of Marly, situated at the northern extremity of the new canton. In their petitions the inhabitants made much of their 'distinction de bourg',[21] despite having claimed in their *cahier* that they were nothing but 'un faible village assez misérable',[22] but all to no avail. Marly was not only more urbanised, it was bigger than Villepreux. Allan, too, must have experienced some misgivings following its strategic decision to cleave to Montélimar and the Dauphiné. When the cantonal seats in the district of Montélimar were announced, it found itself subordinated to Donzère, a distant riverside *bourg* with which it had few links. Although there is no evidence that the villagers protested the decision, relations with Donzère were never more than perfunctory and would break down completely during the royalist reaction of 1796–7 (see p. 147). As for Roquelaure, it was too close to the regional capital of Auch to have had much hope of preferment under the new regime. The municipality responded phlegmatically to the creation of the department of the Gers on 27 April 1790, and seems to have been unmoved by the news of its incorporation, along with twenty other villages, in a greater Auch canton.

Most of the inhabitants of Saint-Alban spent the autumn and winter of 1789–90 thinking about little else but food shortages. In this highland parish severe frosts in mid-June had depleted the rye harvest, while the demand for homespun woollens had contracted almost to nothing. On 6 December the *consuls* reported baldly that the poor were beginning to die of hunger.[23] Nevertheless, news from the National Assembly continued to filter into the village throughout the autumn via a correspondence committee established in Mende. And the news that the deputies sent back to their constituents was not very encouraging. The Gévaudan, they reported, was likely to be dismembered, since the Committee on the Constitution took the view

---

[21] A. C. de Villepreux, 29 October 1790.
[22] See M. Thénard, *Bailliages de Versailles et de Meudon: les cahiers des paroisses avec commentaires accompagnés de quelques cahiers de curés* (Versailles, 1889), p. 90.
[23] See P.-J.-B. Delon, *La Révolution en Lozère* (Mende, 1922), p. 50 and note 2.

that the old province of Languedoc could be converted into six departments but not seven. A vigorous rearguard action waged notably by Jean-Joseph Rivière, the third-estate deputy for Mende, warded off this prospect, with the result that in January 1790 it became known that a department of the Gévaudan would, after all, come into being with only a small loss of territory along the northern frontier. The Saint-Albanais, like everyone else, were spectators to this struggle. They became involved only when reports of the National Assembly's decree of 5 February 1790 dividing the Gévaudan into seven districts began to circulate.

If Saint-Alban harboured thoughts of becoming the seat of a District administration, it could only have been in the context of irreconcilable differences checkmating the ambitions of the two principal contenders: Saint-Chély-d'Apcher and Le Malzieu. When the inhabitants of Le Malzieu discovered that the weight of opinion in this corner of the Gévaudan favoured Saint-Chély-d'Apcher, the hopes of Saint-Alban also collapsed. Nonetheless, the Saint-Albanais had a crisper agenda as far as the cantonal seats were concerned: they wanted to contour the new canton around their old seigneurial jurisdiction. In this they were only partly successful, however. One of the parishes previously subject to the barony of Saint-Alban 'escaped', so to speak, leaving a canton comprising no more than the parishes of Saint-Alban and Sainte-Eulalie. Since the latter was little more than a hamlet, the inhabitants of Saint-Alban entered the new regime with the dubious satisfaction of forming a canton all on their own. While this enabled them to nominate the Justice of the Peace more or less at will, it imposed financial burdens on the parish and created an anomaly that would not survive the judicial reorganisation of the Year Ten (1801–2).

SELF-RULE

In February and March 1790 towns and villages all over the country set about the business of electing municipal councils. The meetings called for this purpose were, in the majority of cases, the first properly constituted assemblies to have taken place for a year – a year that had seen a quite extraordinary jumble of ideas course through country dwellers' minds. These meetings provide a final opportunity to take stock of agendas as our villagers stood on the threshold of an event now routinely described in the public prints as a 'Revolution'. As far as we can judge they were well attended. The controversial distinction between 'active' and 'passive' citizenship which the National Assembly had fleshed out in late October 1789 was poorly understood and unevenly implemented. Until new municipal institutions had come into being, there was really no body, or bodies, that could be safely entrusted with the execution of laws. A royal Declaration of 20 November instructing Provençal communities to perpetuate their *consuls* in office until such time as the new municipalities took over was a tacit admission of this fact. Disenfranchised 'citizens' would not constitute a very prominent feature of the village political landscape in any case. Passive households could be counted on the fingers of two, three or four hands in Allan, Roquelaure and Saint-Alban, and they were scarcely more numerous elsewhere. Only in Villepreux and Châtelaudren is it possible that the poor felt excluded almost from the beginning (see table 3).

One way of measuring attitudes at this juncture is to look closely at who was elected. In general the picture is one of continuity; only in Neuviller and Rennemoulin – the small satellite hamlet of Villepreux – did established elites fracture. 'Politics as usual' would be a fair description of events in Roquelaure. The village intelligentsia had long practised a cosy system of office rotation, and in 1790 there was no pressure from anywhere to alter this custom. Joseph-Marie Barrué, previously first *consul*, became mayor and his entire municipal team can be identified as one-time office holders. Even the 'notables' had all been *jurats* at some point in the 1770s or 1780s. Châtelaudren's elite of merchants and liberal professionals likewise migrated directly from the *général* into the municipality with barely any loss of administrative continuity. The only semi-casualty en route was *recteur* Gilles Le Corvaisier, who was chosen as a 'notable' but not as a municipal officer. In Saint-Alban political authority was an attribute of kinship, although this is to read the politics of the village backwards from 1793, when the animosities between resident bourgeois families became so intense as to expose the structuring of power to view (see pp. 189–91). Atrasic, the serving first *consul*, glided effortlessly towards the mayorship and carried with him Jean-François Polge, his cousin, who took over as *procureur*. Most of the municipal officers appear to have been drawn from the hamlets, which, in this dispersed habitat parish, may indicate a bid by outlying voters to redress the political balance. The official record of the election has not survived, unfortunately, although a document drafted by the parish priest informs us that several of the most distant hamlets used the occasion of the electoral assembly to give voice to a separatist agenda. They wanted to break away from the mother church and form a parish in their own right. Such tensions rooted in '*bourg*–hinterland' polarities were commonplace in the thinly populated highlands of the Massif Central.

Kinship also cemented power structures in the village of Allan. Gathered together in the hall of the chateau on 21 February 1790 because neither the 'maison de ville' nor the church was large enough, 125 male heads of household chose Jean-Baptiste Gouteron and his cousin Joseph Laurans to be their mayor and *procureur* respectively. Gouteron, a merchant, moneylender and owner of land, lived in the hamlet of Les Mèges and was one of the wealthiest men in the parish, whereas Laurans had been acclaimed for his role as the village's envoy to Aix during the litigation with the seigneur. He represented the *castrum* or the core village. Neither was a stranger to local office holding, and Gouteron had even worked for the seigneurie on a contractual basis. This draws attention to one of the paradoxes of village politcal life during the early years of the Revolution. Even in localities where relations with seigneurs had been strained, contamination by seigneurialism did not automatically exclude from local office. In view of the institutional and economic omnipresence of seigneurial authority, villagers adopted a pragmatic attitude – providing always that proprieties were observed. In 1780, when Gouteron was farming seigneurial dues whilst simultaneously an officer in the seigneurial court, he would stand down 'se trouvant suspect'[24] when the cases of defaulters were heard.

Seigneurial power could not have lasted for as long as it did without enlisting men of substance, or talent, at the village level. But equally such men were generally good at sensing the winds of change. The senior judicial representative of the seigneur of Allan in 1789 was Jean-Baptiste Biscarrat. He had acquired the office of *châtelain* in 1777 and in this capacity had legally authenticated each page of the community's lengthy *cahier de doléances*. Nevertheless, he plainly enjoyed the confidence of the villagers and they sent him as one of their delegates to the *sénéchaussée* assembly in Arles. During the summer crisis in the village he speedily divested himself of the trappings of seigneurial office, and for his pains was made commander of the National Guard. A bid to become the first Justice of the Peace of the canton failed completely in December 1790, but his home village recognised his talents by making him *procureur* in place of Laurans, whose zeal had ebbed in the face of the Civil Constitution of the Clergy. Thereafter Biscarrat's career in the service of the Revolution fairly took off. It would conclude with his appointment to the mayorship of Allan during the Hundred Days.

It was the failure to observe proprieties, indeed the lack of any kind of dividing line between the seigneurial and the civil (or the ecclesiastical), that caused such trouble in Neuviller. Throughout the year 1789 Joseph-Etienne Seignelay, the parish priest, had done his utmost to keep control of the village in conjunction with the officers of the *prévôté* court. These

[24] A. D. de la Drôme, B 1340, Registre à l'extraordinaire, 14 January 1780.

efforts had not entirely succeeded, as our analysis of the *cahier de doléances* has revealed, and the news that the municipal assembly (over which the *curé* presided in the absence of the seigneur) was to be replaced by a body elected on a broader franchise was therefore not especially welcome. Accordingly, on 7 February 1790, Seignelay 'fixed' the municipal election with the help of the village poor, who had been reminded several days beforehand that applications to the fund established by prior Rosselange for charitable relief required the endorsement of the incumbent. On the day of the election, the village schoolmaster planted the ballot box on the altar table and provided a helping hand for anyone unable to write out his voting slip. The result was not unexpected, therefore: Antoine Prost, the seigneurial *maire*, became mayor, Seignelay got himself elected as *procureur*, while the municipal officers and the *notables* were mostly fairly pliant individuals.

'Fixed' elections were not unusual, of course. But in Neuviller there existed a rival source of authority in the shape of the National Guard, which had come into being at some point during the previous summer. It is the confrontation between these two bodies that enables us to explore the popular mood at a time when agendas were evolving against a backdrop of institutional disarray, even incoherence. The attitude of the priest Seignelay is not difficult to understand: he had arrived in the village in 1779, no doubt with the blessing of La Galaizière *fils*, and in 1791 would describe the land redistribution as 'la belle opération du 15 décembre 1770'.[25] As well he might, since it had nicely rounded the lands belonging to the parish church. The village schoolmaster was a docile adjunct to the *curé*, a normal state of affairs in the eighteenth century, while Prost, the *maire*/mayor, had an obvious interest in upholding the edifice of seigneurial power. One of his main duties in 1789–90 was to keep account of the payment of feudal dues. Neuviller's National Guard was dominated by the Dieudonné clan, of which there were three separate households in 1789. The prime movers were Pierre Dieudonné *père* and his two sons, Pierre and Liboire. A barrister by profession, Dieudonné *père* served as clerk (*greffier*) both to the seigneurial court and to the municipal assembly, an overlap that would not have been tolerated in the more structured environment of the southern village. Why he gravitated into the camp of the Revolution is impossible to judge; there is nothing known about his background that would help us to explain such a move. His family seems to have been one of the main beneficiaries of the land redistribution of 1770–1, and his 'populism' in 1789–90 sits uneasily

---

[25] A. D. de Meurthe-et-Moselle, 1Q Supp 170, petition of J.-E. Seignelay to the Administration of the Department of the Meurthe, Chaumont, 1 January 1791.

with his record as an encloser and would-be engrosser. Opportunism is probably the best answer, or else a clash with the *curé* in the municipal assembly.

As commander of the National Guard, Pierre Dieudonné *père* took it upon himself to mobilise opposition to what a petition laid before the National Assembly described as the 'municipalité fabriquée par le curé le sept février dernier'.[26] And indeed, the municipal election was rerun on 18 May in the presence of forty-one out of an alleged seventy-six active citizens. No doubt this assembly was 'fixed' to some degree as well, but it does enable us to catch a glimpse of the specific points at issue. The villagers, it was alleged, were worked up about five matters: La Galaizière's bullying land redistribution; the alienation by *triage* of a portion of their commons; the misappropriation of a charitable bequest; the inclusion of noble and ecclesiatical property in the tax net; and the redemption terms for non-extinguished feudal dues. The first two items are already familiar to us, but no one had yet dared to raise the question of how the proceeds of prior Rosselange's legacy to the poor were being disbursed, or not disbursed, while items four and five were additions to the agenda arising directly from the dynamic of Revolution. *Curé* Seignelay stood accused of withholding or concealing the decrees of the National Assembly, notably those relating to the redemption of feudal dues, and of failing to calculate the tax loading on the property of the seigneur in an accurate and verifiable manner.

At this point the institutional disarray of the spring of 1790 came to the rescue of the 'priest's municipality'. Dieudonné's petition was passed on to the Constitution Committee, which, assailed from all sides and quite unable to verify any of the facts being alleged, 'misunderstood' the situation. Triumphantly, Seignelay brandished a letter signed by Target, no less, that exonerated his municipality. A few days later the mayor called the villagers to an open-air meeting in order to hear a reading of the new tax roll. Prudently he decided to conduct the exercise from an upstairs window. A riot broke out nevertheless, which ended with the National Guard arresting and detaining the *curé*. He was released from the guardhouse after a couple of days, but only because a celebrant was required in church for the Mass of the Fête Dieu. Shocked by his treatment, Seignelay brought a suit before the Chambre des Comptes of Nancy, which had no love for the new regime, and was happy to oblige with an *arrêt* condemning the National Guard of Neuviller to punitive damages. Only with the establishment of the new

[26] A. N., DIV 43, 'A nos seigneurs de l'assemblée Nationnalle, séante à Paris, supplie très humblement la Communauté et Garde Nationnalle du bourg de Chaumont sur Mozelle' (n.d.).

District administrations in late June 1790 did the counter-municipality organised by Dieudonné win some much needed support. But the overall political context was scarcely favourable to village militias that presumed to question established authority. That August the Marquis de Bouillé crushed 'disorder' in the regiments garrisoning Nancy, an act that launched a 'moderate' counter-revolution throughout the region. There were still two municipalities disputing furiously in Neuviller at the end of the year. By that time, however, Dieudonné *père* had secured himself an alternative power base in the cantonal ballot for the Justice of the Peace.

The example of the rival municipalities in Neuviller tells us almost as much about the manipulation of peasant agendas as about the agendas themselves. If we want to find out what villagers thought about enclosures and common rights, we need to explore the transcripts of the cases brought before Dieudonné in his capacity as Justice of the Peace, not the petitions that he penned on behalf of the National Guard and its puppet municipality. It is nevertheless clear that the signal to elect municipalities was given at a moment when country dwellers everywhere were clinging to the decrees of the National Assembly in daily expectation of decisions of infinite importance to their lives. Villagers were waiting to hear which dues and monopolies had been abolished outright and which were subject to compensation; they were waiting to hear whether transactions relating to common land which had been agreed under seigneurial duress could be reopened; they were waiting for news about the tithe; for information about the siting of the new courts. Your duty, urged Durand de Maillane in a letter despatched to the *consuls* of Grignan for onward transmission, is to contain spirits 'dans une juste patience'.[27]

This was easier said than done. After the shocks of the summer and early autumn of 1789, the deputies of the National Assembly found succour in a vision of burgeoning national unity: 'Devenue [*sic*] frères avec tous les français des provinces les plus éloignés avec qui nous étions cy devant comme étrangers et quelquefois comme ennemis,' continued Durand de Maillane, 'nous ne serions pas excusables de ne pas vivre avec nos compatriotes avec plus de fraternité que par le passé.'[28] All that remained was for country dwellers to play the part allotted to them. Viewed from the level of the village, however, the birth of the 'nation' was an altogether more discordant, even traumatic, process. Insecurity was rife, as was the non-payment of taxes and the withholding of feudal dues. Supposedly a solution to the problem of insecurity, the National Guard displayed a worrying

[27] A. C. d'Allan, AA 12, circular dated 11 December 1789.   [28] *Ibid*.

propensity to become a source of disorder in its turn. The case of Neuviller has been mentioned, and the National Guard of Châtelaudren would also pursue its own 'policing' agenda the following year with punitive forays into neighbouring parishes. Nor would Durand de Maillane's expectation that villagers would continue to pay 'droits utiles' be fulfilled in either Allan or Saint-Alban. Non-compliance began early in Allan as we have seen, and it continued with even greater collective determination once the conclusions of the Feudal Committee as to what constituted a reimbursable due (embodied in the decree of 28 March 1790) became known. In Saint-Alban the main phase of resistance occurred later, that is to say after May 1790, when the villagers finally grasped that escape from their heavy *champart* via redemption would not be a viable option for the majority. Demands to see title deeds were followed – in the spring of 1791– by threats to set light to the chateau. In neither instance did the seigneurs, or their agents, find the new municipalities conspicuous in upholding the letter of the law.

In some villages, of course, the tithe – not seigneurial dues – was the key issue. To judge from the minutes of the municipal council of Roquelaure the subject was not raised for discussion at any point during the first year of the Revolution, but this silence is deceptive and quite possibly contrived.[29] At least three parties in the village were monitoring closely the work of the National Assembly. The great mass of households, among whom numbered many sharecroppers, were waiting for the National Assembly to make good its promises of the previous August in the firm expectation of a tangible reward for their 'patience' by the time of the next harvest. The bourgeois elite of the village also objected to the tithe in principle, and stood to gain in material terms should the Assembly decide on a policy of outright abolition. Their stance was complicated, however, by the fact that the farmers of the tithe had often been drawn from this milieu in the past. In fact two resident bourgeois had signed a nine-year contract to collect the tithe owned by the Chapter of Auch throughout the parishes of Roquelaure and adjacent Arcamont in 1785. No doubt the risk they had taken was reflected in the price, for the Chapter had covered itself by inserting into the contract a disclaimer 'sans que les preneurs puissent prétendre aucune indemnité pour le refus de la cote de la dixme'.[30] As a result of the municipal election held in February 1790, one of those tithe farmers had become a *notable*. The third party to have an interest in the matter was the seigneur. The land clearance edict of 1766 had encouraged the Comte Dubarry, among others, to bring

[29] A. D. du Gers, E Supplément 1010³.   [30] A. D. du Gers, G 37, Baux à ferme, 1767–1790.

much new land into cultivation on the promise of a fifteen-year exemption from the tithe. Since 1781, however, these wheatfields and vineyards had fallen within the scope of the tithe farmers' contract. The Dubarry family had long since disposed of the seigneurie of Roquelaure, of course, but the issue of tithing cleared land continued to rankle. Celès de Marsac, the new seigneur, was a senior magistrate in the Parlement of Toulouse – the body which the archbishop and Chapter of Auch blamed for their enforcement difficulties during the 1780s.

As far as the tithe is concerned, then, both agendas and the social forces harnessed to those agendas tended to evolve. In the 1780s there were few, if any, calls for the abolition of the tithe, but rather cross-community support for a reduction in its weight and for the restitution of straw. In the summer of 1789 the issue of abolition entered the realm of practical politics, and for the next eight or nine months the villagers of Roquelaure were on tenterhooks to know whether the tithe would be extinguished outright or terminated by means of redemption payments on a par with feudal dues. The verdict of the National Assembly was enshrined in a decree that received the Royal Assent on 22 April 1790: the tithe would remain in place for one more year and be paid to the Nation since the property of the church had been confiscated. Thereafter it would lapse without compensation. At this point the issue switched again as the implications of abolition sank in, and individual villagers settled down to work out their gains and losses. It began to dawn that the law said nothing about how the benefits of abolition were to be distributed, whether in 1791 or years beyond. Croppers naturally assumed that the terms of their (usually verbal) contracts would be lightened in proportion to the amount of the tithe they paid, but landowners did not view the matter in this light at all and exploited their dominant position in the new District and Department administrations to assert that the tithe was a charge on the land whose abolition could only benefit the owners thereof. Before the year was out, the National Assembly had confirmed this interpretation with a decree declaring that 'tenants and sharecroppers of holdings whose yield was liable to the ecclesiastical or infeudated tithe shall pay to the proprietors the value of the tithe with effect from the harvest of 1791'.[31] Village solidarity crumbled.

Between 1787 and 1790 the System changed in France, and the aim of this chapter has been to lay bare the process whereby the inhabitants of six small localities came to understand that a definite break with the past

[31] See P. M. Jones, *The Peasantry in the French Revolution* (Cambridge, 1988), p. 99.

was both feasible and likely to take place. The process was not continuous, nor was it seamless. Moreover, villagers' awareness of the changes to the political landscape developed at different speeds. It is nevertheless possible to identify certain familiar landmarks: the intellectual ferment released by the invitation to draw up *cahiers de doléances*; the threat, even the reality, of civil disorder in the summer of 1789; and the heaving into place of the building blocks of the new administrative regime during the late winter and spring of 1790. An important message emerging from our analysis, however, is that the apprehension of change was not nurtured overnight, in 1789. The Pre-Revolution had a rural dimension, and to neglect this fact is to run the risk of misunderstanding the multiple ways in which country dwellers disengaged mentally from the *ancien régime*. The Calonne–Brienne local government reform was crucial to this process, as we have seen, but so was the campaign to 'regenerate' Provincial Estates in Brittany, Provence and Languedoc.

A second and no less important conclusion that can be drawn from the evidence presented in this chapter is that villagers actively participated in the process of disengagement from the governing structures of absolute monarchy and the 'society of orders'. While events acted upon them, they also acted upon events. Agendas constructed initially on the theme of 'burdens' were replaced by agendas rooted in 'opportunities'. Nonetheless, no single narrative of agenda formulation will suffice if we wish to capture the range of positions adopted by villagers. Only in the loosest and most unhelpful sense had a common national agenda been forged by 1789 (e.g. all country dwellers called for a fairer distribution of taxation). By way of illustration one might recall the obsession with the tithe in Roquelaure, whereas the inhabitants of Châtelaudren showed no interest in the subject; or the preoccupation with seigneurial dues and monopolies in Allan, issues that the inhabitants of Villepreux could afford to regard with a large measure of indifference. Multiple agendas, then; but we have also identified disguised agendas and sectional agendas, which serve as a reminder that the 'whole village' approach can take us only a part of the way. Deliberation in the presence of the seigneurial judge was not necessarily conducive to a free exchange of opinion, but then neither was deliberation in the presence of municipal officers and *notables* recruited from among the principal tenant farmers of a village. Some villagers cut loose from their old-regime moorings quicker than others. Seigneurial officials faced hard choices early on and had to make speedy decisions, while the destitute poor probably grasped the magnitude of the changes taking place only when the flow of alms from long-established ecclesiastical institutions started to run dry.

Do these conclusions invite a reconsideration of peasant behaviour at the outset of the Revolution as traditionally understood? According to Georges Lefebvre the intervention of country dwellers was spurred by a socio-economic crisis of the late *ancien régime* in which the heavy and rising burden of seigneurial dues bulked large.[32] It was marked out by set-piece events: the Great Fear, the agrarian uprisings of 1789 and the tenacious and all-consuming struggle against feudalism. Taken together, these events can be said to differentiate country dwellers from other actors in the drama; indeed, to vindicate the notion of an independent, even autonomous, peasant revolution. Micro-history tends always to blur the outlines of grand narratives, and so it is in this case. For a start, we have not uncovered much evidence of an escalation of seigneurial dues, save, perhaps, in the case of Saint-Alban. By contrast, quite different villages appear to have been sensitised to the 'problem' of seigneurialism as a consequence of the loss, decline or withdrawal of reciprocal services. This is Tocqueville's argument: lordship came to be viewed as a system of public power that had jettisoned its public responsibilities.[33] In this scenario the so-called crisis of the *ancien régime* becomes short-term and mainly political, rather than long-term and mainly economic. True, each of our six villages suffered penury in varying degrees following the adverse harvest and climatic conjuncture of 1788–9. But this hardship has not been analysed in any detail, because it does not appear to have been the ingredient crucial to an explanation of the evolving attitudes of the Pre-Revolution.

For all its salience in the story of how country dwellers entered the Revolution, the Great Fear did not grip the whole of France – a fact that Lefebvre willingly acknowledged. Châtelaudren was not affected in any way, nor was Neuviller on the other side of the kingdom. The rural panic attack that affected this part of Lorraine occurred in July and early August 1790 and seems to have owed more to anxieties stemming from the continuing political power vacuum (filled by the National Guard of Neuviller, among others) than to the activities of 'brigands' in the pay of a vengeful aristocracy. Only in Allan were agendas sharpened exactly in the way described by Lefebvre, that is to say by a palpable and very real Fear followed by an invasion of the chateau. On the evidence of our villages, 'collective bargaining by riot' was not a common occurrence in any case. More was achieved by stonewalling, by selective non-compliance and by

---

[32] For the classic statement, see G. Lefebvre, 'La Révolution française et les paysans', reprinted in *Etudes sur la Révolution française* (Paris, 1954), pp. 246–68; also P. M. Jones, 'Georges Lefebvre and the Peasant Revolution: Fifty Years On', *French Historical Studies*, 16 (Spring 1990), 647.

[33] Tocqueville, *L'Ancien Régime*, pp. 36–41.

negotiation backed by the possibility of force. Georges Lefebvre goes on to argue that the glue which bonded villagers together for the first three years of the Revolution was anti-seigneurialism. A negative agenda, therefore, and one to which even peasants untouched by seigneurialism subscribed, or so he implies. Our close-focus study of six villages spells difficulties for this convergent vision. For while most villagers were touched by seigneurialism the issue scarcely acted as a fixative to the degree that Lefebvre would have us accept. After the autumn of 1790 there was very little left that was even remotely 'seigneurial' about peasant agendas in Villepreux. More pressing matters had intruded, and so it was in other villages. The anti-seigneurial struggle – where it applied – was pursued concurrently with other objectives.

CHAPTER 4

A new civic landscape

In the closing months of 1814 the mayor of Neuviller received an administrative instruction to revert to pre-revolutionary usage as far as the name of his village was concerned. A municipal seal arrived which was inscribed 'Chaumont-sur-Moselle'. Maurice Jordy, the mayor and new owner of the chateau, demurred, albeit circumspectly. Choosing his arguments with care, Jordy pointed out that the descendants of the Chaumont de La Galaizières no longer possessed any property in the village, which featured in all the postal directories as 'Neuviller-sur-Moselle'. Moreover, the name 'Chaumont' had caused endless confusion to the authorities, with mail being misdirected to Chaumont-en-Bassigny. He did not, at this stage, explain the circumstances that had prompted the change in the first place; nor did he disclose the real reasons for his reluctance to contemplate a switch of nomenclature. With the return to power of Napoleon a few months later, the whole matter could be safely ignored, or so it seemed. The white flag of the Bourbons was lowered from the church tower and replaced with the tricolour, the seal pushed to the back of a drawer. Military defeat at Waterloo would turn the wheel of fortune in favour of the Bourbons once more, however. In the face of renewed pressure from the subprefect of Lunéville, Jordy now spelled out the reasoning behind his opposition to the proposed name change. Such a policy 'rappelloient des temps qui doivent être oubliés'.[1] This time the reference was impossible to mistake and the subprefect referred the matter to his administrative superiors. In Nancy wiser counsels were brought to bear on the issue. On 14 October 1815 the prefect ruled that it would not be expedient to force a name change on the inhabitants of Neuviller 'qui rappeleraient des tems de la féodalité ou des privilèges seigneuriaux. Les malveillants ne manqueraient pas d'en profiter pour alarmer les habitans des campagnes.'[2]

[1] A. D. de Meurthe-et-Moselle, 1M 625, Mayor [Jordy] of Neuviller to the prefect of the Meurthe, Neuviller, 28 September 1815.
[2] Ibid., Prefect of the Meurthe to subprefect of Lunéville [draft], Nancy, 14 October 1815.

Plainly, by 1814 the villagers of Neuviller had constructed a new identity
for themselves. The stages in this protracted process are not well documented, but stray indications of their developing maturity and independence of thought can be found in the minutes of municipal council meetings. On 16 December 1809, for example, councillors recorded their surprise
at the 'complaisance' of their predecessors in the face of the demands of
La Galaizière father and son in the 1750s, 1760s and 1770s, adding 'cela
nous rapel fort bien comme les abitants des campagnes étoient mené par le
cidevant seigneur'.[3] To force a name change on the villagers was therefore to
reinvest them with a patrimonial identity; an identity rooted in hierarchy,
submission, even coercion. While few villagers in 1814 had personal experience of the 'slave labour' schemes of Chancellor La Galaizière, or even
of the land amalgamation pushed through by his son, the role of 'vicarious memory' in fixing emotional attachments and the sense of belonging
should not be underplayed. As France, or, more accurately, the French,
returned to Bourbon rule, the inhabitants of Neuviller defined a hard-won
identity by 'remembering' – no doubt selectively – the arbitrary conduct
of their seigneurs. Mayor Jordy's position was more ambiguous, however.
For remembrance of the past also served to reactivate memories of how he
had systematically bought up the lands and prerogatives of the outgoing
seigneur. For both public and private reasons, therefore, he recommended a
policy of 'forgetting'. Neuviller was not, in any case, a relict name evoking
memories of the Terror, as the subprefect must finally have grasped. The
excrescence – if excrescence there was – lay in the name 'Chaumont', which
had been imposed by royal Letters-Patent in 1776.

   Few villagers experienced a crisis of identity as prolonged or as contested
as those of Neuviller, of course. After the seigneur's enclosure operation and
concomitant partition of the commons in 1771, they even had difficulty in
recognising the physical landscape of their parish. For the majority, the
value shift of these years occurred primarily in the mental sphere, and it
is chiefly in this rhetorical sense that the term 'landscape' is employed in
the present chapter. The aim is to chart the evolving mental landscape of
our villagers, particularly in those areas touching on the state and their
role within it. A new 'civic landscape' did not spring into shape overnight.
Indeed, some of its key features can be identified – in outline – even before
the events of 1789–90 opened up a larger field of political opportunity. One
of the advantages of a longitudinal study of village life is that it can capture
in close-up every halting expression of civic awareness, and the pattern that

[3] A. D. de Meurthe-et-Moselle, N[on] C[oté] G3 94/1/1.

emerges is scarcely even or linear. Whilst the early revolutionaries clung wishfully to the metaphor of 'instantaneous regeneration' and its human operative the 'new man', reality usually turned out to be more prosaic. Men could reinvent themselves over time, in the sense of growing into roles that would have been literally unthinkable before the breakthrough of 1789. Chapter 5 will provide a number of examples. Yet the growth of civic awareness and responsibility as a phenomenon should not be thought of as a single-speed, incremental process.

By the end of the Empire all six villages possessed a civic landscape which their inhabitants could recognise and identify with, however confusedly. Some Bourbon officials may have hankered for a return to the old ways, but they were soon made to realise that the substance of the revolution in the village – mediated by the Napoleonic Codes – was untouchable. Yet this residual civic landscape (abolition of rank and privilege, institutional uniformity, universal taxation, equality before the law, careers open to talent, the common obligation of military service, the inviolability of property, trial by jury, etc.) did not evolve in a painless and predictable fashion over three decades. It was often challenged, and even disappeared from view altogether as partisan definitions of civic responsibility momentarily obscured the landscape. The formulary of civic zeal during the Year Two (1793–4) was far removed from that of 1790, the mix of ingredients by the advent of the Empire far removed even from the modes of public expression and devotion approved during the Directory years. Multiple landscapes, then, that were subjected to weathering, erosion and intermittent seismic movement. But did the events of these years fail to leave any impression on men's minds? Assuredly not. Between the late *ancien régime* and the early Restoration the village community was subjected to a series of vigorous mental exercises inviting members to reassess their expectations and responsibilities, and also their social ties. Much was tried and much was discarded, but certain habits and practices endured. The purpose of this chapter is to weigh up the changes and to identify the permanent features of the new civic landscape.

RIGHTS

Some villages had a civic 'advantage' over others even before the passing of the *ancien régime*, and nowhere is this more apparent than at the level of institutions. Southern villages, as noted in chapter 2, were usually structured in a manner that facilitated identification of the general good and the formulation of public policy. The same was true in Brittany. Legally trained

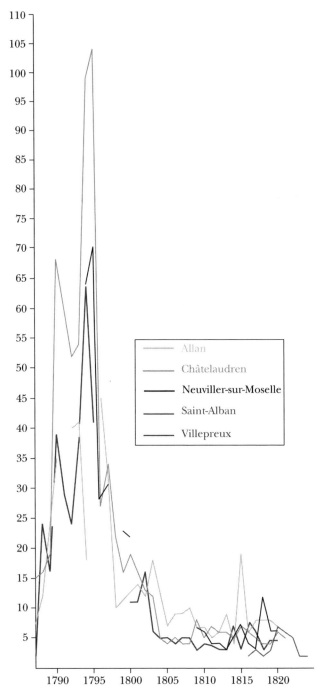

Figure 5. Frequency of deliberative assemblies in case-study villages, 1787–1820

Legend:
- Allan
- Châtelaudren
- **Neuviller-sur-Moselle**
- Saint-Alban
- Villepreux

elites, regular meetings, a clearly articulated division of responsibilities – in short a whole 'administrative routine'– ensured that the inhabitants of Châtelaudren, Roquelaure, Allan and, potentially, Saint-Alban were well placed to absorb the civic culture of the Revolution. Elsewhere villagers waited upon the Calonne–Brienne local government reform for their first lessons in public-spiritedness. When the inhabitants of Villepreux gathered after Vespers on Sunday 12 August 1787, the *sindic* informed them that they were to elect a municipal body paying no attention to rank or to precedence. This body was to meet weekly, henceforward, recording its deliberations in a register purchased for the purpose. In Villepreux, 'administrative routine' was invented overnight, then. The new municipal officers scarcely knew why they had been called into existence, but they convened, each Sunday, for the next six months if only to sign the register as proof of their diligence. The circulars of the *élection* assembly of Saint-Germain-en-Laye were dutifully transcribed, too, but no other business was transacted until the Great Fear produced a flurry of activity.

Still, the right to meet collectively, even when there was nothing much to talk about, was an important feature of the civic landscape now taking shape. In four out of the six villages on which this study is based the intensity of collective life – as measured by the frequency of council meetings – dramatically increased with the onset of revolution (see figures 4 and 5). If sufficient documentation existed to permit a comparison, it would almost certainly show that collective life in Roquelaure and Saint-Alban followed a similar trajectory. In Villepreux and Neuviller, where the practice of formal assembly was virtually non-existent before 1787, the new regime was greeted by a veritable outpouring of collective expression. During the first full year of revolution the mayor and municipal officers of Villepreux gathered on no fewer than forty-four occasions, a figure that reached sixty-two during the year of the Terror. In Neuviller, too, the representatives of the community made trenchant use of the right of assembly (sixty-four meetings in the Year Three, 1794–5). Where regular assembly had been customary prior to 1789 the effect was not quite so dramatic. Analysis of the deliberations of the *consuls* of Allan reveals on average a tripling in the incidence of meetings during the first three years of the new regime (1789 excluded), compared with the last three years of the old. By the same measure, the intensity of collective life in Châtelaudren quintupled.

Indeed, frequency of assembly was used as a kind of barometer by the revolutionaries themselves. When expressions of civic zeal threatened to exceed the norms laid down by legislators in Paris, there was always a temptation to release some of the pressure, either by curtailing the number of occasions for assembly or by limiting the right of access. In 1795 the Thermidorians lowered the pressure by removing the rights of most villagers to hold deliberative assemblies altogether. The Constitution of the Year Three (22 August 1795) revised the 1789 Municipal Law, which had granted powers of self-rule to virtually any locality capable of drawing up a petition, and focused the energies of government on the cantonal seats instead. After the frenzies of the Terror and Dechristianisation (see pp. 210–13), the thinking seems to have been that the quality of civic experience counted for more than the quantity. Bonaparte and his fellow Consuls diagnosed the problem rather differently and concluded that the effervescence of revolutionary political culture (passion, parties, factionalism) stemmed from an overreliance on the electoral principle. Within months of the Brumaire *coup* (10–11 November 1799), therefore, legislation reinstated the village mayor and council, but these 'representatives' were henceforth appointed by government. Doubts expressed in the Tribunate were soothed away with the assurance that democratic elections could be restored once an 'esprit national'[4] had been forged. In 1800, after an interruption of four and a half years, then, every village in the Republic recovered a separate organ of administration. Yet the right – even the obligation – of assembly had been curtailed in the meantime. Ever since Brienne's shortlived local government reform, villagers had been entitled to assemble more or less at will. Even the cantonal municipalities established towards the end of 1795 were restricted only in the sense that a minimum number of meetings per month was stipulated. By contrast, the village assemblies of the Consulate and the Empire were called infrequently, at the behest of the prefect, and usually at appointed seasons of the year.

In view of the Thermidorians' determination to aggregate – and confine – political expression to centres of population enjoying cantonal status, historians sometimes argue that the real rupture in the trajectory of civic life at the level of the village occurred in 1795 rather than in 1789.[5] The civic landscape across much of rural France certainly decayed during the early years of the Directory, although other factors conspired to produce this result. In the south, in villages such as Roquelaure, Saint-Alban and Allan, well-rooted traditions of assembly probably did mitigate the impact of the

---

[4] *Réimpression de l'Ancien Moniteur* (32 vols., Paris, 1840–7), XXXII, p. 225.
[5] See Fournier, *Démocratie et vie municipale en Languedoc*, II, pp. 376–9; S. Bianchi, 'Pouvoirs locaux et pouvoir central en milieu rural dans le sud de l'Ile-de-France, 1787–1802', *Annales de Bretagne et des Pays de l'Ouest*, 100 (1993), 528–32; *Les Bretons délibèrent*, p. 6; J.-L. Clade, 'La Vie municipale dans la région de Rougemont (Doubs) de l'Ancien Régime à la Restauration (1720–1820)' (3 vols., dissertation, University of Besançon, 1983), I, p. 210.

Municipal Law of 1789. It is even possible that the structuring of the new municipal councils actually narrowed the basis for representative democracy, notably in Roquelaure where a vigorous culture of general assemblies persisted, as we have seen. Neither Roquelaure nor Allan was a *chef-lieu de canton* and the loss of municipal autonomy in 1795 struck contemporaries forcibly. For the first time in more than a century the bells used to summon council meetings fell silent. The interests of the villagers of Roquelaure competed for attention alongside those of nineteen other rural communes in an oversized canton labelled 'Auch nord'. Needless to say, the enlarged municipality held its meetings in Auch and was dominated by the resident bourgeoisie of the capital. No doubt the opacity of the civic life of the village in these years stems in part from the less than adequate documentation available to us. Even so, few divisions appear to have disturbed the public demeanour of this stolidly republican canton, and the villagers of Roquelaure gave no hint that they objected to the relocation of political power.

Not so those of Allan who had long grumbled about their absorption into a canton whose centre of gravity lay on the banks of the river Rhône. The canton of Donzère was not so much populous as far flung: at over two hours' march, the *chef-lieu* was not easily accessible to country dwellers who wished to make the round trip in one day and before nightfall. Moreover it was foreign territory, and still perceived as such, despite the patriotic *élan* of 1790 that had prompted the villagers of the Terres Adjacentes to join their future to that of Montélimar and the department of the Drôme. Thus, when Donzère and the neighbouring *bourg* of Châteauneuf-du-Rhône succumbed to the politics of moderation and then outright royalism, the die was cast (see p. 147). After 1793 the inhabitants of Allan avoided contact with those of Donzère as far as possible. Indeed, they honed their own civic identity on the developing reputation of the riverine *bourgs* as havens of malevolent royalism. With the onset of the post-Thermidor reaction relations broke down completely, to the extent that peasants from Allan faced taunts and gibes should they appear in the streets of the *chef-lieu*. The withdrawal of municipal autonomy in late 1795 was therefore a bitter blow. But the village elders responded in a characteristically resourceful fashion: they simply continued to hold meetings in the 'maison commune' in a manner reminiscent of the old *conseil politique*. Throughout the Years Four, Five and Six (late 1795 to late summer 1798), in consequence, the civic life of the village – or at least one of its key components – continued more or less uninterrupted. The *agent* and *adjoint*, as the elected officers of the commune were now known, presided over more than ninety deliberative assemblies during this period. Only when major issues (taxation, requisitions) were scheduled for discussion did they make an effort to attend the sessions of the 'official' cantonal municipality in Donzère.

The Constitution of the Year Three administered something of a shock to the 'body politic' as fashioned by the early revolutionaries, then. Even villages with no antecedent traditions of assembly had grown used to exercising a small portion of national sovereignty on a par with the towns in whose shadow they had vegetated for so long. The elite of Villepreux reacted with dismay when higher authority took away what had been put in place only five and a half years earlier, but here dissimulation was not a viable option. Unlike the cantonal municipality of Donzère, the 'municipal administration of the canton of Marly' (to use the more exact and evocative official title) was well organised, vigilant and unshakably Directorial as befitted an organism operating under the direct gaze of government. On 10 Floréal V (29 April 1797), the representative of the village of Louveciennes was reprimanded for having permitted an 'unconstitutional' assembly to take place in his commune. The following year it was the turn of Jean-Germain Prissette, *agent* of Villepreux, who found himself in deep water on presenting a list of *gardes-champêtres* for endorsement. Someone noticed that the list appeared to have been drawn up 'en assemblée de commune'. Prissette was obliged to admit that he had indeed called an informal meeting of landowners and tenant farmers, 'mais que cette assemblée n'est point communale, et n'en peut avoir les caractères, attendu qu'une assemblée communale suppose la convocation de tous les citoyens actifs'.[6]

Elsewhere the impact of the constraint placed upon the right of assembly was minimal. Both Châtelaudren and Saint-Alban constituted cantons unto themselves to all intents and purposes. In spite of all their efforts, the bourgeoisie of Châtelaudren never succeeded in extending their rule over the *hobereaux* and well-to-do farmers of neighbouring Plélo. In 1795 Plélo briefly succeeded in obtaining a canton of its own, leaving Châtelaudren with no more than two satellite localities under its direct control. Accordingly, the minutes of the municipality betray few signs of the coming into force of a new constitution. Like Allan, Châtelaudren continued to take pride in its status as a patriotic outpost in a landscape ravaged by royalism. Situated in a poorly accessible corner of the central highlands, Saint-Alban was unencumbered by rivals who might have stimulated a reflex of civic zeal. Of all the villages covered in this study it proved the most reluctant to embrace the new sense of belonging. In a canton comprising just one

---

[6] A. D. des Yvelines, 23 L2, 25 Floréal VI.

other commune (the settlement of Sainte-Eulalie, whose male inhabitants absented themselves during the winter months), Saint-Alban's quarrelsome and inward-looking bourgeoisie were left to their own devices (see pp. 189–93). On receipt of the legislation setting up canton-wide administrations, the municipal council simply noted that neither the *agent* nor the *adjoint* of Sainte-Eulalie had turned up, 'quoique dument invités'.[7] Continuity of assembly was also maintained at Neuviller, although the character of deliberations altered owing to the presence, intermittently, of representatives from the ten other communes of the canton.

The Constitution of the Year Three had concentrated the deliberative energies of Frenchmen. Ubiquitous village assemblies – those most vigorous and vital organisms of the Revolution – disappeared, to be replaced by an altogether more artificial, and docile, construction: the cantonal municipality. In effect about 87 per cent of villages had been deprived of their mayors, municipal officers and aldermen. This loss of the right to assemble was not absolute since the Constitution introduced a system of annual renewals that made necessary a provision for 'communal assemblies'. Nevertheless, the right of the sovereign Nation to gather at will and deliberate had been severely curtailed at the base. Little wonder if the growth of civic awareness faltered in consequence. Refusal of public office, and absenteeism, became the bane of the Directory. The reinstatement of municipal councils in 1800 ought therefore to have been greeted with some satisfaction. It was, after all, a tacit admission that some local matters should only ever be handled locally, and, more obliquely, a recognition of one of the enduring civic achievements of the revolutionary years. Yet close inspection of the municipal registers of the Napoleonic period (they survive for four out of the six villages) reveals a situation in flux. The restless, protean civic culture of the early 1790s did not revive. Instead a refashioned civic landscape started to take shape at village level which was more dutiful, oligarchic, homogenising and passive.

Of course the regime had suspended the process of popular election in very large measure, estimating, perhaps correctly, that the hustings and party divisions posed the main obstacle to the evolution of a consensual civic culture. But the restored municipal councils – if we can judge by their minutes – lacked many of the attributes of their predecessors. They met spasmodically, as noted, and their deliberations rarely convey a sense of business being generated from below, that is to say from a constituency of interested and empowered citizens. Indeed, the label 'citizen' dropped out

---

[7] A. D. de la Lozère, L419, 10 Frimaire IV.

of use altogether in 1804. From 1806 onwards, the worthies of Châtelaudren feature in the minutes with the courtesy title 'Sieur' attached to their names just as they had done prior to the Revolution. The decentralisation of power and responsibility that had characterised the first three years of the Revolution had ebbed considerably by this date in any case. The trend towards a professional tax administration which had been so conspicuous, and contentious, at the end of the *ancien régime*,[8] resumed in 1797 with Ramel's reforms. It would issue in the setting up of the Direction des Impositions Directes on the morrow of the Brumaire *coup*. After 1802 the tax collectors of Allan ceased to present their accounts for inspection, an auditing responsibility that the village council had exercised for as long as anyone could remember. Taxes, loans, budgets, in fact public expenditure of any type, fell within the purview of the prefect – leaving local officers in a rather indeterminate position. Did they exist in order to 'represent' the interests of villagers to the higher authorities, or were they 'administrators' to all intents and purposes, representing the wishes of the subprefect and the prefect to their 'administrés'? The regime chose to leave this question unresolved. It would be an exaggeration, however, to imply that the right of assembly became worthless under the Consulate and the Empire because village councils acted as little more than rubber-stamp bodies. Centralisation, in the hands of Napoleon's prefects, tended to hide a great deal from view; yet the episode of the Hundred Days would demonstrate that the democratic culture of the revolutionary years still had its partisans (see pp. 197–9). Nonetheless, the so-called municipal 'deliberations' of the 1800s and 1810s do often resemble a record of administrative bookkeeping and not much else.

In the late eighteenth and early nineteenth centuries, voting was a collective practice and one well suited to the inculcation of new norms of behaviour and belief. Admission to the vote, moreover, signalled a claim to belong that had been accepted, a right of citizenship. By examining both the theory and the practice of voting, therefore, it should be possible to explore another dimension of the civic landscape that helped villagers to make sense of their lives. But voting, or rather the collective practice of elections, should not be construed as the key denominator of citizenship that it has since become. The rites of passage connecting the village to the wider polity were many and varied. Voting was a spasmodic and gendered activity that involved minorities for the most part. Indissolubly associated with the

---

[8] See M. Kwass, *Privilege and the Politics of Taxation in Eighteenth-Century France: Liberté, égalité, fiscalité* (Cambridge, 2000).

Revolution, to be sure, it should be weighed in the balance alongside other no less potent mechanisms for cementing allegiances.

The onset of Revolution in 1789 served to obscure the *ancien régime* discourse on citizenship, both in the minds of contemporaries and in those of historians subsequently. Yet all village communities applied rules restricting access, whether to political power or to material assets such as collectively owned pastures or woodland. In the east it was often necessary to 'buy in' to the community by paying a 'fine' to the titular seigneur. In Provence, as we have already noted, village *consuls* tended to reserve the status of 'habitant' to those owning land, a widespread practice. The Gascon village of Roquelaure was particularly prone to membership disputes for the reason that many of its landowners were non-resident, whilst the resident parishioners counted a large number of non-landowning sharecroppers in their midst. Like farm servants, vagabonds, boarded-out foundlings and some beggars, croppers were routinely disempowered on the grounds that they were marginal and all too often fleeting members of the community. The *forains*, too, lived in trepidation that their interests might be overlooked. Since 1745 they had had a mandated *sindic* whose job was to attend whenever an *assemblée générale* was called. Notions of citizenship were also shaped from above, however. And during the climactic decades of the *ancien régime* an administrative definition of citizenship had been gaining ground which, as Michael Kwass has underlined, linked the attributes of the citizen to those of the taxpayer.[9]

Thus the Calonne–Brienne local government reform of 1787, which marked the start of the modern electoral history of the village, dispensed the 'right' to 'vote' to members of the new municipal assemblies on condition of a robust fiscal qualification. Yet the tax threshold (10 *livres*) was less important than the implication that all previous rules for assessing 'worth' were now deemed to be redundant. In Roquelaure, for instance, sharecroppers were no longer disenfranchised by mere fact of their 'condition'.[10] Since the tax rolls of this village have not survived it is difficult to follow up the implications of the reform, but in neighbouring localities croppers *did* vote. In fact one even secured election, to the astonishment and scandal of contemporaries. Even before the ending of the *ancien régime*, therefore,

[9] *Ibid.*, p. 169.
[10] See the text of the edict of 12 July 1787 applicable to the *généralité* of Auch, *Assemblées municipales*, article VI: 'l'assemblée de la paroisse sera composée de tous ceux qui payeront dix livres et au-dessus, dans ladite paroisse, d'imposition foncière ou personnelle, de quelque état et condition qu'ils soient'. Cited in J. Arrivets, 'L'Assemblée provinciale de la généralité d'Auch: essai historique', *Bulletin de la Société d'histoire et d'archéologie du Gers*, 33 (1932), 257.

Table 3. *Active and passive citizenship in case-study villages and adjacent hamlets, 1791–2*

Village	Total households	Total actives	Total passives	Passives as % of total households
Allan	251	243	9	4
Châtelaudren	212	107	66[a]	31
Neuviller-sur-Moselle	117	84	22?	19?
Roville-devant-Bayon	42	45	0	0
Saint-Alban [*bourg*]	100?	87	19?	13?
[*commune*]	400?	322	70?	18?
Roquelaure	202	192	23	11
Villepreux	200	150	32	16
Rennemoulin	24	17	7	29
National average[b]	6,222,000	3,777,000	2,450,000	39.4

Notes
[a] Figure includes beggars
[b] Estimates based on a total population of 28 million

egalitarian notions of individual worth were in play that we more readily associate with the period of the Revolution. To be sure, citizenship was not yet defined as a nebulous bond establishing a direct and personal contract with the state – the revolutionary 'nation' was still waiting in the wings. Nevertheless, as one Third Estate *cahier* would put it, 'He is not a citizen who does not pay his taxes.'[11] The legislators of the National Assembly built unblushingly on this legacy.

Perhaps unaware of these antecedents, historians have made too much of the 'active/passive' distinction. Pegging 'rights' to taxes was less a blow against the poor than one against a tradition that linked representation to rank and estate. On the evidence of the villages examined in this study, the great majority of adult male householders were entitled to participate in the electoral process at the lowest tier, either because they paid the equivalent of three days' labour in direct tax (between 2 and 3 *livres*), or because the rolls of potential voters were simply copied out from pre-existing lists of households with widows and spinsters excluded. The figures given in table 3 are approximate and subject to error; yet they do indicate that even in the polarised villages of the district of Versailles between two-thirds and four-fifths of adult males possessed the right to vote for mayors, municipal

---

[11] Markoff, *The Abolition of Feudalism*, p. 142.

officers, aldermen, Justices of the Peace and their assistants.[12] Of course, 'fiscal citizenship' was simply one definition among many. Robespierre was not alone when he protested in 1791 that 'ce n'est point l'impôt qui nous fait citoyens'.[13] And besides, the attempt to filter political rights through the net of taxation was abandoned completely the following year. With the possible exceptions of Châtelaudren and Villepreux, however, it seems unlikely that the advent of universal manhood suffrage widened perceptibly the sense of belonging to the Nation. Possessing the vote and using the vote were two very different matters, as we shall see. After the local authority renewals of the autumn of 1792, the opportunities for electoral participation at the village level would in any case be sharply curtailed.

The Constitution of the Year Three steered clear of the ambiguities of 'passive' and 'active' citizenship even though the latter term had taken root in village political culture. Rather it defined a French citizen as a resident, adult, taxpaying male who had fulfilled all his other civic responsibilities. Thus qualified he was entitled to vote in the canton-wide primary assemblies which would henceforth replace nearly all other types of electoral assembly. Since none of the Napoleonic Constitutions, nor the Constitutional Charter issued by the Bourbons in 1814, makes any mention of a taxpaying franchise, one might suppose that the story of citizenship graduated against pecuniary contributions to the running costs of the state ended in 1799. But in fact Napoleon resuscitated the concept of 'active' citizenship as part of his bid to liberalise the Empire following his escape from Elba (see pp. 135–6). Villagers were once again invited to elect their mayors and assistants (*adjoints*) in assemblies composed of 'active' citizens summoned in accordance with the Municipal Law of 1789.

Conditions of access to the vote varied, then. At intervals whole categories were excluded: vagabonds of no fixed address, those in service, the very poor, migrant workers, ex-nobles, the kith and kin of *émigrés*, refractory priests, and so forth. Each category of exclusion provides clues as to how villages construed their civic landscape, and how governments sought to direct the process from above. Nevertheless, it is the mere fact of elections that should hold our attention. For a long decade (1787–1802) elections impinged on the village, often shaping the views of those who did not participate every bit as much as those who did. By the time the structural reforms approved by the National Assembly were fully in place, a huge slice of public life had been opened up to appointment on merit, and the

---

[12] See P. Gueniffey, *Le Nombre et la raison: la Révolution française et les élections* (Paris, 1995), pp. 89–91.
[13] *Oeuvres de Maximilien Robespierre* (10 vols., Paris, 1950–67), VII, p. 162.

sanction of electoral accountability became the essential mechanism for the assessment of worth. Mayors, municipal officers, procurators and aldermen (*notables*) were subjected to election, as we already know, but so were officers in the National Guard, Justices of the Peace and their assistants (*assesseurs*), District and Department administrative personnel, civil court judges and parish priests as stipulated by the terms of the Civil Constitution of the Clergy. Solely from the perspective of elections, then, the years 1790 and 1791 involved a steep learning curve. Villagers were constantly being enjoined to attend assemblies, whether to elect local officials, or to nominate 'electors' who would travel to the nearest town in order to participate in the tiered process designated for the selection of higher officials and deputies.

For many the learning curve was too steep. The exercise of rights carried with it attendant responsibilities, not to mention physical effort, expense, even risk. When the word came through that a primary assembly would be held in Marly on 26 August 1792 to choose deputies for the National Convention, the mayor of Rennemoulin (satellite hamlet of Villepreux) in-structed his twenty-four voters to gather at 6.00 am in readiness for the long march to the *chef-lieu*. After a wait of an hour and more, about half turned out; further procrastination then ensued, after which just three or four agreed to accompany the mayor. This was not untypical, and researchers have widely documented the swift transition from majority to minority par-ticipation between 1790 and 1792. Insofar as the practice of voting resisted erosion, it was at the most local and familiar levels. Even so, municipal renewals attracted fewer and fewer voters after the initial breakthrough of February 1790. No more than twenty-five participated when the munici-pality of Châtelaudren was reconstituted on 9 December 1792, that is to say barely one-sixth of the electorate. But do such figures indicate a waning enthusiasm for participatory democracy? Not necessarily. While some vil-lages were voluntarily falling out of step with the Revolution – Saint-Alban (see pp. 182–5) would be a case in point – this scenario cannot be applied to Rennemoulin and its larger neighbour Villepreux, to Châtelaudren, or to Neuviller. Villagers seem to have developed a functional attitude towards electoral assemblies. When they had something to say, or rather to signal, to the higher authorities they attended in large numbers. When they perceived an assembly to constitute a kind of 'civic test', they likewise turned out in force. All twenty-four families of Rennemoulin took the trouble to send a representative to Marly on 7 July 1793 when voting on the Constitution of 1793 was the order of the day. They even took the precaution of drawing up a list of attendance. Similarly the inhabitants of Neuviller (a cantonal seat admittedly) packed into the assembly convened to sanction the Constitution of the Year Three mainly, it seems, because they wanted to protest against the decree of the Two-Thirds.

Elections were not just a matter of turning up. A whole 'science' of representative government had to be acquired and internalised by would-be voters, a 'science' comprising jurisprudence and civic etiquette in uneven and shifting proportions. For a start, the very language of elections was a puzzle to many villagers. What was a mayor? As far as the inhabitants of Neuviller were concerned, the 'maire' was an enforcing agent of the seigneur whose mandate originated in the purchase of his office. What was a municipal officer? Again, villagers would not readily have grasped the connotations of the term save perhaps in the south of the country. Anticipating confusion, the National Assembly decreed that these labels, and only these labels, would be legally recognised throughout the length and breadth of the kingdom. Everyone would begin on the same page of the civic primer, so to speak. Even so, the first village elections were cumbersome and fumbling affairs, during which voting regulations often had to be explained line by line. The mayor was supposed to be elected by 'scrutin individuel à la pluralité absolue' whereas municipal officers were subject to 'scrutin de liste double', but no one took much notice of these concepts at Neuviller on 7 February 1790, even though the 'président d'âge' who was in charge of the proceedings did his best to explain them. Understanding was an even bigger challenge in Châtelaudren and Roquelaure, where the linguistic idiom of many of those attending electoral assemblies was not French.

It would also be many years before a common practice on voter secrecy could be adopted. The Calonne–Brienne reform permitted out-loud voting, which was the practice followed in Villepreux in order to bring into being the Municipal Assembly of 1787. But traditions in the *pays d'états* varied, and the revolutionary legislatures fought shy of imposing a common template. Vote by public acclamation was favoured by the assemblies of the Paris Sections during the Year Two, but not, it seems, at village level, where chorused expressions of the General Will were confined to civic festivals (see p. 152). In Allan secret voting (i.e. written ballot slips drawn up and deposited confidentially) predominated, a reflection no doubt of the jurisprudence of the old Parlement of Provence. But widespread illiteracy militated against this becoming civic 'best practice'. In most of our villages the scrutineers were employed in writing out large numbers of ballot slips on behalf of voters who were not adept with the quill. The opportunities for abuse that this system generated were legion, of course. Yet allegations of abuse provide some of the best accounts of the reality of elections at village level. They seem to have been noisy, hectoring, quasi-tribal affairs, during which acts of defiance, and even bloodshed, sometimes threatened to derail proceedings. Witness the official transcript of the primary assembly held in Saint-Alban to elect the Justice of the Peace on 10 Brumaire IV (1 November 1795). It describes the general clamour and disorder, as furiously disputing parties hemmed in the electoral bureau and impeded the work of the scrutineers 'à tel point qu'ils ne pouvaient remplir leur charge puisqu'ils étaient la plus part apuyés sur le derrière de leurs chaises, et les remuoient pour les empecher d'écrire'.[14]

The didactic impact of elections stemmed from their repetition. Cumulatively, if not individually, they brought home in a tangible manner what it meant to be a citizen in possession of rights. And lest there be any misapprehension as to the contractual nature of the new citizenship, voters were required to swear a civic oath. Indeed, the oath requirement can be construed in a negative fashion in order to demonstrate the meaningful nature of electoral participation. Villagers were reluctant to forswear themselves and generally sought to avoid a public affirmation of beliefs to which they did not in fact subscribe. When on 21 June 1791 the active citizens of the canton of Châtelaudren gathered to choose electors, the 'président d'âge' (an inhabitant of Plélo) preferred to step down rather than repeat the prescribed protocol. The 'hatred' oath which the Directory introduced to sustain its own carefully positioned conception of citizenship focused men's minds even more. Unsurprisingly, the officers of the cantonal primary assembly of Saint-Alban neglected to enforce the oath in either the Year Four or the Year Five (1796–7), but the Fructidor *coup* triggered a general tightening of civic discipline. On 2 Germinal VI (22 March 1798) voters arrived to find the following written out in large letters and prominently displayed: 'Je jure haine à la royauté et à l'anarchie, fidélité et attachement à la République et à la Constitution de l'an trois.'[15] The requirement to repeat out loud this oath before writing out a ballot slip (or causing one to be written) caused consternation.

After 1792 the electoral learning curve was interrupted in most villages for the duration of the Terror. The Law of 14 Frimaire (4 December 1793) ratified what had been happening informally through much of rural France, namely the elevation of a more disciplined version of civic culture that left no room for dissent and little room for differences of opinion about the 'worth' of individuals. Only in Châtelaudren were the voters called out to select a mayor (and four *notables*) during the Year Two, an electoral practice that endured largely because few *représentants-en-mission* ever passed that

---

[14] A. D. de la Lozère, L 869, 10 Brumaire IV.   [15] A. D. de la Lozère, L 870, 2 Germinal VI.

way. The major and enduring interruption of electoral practice occurred with Napoleon's conquest of power, however. In the aftermath of the Constitution of the Year Eight (promulgated on 13 December 1799), just one public official still looked to a local electorate for his mandate: the Justice of the Peace. But even this gross restriction of one of the founding principles of the early Revolution appeared insufficient once Napoleon had secured his position. The Constitutional revision of the Year Ten (4 August 1802) extended the mandate of the Justice of the Peace to a term of ten years and curtailed freedom of choice in a manner reminiscent of the practices of the *ancien régime* (the voters were to designate two candidates, one of whom would be appointed by the First Consul).

For a long decade after 1802 there were no more elections in the village, then. Had an integral part of the post-1787 civic landscape been rooted out, or merely obscured by the enhancement of other civic virtues? A partial answer can be found in the events of 1815. On 13 March 1815 the recently returned emperor issued a decree reconvening the electoral colleges, which the prefect of the Côtes-du-Nord proceeded to gloss in glowing terms before transmitting it to all the communes of his department. The copy received in Châtelaudren extolled the 'eternal principles' of 1789, adding 'l'Empereur reconnoît ces DROITS DU PEUPLE ACQUIS PAR VINGT-CINQ ANS DE COMBATS; il s'élève contre le principe que LA NATION EST FAITE POUR LE TRÔNE, NON LE TRÔNE POUR LA NATION. Il veut s'entourer des Collèges électoraux, POUR CORRIGER ET MODIFIER NOS CONSTITUTIONS SELON L'INTÉRÊT ET LA VOLONTÉ DE LA NATION.'[16] What this amounted to in the present context was an admission that a gulf had opened between the state and the individual. More tellingly, it amounted to an oblique admission that the neutered Napoleonic interpretation of citizenship would not prove strong enough to mobilise the energies of the nation in readiness for the struggle that lay ahead. One tangible result of this recognition was the decree of 30 April which gave back to (male) citizens the right to elect their mayors and *adjoints*.

Historians have largely overlooked the momentary redrawing of the civic landscape of the village during the Hundred Days. Yet despite the confused state of allegiances in large parts of the country – and the evident distaste of the prefects – unmistakable signs of the political culture of the 1790s did briefly manifest themselves. In Châtelaudren and the other villages

---

[16] A. N., F^{1c} III Côtes-du-Nord 5, printed poster headed 'Le Préfet des Côtes-du-Nord, Baron de l'Empire, Officier de la Légion d'honneur à MM. les Propriétaires et Habitans du même département' (Saint-Brieuc, 1815).

and small towns of the Côtes-du-Nord the municipal elections never took place, for the reason that the prefect secured a stay of execution from the Minister of the Interior.[17] But electoral assemblies convened in Neuviller and its satellite hamlet of Roville, in Roquelaure, in Saint-Alban and in Allan, where the forty-odd deliberants were referred to as 'citoyens actifs'.[18] In Villepreux the offices of mayor and *adjoint* changed hands as well, but it is not clear whether an election was ever held in this locality.

RESPONSIBILITIES

In order to be admitted to the vote, citizens were bound to accept enrolment in the National Guard. Although the early legislators never promulgated a Declaration of Duties, it was understood almost from the outset that the French, in revolution, had acquired responsibilities as well as rights. Service in the National Guard translated in a simple and practical manner the common obligation of defence of the fatherland. The swearing of an oath of adhesion likewise expressed this ethic of solidarity. The terms of the Constitution of 1791 left no room for equivocation: 'Pour être citoyen actif, il faut... Etre inscrit dans la municipalité de son domicile au rôle des gardes nationales; – Avoir prêté le serment civique.'[19]

How far this disembodied site of obligation and belonging – the fatherland – made sense to villagers *prior* to 1789 can only be guessed at, however. Reform legislation from the time of Necker's provincial assemblies (1778–9) onwards was often predicated on the existence of a place of reference lying beyond loyalty to the monarchy, but the word 'patrie' appears never to have entered village-level discourse. The notion of the 'nation' as an extra-local construct that expected as well as provided seems to have been a product of the first year of the Revolution. The early history of the National Guard is apposite in this respect, for it would express more fully than perhaps any other post-1789 institution the burgeoning apprehension of civic solidarity. Indeed, at village level the National Guard probably involved more people in more sustained mental (and physical) exercise than any other creation of the revolutionary era. Moreover, it was virtually the only institution to have an uninterrupted history spanning all regimes up to, and including, the Bourbon Restoration.

The first village militias carried little of this promise, though. When on 16 August 1789 the *consuls* of Allan decided to set up a 'garde', their main

---

[17] *Ibid.*, Prefect of the Côtes-du-Nord to the Minister of the Interior, Saint-Brieuc, 29 May 1815.
[18] A. C. d'Allan, N[on] C[oté] Délibérations municipales, 22 May 1815.
[19] Titre 3, section II, article 2.

concern was to protect property in a context of crumbling seigneurial authority and mounting lawlessness. The same motivation lay behind the decision taken in Villepreux on 29 July 1789 to create a 'milice'. In Châtelaudren,
on the other hand, a general assembly of inhabitants convened on 4 August
with the explicitly political purpose of offering rhetorical succour to the
embattled National Assembly ('tous les hommes devenus militaires doivent
s'armer pour la sûreté de cette auguste assemblée, le maintien de leurs droits
et de l'ordre publique').[20] In the absence from Brittany of the Great Fear, it
was perhaps easier to focus on abstract solidarities. But events were moving
fast and the other villages swiftly fell into line. A week after their initial
decision, the *consuls* of Allan acknowledged the wave of enthusiasm that
had greeted the initiative and labelled their creation 'un régiment des soldats de la Nation'[21] instead. While the threat to law and order continued to
cause anxiety, the symbolic spectacle of armed citizens forming a common
rampart in defence of new-found freedoms was acquiring potency.

In origin the National Guard was truly popular, then. It took shape on
the ground without any legislative sanction, and it involved everybody. In
the years prior to the emergence of village-level Jacobinism, the incidence
of National Guard formations probably provides the best indicator of the
contours of rural patriotism. Where detachments only belatedly came into
being, the zeal of villagers for the new regime was open to question. In the
canton of Châtelaudren, for instance, the inhabitants of Plélo showed no
interest in following the example of the *chef-lieu*. Only in the autumn of 1791
did the mayor of Plélo take steps to set up a 'phantom' National Guard,
having learned that membership was a condition of access to the vote.
Mass involvement, during these early years, drove home the implications
of the civic landscape in which French men and women were now living
in no uncertain fashion. Service in the National Guard, or a contribution
to its running costs, was a collective burden. When widow Vaast, a poor
washerwoman, complained that she was quite unable to pay 15 *sous* per week
in lieu of guard duty, the municipality of Rennemoulin replied sharply that
the duty in question was an expression of solidarity. If she petitioned for
immunity, others would try to do the same, with the result that 'la garde
tombera'.[22]

Mass incorporation, while understandable and even desirable in the conditions of 1789, did not fit well with the model of civic activism that
the National Assembly was endeavouring to construct, however. Almost

---

[20] A. D. des Côtes-d'Armor, 20G 42.   [21] A. C. d'Allan, BB 3–4, 23 August 1789.
[22] Tambour, *Les Registres municipaux de Rennemoulin*, p. 81.

overnight and without anyone's say so, a luxuriant growth of regiments, battalions and companies had sprouted in the village. Each formation had been equipped with 'officers' elected, for the most part, in unsupervised general assemblies. Whilst most of these formations expressed ostentatious loyalty to the new – and properly constituted – local authorities, some did not. The National Guard of Neuviller is a case in point, as we have seen. They were also arming themselves. In fact weaponry was fast becoming a hallmark of citizenship. At Neuviller the guard grumbled, in the summer of 1790, that they possessed no firearms, while that of Villepreux relied on forty-one pikes until the news of the king's flight persuaded the municipality to agree to an urgent purchase of thirty-one muskets. Allan, by contrast, despatched to the royal manufactory at Saint-Etienne an order for thirty-four muskets within weeks of setting up its guard. Flush with funds, or rather the expectation of funds, following its victory over the seigneur, the municipality incurred a bill of 683 *livres*. By 1792 the commune was formidably armed: an inventory taken that summer mentions 85 muskets, 36 pistols, 24 sabres, 4 halberds and many pounds of lead shot and powder. This 'gun culture' probably predated the Revolution, since the *gardes-champêtres* had been in the habit of carrying firearms wherever they went. Nevertheless, the villagers' self-image as embattled republicans who needed weapons for their own protection as well as that of the fatherland came to represent something of a headache for the higher authorities. In August and September 1815, following the Hundred Days, they would be systematically disarmed.

It appears that the National Guard came to be something of a headache for the deputies of the National Assembly, too. Despite advice on reorganisation flowing in from all quarters, they ruled that the diversity of the institution should be allowed to continue for the time being (decree of 2 May 1790). In fact the task of disciplining the Guard and of confining membership to 'active' citizens was mainly consigned to the Legislative Assembly (decrees of 29 September and 14 October 1791). Nevertheless, an important lesson had been learned. The National Guard was too powerful an instrument to be left to its own devices. All future regimes would seek to fashion it in their own image. The belated attempt to close off access to those whose citizenship was merely 'passive' barely outlived the Legislative Assembly, of course. But as the poor were readmitted, whole categories of 'political' offender were expelled. The all-inclusive institution that helped to consolidate the transition of 1789 would not be seen again. On 4 September 1792, when the National Guard of Villepreux was reconstituted following a period of inactivity occasioned by the harvest, a general assembly of villagers resolved that two individuals of noble origin would no longer be welcome 'attendu qu'ils ont donné jusqu'à ce jour aucune preuve de civisme'.[23] The following year the municipality of Saint-Alban weeded its Guard of 'suspects', 'fanatisés', Maximum infringers, kinsmen of *émigrés*, and those believed to be protecting deserters. No legislation underpinned these measures, merely *arrêtés* promulgated by the *représentants-en-mission*.

Not until well after Thermidor, in fact, did legislators return to the question. A decree promulgated on 28 Prairial III (16 June 1795) restored access to the National Guard, but with notable exclusions (servants, day labourers, migrant workers, etc.), and reactivated the practice of annual election to officer grades. This measure set the tone for the whole of the Directory and even the Consulate, although the progressive militarisation of the state and of society steadily tugged the National Guard away from its original moorings. At the level of the village, activity waxed and waned with each crisis and emergency. The initial enthusiasms of 1789 wore off swiftly. Constant guard duty and night patrolling triggered discontent and recrimination. By mid-November the guardsmen of Villepreux were clamouring to stand down; by April of the following year the grumbling of their counterparts in Châtelaudren had also reached a crescendo. But the municipality was unrepentant and reminded everybody of their collective obligations. Finally, in late July and with the harvest impending, the municipal council voted to discontinue regular guard duty and to substitute intermittent weapons training instead. And so the pattern continued: reactivation in Villepreux following the flight of the king; in Châtelaudren following the outbreak of war in the spring of 1792; quiescence throughout the autumn and winter; renewed activity in response to the recruitment disorders of March 1793, and so forth.

One striking thread of continuity should not be overlooked, however. From the earliest months of the Revolution until the early months of the Empire, villagers routinely gathered to elect officers for their National Guard detachments. Furthermore, they gathered in assemblies consistently more popular in character and composition than those called – when they were called – to renew civil and judicial authorities. One hundred and forty-eight 'active' citizens accompanied by their grown-up sons turned out to renew the officer corps of the National Guard of Allan on 14 March 1792 compared with 117 for the renewal of the municipality some seven months later. In Châtelaudren, where participation in municipal elections had dwindled, as we have seen, the disparity was even greater. The

[23] A. C. de Villepreux, D2, 4 September 1792.

implication seems to be that the National Guard acted as the prime vector of democratic political culture at village level. In the spring of 1790, for example, a vigorous polemic took place within the ranks of the National Guard of Châtelaudren. The ordinary troopers wished to determine the number of officers and the mode of selection as they saw fit, and they prevailed upon the municipality to hold a fresh electoral assembly. As a consequence, the commander and his senior officers were chosen by simple majority voting, while the *sous-officiers* were nominated by 'acclamation'.

Oath taking was another means by which villagers were induced to confront and comprehend their civic landscape. Public officials engaged their responsibilities, and even their lives, repeatedly during the revolutionary climacteric. Indeed, the returning Bourbons acknowledged the degree to which relations between individuals and the state had altered during these years when they, too, prescribed an oath of allegiance. Ordinary villagers swore a rich variety of oaths as well, usually simultaneously and usually in the context of public pageants or 'fêtes civiques' whose characteristics will be explored under a separate heading. Before 1789 oathing was a negligible activity; after 1789 it became ubiquitous. Individual community leaders might swear oaths of loyalty or allegiance three or four times a year over a lifetime of public service: to the trinity of the early Revolution (Nation, Law, King); to Liberty combined with Equality from the summer of 1792; to the Republic One and Indivisible in 1793 and 1794; to the Constitution and the Republic from 1795; *against* both Monarchy and Anarchy in 1798; *in support* of the Republic and the Representative System in 1800; to the Emperor and the Constitutions of the Empire in 1804; to His Majesty Louis XVIII in 1814; to the Emperor and the Constitutions of the Empire (again) in 1815; and finally to the King and the Constitutional Charter in 1820.

The puzzle of oath taking is that it was plainly a meaningful exercise to many individuals. Priests were not alone in supposing that the moral imperatives of revolutionary politics might endanger their eternal souls. Yet men solemnly (or is it just the *procès-verbal* that is solemn?) engaged their responsibility to uphold propositions that were plainly antithetical. How could a seasoned revolutionary such as Augustin Enjalvin of Saint-Alban – known locally as a 'patriote enragé'[24] – swear to defend Liberty and Equality unto Death in 1792, take an oath of allegiance to Napoleon when made Justice of the Peace in 1811, and declare his adhesion to the King and the Constitutional Charter when reappointed mayor of Saint-Alban in 1821 under the benevolent gaze of the subprefect ('reconnu pour bon

---

[24] A. D. de la Lozère, L 520*, 21 Ventôse II.

royaliste')?[25] Perhaps the answer is 'because he *was* a seasoned revolution-ary'. Men who changed their convictions over a span of thirty years were not simply weathervanes. Moreover, individuals such as Enjalvin and his older brother Jean-Jacques were bred to the role of political leadership – a phenomenon that we shall need to explore in chapter 5. Their participa-tion in the exercise of political power was cradled in a web of expectations which left precious little room for free will. As principal actors in their local communities, they were expected to hold office, and, by the same token, the higher authorities had little choice but to confirm their appointment. In these conditions, oath taking became a ritual act of complicity intended to conceal more than to reveal. The responsibility engaged was not to this or that regime, but to an administrative system which had evolved since 1789 and which now commanded its own loyalties.

Impromptu gestures of solidarity studded the early years of the Revo-lution and reached a peak during the emergency conditions of the Terror. On learning of the king's flight, the National Guard of Villepreux swore not to abandon their posts, 'no matter what disorder might ensue'.[26] A couple of years later the villagers subscribed 2,267 *livres* in order to fit out twenty-seven volunteers who had offered to go and join the forces that were trying to quell the Vendée insurrection. Provision was made to look after their farms and to bring in the harvest during their absence. Châtelaudren answered the call of the Vendée, too. On 13 May 1793 the municipality selected by ballot six of its national guardsmen for the duty, only to run into criticism from those who had *not* been chosen. In the end fourteen young men set off. Servicing the war effort, by 1793, was in fact becoming the ultimate expression of civic responsibility. Villages supplied men (aptly dubbed 'défenseurs de la patrie'), they supplied equipment, they hauled down their church bells in order to supply gun metal, they established premises in which to manufacture saltpetre for gun powder, they answered requisitions. All of these activities remained quasi-voluntary, thus preserv-ing the notion of patriotic sacrifice. Not until 1798 would the government resort to systematic conscription in order to replenish the armies. As for Napoleon's 'blood tax' mode of recruitment, which left villagers with very little control of the process, it was still some way off.

Nevertheless, villages variously construed their responsibilities in mat-ters of military supply. Saint-Alban practised studied recalcitrance when confronted with the manpower needs of the Republic and the Empire. Far

---

[25] A. D. de la Lozère, 2Z 12, 1 August 1815.
[26] A. C. de Villepreux, D1, Municipalité, délibérations, 23 June 1791.

removed from any frontier, the village lay in the heart of a vast upland region whose population would resist conscription with legendary cunning
and obstinacy. When muster agents for the so-called 'levy of the 300,000'
arrived in the district in April 1793 they were confronted by crowds of
young men shouting 'Vive le roi! au diable la nation! vivent les émigrants!
ça n'ira pas!'[27] A full-scale insurrection was averted – just – although the ill-
feeling would feed into the Charrier uprising a couple of months later (see
pp. 183–5). The 'volunteers' who did finally set off from Saint-Alban and
surrounding villages were miserably clothed and equipped by comparison
with those of other departments, and most took the earliest opportunity
to return home. The outcome of the *levée en masse* (23 August 1793) was
scarcely more reassuring. About 400 of the 700 strong contingent of recruits from the Lozère were reported to have deserted by Prairial II (June
1794), including, the *comité de surveillance* of Saint-Alban noted grimly,
'une grande partie des recrues de la levée en masse de cette commune'.[28]
The only way the authorities could think to stem disaffection on this scale
was to drive a wedge between villagers. On 25 July 1806 the subprefect
of Marvejols reported that a free billeting system (*garnisaires*) which the
prefect had introduced two months earlier was beginning to produce satisfactory results. Faced with financial ruin (i.e. the costs of billeting), the
larger taxpayers of Saint-Alban and neighbouring villages had started to
use their influence to ensure that deserters and draft-evaders surrendered
to the appropriate authorities.

The larger picture reveals Saint-Alban as exceptional, however. No other
village displayed such reckless and persistent disregard for the responsibilities of citizenship. Neuviller, Châtelaudren, Allan and Roquelaure were
all situated on, or close to, military highways. All could perceive, however
dimly, the link between military preparedness and their own wellbeing.
Neuviller would be threatened with invasion both in 1792–3 and in 1799,
and, in common with Allan and Villepreux, would be occupied by Allied
troops in 1814 and again in 1815. It is unsurprising, therefore, that the
creeping militarisation of civic life encountered fewer obstacles in the east.
The inhabitants of Neuviller would respond promptly and energetically to
military manpower levies. Indeed, the department of the Meurthe ranked
alongside the Vosges in its enthusiastic acceptance of the military responsibilities attaching to citizenship. Proximity to one of the major theatres of
military operations brought other obligations, however. Throughout the
Directory, but particularly during the Years Seven and Eight (1798–1800),

---

[27] Delon, *La Révolution en Lozère*, p. 254.   [28] *Ibid.*, p. 263.

the farmers and vine growers of Neuviller were taxed with a steady stream of military requisitions (carts and draft animals, saddle horses, fodder, shoes, even manual labour). None of the other villages experienced anything comparable to these exactions, and Saint-Alban was asked to contribute little or nothing. These requisitions engendered grumbling, stonewalling and, in the case of the cavalry mounts, deep resentment. But never once did the inhabitants of Neuviller fail to meet their allotted quota. Somehow, conscripted labour to fortify the bridge at Kehl in the face of an Austro-Russian advance (21 Vendémiaire VIII/13 October 1799) was not the same as the *corvée* labour ruthlessly extracted some forty years earlier by Chancellor Chaumont de La Galaizière.

RITUALS

Historians rightly emphasise the 'transfer of sacrality'[29] from the old regime to the new. In this area the debt owed by students of the village to the analytical methods of social anthropology is both conspicuous and enriching. But the notion of 'ritual' needs to be enlarged for present purposes. It must embrace space and sound as well as objects and practices. The festivals of the Revolution, Consulate and Empire naturally invite our attention, not least because they provide a sensitive gauge for the measurement of shifts in civic culture across the climacteric. However, the symbolism of space and sound in the village also altered during this period. In adopting the new practices of representative assembly, villagers also displayed a new sense of space, and a new sensibility to the aural indicators of public life. In like manner, objects and artefacts were endowed with new meanings. Indeed, the Revolution promoted to near cult status a succession of objects whose mnemonic properties would enable villagers to connect with the mythic landscape of rights and responsibilities that was developing around them.

Representational space was nowhere clearly defined at the end of the *ancien régime*. Only the village of Allan seems to have possessed a 'maison commune', but it was small and cramped in keeping with nearly all of the dwellings in the *castrum*. Assemblies took place in church, in the chateau, or in the open air. Royal legislation dating back to 1559 favoured open-air meetings and in 1608 Sully had specified the planting of elms to provide shelter in front of parish churches. Only in the village of Roquelaure, however, is there evidence of a long-standing tradition of assembly *sub ulmo*. On 25 February 1785 the *conseil politique* authorised repairs

---

[29] See M. Ozouf, *Festivals of the French Revolution* (Cambridge, Mass., and London, 1988), pp. 262–82.

to the stone seating that ringed the 4.3-metre trunk of a colossal elm tree whose branches virtually covered the 'place de l'Espérou' (see map 7). It is likely that village assemblies took place on this spot, which is only a few metres from the church; it is certain that the spot subsequently became the prime arena for the public spectacles of the Revolution. In November 1793 the Roquelaure Jacobin club ordered that the statues and sacred vessels of the church be deposited beneath the elm in readiness for ritual destruction. Elsewhere, however, the corporate life of the village tended to hover uncertainly between the territory of the seigneur (chateau, courthouse) and that of the *curé* (church, churchyard, sacristy). The infrequent assemblies of the inhabitants of Neuviller before the Revolution took place in the principal room of the chateau, but the first municipality of the village was actually elected in the church, as already noted. Thereafter it appears to have held meetings in the house of the mayor Antoine Prost, a privatising of the public domain entirely consistent with what we already know of the history of the village. The Napoleonic *conseil municipal* was still meeting in the house of the mayor in 1811, although by this time the mayor was Maurice Jordy and his 'house' the chateau! Not until the Second Empire would the villagers construct a *mairie*, thereby establishing a truly independent public space.

Both the municipal assembly of Villepreux and its linear successor the revolutionary municipality made use of the church for their meetings. But there seems to have been a widespread apprehension that the church was not a satisfactory place in which to conduct essentially secular business. On the other hand, the choice of large buildings was limited in most villages until the sales of *biens nationaux* had started to take effect. The municipality of Villepreux remained peripatetic until a room in a house belonging to the churchwardens became available in 1792. The following year the effects of Dechristianisation substantially enlarged the scope for civic space, and the municipality moved to the presbytery hard on the heels of the departing juring priest. Something of the sort happened in Roquelaure, too. Initially the newly founded Jacobin club held its meetings in the church, but with evident reluctance on the grounds that 'il n'étoit pas bienséant que l'église de notre paroisse servît pour le culte et pour y discuter des matières profanes'.[30] A switch to a private venue scarcely proved satisfactory, either. Once the parish priest had abjured, however, the tension between the sacred and the profane no longer applied, and the club felt able to reoccupy the 'ex-church' and to invest it with an alternative sacrality. Not only were the

---

[30] A. D. du Gers, L 699*, 26 May 1793.

statues removed from their niches; for good measure the lead coffins of the dukes of Roquelaure were also dragged out of the crypt.

Large open-air spaces were not, by and large, a characteristic of our villages. Allan and Roquelaure were still encircled by walls, and only Châtelaudren possessed a marketplace properly speaking (see plate 3). The 'place publique' that all six would boast during the Revolution was usually little more than a constricted intersection of alleyways made even more congested by civic clutter (Liberty Trees, Holy Mountains, etc.). The 'place de l'Espérou' in Roquelaure was tiny and quite unsuited to the large-scale pageantry, not to mention the dancing, games and festive bonfires that would develop after 1789. Accordingly most village councils sought an extension of civic space outside their built-up territory, and if the space thus commandeered had previously belonged to a rival source of authority so much the better. The inhabitants of Allan took to meeting on the seigneurial rabbit warren (*garenne*) just outside the walls of the *castrum* for purposes of display and celebration (see map 6). This was the site where 'citizens of both sexes'[31] (to quote from the *procès-verbal*) gathered to make the first of many declarations of allegiance to the Nation, the Law and the King on 6 April 1790. Their counterparts in Neuviller carried out a very similar conquest of space, but not until 1792 when La Galaizière *fils* emigrated and the walls of his park were broken down. Villepreux possessed a smallish square directly in front of the church. Once the market cross had been demolished, there was just enough room to plant a Liberty Tree and, in due course, to construct a Holy Mountain. But large assemblies such as those prescribed for oath taking and other exercises associated with the sovereignty of the people demanded an open space, both physically and metaphorically. The municipality designated for the purpose a spot just outside the village known as 'la demie lune' (see map 3). Originally a meeting-point for royal huntsmen, the 'demie lune' had been planted with a double ring of poplars and therefore resembled a purpose-built Champs de Mars. Decades after the Revolution it was still known as the 'pré de la fête'.[32] Marketplaces were already public space, of course, but their conversion into 'civic' public space rarely proved straightforward. The municipality of Châtelaudren complained of damage to the Liberty Tree caused by stock, and once that precious symbol of regeneration had been fenced in they complained that villagers were hitching their horses to the rails. The effluvia of the marketplace would also offend republican sensibilities. In the end a solution was found in the separation of

---

[31] A. C. d'Allan, RV 2, Délibérations municipales, 14 July 1790.
[32] A. D. des Yvelines, 2Mi 115 T.

functions. Flush with funds from the municipal *octrois*, the council voted in 1806 to clear the site of the old chateau and to create a public promenade (see map 4).

One of the changes remarked upon by travellers returning to France in the late Directory years was the absence of those aural indicators of public life that everyone had taken for granted just a decade or so earlier. Chateaubriand noted the empty bell towers as he sped through the countryside from Calais to Paris.[33] Day and night were no longer segmented by the tolling of church and monastic bells: clocks no longer chimed the hours. The new civic culture appeared to be one of open space and silent communion. Appearances can be deceptive, as we shall see. The revolutionaries simply celebrated time differently and employed different means in order to render it audible. Nevertheless, the observations of travellers hold good inasmuch as the ringing of church bells did largely cease for a long spell between 1793 and 1800, and at intervals was even criminalised. Only once the Concordat had been signed would the aural culture of the village recover some semblance of *ancien-régime* familiarity.

Bells were sophisticated signalling devices. Although their connotations remained unmistakably religious, they could be used to serve multiple social purposes. In 1620 Allan possessed three, each with a different pitch, and it was agreed that the middle bell would henceforth be assigned exclusively to the needs of the Calvinist minority. Villagers listened intently to bells, then. A fire or storm bell was not the same as an Angelus bell, either in pitch or in the number of chimes. In 1796, in view of the large number of families now residing outside the *castrum*, the elders of Allan resolved that the *agent* and the *adjoint* would be alerted by fifteen tolls, whereas thirty tolls would signal a full meeting of the council. In Saint-Alban, on the other hand, a single, slowly tolling bell was rung to orientate travellers during snowstorms. Nevertheless, the bell tower of the parish church served primarily to demarcate a religious landscape, a territory of grace. This point was well understood by the revolutionaries, and was one that they were bound to challenge once it became evident that religious and civic identities could not be combined.

Even before the upset of the Civil Constitution of the Clergy and the clerical oath there was a move afoot to make the functioning of village-level political life less dependent on the ringing of church bells. On 5 August 1790 the municipality of Roquelaure decided to buy a drum, including in

[33] F.-R. de Chateaubriand, *Mémoires d'outre-tombe* (4 vols., Paris, 1948), II, p. 12. See also P. Usteri and E. Ritter (eds.), *Henri Meister: souvenirs de mon dernier voyage à Paris [1795]* (Paris, 1910), p. 51.

the budget a sum to meet the cost of sending a lad to Auch to be taught how to beat it ('battre la caisse').[34] The National Guard of Châtelaudren took a similar step the following year. Although drumming up assemblies tended to be less effective than ringing bells, the resonance of the drum quickly became an audible symbol of the quasi-military forms of engagement favoured by the new regime. During the early months of 1790 bells were still being rung in order to summon the inhabitants of Allan to meetings. By June bell ringing and drumming accompanied verbal announcements by the *valet de ville*, but by December of the following year just a drummer and the *valet* would go round the streets. In Villepreux, too, an implicit rivalry of bell and drum developed which would last until the autumn of 1793 when the Dechristianisation campaign brought the experiment with a church harnessed to the needs of the state to an abrupt halt. In the small print of an *arrêté* imposing the revolutionary calendar, *représentant-en-mission* Crassous effectively anathematised bell ringing: 'la cloche ne sonnera jamais que pour les assemblées-générales de la commune, ou dans le cas d'accident. Elle ne peut rappeller aucune idée de culte.'[35]

This was the position that the Directory adhered to, albeit waveringly, over the next five years. The changing timbre of public life was underlined by the fact that many villages had already handed over their bells by this date, in any case. Allan gave up two of its three bells (the chateau having already been stripped) in November 1793; likewise Saint-Alban, despite considerable popular reluctance. It would subsequently transpire that the municipality had withheld at least one of its bells, and, in the propitious political climate of the spring of 1797, planned to resume bell ringing. Permission was sought, and obtained, from the neo-royalist Central Administration of the Lozère which, entering into the subterfuge, endorsed the reinstatement of 'une cloche pour servir aux usages purement civils'.[36] The Years Four and Five (1795–7) witnessed a partial retreat from many of the denominators of village civic culture, as we have noted. On 24 Ventôse V (14 March 1797) the cantonal municipality of Donzère agreed to reactivate the practice of ringing a bell at dawn in response to a request from agricultural day labourers. Again the subterfuge was transparent, and it would be denounced on the morrow of the Fructidor *coup* as a preliminary step towards the resumption of public worship. Not surprisingly, therefore, the wholesale purges of local government personnel during the early months of the Year Six (late 1797) were accompanied by a general reminder that, insofar as bells had any role

[34] A. D. du Gers, E Supplément 1010³.
[35] See *arrêté* of 23 Ventôse II in Tambour, *Les Registres municipaux de Rennemoulin*, p. 201.
[36] A. D. de la Lozère, L 420, 12 Floréal V.

to play, it was a secular one. For good measure, the *agent* of Allan removed the clapper from the village's one remaining bell and locked it away in the 'maison commune'. Village life resumed to the patriotic beat of the drum.

The ritual beating of the drum calling villagers to their civic devotions helped to anchor them within the new landscape. The ritual artefacts of the new regime – cockades, flags and sashes of office – performed a similar role. They served as powerful fixatives sealing belonging, authority and a common fund of memory. In keeping with municipalities all over the country, the newly elected officers of Allan hastened to order seven sashes of office in the early months of 1790. They cost 140 *livres* and were delivered on 10 July, just in time for the Fête de la Fédération. The tricolour sash, like the tricolour flag, would carry a huge emotional charge. When in 1794 Raymond Monier – the *agent national* of Allan – was called out to break up a tavern brawl, the combatants refused to acknowledge his presence since he was not wearing his sash. He returned to collect it; whereupon the most pugnacious of the participants – a wheelwright named Robin – retorted that while he respected the sash as a mark of office, he could not respect the person wearing it. Woven into a few strips of ribbon could be found the concentrated energy and authority of the Nation: transgressors beware. The loss or withdrawal of the sash of office gave pause for thought, therefore. Following the recasting of local government foreshadowed in the Constitution of the Year Three, the cantonal administration of Neuviller instructed their nine constituent municipalities to surrender their sashes of office. The order acted as a powerful, and dispiriting, reminder of the relocation of popular sovereignty.

The symbolism of cockade and flag was less straightforward. Most villagers had stumped up to purchase flags of various colours and designs for the National Guard battalions before expenditure on sashes of office became an issue. However, the National Assembly complicated the symbolism of the flag with its Martial Law legislation. On 9 May 1790 the mayor of Châtelaudren was instructed to acquire both red and white flags 'pour servir au besoin suivant l'esprit de la loi martiale'.[37] Subsequently the colour red became linked to militant Jacobinism, while white would be employed as a signal of allegiance to the Bourbon dynasty. In 1793 a detachment of the National Guard of Saint-Alban used the red flag to terrorise the inhabitants of the village of Les Faux in a dispute over common land. The flag was left fluttering from the chimney of the village bread oven to the scandal of the whole neighbourhood. The equivocal legacy of the Liberty

---

[37] A. C. de Châtelaudren, Municipalité, délibérations du Conseil municipal, 1790–an II, 9 May 1790.

Bonnet also stemmed from the colour red. On 30 Ventôse V (20 March 1797) the Administration Cantonale of Marly ordered that all representations of the Liberty Bonnet throughout the canton be repainted 'aux trois couleurs nationales'.[38] With the primary assemblies about to convene, the Directory was anxious to draw a distinction between its civic culture and that of Revolutionary Government. White as opposed to tricolour cockades would attract the death penalty during the Terror (decrees of 8 July 1792 and 19 March 1793). In fact, one Saint-Albanais paid with his life for fixing a white cockade to his jacket and taking up arms against the Republic during the Charrier insurgency. By 1815, therefore, there could be no doubt what these colours signalled. In that year villagers needed to look no further than their bell towers in order to know who was in power. If the tolling of bells offered no clue, the ensign fluttering from the flagpole most certainly would.

The 'memory objects' of the Revolution did not automatically trigger a common or an enduring reflex of allegiance, then. Some were bitterly contested, and some awakened aspirations for a civic order that would prove ill founded and ephemeral. The shrines to the Holy Mountain are a case in point. Erected, for the most part, during the climactic phase of the Terror, the majority had been scheduled for demolition within a year. Châtelaudren seems to have begun to dismantle this artificial addition to the landscape planted in the middle of its marketplace at the end of Ventôse III (March 1795), and a few weeks later the municipality of Villepreux invited tenders for the purchase of the picket fence and gate surrounding its 'former Mountain'.[39] The so-called Altars to the Fatherland, which a decree of 26 June 1792 had imposed on every village in France, did not prove much more durable either. By contrast, Liberty Trees put down deeper roots – metaphorically if not physically. They would become a constant of the civic culture of the 1790s and early 1800s.

Tree symbolism has a long history and one that scarcely calls for much explanation. The notion of the tree as a 'living shrine'[40] exists in a number of indigenous cultures where it is understood as a representation of the identity, longevity and wellbeing of the village. In the conditions of revolutionary France, the 'tree of liberty' depicted the rediscovery and regeneration of the Nation. Villagers planted Liberty Trees as a gesture of fraternity, of a desire to participate jointly in this sacred endeavour. They also planted them to commemorate the salient and joyful events of 'their' Revolution. The fact

---

[38] A. D. des Yvelines, 23L 1, 30 Ventôse V.   [39] A. C. de Villepreux, D2, 10 Germinal III.
[40] See F. de Boeck, 'The Rootedness of Trees: Place as Cultural and Natural Texture in Rural South West Congo', in N. Lovell (ed.), *Locality and Belonging* (London and New York, 1998), p. 25.

that most Liberty Trees were *not* living shrines in the physical sense does not appear to have mattered, not at the outset at least. They were memory-unifying and homogenising objects, after all. The earliest Liberty Trees, particularly in the southwest of the country where the custom originated, were little more than poles painted or festooned with appropriate symbols. Roquelaure had one such, to which a second was added in June 1793. In the minds of the local Jacobins, if no one else, it symbolised the return of unity and unanimity to the village following an outbreak of 'aristocratie' (religious dissidence). During the course of that decade the villagers of Allan planted three tree symbols: one in 1794, one in 1797 and one in 1798. The most impressive was the thirty-foot pine planted on 3 Prairial V (22 May 1797) following receipt of the news of the Peace Preliminaries of Leoben. It was painted in the 'three national colours' and crowned with a Liberty Bonnet, also in tricolour livery. The neo-Jacobin revival unleashed by the Fructidor *coup* triggered a spate of tree plantings and replantings throughout the Republic linked, for the most part, to the reinvigorated calendar of civic festivals. The inhabitants of Allan chose this moment to make a doubly symbolic gesture: they planted another tree, but on the site of the old seigneurial bread oven. Unlike Sully's elms, none of these trees survived for long and there appear to have been no replantings after the Year Eight (1799–1800), a fact significant in itself. The last replanting took place in Roville, the hamlet adjacent to Neuviller, a few months after Napoleon's *coup d'état*.

Nothing captures more dramatically the unevennesses of village-level ac-culturation than the ritual of the civic *fête*, however. Between 1789 and 1820 villagers learned to demonstrate their loyalties publicly in a manner quite alien to the habits of the *ancien régime*. But the deities invoked during these years were many and various. The *fête*, like the public oath of allegiance that so often accompanied it, therefore represents something of a conundrum. How can we make sense of the fact that, at different times, villagers paraded, unblinking, their loyalty to abstractions as diverse as the Law, the Nation, the Republic, the Sovereignty of the People, Victory, Saint Napoleon and Saint Louis? The earliest *fêtes* were *fédérations*, in fact; that is to say im-promptu and somewhat nervous expressions of solidarity between villages and between towns and villages at a time when the birth of the Nation was by no means a foregone conclusion. On 13 December 1789 the *consuls* of Allan despatched delegates to a huge gathering of national guardsmen beneath the walls of Montélimar. The purpose? To swear an oath of fidelity to the Law, and to express solidarity with the representatives of the Nation in their efforts to reform the kingdom. On 9 February the municipality of Châtelaudren chose one of its number to attend the Pontivy Assembly. Again, expressions of joy at what had been achieved since the previous summer were mingled with apprehension for the future. Roquelaure likewise sent a delegate to the 'pacte fédératif' called by the town of Auch on 4 July 1790.

Regeneration as an attainable short-term goal still commanded widespread public support during the first full year of the Revolution, though. Indeed, with the approaching anniversary of the fall of the Bastille, many French men and women were willing to believe that the Revolution had already reached its terminus. The *fête de la fédération* of 14 July 1790 was the first nationwide civic pageant of the era. While it tended to disguise gaps that had opened between rival political agendas, there can be no doubting that the event was attended by deep emotion and an authentic spirit of fraternity. The choreographed element of the *fête* was confined to synchronised oath taking throughout the length and breadth of the kingdom, but no other collective exercise could have better conveyed the message that France was now a land of liberty and unity in which all artificial divisions had been removed. On the appointed day and at the appointed hour, the inhabitants of the hamlet of Rennemoulin stood shoulder to shoulder: the miller Robine whose property had been invaded by the poor during the *guerre des farines* of 1775, Jérôme Sénéchal the principal tenant of the royal domain who controlled most of the arable land of the parish, and the dozen landless or virtually landless 'pères de famille' who were hoping to dispossess him. The adult male inhabitants, that is; when some of the womenfolk presented themselves with every intention of taking the oath, they were turned away. This early reminder of one of the most persistent ambiguities in the new concept of citizenship was partially remedied eleven days later when the whole ceremony was rerun as a result of protests by the wives and grown-up daughters. Even so, only a 'representative woman' (wife of the municipal *procureur*) was permitted to swear the oath.[41]

In view of the capacity of festivals to capture the lineaments of civic culture as they evolved over time, it is worth exploring the *mise-en-scène* of the ceremonies organised to mark the first anniversary of the Revolution in more detail. To judge from surviving *procès-verbaux*, the *fête* held in Allan was the most elaborate. It began with beating drums as the National Guard marched around this hilltop village at dawn on 14 July. The local authorities then gathered, and at the stroke of 10.00 am they set off from the 'maison commune' (relabelled 'hôtel de ville') in procession to the church, trailing

---

[41] See Tambour, *Les Registres municipaux de Rennemoulin*, pp. 54–8.

behind them the bulk of the population. During Mass the *curé*, Reynaud, delivered an 'edifying sermon' in which he explained both the rights and the duties enshrined in the oath. Flags deployed, the municipality and the National Guard then exited the church and led the population ('soit hommes, garçons, femmes et filles de tous les âges')[42] outside the walls to the *garenne* or rabbit warren where the oath was to be administered as the village clock struck 12 noon. While everybody waited, the mayor made a speech ('plein de patriotisme'), followed by the commander of the National Guard, the sergeant-major and the captain, one after the other. The hour having come, the mayor raised his hand to the heavens and took an oath to the Nation, the Law and the King which was repeated in unison by all those present. The authorities then returned to the 'hôtel de ville' in order to divest themselves of their sashes before presiding over a 'diner civique' available to all at a fixed cost. With Vespers approaching the municipality returned once more to the 'hôtel de ville' in order to retrieve their sashes, and processed into the church at 5.30 pm in the company of the National Guard and the Confraternity of the Holy Sacrament. By the time Vespers and a solemn *Te Deum* had been sung it was 7.30 pm, and the municipality once more led the villagers outside the walls to a spot where a festive bonfire had been laid. It was lit by municipal officers bearing torches, each in turn, and the rest of the evening was spent making music and dancing 'farandoles'.

At least two elements are worth retaining from this account: the pre-occupation with open space and the way in which religion impregnated all forms of collective expression. In Villepreux, too, the articulations of the *fête* were a large open space ('la demie lune') and the parish church. The pattern was sensibly the same in Châtelaudren: an initial procession to the parish church of Saint-Magloire where the rector delivered a 'dis-cours analogue aux circonstances', followed by an escorted procession to the marketplace where the 'hôtel [*sic*] de la patrie' had been erected.[43] In neither Villepreux nor Châtelaudren was provision made for an 'après fête' of popular amusement (bonfire, music, dancing, games), however. It would be useful to explore how much this first festive experiment of the Revolu-tion owed to older ritual practices, but such an exercise fails for want of evidence. All we know is that the villagers of Allan were well used to ambu-latory processions, which figured prominently in their ritual of intercession for rain during the summer months.

[42] A. C. d'Allan, RV2, Délibérations municipales, 14 July 1790.
[43] A. C. de Châtelaudren, Municipalité, délibérations du Conseil municipal, 1790–an II, 14 July 1790.

On the other hand, it *is* possible to trace the way these *fêtes* evolved subsequently. When the inhabitants of Rennemoulin reassembled for the second anniversary of the taking of the Bastille, the *mise-en-scène* was essentially the same, but the phrasing of the civic oath had grown longer and more laborious. Now it included an undertaking to uphold the free circulation of grain and the prompt payment of taxes – an oblique admission that the regeneration of France was proving a harder task than anyone had anticipated only twelve months previously. The following year the municipality of Rennemoulin did not bother to hold a *fête de la fédération* at all. The partnership role envisaged for the clergy would prove an embarrassment for all parties by this date, too. When the mayor of Châtelaudren approached rector Gilles Le Corvaisier with a view to his participation in the programme of events scheduled for 14 July 1791 he was rebuffed. Le Corvaisier, a non-juror, stated categorically that he wanted nothing to do with the ceremony, although he would not stand in the way of a juring priest being brought in from the outside. The municipality had to content itself with this arrangement; and the *procès-verbal* contains other signs that the *fête de la fédération* was no longer performing a solidifying role. The municipality offered citizens a bonfire to round off the day's events, but those who failed to illuminate their houses would be liable to a fine of 3 *livres*.

By 1792 the style of civic behaviour associated with the impulse to 'federate' had almost run its course. As in Rennemoulin, the municipal officers of Châtelaudren made no effort to celebrate the second anniversary of the taking of the Bastille, yet they had gone to some trouble to arrange a Liberty Tree (and Bonnet) planting ceremony just three weeks previously. Allan stayed loyal to the *mise-en-scène* of 1790, but there had been defections and shifts in public taste here, too. Reynaud, the long-serving parish priest, had been ordered out of the village at the start of the year, which provided a pretext to curtail the public role of the clergy. While Raspail – his juror replacement – officiated at the ceremony, it was in a subordinate rather than partnership capacity. He was required to celebrate the principal Mass in the open air and in front of an Altar to the Fatherland which had been constructed for the purpose on the *garenne*. The *procès-verbal* also records the absence of the municipal *procureur* 'quoy qu'invité'.[44] Clearly the civic landscape was no longer as firmly demarcated in men's minds as it had been in 1790.

Despite the best intentions of legislators, the festive impulses of the early years of the Revolution were never harnessed to a state-sponsored

---

[44] A. C. d'Allan, RV2, Délibérations municipales, 14 July 1792.

programme of public pageants. The National Convention prescribed nationwide festivals to mark the overthrow of the monarch and the Montagnard victory over the Gironde, and in recognition of the Supreme Being (to be held on 23 Thermidor, 12 and 20 Prairial respectively), but they made only a small impact at village level. Such *fêtes* as took place during the Year Two (1793–4) were largely spontaneous and undirected by any higher authority, which may mean, of course, that they can actually provide a better insight into the revolutionary imagination at the grass roots. Certainly it comes as no surprise to discover that the villagers of Allan responded to the legislation requiring the destruction of seigneurial title deeds with a lavish *fête* on 7 Nivôse II (27 December 1793). Drums, flags and municipal sashes were much in evidence as a pyre of old parchments was built on 'la place où il est planté l'arbre de la liberté'.[45] But the fire risk was too great and the bonfire was eventually transferred to an open area outside the walls. This symbolic and, to all appearances, uncompromising attempt to put the past beyond reach would become the subject of a polemic during the Restoration, and only then was the 'inside story' of the auto-da-fé of 1794 disclosed. The municipality, *in collaboration* with the caretaker of the chateau, sorted through the parchments before consigning a proportion of them to the flames. For a village steeped in the culture of Roman Law and one, moreover, which had won a signal victory in the courts on the strength of title deeds, it would have been foolhardy to behave otherwise.

Allan, Châtelaudren and, to a lesser degree, Villepreux developed a vigorous festive culture during these years. By contrast the villagers of Saint-Alban were proving reluctant converts to the ethos of the Nation, as we know. It is not even certain that a *fête de la fédération* was held in the *bourg* in 1790. The newly elected administrators of the Lozère chose instead to invite everyone to a rally at a windswept spot on the Causse de Sauveterre. As for Neuviller and Roquelaure, there is insufficient evidence on which to base a judgement, although the general demeanour of these villages argues in favour of a dutiful attitude towards public ceremony at the very least. The real test, however, would begin towards the end of 1795 when legislators returned to the task first espied in 1791, that of actively building the *fête* into the civic landscape of a regenerated Nation. With public-spiritedness in general retreat following the excesses of the Terror, though, the signs were scarcely propitious.

The *fêtes* of the Directory were driven from above. As such they inherited and perpetuated the secularising animus of their immediate

---

45 *Ibid.*, 7 Nivôse II.

predecessors, and made more explicit their pedagogic and militaristic appeal. Directorial *fêtes* commanded attendance, they did not 'invite' it. This would raise an ambiguity that the regime never satisfactorily resolved. How far ought the civic culture-in-the-making to compromise with popular culture of ancient provenance? If the *fête* was a 'school of citizenship', did its pupils need 'out of hours' amusement, or would an unadulterated diet of civic catechisms and gawping displays of military firepower suffice? The continuing skirmishing with the Catholic church made the dilemma especially acute. For once the regime had retreated from the coercive policies of the Terror, it was obliged to function in an environment of cultural pluralism. But a situation of *de facto* pluralism in which civic culture was nurtured on *décadis* while popular culture flourished on Sundays and patron saints' days was not an option, or at least not an option acceptable to Paris for much of the period under review.

Yet it would be wrong to imply that villagers jibbed at this heavy-handed attempt to direct their festive lives. With the exception of Saint-Alban, where the obligation to hold *fêtes* was largely ignored between 1795 and 1799, they fell in with it dutifully enough. But were the *fêtes* of the Directory popular and well attended? Here we face a problem of evidence, for while the occasions licensed by the regime for festive activity were extremely numerous, the administrative transcripts or *procès-verbaux* tend to adhere to a common template and often conceal more than they reveal. Much depended on where and when they were held. In the conditions created by the Constitution of the Year Three, the villagers of Villepreux were no more inclined to trek to the seat of the canton for a *fête* than they were in order to vote. At Neuviller (which *was* a cantonal seat) only the stern intervention of *commissaire* Jordy ensured a respectable turn out for the festival commemorating the founding of the Republic on 1 Vendémiaire V (25 September 1796). The custom, we learn from an unusually frank *procès-verbal*, 'est dans les campagnes de n'observer aucune fête pendant le cours des travaux'.[46] Some *fêtes* exerted a greater attraction than others, however. The festival of Youth, which the Directory had scheduled for 10 Germinal IV (30 March 1796), proved a resounding success in Neuviller, perhaps because it fell in the agricultural dead season but more likely because of the generous allowance made for competitive games and the mingling of the sexes. Young men and women from surrounding villages turned out in force to enjoy a day of running races and skittles in the park. *Commissaire* Jordy found an opportunity to deliver himself of a speech on 'la morale et les

---

[46] A. D. de Meurthe-et-Moselle, L 2943bis, 1 Vendémiaire V.

devoirs du citoyen',[47] and as night fell everyone repaired to the 'auditoire' of the chateau for 'un bal' funded by the municipal administration. Even if Jordy's words were lost in the hubbub, no one could have failed to grasp the lesson that the Nation was now dancing in the place where the seigneur's judicial officers had once browbeaten and intimidated the community.

The energy and determination with which the Directory repackaged the festive culture of the Revolution is impressive. Moreover, the signs suggest that by the Year Six (1797–8) a balance of ingredients that was acceptable to most parties lay within sight. Villagers could stomach the ponderous ceremonies and the preaching, provided that there was also an opportunity for some light-heartedness. The *fête* marking the Just Punishment of the Last King (2 Pluviôse) went down badly because it was such a grim-faced affair. Likewise the solemn ceremony held on 30 Prairial VII (18 June 1799) in Marly to honour the memory of the murdered Rastadt envoys. It was supposed to be sombre, silent and vengeful, though the youth of the neighbourhood still closed the day with dancing. The *commissaire* of Châtelaudren would put into words the synthesis that the regime was moving towards. On learning that the Directory had just instituted a festival of the Sovereignty of the People (30 Ventôse), he stressed that the *mise-en-scène* ought to include 'dancing and games',[48] for these activities, too, had a role to play in sustaining public support for the institutions of the Republic. The requirement for school teachers and their pupils to attend civic *fêtes* should also be seen in this light. From 23 Thermidor VI (festival commemorating the Insurrection of 10 August) onwards, they were regular additions to the cast list for the public celebrations organised in Châtelaudren. But the willingness of the regime to enter into a relationship of complicity with salient features of popular culture was not unconditional. Only on *décadis* and national *fête* days were dancing and games dubbed patriotic activities. Moreover, games that did not involve discipline and physical prowess were frowned upon, and the goose game ('jeu de l'oie') was strictly forbidden 'comme contraire à tout principe de moralité et de sensibilité, comme propre à faire contracter à la jeunesse la férocité, source de tous les maux de la société'.[49]

Presumably military display did not encourage ferocity. At any event, the gradual introduction of military values as one of the principal denominators of citizenship is fully reflected in the festive culture of the Directory. The Thermidorians had established a festival of Victory as early

---

[47] *Ibid.*, 16 Ventôse IV.
[48] A. C. de Châtelaudren, Municipalité, délibérations du Conseil municipal, 1790–an II, 21 Ventôse VI.
[49] A. D. des Yvelines, 23 L 1, 5 Floréal VII.

as 30 Vendémiaire III (21 October 1794), but it is the trend at the local level that is most revealing. Situated on the supply line between Paris and Brest, Châtelaudren had long been accustomed to troop movements. Even during the early years of the Revolution, its public ritual had evinced a military quality. The *fête de la fédération* of 1790 closed with bell ringing *and* cannon salvoes. From the start of the Year Six (September 1797), however, the martial symbolism became increasingly pronounced. The festival for the founding of the Republic of that year was punctuated by cannonades and the set-piece pageants included a 'promenade militaire et civique'[50] to the sound of music and drums. Thereafter, a military tatoo, or manoeuvres, featured routinely in the bill of fare. Essentially passive admiration for the feats of the Republic's generals was growing in Allan, too. On the occasion of the festival of the Sovereignty of the People (30 Ventôse VI/20 March 1798) cries of 'Long live the Republic!' were followed by cries of 'Long live our brave defenders, long live Bonaparte!'.[51] The regime pandered to this trend, of course, by organising sumptuous funeral ceremonies for generals Hoche and Joubert. The inhabitants of Villepreux were convoked to replica events in the 'temple décadaire' of Marly on both occasions.

Some measure of the importance which the Directory attached to *fêtes* as a tool of civic transformation can be found in municipal budgets. By the end of the Year Seven (September 1799) the cantonal municipality of Châtelaudren was earmarking 300 *francs* a year for 'frais des fêtes nationales' compared with 200 *francs* for 'frais des écoles primaires'.[52] The Consulate, by contrast, would scale down this massive investment. On the day Bonaparte was installed as First Consul, a law abolished all *fêtes nationales* save for two (the anniversaries of the taking of the Bastille and the founding of the Republic). Châtelaudren's municipal budget for the Year Twelve (1803–4) made no allowance for expenditure on *fêtes*, but set aside 800 *francs* for 'frais de culte, de loyer [de la] maison curiale, entretien de l'église'.[53] It must be emphasised, however, that neither the Consulate nor the Empire dispensed with festive public ritual. All post-1789 regimes – even the restored Bourbons in 1814 – acknowledged that it had a part to play in shaping the civic landscape. Bonaparte's role was to fashion a polity in which civil authority once again enjoyed spiritual endorsement, as is well known. Indeed, our micro-historical approach makes it possible to chart this process in detail.

---

[50] A. C. de Châtelaudren, Municipalité, délibérations, an II–an VII, 2 Jour Compl. V.
[51] A. C. d'Allan, RV2, Délibérations communales, 30 Ventôse VI.
[52] A. C. de Châtelaudren, Municipalité, délibérations, an II–an VII, 3 Fructidor VII.
[53] A. C. de Châtelaudren, Municipalité, délibérations, an VII–1822, 15 Pluviôse XIII.

When the villagers of Allan assembled on 10 Brumaire VI (31 October 1797) in order to celebrate the signing of the Treaty of Campo-Formio, they listened as General Kellermann's letter was read out, whereupon someone suggested that a *Te Deum* be sung. Such a manifestly religious mode of thanksgiving threw the local authorities into confusion. Neither the *agent* nor the *adjoint* was willing to risk inviting an ecclesiastic to act as celebrant, and yet there was significant public support for the idea. In the end, the *adjoint* agreed to officiate, and those villagers who wished to do so filed into the Temple of Reason. As the *Te Deum* was being sung, however, the National Guard provided a musket-fire accompaniment outside the porch. This thinly veiled bid to realign civic and religious culture turned out to be premature. Even in the early years of the Consulate (Years Eight and Nine) public ceremony remained entirely secular. Not until the Year Eleven did the annual *fête* in honour of the founding of the Republic incorporate a *Te Deum* in Châtelaudren. The turning-point seems to have been reached just a few weeks earlier when news of the *senatus-consultum* proclaiming Napoleon Bonaparte Consul for Life (14 Thermidor X/2 August 1802) arrived in the village. The programme for the ensuing *fête* specified a *Te Deum* 'qui sera chanté en action de grâce en l'église de Saint Magloire'.[54] Of course the Concordat had come into force in the meantime. Nonetheless, after an interruption of a little over eight years, the church had been reinserted into the civic landscape of the village.

By the time of the Empire, therefore, the history of the village *fête* had almost turned full circle. The regime had accepted the utility of public ritual at the level of the village, but for purposes somewhat removed from those which had motivated the desire to federate and to celebrate in 1789–90. The *fête* was no longer a weapon of war against an old order, but rather a buttress to the new social order constructed since 1789. The purpose of pomp and ceremony, declared Portalis, the Minister of Ecclesiastical Affairs, in 1806, was to mould civic character. No one would have dissented from this statement at any point in the 1790s. But pomp and ceremony, he continued, could have no purchase on the body politic 'si elles ne se rattachent aux pompes et aux cérémonies de la religion'.[55] Whereas the early revolutionaries had enlisted the church to help them prise open the old order, Napoleon's high officials of state intended to use it in a consolidating and stabilising role. Portalis went on to propose just two national festivals constructed around this vision. One would commemorate the Concordat on 15 August, which, by happy coincidence, was Napoleon's

---

[54] *Ibid.*, 26 Thermidor X.   [55] *Gazette nationale, ou Le Moniteur universel*, 22 February 1806.

birthday as well as the Feast of the Assumption. The other, in December, would recall the Imperial coronation, that is to say 'le rétablissement de ce Gouvernement vraiment national qui donne un père à la patrie'.[56]

We can only guess at what the villagers of Châtelaudren and Saint-Alban might have been saying to one another as they assembled on 15 August 1806. In the space of a single lifetime they had witnessed the beatification of the Law, the Nation, the Republic and now the person of the Emperor. The *procès-verbaux* describing these annual ceremonies are robotic, the *mise-en-scène* laid down in advance by the subprefect. They do not exude warmth or popular commitment. The *fêtes* were not held at all in Villepreux, nor in the village of Allan, which did, however, mark Napoleon's marriage to Marie-Louise with a procession, a Mass, an emblematic civil marriage and a 'bal champêtre' on 10 May 1810. Perhaps we should not be looking for meaning where there is little or none to be found. If, to borrow from Durkheim, the village *fête* had become scarcely more than a ritualised opportunity for community expression, it is not too surprising to find the inhabitants of Châtelaudren hailing Napoleon Bonaparte as 'notre Empereur et roi' on 5 December 1813 and turning out for 'la fête de la Saint Louis' on 25 August 1814 barely nine months later.[57] The Bourbons recognised the oath, as we have seen, and in so doing they tacitly recognised the civic landscape that had taken shape over the preceding twenty-five years. The same applies to the practice of the *fête*. Once the First Consul had reintegrated the Catholic church, there was little or nothing in the symbolism of the civic *fête* to which the Bourbons could take exception. Apart from the change of deity, the *fête de la Saint Louis* held in Châtelaudren in 1814 and subsequent years adhered closely to ritual practices elaborated under previous regimes.

According to Franz Kafka, 'Every revolution evaporates and leaves behind it only the slime of a new bureaucracy'.[58] Was a new bureaucracy therefore the only enduring outcome of the effort to locate villagers in a new civic landscape? The signs are not very encouraging, it has to be conceded. French men and women were united in a common project of civic renewal for about a year or eighteen months following the dramatic events of the summer of 1789. But when the rhetoric of 'regeneration' encountered insurmountable political obstacles, that unity of purpose broke down. The civic landscape glimpsed from the steps of Altars to the Fatherland all over France on 14 July 1790 quickly disappeared into the mist. Subsequent

---

[56] *Ibid.*
[57] A. C. de Châtelaudren, Municipalité, délibérations, an VII–1822, 5 December 1813 and 22 August 1814.
[58] *Penguin Dictionary of Modern Quotations* (Harmondsworth, 1980).

reappearances proved to be problematic, partisan or ephemeral. We must, in consequence, reject the notion of a linear development of civic awareness. Over the years much was added and much was discarded, so much so that our villagers could have been forgiven for not knowing what to believe in, or what to hold dear. Even the Declaration of the Rights of Man, that founding statement of beliefs intended to bind the new community together, ceased to feature as a preamble to constitutional texts after 1795.

Yet this is to argue that the crisis of identity of the inhabitants of Neuviller which served as an introduction to the present chapter was somehow abnormal. Perhaps it was abnormal in its intensity and in the acuity with which the issue of identity was posed in 1814–15, but a long-term, and no doubt enduring, shift in perceptions *had* taken place in all six villages. In its mental dimension, the village was not the same place in 1815 or 1820 as it had been in 1760 or 1789. For a start, the selective game of remembering and forgetting had filtered memories, alternately distorting or homogenising, to produce a mythic collective memory of what the *ancien régime*, or the Revolution, had really been like. And of course this process had been buttressed by a more physical exercise of remembering and forgetting inasmuch as the villagers of 1815 or 1820 were not, by and large, those of 1760 or 1789. Most, by 1820, would have been reliant on 'vicarious memory' for their apprehensions of the *ancien régime* and the Revolution. What, then, would such individuals have recognised when reflecting, vicariously or otherwise, on three or four decades of 'memorable' change?

They would have recognised a new bureaucracy, and its by-product a near total uniformity of institutions, to be sure. But a bureaucracy that both obeyed and enforced the rule of law – not an inconsiderable gain in the eyes of villagers. Whilst the revolutionaries' flawed attempts to deify the law finally found expression in a veritable cult of the law under Napoleon, the advantages to villagers of placing the law outside political and social power structures cannot be overstated. For all their social conservatism the Napoleonic prefects and subprefects were veritable slaves to the letter of the law, and many a villager had reason to be thankful for that fact when battling the attempts of social superiors to overturn the levelling legislation of the revolutionary era. Special pleading now had to be encoded in administrative language or conducted before the courts, and was therefore open to exposure or challenge. Gone were the days when intendants could impose arbitrary tax increases, and powerful seigneurs 'fix' decisions behind the scenes. While doubts can be raised about the willingness of the Napoleonic regime to respect the rule of law in matters of high state, villagers must have experienced a keen awareness that they were now living in a 'lawful society' from which the scourges of iniquitous taxation, arbitrary arrest and partial justice had been largely banished.

Equality in the eyes of the law signalled an end to structural rank and privilege, of course. And in the context of the six villages on which this study is based it implied above all the expunging of seigneurialism from the landscape. Bonaparte and, subsequently, the Bourbons may well have restored noble rank and pretensions, thereby infringing the revolutionary principle of careers open to talent, but equality of opportunity did not mean a great deal at the village level. The crucial issue, after 1800, was seigneurialism, and this pillar of the post-Revolution settlement held firm. One of the most pervasive myths about the *ancien régime* was spun from the thread of seigneurial obligations, and the determination of both Napoleon and the restored Bourbon monarch, Louis XVIII, to resist calls for their reintroduction ensured that a key feature of the new civic landscape survived the passing of regimes unscathed. Likewise the definition of property in general that had been so painfully negotiated between 1789 and 1804. Apprehension about seigneurial dues as Napoleon's armies were scattered was exceeded only by the apprehension of buyers, or holders, of national, that is to say church or *émigré*, property. Yet Louis XVIII's Charter, which was more liberal than any of the constitutions of the Consulate or the Empire, specifically upheld the inviolability of property titles 'sans aucune exception de celles qu'on appelle *nationales*, la loi ne mettant aucune différence entre elles'.[59] Once again, the law intervened to protect the post-revolutionary landscape from what would otherwise have been a disturbance of seismic proportions.

So much for the gains, then; but what had villagers lost? Sovereignty of the people and citizenship had become so dilute as to be virtually meaningless by the end of the Empire. Louis XVIII would find no use for the terms: his Constitutional Charter declared that Providence alone had commanded him to return to France, and that all authority resided henceforward in his person. Whether we date the ebbing of representative democracy from 1797 (the Fructidor *coup*), from 1799 (the Brumaire *coup*) or from the Life Consulship (1802), there can be no doubt that villagers had been substantially disempowered by comparison with 1790 or 1792. How much this mattered depends on the significance one attaches to the vote as a fixative of civic culture. It could be argued that incorporation in the National Guard and participation in national *fêtes* played a more influential role in the process of acculturation. Nevertheless, villagers prized highly the decentralised

[59] *La Charte Constitutionnelle*, 4 June 1814, article 9.

institutions created between 1787 and 1790, and they responded favourably to the downward flow of accountability of locally elected officials. When the Constitution of the Year Three removed the apparatus of self-government from the hands of most villagers, the immediate consequence was a widespread loss of interest in public affairs. From Brumaire onwards Bonaparte worked hard to ensure that democracy would never again figure as an ingredient of mass civic culture. Instead he offered a limp, censitary definition of citizenship that largely hollowed out the meaning of the word. Those excluded were invited to take what succour they could find in the pervasive militarisation of society. Military valour replaced civic virtue as a source of emulation. Yet that was not quite the end of the story. In 1815 – in the hour of his need – Napoleon reactivated the store of memories associated with the revolutionary model of citizenship. And his call was answered: proof that villagers' aspirations towards representative government had not been put to sleep after all.

CHAPTER 5

Sovereignty in the village

As France's legislators cut themselves adrift from the *ancien régime*, many observers sensed the start of an experiment in local power sharing whose outcome could not be foreseen. 'This idea of governing a kingdom of twenty-four [*sic*] millions of inhabitants by municipalities,' commented the American envoy in Paris, 'is so new that all opinions respecting it can only be conjectures.'[1] Yet the idea – with all its imponderables – quickly took root. As doubt mounted about the political infallibility of legislative assemblies, Saint-Just reminded fellow deputies that 'the sovereignty of the nation resides in the communes'.[2] By the end of the first full year of revolution those communes – or villages in this instance – were coming to terms with the fact that the System had indeed changed. Agendas fashioned from the grievances of the *ancien régime* or shaped out of the crisis of 1789 were being overtaken by the flow of events in the manner outlined in chapter 3. Once it became obvious that the institutional grip of seigneurialism had been loosened beyond any hope of recovery, village elites scrambled to disentangle themselves. The new regime would not lack opportunities for advancement, and those travelling the new channels of social promotion could expect to avoid the conflicts of interest that had faced servants of the seigneurial regime. The 'sovereignty' of the village would never be absolute, of course; nor would it always serve as a reliable political compass for legislators. It would nevertheless remain an experience deeply etched into the minds of those men and women who attained maturity just as the 'old' France was ceasing to exist.

The power play of village politics is not easy to decipher, however. While historians from the time of Georges Lefebvre onwards have made a point of stressing the role played by actors in *local* arenas in sustaining

---

[1] J. P. Boyd (ed.), *The Papers of Thomas Jefferson* (27 vols., Princeton, N.J., 1950–97), XVI, William Short to John Jay, Paris, 23 January 1790.
[2] Saint-Just, *Essai de constitution lu dans la séance du 24 avril [1793] à la Convention nationale, & imprimé par son ordre*, chapter II, article VI.

the revolutionary dynamic, few have managed to lay bare the mechanisms involved. 'The micropolitics of rural France in revolution is in many ways still largely unknown to us,' remarks John Markoff.[3] Viewed from the outside, the political life of the village resembles nothing so much as a set of stereotyped responses to external ideological stimuli: a vision of sameness reflected almost to infinity. This is the familiar view, because to obtain any other is an arduous undertaking. Exploring the village from the inside is not only arduous, it risks introducing incoherence where once there was coherence. Every group of villagers operated within a distinctive force field; different groups formulated different agendas for change. How, then, can we compare and contrast villagers' experiences, let alone generalise them? Large-scale generalisation does lie beyond the scope of this study. Nevertheless, it *is* possible to proceed by comparison, and thereby to get a sense of both the shape and the evolution of political life at the level of the village. On the basis of our case studies it may even be possible to identify some of the paths followed by villagers – whether as individuals or as groups of individuals – on the road to explicit political engagement. This chapter builds on the foundations laid in chapter 3, therefore. Within parameters at once thematic and chronological, it tries to lay bare the micro-history of village politics in terms that villagers themselves would have understood.

ELITES AND POWER ARENAS

In an analysis of local power arenas, it makes sense to begin with a discussion of village socio-economic elites. Although the municipal elections of 1790 provided an opportunity to question existing power structures, that opportunity was not taken by and large. Only in Neuviller, as we have seen, did a challenge materialise, although it is perhaps worth adding that a full-blown municipal revolution also took place in the tiny hamlet of Rennemoulin adjacent to Villepreux. Like their counterparts in Villepreux, the inhabitants of Rennemoulin eked out a precarious – and resentful – existence in the economic shadow of the Royal Domain of Versailles. They had protested their impotence in the face of spiralling bread prices during the 'Flour War' of 1775 when miller Robine's grain stocks had been commandeered.[4] They had mounted a challenge again in 1787 on the occasion of the Municipal

---

[3] Markoff, *The Abolition of Feudalism*, p. 310. See also J. Markoff, 'Peasant Grievances and Peasant Insurrection: France in 1789', *Journal of Modern History*, 62 (September 1990), reprinted in T. C. W. Blanning (ed.), *The Rise and Fall of the French Revolution* (Chicago and London, 1996), p. 179.

[4] See C. A. Bouton, *The Flour War: Gender, Class and Community in Late Ancien Regime French Society* (University Park, Pa., 1993), p. 194 and table 4.

Assembly election, but to no real effect. In 1790 the authority of Jerôme Sénéchal, the 'gros fermier' who leased three-quarters of the arable of the parish, was repudiated. He lost the election for the mayorship to Pierre Salles, a smallholder with only a few acres of land. Neither Sénéchal nor Robine featured in the new municipal council.

Continuity is nevertheless the leitmotiv of 1790, a fact revealing in itself. In this respect our findings mirror those of Jean-Pierre Jessenne, whose study of the Artois is currently the only sustained attempt at mapping the transformation of village politics across the watershed of the Revolution.[5] He concludes that old elites survived the transition of 1790 quite well, on condition that they had not compromised themselves in their management of the seigneurial regime. But this does not mean that the 'gros fermiers' of the northern plains and the self-absorbed cliques of village bourgeois in the south sailed the choppy waters of the 1790s totally unopposed, as we shall see. The villages of Roquelaure and Allan provide the best evidence of uninterrupted, or barely interrupted, elite control. In Roquelaure all but one of the posts in the new municipality were filled by men who had served as *consuls*, whether in the 1770s or the 1780s. Only the need to recruit ten *notables* prompted a slight enlargement of the charmed circle of *ancien régime* office holding to embrace a couple of master-craftsmen. Even so, the majority of *notables* were also former *consuls* and *jurats*. There was nothing unusual about this of course; but we find the same power constellation reflected in the membership lists of the *société populaire* in 1793, in the choices made by the communal assemblies of the later 1790s, and, rather less surprisingly, in the municipal councils of the Consulate, the Empire and the early Restoration. To judge from the recorded political history of the village one might suppose that the parish contained just twenty or so families, most of whom resided in the *chef-lieu*. Of the majority of the adult male population – sharecroppers and agricultural labourers – there is scarcely any sign. Yet this elite was not politically unresponsive: it followed the events of the Paris Revolution and the regional revolution closely, in fact too closely, as we shall see. Perhaps the quiescence of the labouring majority stemmed from the fact that their views were being adequately represented. We know from villages elsewhere in the southwest that croppers were not congenitally incapable of expressing their grievances.

Two factors seem to have maintained a unity of outlook among the inhabitants of Allan. For a start there were no deep socio-economic fissures in the parish. By 1789 the villagers no longer counted any liberal professionals

[5] See Jessenne, *Pouvoir au village et révolution*.

in their midst: those who were needed to service the seigneurial court tended to live elsewhere. Instead, leadership was provided by peasant landed families (*ménagers*) and petty traders, most of whom had been established in the neighbourhood for centuries. In the absence of bourgeois cadres they relied heavily on outside 'intercessors' for opinion and advice, as previously noted; nevertheless, they kept a firm grip on the institutions of local government right across the revolutionary climacteric. The onset of the Terror did little to alter the composition of this elite: one municipal officer was recorded as incapable of writing his name in 1790 compared with two or three in 1794. However, the pool of potential village spokesmen had been augmented by the rehabilitation of three or four well-to-do Protestant households. Prior to 1790 they had been excluded from public office. Their presence in the council helped to compensate for the loss, in 1791, of several prominent individuals who were unable to come to terms with the Civil Constitution of the Clergy and the clerical oath. By early 1792 the contours of Allan's revolutionary elite were more or less fixed, therefore. Thirteen of the twenty individuals elected in March of that year to staff the National Guard would go on to become founder-members of the *société populaire*. Among them numbered six Protestants. The other factor that lined up the population of Allan behind its peasant cadres, of course, was anti-seigneurialism. Between 1785 and 1818 the villagers prosecuted, or defended, no fewer than six court cases against their one-time seigneur Madame Lériget de La Faye, wife of Comte Henri de La Tour-du-Pin-Montauban. This long and costly struggle had a regimenting effect as far as leadership roles were concerned, but, by the same token, it ensured that the dynamic of revolutionary politics in the village scarcely evolved beyond a visceral reflex of opposition to all manifestations of seigneurial authority.

The affairs of both Châtelaudren and Saint-Alban were managed by coteries of bourgeois who were living comfortably from the pickings of the seigneurial regime when the Revolution broke. This was all they had in common, however. Whereas the *hommes de loi* and prospering merchants of Châtelaudren formed a fluid, open-minded and well-educated elite, the assorted scriveners, writ-servers and attorneys of Saint-Alban were in-bred, inward-looking and instinctively venal to a degree unusual even among their fellows in neighbouring *bourgs* of the Gévaudan. They were also divided by household into rival clans and, as we shall see, they viewed the Revolution mainly in functional terms. But let us first take a look at the situation in Châtelaudren.

Although the extensive jurisdiction of the Comté de Goello provided employment for a dozen notaries and at least as many judges, procurators and bailiffs, the position of Châtelaudren as a *lieu de passage* ensured that the better sort of merchants and even a handful of master-craftsmen also passed muster as members of the elite. The village even contained two resident noble families who owned farms in neighbouring parishes, a social mix that we have not encountered elsewhere although one entirely in keeping with the complexion of late *ancien-régime* Brittany. Not surprisingly in view of the behaviour of the Breton nobility as an estate, Châtelaudren's titled families dropped out of the power structure in 1790 and would not reappear before 1795. The core of the old *général* weathered the transition to elective power holding almost without upset, however, and it is not too difficult to see why. These were men of talent and connections, after all, and even the humblest villager would have been aware of the role that the courts had played in the local economy. It is true, of course, that no really satisfactory remedy was found for the demise of seigneurial judicial provision, and in the course of 1792 the mercantile character of the village's power elite became more pronounced. Nevertheless, a point of rupture with the traditions of the *ancien régime* was never reached. Even in 1793–4 power did not slide further down the social scale. The personalities of 1790 simply bided their time and sure enough they were recalled to office, albeit by fiat of a *représentant-en-mission*. By 1795 the municipality contained the former *régisseur* of the seigneurie, Jean-Louis Rivot, and a trustee ex-nobleman who was known to be no friend of armed royalism. But there the reaction stopped. It would resume after 1800 once the threat of the *chouannerie* had been overcome. During the Empire power slowly shifted back into the hands of the old seigneurial service bourgeoisie, in alliance, now, with the local nobility.

Some of the leading players in the interminable disputes that wracked the *bourg* of Saint-Alban have already been identified. Here the key to most of the power combinations of the late *ancien régime* and the Revolution can be found in the rivalry of the Atrasic and Mathieu households. Noé-Jean Atrasic owed his wealth, if not his social status, to purchases made by his father, allegedly a miller. Social esteem would only be granted when he secured Félix-Trophime Vincens, scion of a Mende legal family, as a match for the daughter whom he designated heir following the death of his son. By contrast, the Mathieus were a numerous and long-established bourgeois dynasty with offspring ensconced in most of the legal jurisdictions of the neighbourhood. About a dozen other well-to-do families gravitated around these fixed points in the political universe of the parish, and each in turn was able to mobilise a network of clients and kinsmen. The Polge, Marlet and Tardieu families were usually to be found in the camp of Atrasic and his son-in-law, whereas the Enjalvins, Ayralds, Valadiers, Fontugnes and Pelissiers tended to make common cause with the Mathieu clan. All owed their social pre-eminence, and not a little of their economic wellbeing, to the existence of the baronial jurisdiction of Saint-Alban. Or, as a grumbling petition drawn up by inhabitants of the hamlets during the Terror would put it, 'ce sont pour la plupart d'anciens gens d'affaires et agens de l'ancien régime qui...cherchent à se reproduire sous des nouvelles formes et nous vexent plus que jamais'.[6]

The point to note about this elite, however, is that it was divided – irretrievably. Saint-Alban was a community bound together by mutual loathing. The population of the outlying hamlets detested the material and symbolic power of the *bourg*, whereas the well-to-do families of the *bourg* devoted much of their leisure time to in-fighting and the manipulation of external sources of authority. Not surprisingly, therefore, the political tremors unleashed in 1789 tended to follow these fault lines. 'Patriots' contended with 'aristocrats', in a context of decidedly lukewarm support for the Revolution it has to be said, but the suspicion remains that the 'game' being played by the main protagonists and spectated by the bulk of the population was something else altogether. All information about persons and parties emanating from the village of Saint-Alban has to be treated with 'précaution', warned an official of the Central Administration of the Lozère in 1796: 'il existe...des haines invétérées et profondes qui ont souvent produit des éclats facheux'.[7] How far, then, did power slip beyond the grasp of this fractured elite? Only momentarily it would seem. The Terror produced a *frisson* of democratisation – here as elsewhere – inasmuch as several illiterate craftsmen entered the *comité de surveillance*. They were almost certainly handpicked, however, and therefore liege men of their respective bourgeois masters. Only in Germinal II (April 1794) when *représentant-en-mission* Borie curtailed the ascendancy of the Mathieu–Enjalvin clique did some slippage occur: the *comité* was reconstituted so as to ensure a better representation of the hamlets. Mostly illiterate, these 'peasant' members would play a very self-effacing role. The real effect of Borie's intervention was to topple one faction of the bourgeoisie so that it could be replaced by another (see pp. 189–91). But it is the tenacity and constancy of elite micro-politics in Saint-Alban that is so striking. Even though the records of neither the old *conseil politique* nor the revolutionary municipality have survived, we can trace a continuity of factional alignments running from the 1770s

---

[6] A. N., F⁷3681¹⁴, Cultivateurs habitans de la commune de Saint-Alban (n.d.).
[7] A. N., F¹⁹1011, Central Administration of the Lozère to the Minister of the Interior, Mende, 30 Frimaire IV.

until the late 1820s. Most of the actors of the 1770s and 1780s were still on the scenes when the Bourbons returned in 1814. In marked contrast to Châtelaudren, social mobility in Saint-Alban was negligible. Of course, individual members of the elite became skilled at 're-inventing' themselves over time (the case of Augustin Enjalvin has already been mentioned), but the salience of *oustal* (household) culture in the Gévaudan/Lozère ensured that the structure of politics remained basically unaltered.[8]

On the evidence of the events that had taken place in Neuviller during the spring and summer of 1790, one might hypothesise that this village was similarly programmed to descend into internecine strife. In fact a fusion of elites took place. Unlike the tribal groupings of Saint-Alban, the warring parties of Neuviller derived their succour, cohesion and sense of identity from the grand narrative of the Revolution itself. Consequently the party of the *curé* would progressively lose its *raison d'être*. Few administrative papers of any sort survive for the period prior to 1794, and therefore we cannot know by what means the two municipalities elected in 1790 were reconciled. Suffice it to say that by the early months of 1791 only one such body containing an amalgam of the two parties existed. A defamation suit brought before the *juge de paix* makes clear that the old antagonisms had not entirely subsided, though. Antoine Prost publicly labelled François Herbé a thief, and the summonsed witnesses recreated the alignments dividing villagers. But the year 1791 dealt the party of the *curé* two body blows from which it was unable to recover. First, the issue of the clerical oath put Seignelay on the defensive. A restrictive oath, sworn in February, bought some time although it could only prolong his presence in the village by a few months. Second, the seigneurial regime continued to unravel prompting even the most diehard supporters of the ex-seigneur into a posture of compromise. La Galaizière *fils* had disappeared from the scene in any case, and Seignelay would emigrate under the threat of deportation the following year.

Fusion or annihilation, then? Just one of the lieutenants of the former *curé* made the transition, it is true. The remainder retired gracefully as far as we can judge. Antoine Prost, one-time mayor, held no elective office between 1791 and 1797; nor did Claude Hanriot, the caretaker of the chateau. The cadres of the Year Two (1793–4) were therefore drawn overwhelmingly

---

[8] For the *oustal* culture of the southern Massif Central, see P. Lamaison, 'Les Stratégies matrimoniales dans un système complexe de parenté', *Annales: economies, sociétés, civilisations*, July–August 1979, 721–43; E. Claverie, ' "L'Honneur": une société de défis au XIXe siècle', *Annales: economies, sociétés, civilisations*, July–August 1979, 744–59; *La Margeride*, p. 53; P. M. Jones, *Politics and Rural Society: The Southern Massif Central, c. 1750–1880* (Cambridge, 1985), pp. 95–106; P. Maurice, *La Famille en Gévaudan au XVe siècle, 1380–1483* (Paris, 1998); Y. Pourcher, *Les Maîtres de granit: les notables de Lozère du XVIIIe siècle à nos jours* (Paris, 1987).

from the ranks of Pierre Dieudonné's National Guard. Indeed, no fewer than five members of the Dieudonné kin group (three brothers and two cousins) would serve the Revolution in various capacities. Of democratisation there is little sign: all the men managing the affairs of the village during the Terror were either owners of land or master-craftsmen. In spite of intermittent tensions over grazing rights (see p. 252), it is likely that the landless poor connived at this state of affairs. After all, the Jacobin elite of the village delivered on the promise to reallocate the common pastures – one of the issues that had mobilised the needy back in 1790. This much-tempered elite was further stiffened, however, by the arrival of a reinforcement from the outside. Maurice Jordy, who had won his spurs in the training ground of the seigneurie rather like Pierre Dieudonné, took up residence in the village in 1793. He would become *agent national* and subsequently the driving force (*commissaire du Directoire-Exécutif*) behind the cantonal municipality. Given that he was the largest landowner in the parish, neither the Imperial nor the Bourbon regime could afford to ignore him – whatever scruples were raised by his political 'past'.

Only in Villepreux did the continuity of elite control of village life undergo serious modification. Analysis of the abundant fiscal data that have survived for this locality provides a snapshot of the process. When the Municipal Assembly elected in August 1787 convened for the first time it comprised seven individuals who, as we have seen, stood at the helm of local society. They shouldered an average per capita tax burden of 280 *livres*, although the presence of Claude-François Barbé, tenant of the second biggest farm in the parish, undoubtedly inflated this figure. Their linear successors, the municipality elected in February 1790, paid an average of 196 *livres*, even though both Barbé and François Maingot, the miller, had been continued in office. By January 1792, after some refilling of vacant seats, the tax 'profile' of the municipality had dropped to 133 *livres*. However, the really significant rupture occurred towards the end of that year – in December – when a wholesale renewal of administrative elites took place. While a middle-ranking farmer – Jean-Jacques Meunier – was voted into office as mayor, all other posts including that of *procureur* were taken up by craftworkers. Accordingly, the average tax burden plunged to 31 *livres*. This was democratisation with a vengeance, and in a village where the 'camouflage' of seigneurial officeholding which tended to obscure the gulf between the rich and the poor had long since been stripped away. Uniquely among our villagers, Villepreux possessed just one resident *homme de loi* (Jean-Germain Prissette) and he was cleared out of office along with the last of the wealthy tenant farmers and retail merchants in December

1792. Our conviction that ordinary Villepreussiens were using the opportunity afforded by the Revolution to overturn the traditional power elite of their village is reinforced by the fact that nominations to form a *comité de surveillance* – mooted in a general assembly of the commune on 12 May 1793 – reproduced the same pattern. Half of those chosen were modest craftsmen and even wage workers, some of whom could not trace out their own names.

Yet even the municipal revolution of December 1792 did not emancipate the humblest and most numerous stratum: the agricultural day labourers and farm servants (perhaps one hundred households). Like the sharecroppers of Roquelaure, they remained outside the formal power arena. However, there are good reasons for believing that their needs and grievances were acknowledged for a time (see pp. 255–6). We know, for example, that François Hersant, the schoolmaster who kept the minutes of municipal meetings, and also Martin Lemaître, a rope-maker, raised to the status of *officier municipal* in December 1792, were strong advocates of land redistribution. The hegemony of the poor and dispossessed did not endure, of course, but nor was there a complete restoration of the *status quo ante* either. In the spring of 1795 a passing *représentant-en-mission* 'purged' the municipality, thereby facilitating the return to office of several of the big taxpayers who had operated the levers of political power between 1787 and 1790. On the other hand, the bourgeois professionals (Prissette the notary and Mongrolle the barber-surgeon) did not emerge from political retirement until the start of the Directory.

What is striking about the post-Revolution elite of Villepreux is its fluidity, especially when compared to the sedentary elites of Saint-Alban and Allan. The 'gros fermiers' of the Paris Crown could not afford to be sedentary: they moved from leasehold to leasehold. Likewise the victuallers and traders who had made such a comfortable living whilst the royal family and Court had been resident in Versailles. The sequestration and sale of most of the farms of Villepreux (see pp. 249–50) would also complicate the transmission of power and authority. This turnover, alone, helps to explain why only two of the individuals listed among the ten biggest taxpayers of the village in 1818 had a track record of participation in local affairs that can be traced back to the early years of the Revolution. After the Brumaire *coup* we find the fusionist politics of Napoleon Bonaparte at work. As well as being one of the largest landowners in the village, the first mayor of the Consulate was an ex-*parlementaire* and an ex-'anobli'. However, the *adjoint*, an ex-priest who had been elected during the anti-Fructidor reaction of the Year Six (March 1798), was maintained in office. The newly appointed *conseil municipal* was also an amalgam. It included three tenant farmers, Prissette the local epitome of *juste milieu* Directorial politics, Hersant the neo-Jacobin schoolmaster, and Pierre-Adam Labbé, a stonemason who had occupied the post of *agent national* during the Terror.

ROUTES TO POLITICISATION

So much for the elites who would endeavour to shape local power arenas in their own image, then. How was politicisation sustained and deepened once villagers had taken stock of the possibilities of their situation? Institutions such as the National Guard played an unquestioned role, as we have seen; and by late 1792 and 1793 that influence was being relayed by *sociétés populaires* and *comités de surveillance*. Village Jacobin clubs were little more than 'empty institutions foisted on the peasants by outsiders', in the opinion of Crane Brinton,[9] but more recent researchers have concluded that the club movement constituted 'le principal vecteur de l'entrée de centaines de milliers de citoyens – et de quelques milliers de citoyennes – *en politique*'.[10] The import of this judgement is weakened, however, by the fact that clubs did not mushroom in an even carpet across the land. Only 14 per cent of communes ever moved to set up Jacobin clubs, voluntarily or otherwise, and fewer still *comités de surveillance*. On the evidence of this study, only Neuviller was entirely bereft of a *société populaire*, which is surprising in view of the fact that the village lay astride a post road and constituted the seat of a canton. On the other hand, full minutes of club meetings have survived for Roquelaure, but nowhere else. They show that the *société* played an active, acculturating role, particularly from the autumn of 1793. Sessions were open and attendance compulsory (in theory), although the minutes are tantalisingly vague on the subject of sharecroppers. They do not permit us to conclude that the club succeeded in reaching out to these benighted citizens of the hamlets.[11] Circumstantial evidence suggests that the clubs active in Allan and Châtelaudren were far from 'empty institutions', as well, whereas the status of that of Villepreux is difficult to determine, one way or the other. As for the Jacobin club of Saint-Alban, it seems to have taken over the executive role of the municipality and to have become a tool for factional vendettas.

---

[9] See C. C. Brinton, *The Jacobins: An Essay in the New History*, 2nd edn (New York, 1961), p. 39.

[10] J. Boutier and P. Boutry, *Atlas de la Révolution française*. VI: *Les Sociétés politiques* (Paris, 1992), p. 13.

[11] It is significant, however, that the club ordered the reading out aloud of the decree of 1 Brumaire II which appeared to relieve croppers of the obligation to continue paying a tithe equivalent (see A. D. du Gers, L 699* 10 Pluviôse II).

The vigilance committees (*comités de surveillance*) that began to appear at village level during the spring of 1793 conform more closely to Brinton's dictum. Allan, alone, never proceeded to create one, although direct evidence of such a creation is also lacking in the case of Neuviller. Nonetheless, it would be remarkable if the general call to set up *comités* in response to the law of 21 March 1793 produced no echo in Neuviller, since the inhabitants of nearby Roville gathered for this purpose in April. The countryside around Versailles positively heaved with vigilance committees by the spring of 1794: three-quarters of all villages (including Villepreux) possessed such a body. While the early creations (i.e. those of the spring of 1793) were usually elected, either by the municipalities or by general assemblies of all adult males, the later creations (autumn and winter of 1793–4) tended to reflect the imperatives of Revolutionary Government. They were brought into being on the orders of *représentants-en-mission*, or their delegates, and recruited from the membership of the *sociétés populaires*. On the evidence of surviving minute books and *décadi* reports (Roville, Villepreux, Saint-Alban) such bodies *were* usually detached from the general population – necessarily so since their activities had now become largely punitive (arrest of 'suspects', policing of the Maximum, etc.). Nevertheless, we should not discount their role as vectors of politicisation, even if, by 1794, they were mainly preaching to the politically converted. They connected an elite band of villagers to the very heart of the Revolution, more so than the village *sociétés populaires*, not one of which enjoyed affiliation to the Paris Jacobins. Indeed, living just a heartbeat from the centre of power could be decidedly uncomfortable. When on the night of 23–24 Ventôse II (13–14 March 1794) the Hébertistes were arrested on a trumped-up charge of military conspiracy involving the *armée révolutionnaire* of Versailles, the members of the *comité de surveillance* of Villepreux felt the shock wave at first hand.

While clubs, *comités* and, no doubt, the sharp increase in the output of newsprint from 1790 onwards served to accelerate the civic education of country dwellers, it seems likely that the real propellant to political awareness was locked up in more immediate issues and conflicts. At least, this is the conclusion drawn by Guy Ikni on the basis of an in-depth study of the peasant revolution in the department of the Oise,[12] and it is one which our more wide-ranging study substantially endorses. These local issues and conflicts could be quite literally local, in other words unique to a specific village, but on closer examination they usually turn out to

---

[12] See G.-R. Ikni, 'Crise agricole et Révolution paysanne: le mouvement populaire dans les campagnes de l'Oise, de la décennie physiocratique à l'an II' (6 vols., dissertation, University of Paris I, 1993), III, p. 241.

be generic. Take, for instance, the issue of private stalls in church. The privatisation of space in the parish church and the elaborate pecking order that it was intended to signal actualised power hierarchies like nothing else at the end of the *ancien régime*. The removal of benches and the overturning of ancient practices of public ceremony were not uncontentious matters, therefore. On 1 January 1790 the deputy François Ménard de La Groye chuckled in a letter to his wife: 'il sera beau de voir les paisans, devenus officiers municipaux dans leurs paroisses, précéder, en toutes cérémonies publiques, les juges, les gentilshommes, et tous autres'.[13] Most of the legal families of Saint-Alban owned a private stall in their church, and by the summer of 1792 all save Atrasic had agreed to remove them. Needless to say, the struggle to persuade him to comply with the law was spearheaded by a member of the Mathieu clan, and it engrossed public opinion throughout the parish far more than the news of the Paris insurrection against the king. But this was not an isolated incident: the business of pews and precedence excited public indignation in Châtelaudren and Villepreux as well. As for Atrasic, his grandson was still defending the family entitlement to a private pew as late as 1837.

The on-going guerrilla war against seigneurialism is a more obvious example of local-issue politicisation with a wider import, and the case of Allan will serve to show how it operated. Following the happy coincidence of the stunning victory before the Parlement of Provence with the change of regime, villagers resumed their offensive against the absentee seigneur, having persuaded themselves that they occupied the legal as well as the moral high ground. They stopped paying dues and counter-sued Madame Lériget de La Faye for taxes unpaid on *roturier* property which, they alleged, she had passed off as 'noble'. The case that actually went to court in November 1792 claimed arrears of 28,250 *livres*, that is to say a sum equivalent to five times the entire tax burden of the community in the year 1788. In the meantime the villagers had also invaded seigneurial forests and clear felled many hectares of timber. By the autumn of 1792, in fact, it is apparent that the local perception of the Revolution had become indistinguishable from the on-going struggle against seigneurialism.

Madame de La Faye, it will be recalled, was also the owner of the six best farms in the parish, although by this time she had been declared a ward of court having succumbed to a chronic mental disorder. Early in 1793 the village elders agreed on a stratagem that they hoped would force

---

[13] F. Mirouse (ed.), *François Ménard de La Groye, député du Mans aux Etats Généraux: correspondance, 1789–1791* (Le Mans, 1989), p. 167.

her possessions in Allan onto the open market as *biens nationaux*. Since she was 'civilly dead'[14] and since her acknowledged heirs and guardians had not certified their continuing residence in the Republic, they could safely be presumed to have emigrated. In fact her husband, the Comte de La Tour-du-Pin-Montauban, *had* left the country, but their marriage contract kept the dowry legally separate. For a time the stratagem worked: the villagers dug deep into their pockets in order to meet the costs of legal representation, and the Department authorities in Valence were persuaded to place an embargo on Madame de La Faye's property. As they were to learn to their cost, however, litigation and even the decisions of higher administrative bodies could not be isolated from the general political climate. On 15 March 1795 the Comité de Législation reprimanded the Department authorities for ordering the sequestration of Lériget de La Faye's property on a mere 'speculation'.[15] The balance began to swing back in favour of the ex-seigneur's lawyers as the post-Thermidor reaction gathered momentum. The Fructidor *coup* (4 September 1797) handed the initiative to the villagers once more, however. Again, sequestration commissioners appeared to seize the farms, only for the embargo to be lifted a couple of months later as the panic over resurgent royalism died away.

By this date a state of exhaustion had been reached – on both sides. The villagers were heavily in debt and in no mood to renew their pretentions, and in the absence of further communication from the ex-seigneur's lawyers they concluded that the appetite for continued strife had lapsed in this quarter, too. A mistake, for while the Consulate proceeded to lay to rest many old conflicts, many ex-seigneurs interpreted the advent of a more favourable regime as an opportunity to settle old scores with those who had worsted them during the Terror. On 26 December 1801 mayor Gouteron advised his council that fresh charges were about to be laid before the court of Montélimar and that further pecuniary sacrifices would be required in order to rebut them. Madame de La Faye's guardians were now pursuing a claim for 30,000 *francs*, being the value of the timber removed from 'her' forests in 1791. With the odds of winning in the Imperial courts now stacked in favour of proprietors, the community suffered a series of reverses, which a change of regime – in 1814 – did nothing to alter. Quite the contrary, in fact. The final blow fell on 30 August 1817, when the villagers lost their claim for arrears of tax, on appeal, before the Cour Royale of Grenoble. Madame Lériget de La Faye had died three years earlier, and with the Jacobin zealots

---

[14] A. D. de la Drôme, Q 305, Procès-verbal de la municipalité d'Allan, 17 February 1793.
[15] *Ibid*.

no longer in power in the *conseil municipal* the stage was now set for a compromise.

The anti-seigneurial obsession that held the inhabitants of Allan in thrall for a generation and more was unusual in its severity, but it does demonstrate the capacity of this issue to 'fix' attitudes and allegiances. Elsewhere, the rebellion against residual seigneurial authority ebbed away almost completely after the summer of 1792. In Châtelaudren and Villepreux anti-seigneurialism had never been much of a galvanising issue in any case; only in Neuviller did it cast a long shadow comparable in some ways to the scenario we have outlined above. The principal vector of politicisation as far as the inhabitants of Châtelaudren were concerned seems to have been a sense of embattlement in the face of an encircling and increasingly malevolent countryside: a collective 'town versus country' paranoia of a kind that Paul Bois and other historians believe was typical of the Revolution in the west.[16] In Villepreux, by contrast, the vector was land hunger, both as a compound and as two separate issues. While the Châtelaudrinais *all* felt vulnerable in view of the precarious socio-economic, cultural and political geography of their tiny locality, the catalysts of land and hunger *divided* the Villepreux community and created conditions that would make it possible for a radical programme for agrarian reform to emerge (see pp. 179–80).

The inhabitants of Châtelaudren lived out on a limb in all sorts of ways. Their overgrown village sat astride linguistic, episcopal and parochial frontiers (see maps 1 and 4), and yet it was linked by the umbilical of a major highway to the pulses of urban Revolution being generated to the east. As a unit of territory, it was notched into the side of the vast and thickly populated parish of Plélo; as a working community it was almost entirely mercantile and contrasted starkly with the agricultural hamlets and farmsteads and the semi-*bocage* landscape of surrounding parishes. At least Plélo was French speaking, unlike the parish of Plouagat on Châtelaudren's western flank, but it had never been subject to the seigneurial jurisdiction of the Comté de Goello and regarded the 'quasi-town' of Châtelaudren as something of an upstart. The mocking and uncooperative attitude of the inhabitants of Plélo at the time of the flood disaster of 1773 had scandalised the intendant. On the other hand, there were complementarities between town and country. Châtelaudren possessed a market frequented by

---

[16] See P. Bois, *Paysans de l'ouest* (Paris, 1971); M. Faucheux, *L'Insurrection vendéenne de 1793: aspects économiques et sociaux* (Paris, 1964); C. Tilly, *The Vendée*, 3rd edn (Cambridge, Mass., and London, 1976). Note, however, the comments of Jessenne, *Pouvoir au village et révolution*, pp. 84–5, and C. Peyrard, *Les Jacobins de l'ouest: sociabilité révolutionnaire et formes de politisation dans le Maine et la Basse-Normandie, 1789–1799* (Paris, 1996), pp. 147–9.

hundreds of consumers each week, and the fertile countryside of the Breton littoral produced regular surpluses. Châtelaudren also had a resident bourgeoisie capable of supplying the full range of professional services. One further fact, albeit of no great significance before 1788: the 4,354-hectare expanse of Plélo was controlled by the aristocracy. Independent peasant tenures were few and far between; likewise ecclesiastical and bourgeois land holdings. Instead, more than two-thirds of the arable surface of the parish was owned by sixteen resident noble families who had it farmed via cash tenancies or, more commonly, via the system of tenure known as *domaine congéable*.[17]

Breton historians have long sought to explain the manner in which country dwellers were enlisted under the banners of Revolution and Counter-Revolution. How much room for manoeuvre existed between 'bleus' and 'blancs'? Were these affiliations evident from the outset? The inhabitants of Châtelaudren had made their feelings plain even before the Estates General gathered in Versailles, as we know, but opinion in the surrounding parishes still remained fluid and unfocused at the end of 1789. By the end of 1790, however, the inhabitants of Plélo, in particular, had started to turn away from the Revolution. What had happened in the interim? The tergiversations over cantonal status that were mentioned in chapter 3 must have counted for something. Why should a vast, populous and socially superior entity such as Plélo have to play second fiddle to the jumped-up bourgeoisie of a pocket-sized town? But localised sources of dissatisfaction seem to have been capitalised upon by the generality of nobles who showed themselves to be reluctant to accept the verdict of 1789. In the early months of 1790 they mounted a petitioning campaign urging country dwellers to be on their guard against the designs of the towns. Even as late as the spring of 1791 the post office of Châtelaudren would intercept suspicious packages sent out under cover of the former *procureur-général-sindic* of the Estates of Brittany for delivery to neighbouring rural parishes. Yet by this date the confrontation between Plélo and Châtelaudren was already under way.

The first signs of rural disenchantment became apparent in November 1790, when an electoral assembly was called in order to designate a Justice of the Peace for the canton. It resulted in total confusion, with the voters of both Plélo and Plouagat failing to turn up. The Châtelaudrinais had reason to be thankful for this boycott, since they were likely to be vastly outnumbered no matter how the canton was configured. In June 1791,

---

[17] See P. Corbel, 'Production, pouvoirs et mentalités dans une communue rurale gallèse: Plélo' (dissertation, University of Haute-Bretagne, 1980); P. Corbel, 'Gens de Plélo: 1600–1914: une ethno-histoire en cours' (dissertation, University of Haute-Bretagne, 1984).

when a cantonal primary assembly met in connection with the renewal of the legislature, the rural voters did appear in force and bloodshed in the streets of Châtelaudren was only narrowly averted. A similar confrontation took place the following year, when the voters were called out to choose electors who would in turn choose deputies to the National Convention. The activities of Châtelaudren's National Guard (disarming nobles after the Flight, ambushing nocturnal processions of Catholics to outlying chapels, etc.) meant that there was very little love to be lost between town and country by the summer of 1792. The last elections to be held before the 'shut down' of the Terror produced a similar result. In December 1792 the voters of Plélo brought along with them some fifty farm servants to ensure that their candidate for *juge de paix* emerged victorious from the ballot box. Indignant, the bourgeois, the merchants and the craftworkers of Châtelaudren cried foul, but when the election was rerun a couple of months later 308 ballots were cast for the representative of the parishes and only 63 for the nominee of the town.

The 'inconvenience' of elections – to put it no more strongly – in conditions where the opponents of the Revolution were accorded the same rights as everyone else could not have been more conclusively demonstrated. From 1793 onwards relations between 'town and country' would be conducted on the basis of armed reprisals instead. Recruitment for the armies produced clashes towards the end of March, although nothing on the scale of the disturbances occurring in the southeast of the department. Plélo's farmers expressed their antipathy by turning away from Châtelaudren's market, thereby throwing the village into a panic over food supplies. The Monday market of 14 October 1793 was completely deserted, the grain price Maximum having been promulgated two days earlier. The legality of requisitions backed by armed force was questionable, to say the least, but the municipality ordered them nonetheless. A population of eight hundred souls squatting on forty-seven hectares of territory could not survive otherwise. Naturally the 'avide cultivateur'[18] of Plélo was the principal target. The *hobereaux*, their tenants and dependants found refuge in the Counter-Revolution. From the late winter of 1794–5 Châtelaudren lived in fear of attack, an event that finally materialised following the Quiberon landing. On 23 July 1795 the *chouan* army entered the village, ransacking its boutiques and ransoming the few remaining inhabitants. In the orgy of republican counter-violence that followed, punishment squads were sent round the farms with the parishioners of Plélo bearing the brunt of the reprisals.

---

[18] A. C. de Châtelaudren, Municipalité, délibérations, an II–an VII, 10 Fructidor II.

The fact that 'town and country' rivalries evinced this degree of virulence nowhere else is revealing. It tells us something about the human as well as the political geography of Brittany. The villagers of Allan became a foil for the neo-royalists of the *bourg* of Donzère, but here the confrontation was more circumstantial than pathological. The hamlets of Saint-Alban likewise showed signs of restlessness in the face of an overmighty *bourg*. The fact that the dominant families of Saint-Alban also had allies and supporters in the hinterland diffused tensions, however, and prevented a clear-cut geographical alignment from emerging. The alignment that thrust the agricultural labourers and impoverished craftworkers of Villepreux (and Rennemoulin) into the political arena had very different origins, though. It was largely internal to the localities concerned, and had been foreshadowed in the turbulent electoral contests of the early years of the Revolution.

The land hunger of the poor peasants and rural artisans on the plains around Paris scarcely requires further demonstration. It was linked to the presence of the Royal Domain, of course, but it was also linked to the process of land engrossment. This trend towards the consolidation of holdings into ever larger units of exploitation was linked, in turn, to the expansion of capitalist, or surplus generating, cereal agriculture during the 'high farming' decades of the 1760s and 1770s. In fact the pressures of engrossment eased slightly in the years immediately prior to the Revolution, but the damage to the social fabric of rural communities had already been done. The middling peasantry were nearly everywhere in sharp decline, to be replaced by a mass of landless or virtually landless day workers who looked to the two or three 'gros fermiers' in each parish for employment. In Villepreux and also in Rennemoulin about half a dozen 'gros fermiers' managed farms of sizeable dimensions (up to 148 hectares) that belonged to the Royal Domain for the most part. Inevitably, therefore, this focused attention on the likely fate of Civil List properties as the Revolution got under way, and also on the role and responsibilities of big tenant farmers in their respective communities.

The forlorn attempt to enforce a ban on hunting in the Grand Parc had triggered an initial wave of politicisation (see p. 100), but the events of the summer of 1792 simplified the issues and outflanked those local power brokers who were still advocating a policy of caution. With the king and royal family despatched to the Temple, the common people of Villepreux and Rennemoulin began really to believe that they had the support of the politicians in Versailles and Paris for their agenda of land redistribution. The decree of 28 August 1792 granting village communities ownership of 'waste', that is to say uncultivated land, was crucial in this respect. It focused attention on the Civil List properties which included extensive game covers; it seemed to provide some legislative sanction for a policy of partition, and it crystallised public dissatisfaction with the 'gros fermiers' whose leases embraced most of the land in question. Through the autumn and winter of 1792–3 the poor of Villepreux, Rennemoulin and the other villages lying within or adjacent to the Grand Parc followed debates in the National Convention closely in anticipation of follow-up legislation. They were heartened when the discussion broadened to embrace the question of engrossment, and word came through that no farmer in the district of Versailles should have within his control more than 200 *arpents* of arable (the big Villepreux farms ranged from 138 to 351 *arpents*). Finally, they gave notice, in February 1793, that if some land were not parcelled out swiftly they would take it for themselves.

Hunger as well as Jacobin notions of redistributive justice were driving the campaign by this date. A plot sown in the spring might yet yield a harvest of sorts. Also the market at Villepreux was not functioning at all well for reasons already mentioned, and when consumers found it difficult to buy grain on the marketplace of Versailles, too, the focus of public anger switched to the 'gros fermiers'. The rise of socio-economic antagonisms within the community completed the political education of Villepreux's labouring poor. Egged on by public opinion the municipality denounced two of the largest proprietors: Jacques-Nicolas Gravelle-[de]-Fontaine and Henri-Anne Mecquenem d'Artaize. Both were arrested, but whereas Gravelle-Fontaine survived to become mayor and to reinstate his 'particule' after Brumaire, Mecquenem d'Artaize mounted the steps of the guillotine. As for the 'gros fermiers', all were visited in November 1793, that is to say threatened with reprisals should they fail to thresh their grain and bring it to market. The ultimate 'bonheur'[19] was delayed until the spring, however, when land was amputated from the Grand' Maisons tenancy and distributed to the landless families of the village in the form of one-*arpent* plots (see map 3 and p. 256).

Several routes towards politicisation have been examined and others invite investigation. It would be instructive, for instance, to explore the way in which the battle to recover the portions of common forfeited to seigneurial *triage* in 1771 opened the door to village Jacobinism in Neuviller and Roville. Or else the impact on the sharecroppers of Roquelaure of the proprietors' decision to reserve to themselves the proceeds of the abolition

---

[19] On 2 September 1793 an official of the District of Versailles had annotated a petition submitted by the inhabitants of Rennemoulin with the words 'dîtes-leur que bientôt, avant l'hiver, la Convention aura décrété leur bonheur' (see Tambour, *Les Registres municipaux de Rennemoulin*, p. 135).

of the tithe. But in neither case is it possible to identify the key players in the local political arena, or to clarify satisfactorily their motivations. Gaps in the records have to be filled with conjecture, yet there comes a point when plausible guesswork gives way to pure speculation. Most of the landowners of Roquelaure were *forains* and we just do not know what terms they imposed on their tenants. The names of most of the smallholders of Neuviller and Roville are familiar to us, but, again, the role of the larger farmers is difficult to fathom. How much stock did they own? Did they want to enclose their land? Were they prevented from so doing? It makes more sense to change tack, therefore, and to ask how events of nation-wide significance – the external agenda of the Revolution, so to speak – intervened to shape apprehensions and allegiances.

MATRIX EVENTS

Almost all historians concur that it was the decision to impose an oath of loyalty on the clergy that first breached solidarities at the local level. Those villagers who were already looking askance at the flow of events found an issue to rally round and, by the same token, those elites whose conversion in 1789 had never been more than lukewarm found themselves in possession of a handy stick with which to beat supporters of the new regime. Nothing in our close-focus study invites a different conclusion. By the spring of 1792 some of the shortcomings of the Revolution were becoming obvious (the incomplete abolition of seigneurialism, tax disillusionment, the breakdown of charitable relief structures, etc.), but they were all perceived through the filter of the disruption and heart searching stemming from the clerical oath. Only in the case of the village of Roquelaure is it possible to hypothesise a variant scenario, inasmuch as the shock discovery by sharecroppers that they were to continue paying the tithe (or more accurately a tithe replacement) coincided with the repercussions of the deputies' ill-judged policy to force ecclesiastics into line. Yet this is not to suggest that the negatives of root-and-branch reform had begun to outweigh the positives by the spring of 1792. The majority of villagers, as we shall see, were able to overcome the scruples they may have felt as the drama of oath taking and oath refusal was played out.

The incumbents of Allan, Châtelaudren, Roquelaure and Villepreux all declined to take the oath when invited to do so: firmly and unhesitatingly. In Neuviller *curé* Seignelay swore a restricted oath which he withdrew three months later, and in Saint-Alban the elderly Béraud proceeded to take an unrestricted oath, only to change his mind a short time afterwards. Alone among the clergy of our six villages, curate Jean-Jacques Chapdelaine of Villepreux swore the prescribed oath to which he steadfastly adhered thereafter. Lest it be supposed that clerical intransigence automatically propelled country dwellers down the road of resistance to the Revolution, we should bear in mind that only one of our villages (Saint-Alban) ever dabbled in the politics of armed royalism; the rest remained supportive of the new regime, albeit to varying degrees. Indeed, Châtelaudren would become a rampart against Counter-Revolution in its neighbourhood, even though both rector Le Corvaisier and *vicaire* de Keruzec followed the lead of the bishop of Tréguier and refused the oath. Villagers were sensitive to the behaviour of the clergy, then, but not driven by it. Gilles Le Corvaisier was plainly embarrassed that a parting of the ways had been reached and tried to pull out of the civil and religious life of Châtelaudren as gracefully and as uncontentiously as possible. Matters were more finely balanced in Allan, and for a time the defection of the *curé* looked as though it would drive a wedge between the mayor and members of his council. But early in 1792 *curé* Raynaud and his most notorious adherents were expelled from the village and harmony restored. By contrast, the municipality of Villepreux acted decisively to contain the damage caused by Teissier's flouting of the law. When the *curé* sought to justify his refusal of the oath by reading from the pulpit a Pastoral Letter of the archbishop of Paris on Sunday 20 February 1791, a municipal officer and other members of the congregation called him to order. Convicted before the District court of Versailles of uttering statements 'likely to throw timid consciences into a state of alarm',[20] Teissier was sentenced to pay a fine of 20 *livres* in favour of the poor. He seems to have retired to Versailles shortly afterwards, which must have limited his influence. Villagers' sensibilities were soothed by the election of Chapdelaine, the curate, to the parish incumbency a couple of months later.

The process whereby priest applied moral pressure to parishioner could also operate in reverse, however. Simon-Alexandre Béraud of Saint-Alban initially took the oath, a decision that was entirely in keeping with the personal trajectory of this Jansenist-minded cleric whose reform ambitions have been detailed in chapter 3. He was no friend, either, of the bishop of Mende, who had become one of the earliest and sternest critics of the new regime in the region. Accordingly, the *abbé* read out the entire text of the Civil Constitution of the Clergy from his pulpit on 8 December 1790, an act of faith if ever there was one since he was old and ill and could

---

[20] A. D. des Yvelines, 47L 83, Dossiers de procédure.

scarcely make himself heard. When on 20 February he proceeded to take the oath, though, an uproar of disapproval greeted his decision, and he had to be escorted to safety in the sacristy. In this instance, therefore, we are dealing with a population that had already swung decisively against the ecclesiastical politics of the National Assembly, and one angered to discover that its incumbent was not of the same mind. Who or what provoked the swing of opinion? Almost certainly Monseigneur de Castellanne, the bishop of Mende, and his coadjutors, whose sway in the Catholic parishes of the Gévaudan/Lozère had always surpassed that of the civil authority. In January the bishop had issued a warning that elected replacements for regularly ordained clergy would be deemed schismatics and, as such, devoid of canonical authority. The fact that all sections of society from the level of rural parishes upwards heeded this warning indicates where real power lay in the Lozère even after two full years of Revolution. It also helps to explain how the villagers of Saint-Alban could be brought to the very brink of active Counter-Revolution just a year or so later.

The Charrier Revolt of May and June 1793 broke out in the department of the Aveyron, but it was played out very largely on the territory of the department of the Lozère. *Emigré* plotters had long regarded the southern Massif Central departments as fertile territory from which to launch a rural Counter-Revolution. The impact of the oath legislation, the apparent ease with which the peasantry could be mobilised as evidenced in the gatherings at the chateau of Jalès, and the ready tinder of Catholic–Protestant enmity all boded well. An abortive attempt to kick-start a rising occurred in February 1792 when the National Guard of Mende went on the rampage and smashed up the Jacobin club. In Saint-Alban there was casual talk of sending men to reinforce the mutineers, to judge from evidence taken down somewhat later, but the Legislative Assembly reacted energetically, ordering the arrest of ex-bishop de Castellanne among other conspirators. Charrier, however, enjoyed better success, if only briefly. He managed to raise an army of peasants and rural artisans some 2,000 strong and marched it in the name of Louis XVII and the Regent against the towns of Marvejols and Mende. Both capitulated to his forces, which were never defeated in battle. If the rebellion failed, it was for strategic reasons. Unable to synchronise with movements elsewhere, Charrier gave the order to disband the army and went into hiding. With many thousands of republican troops converging on the region from all points of the compass, he correctly judged that, for all its initial success, his rising was doomed to failure.

The Charrier insurrection became the political touchstone of the Lozère. Everyone had to face up to the question 'Where were you during the final

week of May 1793?', and a good many peasants, artisans and priests and
even a few bourgeois had to answer that question publicly. It is for this
reason that we are able to reconstruct, in rough outline, the way the events
of that week impacted on the villagers of Saint-Alban. Charrier's success,
such as it was, owed much to factors that had scarcely been in evidence in
1792. Nearly every parish incumbent had refused the oath and although the
Department authorities had delayed calling electoral assemblies in order to
choose replacements for as long as they dared, many mountain villages on
the border of the Aveyron and the Lozère faced the stark prospect of a
complete breakdown in the provision of parish services. Béraud had died
shortly after retracting his oath, and the fact that no record survives of
the name of his juror replacement is highly revealing. In all probability an
unbeneficed and oath-exempt clergyman named Roux, a long-time resident
of Saint-Alban, maintained continuity, but even he found it difficult to
minister to the needs of a far-flung parish once the deportation legislation
took effect. The other factor that had not been in play in 1792 was military
recruitment. In April 1793 the steps taken to implement the *levée des 300,000*
decree produced a groundswell of resistance in the villages of the Aubrac
plateau and the western flanks of the Margeride.

Capitalising upon heavy-handed attempts by gendarmes to quell the
mountain villages by arresting their refractory clergy and pursuing draft
dodgers, Charrier gave the signal to rise. A squadron of armed republicans
encamped overnight in the village of Rieutort-d'Aubrac on 25 May 1793
was taken by surprise. On the morrow, Charrier despatched a circular
letter to all the surrounding localities urging them to rally to his standard.
Significantly, he would label his forces 'l'armée chrétienne du Midi',[21] and
in his rallying cry the defence of religion featured prominently alongside
loyalty to the monarch-in-waiting. The mayor of Montivernoux read out
Charrier's proclamation to the assembled village (the 26 May was a Sunday),
but in Saint-Alban Jean-Jacques, the elder of the Enjalvin brothers, was in
charge and he managed to deter an immediate mobilisation. Public opinion
was nevertheless divided, particularly in the hamlet of Les Faux where both
the Enjalvin and the Atrasic–Vincens owned farms. While the Enjalvin
brothers were resolute in their opposition to Charrier from the outset – to
judge from later depositions – those close to Noé-Jean Atrasic seem to have
been *attentiste* in outlook, or frankly sympathetic to Charrier. According
to one overheard conversation, François Veissière, a *laboureur* of Les Faux,
urged others to travel to Rieutort, while his wife declared 'que la nation

[21] See Delon, *La Révolution en Lozère*, p. 320.

étoit dans son tort davoir détruit la religion et détruit les prêtres, et que la
Nation netoit pas la Religion'.[22] The behaviour of Atrasic and his son-in-
law also gave grounds for suspicion. One of the charges levelled at the pair
during the Terror asserted that they had sent a female runner with a letter
for Vincens *père* in Mende on learning that Charrier's forces had entered
the town. The runner was intercepted by armed troopers who, having
opened the letter, warned that both she and its authors risked having their
heads cut off. But such was the mesh of kin links between the bourgeois
households of Saint-Alban that even the Enjalvin were unable to escape
contamination by association. As the fifty-two able-bodied menfolk of the
village of La Malène marched across the Causse de Sauveterre on their way
to join Charrier, they were halted by republican cavalry. Nearly all were
subsequently executed, including Jacques-Philippe Polge, public notary of
La Malène and brother-in-law of Augustin Enjalvin *cadet*.

The Charrier affair was a Vendée in the making, but the Republic learned
the lessons of the previous March and sent in troops from all quarters.
Even the villagers of Allan on the far side of the Rhône were urged to
mobilise 'pour arrêter les ravages que commet [*sic*] des rebelles dans le
département de la Lozère'.[23] The elites of Saint-Alban could also afford to
breathe a sigh of relief that they had not been more exposed. In view of his
status as a rebel sentenced to death for bearing arms against the Republic,
Polge's property in Saint-Alban became liable to confiscation, although his
sister (Augustin Enjalvin's wife) managed to lease it back from the Nation.
Exercising sovereignty in the village was not a duty to be treated lightly. A
misreading of power signals cost forty-seven men of La Malène their lives,
and it is likely that Polge – the only bourgeois to be captured – bore a heavy
weight of responsibility for what happened. In Saint-Alban, on the other
hand, the very disunity of the bourgeois elite helped to paralyse the reactions
of the population and to prevent a mobilisation whose consequences could
have been extremely serious.

While the scaffolds erected in Florac and Mende were busy despatch-
ing the Malenais and other captured rebels, the news of the Montagnard
victory in the National Convention began to spread through the departments. Once again village elites would be called upon to exercise finesse and
judgement. Federalism – the reflex of hostility and even of resistance to the
exaggerated exercise of popular sovereignty by the Paris Sections – was not
confined to major centres of population as historians have too frequently

[22] A. D. de la Lozère, L 520*, 26 Ventôse II.
[23] A. C. d'Allan, RV 2, Délibérations municipales, 2 June 1793.

supposed.[24] Although nearly always derivative in character, village-level Federalism nonetheless testifies to the impact that issues of sovereignty could make at the local level. Châtelaudren and Roquelaure both openly declared their support for the expelled Girondin deputies, and there is reason to believe that Neuviller did likewise. Saint-Alban was too preoccupied by repression and by the famine left behind by departing republican troops to take much notice of events in Paris, whereas the villagers of Allan either misunderstood the issues or, more probably, constructed a deliberately ambivalent stance. Only in Villepreux, as we might expect, did the actions of the Mountain and the Sections elicit no critical comment whatsoever.

A historic outpost of Provence, the village of Allan absorbed both northern and southern influences – in matters relating to politics as in so much else. Usually these pressures acted in concert, but the refusal of the Marseillais to accept the authority of the purged Convention produced a dilemma in the minds of villagers. Valence gave a lead when a 'congress' of delegates drawn from forty-two Jacobin clubs helped to swing the authorities decisively in favour of the Mountain, but matters were not so clear cut in the south of the department, where the town of Montélimar continued to hesitate. On 23 June 1793 the inhabitants of Allan gathered in an open assembly and were invited to declare 's'ils voulaient être royalistes ou republicains, et tous ont criés à haute voix être republiquains'.[25] This was scarcely a ringing declaration of faith in the Mountain, and when a summary of the meeting was sent in to the Department an unknown administrative hand wrote in pencil the annotation 'se réserve'.[26] Nevertheless, General Carteaux's march southwards in order to intercept the Marseille Federalists soon concentrated minds both in Montélimar and in the surrounding villages.

By contrast the mercantile bourgeoisie who had ensconced themselves in office in Châtelaudren disavowed the purging of the Convention, swiftly and decisively, on 9 June. In this they were surely influenced by the fact that the Girondist Departmental administrator Olivier Rupéru, whose widowed mother was still living in Châtelaudren, numbered among the fugitives. A parallel can be drawn with the villagers of Neuviller, whose opinions seem

---

[24] See G. Lefebvre, *The French Revolution from 1793 to 1799* (London, 1967), pp. 56–8; A. Soboul, *The French Revolution, 1787–1799* (London, 1974), pp. 317–19; D. M. G. Sutherland, *France 1789–1815: Revolution and Counter-Revolution* (Fontana, 1985), pp. 175–91. But note the corrective in A. Forrest, 'Federalism', in C. Lucas (ed.), *The French Revolution and the Creation of Modern Political Culture*, II: *The Political Culture of the French Revolution* (Oxford, 1988), p. 311.

[25] A. C. d'Allan, RV 2, Délibérations municipales, 23 June 1793.

[26] A. D. de la Drôme, L 186, Relevé des voeux de diverses communes du département de la Drôme sur l'état actuel de la République [n.d.].

to have been coloured by the tirades launched against Marat and the Paris 'anarchists' by the local deputy, Jean-Baptiste Salle. Both Châtelaudren and Neuviller took their political cue from neighbouring towns (respectively Saint-Brieuc and Vézelise), and the retreat would be sounded in these quarters, too. The municipality of Châtelaudren tersely acknowledged its political 'mistake' in a note squeezed into the minute book between the deliberations of 15 and 21 July 1793: 'le Conseil général assemblé a rapporté et rapporte ses arrêtés du 9 juin et du 10 juillet dernier comme étant contraires à l'intérêt public'.[27] The mistake went unpunished, whether in Châtelaudren or Neuviller, and we are bound to ask why. The most plausible answer is that the summer of 1793 was not a time to squander the resources of the Revolution in 'front-line' villages. Châtelaudren lay within the danger zone should the Vendeans have succeeded in crossing the Loire and attempting a march towards the Channel, whereas Alsace and Lorraine were being steeled for an invasion following the capitulation of Mainz. In the more sheltered southwest, by contrast, political sectarianism knew no limits.

The Federalism of Roquelaure reflected the bitter power struggles dividing supporters of the Revolution in nearby Auch. Even after the Republic had been 'saved', it remained a subject for recrimination within the village elite, indeed arrest, although the demonisation of the Gers Federalists owed much to the single-mindedness of *représentant-en-mission* Dartigoeyte. A Gascon speaker from the adjacent Landes department, Dartigoeyte had received a frosty reception in Auch when sent out on his first mission of political proselytism in April–May 1793. By the time of his return in early September he had persuaded himself that the sins of sectarianism were uniquely lodged in the administrative corps of the towns. 'J'ai vu un grand nombre de citoyens des campagnes,' he reported, 'ces derniers valent mieux que les villes. C'est le peuple de la campagne qui a déjoué le fédéralisme.'[28] The sharecroppers, he added tellingly, had remained on the sidelines by and large, but their support for the Mountain could be secured if only something could be done about the law that attributed the value of the tithe to the landowners. It is true that an almost visceral hostility to Parisian Jacobinism had permeated all echelons of the administration in Auch, not to mention the *société populaire*, by May 1793. In fact the club in Roquelaure seems to have been set up towards the end of that month as a Girondist offshoot of the mother club in Auch.

---

[27] A. C. de Châtelaudren, Municipalité, délibérations du Conseil municipal, 1790–an II, 15–21 July 1793.
[28] M. Müller and S. Aberdam, 'Conflits de dîme et révolution en Gascogne gersoise, 1750–1800' (dissertation, University of Paris I, 1971–2), p. F26.

When the news of the events of 31 May–2 June came through the party fighting began in earnest. A congress of *sociétés populaires* gathered in Auch on 17 June in order to declaim against the Convention, and Girondist sympathisers in the Department and the municipality set about ousting their political opponents. By mid-July tensions in the town had reached such a pitch that the municipality had loaded cannon positioned outside the *hôtel de ville*. In Roquelaure, we surmise, dissension had also broken out. Certainly the club held no regular meetings between 7 July and 20 October, which seems to indicate that disagreements had splintered what had been a tightly knit elite until this point. The most prominent Federalist was Charles Chapoteau, the constitutional cleric, but it is not possible to identify who his allies were, or indeed his main opponents. When the Convention counter-attacked in late July and summoned the principal Girondist sympathisers of Auch to Paris, the edifice of Gers Federalism swiftly crumbled. All the clubs were reconstituted as *sociétés montagnardes*, yet a legacy of bad feeling continued to strain relations between the club members of Roquelaure. Chapoteau endeavoured to cover his tracks with an energetic display of orthodox Jacobinism, only to fall foul of the move towards Dechristianisation. Although he willingly abjured on 1 Frimaire II (21 November 1793), the criticism directed against him on that occasion clearly drew on the enmities of the previous summer. Shortly afterwards, he was arrested. In the Gers there was never any question of forgiving those who had 'mistakenly' presumed to question the locus of national sovereignty. Federalism had traumatised the department. In late Ventôse II (mid-March 1794), as the village elite of Villepreux wondered anxiously where the blow against the Hébertistes would fall next, the Jacobins of Roquelaure were being enjoined, once again, to root out the Federalists from their midst.

The Federalist Crisis of the summer of 1793 illustrates the way agendas formulated well beyond the confines of the village could produce extremely varied responses and consequences. The Dechristianisation Campaign is another case in point, but one that will be explored from a rather different perspective in chapter 6. The Terror produced a politics of slavish conformism in the village, particularly once legislators had resolved – in the law of 14 Frimaire – the ambiguities that had bedevilled the concept of sovereignty since the very start of the Revolution. On the evidence of 1793 – the Vendée, Charrier, Federalism, foreign invasion – one conclusion seemed inescapable: political power would have to be concentrated as well as streamlined. But the concentration of power led ineluctably to the abuse of power. Even as they toured the countryside setting up the institutions of the 'republic in the village', many *représentants-en-mission* were painfully aware of the paradox. And what was done could not easily be undone: coteries of militants who took risks, even exposed their lives, for the Republic in the course of the Year Two were not likely to disband following a mood swing or a relaxation of policy in Paris. In this sense the Year Two had an 'afterlife' in the village, and one that contributed largely to the chronic instability of the Directory regime between 1795 and 1799. In the judgement of Bonaparte's Consular advisers the only solution, as we shall see, was to try to kill off village politics at its source.

Kinship in politics was initially perceived as comradeship, then as protection, before becoming an invitation to practise the abuse of power. The early revolutionaries had not worried unduly about it, any more than had the officials of the *ancien régime*. They were more concerned to legislate incompatibilities of office, as between, for example, public notary and Justice of the Peace. Yet parish priests could be elected as mayors or municipal councillors, and, in the conditions of 1790, they frequently were.[29] Kinship became a source of concern only when the power base of the Revolution at the local level narrowed. Another look at the situation in Saint-Alban will illustrate the problem.

On 9 Prairial II (28 May 1794) *représentant* Borie, who had been entrusted with the implementation of Revolutionary Government in the departments of the Gard and the Lozère, confided in the Committee of Public Safety that there were far too many *comités de surveillance* in the countryside: 'que c'est dans ces comités où se sont glissés des hommes perfides et je sens maintenant, plus que jamais, l'utilité de réduire les comités [à un] par canton'.[30] Borie was on his way to Saint-Alban where he would uncover intimidation, graft, racketeering and persecution on such a scale that the episode would become known throughout the neighbourhood as 'la fameuse affaire de Saint-Alban'.[31] In his final report, penned on 24 Prairial (12 June), the *représentant* announced: 'il n'est peut-être pas de commune dans laquelle les droits sacrés que la loi garantit à l'homme libre ayent été plus ouvertement violés qu'à Saint-Alban'.[32] Household rivalries, as we might well suppose, lay at the heart of the problem. Having 'captured' the municipality, probably in the aftermath of the Charrier insurrection, the Mathieu–Enjalvin

---

[29] A law of 24 August 1790 declared the offices of parish priest and mayor incompatible, but it was not always adhered to by voters.

[30] See F.-A. Aulard (ed.), *Recueil des Actes du Comité de Salut Public avec la correspondance officielle des représentants-en-mission et le registre du Conseil Exécutif Provisoire* (30 vols., Paris, 1889–1951), XIII, 9 Prairial II.

[31] A. D. de la Lozère, L 528, letter dated 20 Messidor II.

[32] A. N., F⁷3681¹⁴, *arrêté* of Jean Borie, *représentant-du-peuple*. See also A. N., DIII 138.

faction proceeded to create a *comité de surveillance* in its own image. As constituted on 20 October 1793, this body comprised the two Enjalvin brothers (one of whom was mayor, the other a former mayor), the two Mathieu brothers (Jean-Antoine being the Justice of the Peace), their uncle (*assesseur* to the *juge de paix*), Etienne Valadier (municipal officer and a germane cousin of the Mathieu brothers), Jean-Jacques Fontugne (uncle of Valadier), Martial Pelissier (brother-in-law of Fontugne and uncle of Valadier), Etienne Polge (father-in-law of the younger Enjalvin) and so on. The only member indisputably unrelated to any of the others was François Farges, a peasant farmer from one of the more distant hamlets. Needless to say, the first item on the committee's schedule of priorities was to arrest Atrasic and Vincens under the catch-all terms of the Law of Suspects.

Until the law of 14 Frimaire II was promulgated, there was nothing illegal about such a concentration of power, it should be emphasised. Asked whether the *comité* and the municipality constituted an overlapping cell of kinsmen, Etienne Valadier agreed, while pointing out that 'il n'y avoit pas incompatibilité d'après la loi du 17 september [the Law of Suspects]'.[33] In the conditions prevailing in the autumn and winter of 1793, however, the almost inevitable consequence was systematic abuse of power. First *représentant* Châteauneuf-Randon and then *représentant* Borie began to uncover overwhelming evidence of a long list of misdemeanours. Whether jointly or separately, members of the municipality and the *comité* of Saint-Alban stood accused of negligence (failure to complete the tax rolls), sharp practice (failure to notify voters of meetings in advance), intimidation (in the conduct of electoral assemblies), fraud (at the time of recruitment), embezzlement (proceeds of subscriptions), bias (allocation of requisitions), theft (salt, firewood) and the imposition of arbitrary taxes. The Enjalvins, the Mathieus, Valadier, Pelissier and several others were arrested in order to be dealt with by the local courts, while Jean-Antoine Mathieu, the Justice of the Peace, suffered the dishonour of transfer before the Revolutionary Tribunal.

In a culture where 'face', that is to say reputation, counted for everything, Noé-Jean Atrasic and his son-in-law must have laughed aloud at the prospect of Jean-Antoine Mathieu being escorted to Paris, perhaps never to return. It was ample compensation for the insulting letter that the *juge de paix* had addressed to Atrasic in which he contrasted his own bourgeois lineage to the humble and uncouth parentage of his opponent ('nos conditions ne sont pas du tout égales, vous êtes le fils d'un meunier je suis le

[33] A. N., F⁷3681¹⁴, interrogation of Etienne Valadier, 12 Messidor II.

fils d'un avocat', etc.).[34] Ironically, it had been the constitutive law of Revolutionary Government (14 Frimaire) that had redressed the balance in the village. A partial renewal of the membership of the *comité de surveillance*, prompted by much tighter rules on pluralism and prohibited degrees of kinship, loosened tongues. Atrasic and Vincens managed to secure provisional release from prison, and Borie's determination to set the commune to rights completed their re-invention as 'oppressed patriots'.[35] To ask which of the contending groups actually was the most patriotic is probably a misplaced question, for the reasons mentioned earlier. But in the politically expedient context of the Year Two it appears more than likely that *représentant* Borie had ordered the arrest of the 'wrong' men.

The virulence of factionalism in Saint-Alban was exceptional without a doubt; not so much for the fact of its existence as for the fact that it constituted a 'lifetime' experience for the main protagonists, and structured the politics of the village for the rest of the decade and into the next. Nonetheless, a safe generalisation can be made that Jacobinism exploited the bonds of kin and client more than any other creed of the Revolution, or of the Counter-Revolution. Every village may not have contained teams of 'ins' and 'outs' in the manner of Saint-Alban, but everywhere the experience of the Year Two proved formative in the sense that it left behind a residue of allegiances and alliances. Indeed, the structuring of village politics would become mutually reinforcing: in each crisis the higher authorities drew from a perceived constituency of tried and trusted men (proto-royalists, Directorial republicans, neo-Jacobins) the cadres they needed for local office. The process is best exemplified by the aftermath of the Fructidor *coup* (4 September 1797). In most of our villages fractions of the power elite yielded – more or less gracefully – to other fractions of the elite as an atmosphere of expectant royalism gave way to one of resurgent Jacobinism. In Châtelaudren, where there were no visceral animosities, Louis Le Breton and Jean-Baptiste Clouient, two stalwarts of the period of the Terror, returned to office; in Villepreux safe pairs of hands were found in the shape of Jean-Germain Prissette, the notary, whose non-sectarian Jacobinism had matured into Directorial republicanism, and Gilles Cottereau, one of the craftworker militants of the municipality of the Year Two. The village of Allan already boasted a Jacobin leadership when the *coup* hit home, but the purging of the entire cantonal administration owing to the flagrant royalism of Donzère momentarily unsettled it. *Agent* Gouteron was replaced

---

[34] A. N., F⁷3681¹⁴, *procès-verbal* of *commissaires* J.-B. Filhon and M. Martin, Saint-Alban, 18–20 Pluviôse II.
[35] A. D. de la Lozère, L 524, 12 Germinal II.

by a wealthy Protestant *ménager* and trader, while the post of *adjoint* went to another well-to-do peasant farmer. In terms of political affiliation, these were more or less interchangeable appointments. The entire elite of Allan, whether Catholic or Protestant, seems to have functioned on a 'toujours à gauche' basis. When the officer corps of the National Guard was renewed a month or so after the elections of the Year Six, twelve of the nineteen posts were filled by men who had helped to found the *société populaire* in 1793.

Predictably, the biggest upsets of the Directory years occurred in Saint-Alban. Having escaped the clutches of the Revolutionary Tribunal, Jean-Antoine Mathieu returned to the village kitted out in the moral armour of a victim of 'la faction de l'exécrable Robespierre'.[36] There was a brief internecine struggle with his uncle – Placide Mathieu – in the spring of 1795, as he tried to recover the post of Justice of the Peace, but then it was back to business as usual. Major clashes occurred in Brumaire IV (November 1795) (*juge de paix* elections), Germinal VI (March 1798) (legislative and communal elections) and Nivôse X (late December 1801) (fresh *juge de paix* elections occasioned by the reform of the Year Ten). Although there were a few defections in the ranks, party discipline held remarkably firm, and replicated the alignments of 1793–4. In the aftermath of the Fructidor *coup*, the central administration of the Department cashiered the cantonal municipality of Saint-Alban for failing to implement the proscription laws against returned *émigrés* and priests, and also because '[elle] se trouve composée des membres proches parens ou aliés entreux'.[37] This action, in turn, set the scene for the disruption of the cantonal primary assembly three months later. Reluctant to countenance Vincens as president of the assembly and having failed to disenfranchise and dislodge Atrasic by means of a procedural manoeuvre (an allegation that he was the nephew of an *émigré*), the 'neo-Jacobins' walked out and set up a schism electoral body of their own. The ringleaders, needless to say, included Pierre-Augustin Mathieu, the younger Enjalvin, Jean-André Constand and François Farges – all of whom had been members of the *comité de surveillance* set up in the commune in October 1793. Noé-Jean Atrasic made one final attempt to wrest meaningful power from the hands of what must have seemed like a mafia of bourgeois opponents: in 1801 he challenged the incumbent Jacques-Philippe Ayrald (a kinsman of the Enjalvin) for the post of Justice of the Peace. The challenge was lost, or so he claimed, because Ayrald's principal backer was none other than Jean-Antoine Mathieu. As the returning officer for those voting

[36] A. N., DIII 138, J.-A. Mathieu *ex-juge de paix* to the administrators of the District of Saint-Chély-d'Apcher, 4 Ventôse III.
[37] A. D. de la Lozère, L 420, 12 Frimaire VI.

in the *bourg*, Mathieu took great care not to open his ballot box until the results of all the neighbouring villages were known. 'Tenon l'oulet, nous escaparo pas,'[38] he was overheard to exclaim in patois after calculating the spread of votes on a table-top in Favier's tavern.

This constant rotation of elites, whether in Saint-Alban or the other villages, suggests that we should return to the question first raised in chapter 4. Did the local power arenas of the Revolution and post-Revolution actually function in accordance with the norms of 'choice'? In nearly every case they appear to have been structured around dynasties of power brokers who both expected and duly received the endorsement of 'their' electorate. None of the parties to the exercise seem to have enjoyed much room for manoeuvre. It was rare for elites, collectively speaking, to be dislodged, and certain families – within those elites – were predestined to appear and reappear in every power combination. Voters and office holders played roles assigned to them, then, but so too did the higher authorities. Their freedom of manoeuvre was curtailed by the fact that, in any given village, the choice of suitable candidates for office was extremely limited. Candidates' moral and political qualities had therefore to yield in the face of social, cultural and economic imperatives. On 21 Prairial X (10 June 1802) the prefect of the Lozère advised the Minister of the Interior that the sixty-year-old citizen Atrasic was legally trained, 'un des plus riches propriétaires du canton', and that 'il jouit d'une bonne réputation': ergo, he was a fit candidate for the post of Justice of the Peace.[39] While the first two statements were almost certainly correct, the third was not, and it is likely that the prefect knew as much. Mayor Enjalvin scarcely enjoyed a better reputation for that matter. But in the sphere of local government the regime – each regime – had to take what was on offer, or else open up power arenas to the vagaries of popular election.

SOVEREIGNTY SUBLIMATED

In the midst of all the alarms caused by the brigand threat, the inhabitants of Allan may not have paid much attention on 12 October 1799 to an assortment of cavalry and carriages waiting to ford the swollen waters of the river Jabron. General Bonaparte had returned from Egypt. A month passed, bringing with it the news of the Brumaire *coup* and the abolition of the Directory; then another month, by which time the outlines of the new

---

[38] A.N., F^{1c}III Lozère 1, Atrasic to *citoyen* Osty *sous-préfet*, Saint-Alban, 17 Ventôse X.
[39] A. N., F^{1c}III Lozère 1, prefect of the Lozère to the Minister of the Interior, 21 Prairial X.

regime had started to become clearer (promulgation of the Constitution of the Year Eight). Yet no word emerged as to the future shape of local government: the municipal administration of Donzère continued in office, therefore, issuing futile orders to apprehend highway robbers, allocating requisitions and apportioning taxes. Finally, at the end of March 1800, the news reached them that there were to be no more canton-based municipalities made up of elected agents of the villages, but instead mayors and *adjoints* for each commune who would be nominated by an official called a prefect.

The law of 28 Pluviôse VIII (17 February 1800) curtailed the experiment in village-level sovereignty that had been running, haphazardly, for a decade. In the verdict of many historians it also sounded the death-knell of village politics.[40] By removing the passion from public life, Bonaparte privatised politics and invited oligarchies to resume the exercise of power. There is much truth in these observations, as anyone who reads the transcripts of village council meetings over a thirty-year period must acknowledge. The vitality and spontaneity of the deliberations drafted in the early 1790s is entirely absent from the truncated and essentially 'managerial' deliberations of the 1800s and 1810s. There are no general assemblies, only 'reinforced' assemblies in which decision making is shared with major taxpayers. There is little petitioning, either, an exercise that carried a connotation of insubordination in the prefectoral mind. Yet the retreat from sovereignty had been under way for some time, as other chapters of this study have made clear. Moreover, Bonaparte's cronies in the new legislative bodies sweetened the pill by restoring at least the semblance of local decision taking. Villages such as Allan, Roquelaure and Villepreux, which had been sucked into cantonal municipalities in 1795, could take satisfaction in the fact that they would now have their 'own' mayors, even if these individuals received their mandates from above.

The trend towards oligarchy was not an invention of the Consulate and the Empire, either. As the analysis of elites at the start of this chapter demonstrated, there was no sudden or brutal ousting of the cadres of previous regimes. In truth even the architects of Revolutionary Government found it expedient on occasion to retain the services of former nobles and 'bourgeois specialists', whether at the national or the local level. During the Year Two the saltpetre workshop of Saint-Alban had been run by Jean-Adam Molette-Morangiès, brother of the one-time seigneur. In the

---

[40] See the commentary in C. Guionnet, *L'Apprentissage de la politique moderne: les élections municipales sous la monarchie de juillet* (Paris and Montréal, 1997), pp. 41–2, 111.

department of the Meurthe the incoming prefect introduced himself to the new mayors – Jordy of Neuviller included – with a justification of his criteria of choice and a proposal for partnership in the selection of municipal councillors. The choices made had been determined not by socio-economic categories, but by the need to harness 'civisme' and 'lumières'. As for the councillors, 'vous donnerez une préférence particulière aux citoyens qui, réunissant à ces titres [i.e. 'moralité', 'civisme', 'talents'] celui d'acquéreur de domaines nationaux, ont aussi donné un gage de plus de leur attachement à la Constitution'.[41] Maurice Jordy met all of these criteria nicely and, notwithstanding his 'past' as a revolutionary, remained in office without interruption from 1800 to 1815. If the regime had wanted to boost oligarchy further, or to remove the rotten timbers of the Revolution from the ship of state, the opportunity occurred in 1808 when village mayorships fell due for renewal. But our study suggests that village-level elites were left to evolve by and large. Michel Gouteron of Allan and Augustin Enjalvin of Saint-Alban both served the full term (i.e. they were continued in office in 1808 and again in 1813), whilst François-Honoré Corbel's tenure of the mayorship of Châtelaudren was interrupted only by his death in 1809. The post of mayor of Roquelaure certainly changed hands, although it is not easy to identify the incumbents and therefore to sort out the factors in play. As for Villepreux, where a more fluid elite afforded a greater freedom of manoeuvre, the smooth transition of 1800 hesitated in 1808 when Gravelle-de-Fontaine was ousted in favour of Jean Brault, a man who had first held office in the Municipal Assembly of 1787 and who was identified with the earliest years of the Revolution. Again, though, the thinking behind the prefect's decision is hard to penetrate.

What about the passion for politics? After 1800, and more especially after the signing of the Concordat (see p. 223) and the Justice of the Peace elections of 1801–2, public quiet did descend upon the village. It lasted for about a decade, and like all silences is difficult to interpret. The gradual sublimation of peasant Jacobinism into a populist strand of Bonapartism must be accounted a factor in this relative quiescence. Rural Bonapartism would become one of the most pervasive, yet least understood, political affiliations of the nineteenth century. Old soldiers returning to the villages after the campaigns of the First and Second Coalitions seem to have acted as the principal vectors of this democratic republicanism and caesarism. Yet it was an unstable mix: on the evening of 7 February 1801 a fracas occurred

---

[41] See C. Pfister, *Les Elections à Nancy et dans le département de la Meurthe sous le Consulat et le Premier Empire, 1799–1815* (Nancy, 1912), p. 19, note 2.

in one of the taverns of Villepreux when a veteran expressed his amazement on learning that Jacques Cochard had been continued in office as *adjoint* of the commune: 'c'est un prêtre qui devait être guillotiné il y a dix ans,' adding for good measure, 'il était un des auteurs de la machine infernale'.[42] Such sentiments would be driven out of the public sphere as the regime secured its hold. This raises the question of unreconciled, underground Jacobinism in the village – a question that can only be answered in relation to the events of 1814–15.

The 'collective anaesthesia'[43] of the Empire began to loosen its grip from 1810 or thereabouts. The dearth of the agricultural year 1811–12 brought forth crowd reflexes, and rhetoric, reminiscent of the Year Two. Châtelaudren, the village most vulnerable to harvest shortfall and the breakdown of supply mechanisms, experienced disturbances in its marketplace, and a grain price ceiling – or Maximum – was imposed on 4 June 1812. Is it just coincidence that the 15 August Festival of Saint Napoleon of that year was celebrated with less than the usual pomp and circumstance? Was the gilding of the Empire wearing off? Within a matter of months unsettling rumours of military reverses began to circulate. The villagers of Neuviller would have learned the news that the Grande Armée was retreating from Russia around 21 December 1812, following the receipt of reports to that effect in Nancy. Napoleon's post haste return to France was even known to a few people in the Lorraine capital by that date. Increasingly urgent calls for men and materials over the next few months left no doubt that the Empire was in a state of crisis in any case. Neuviller, the most easterly of our villages, bore the brunt of the requisitions, to which it responded energetically in the knowledge that it straddled one of the main invasion routes. Skirmishing took place in the neighbourhood on 11 January 1814 as French forces continued their orderly retreat. But once the bridge over the Moselle at Flavigny had been blown up, the village was left wide open to occupation by the Russians. As the Allied advance progressed, the villagers of Villepreux were next to feel the weight of occupation. By early April 1814 the 150 inhabitants who had not fled the village were providing quarter for 160 *cuirassiers* of the Russian Imperial Guard. Allan, Châtelaudren, Roquelaure and Saint-Alban, by contrast, all emerged physically unscathed from the military operations attendant upon the First Restoration, although Auch would be occupied by English soldiers and Allan would play host to foreign troops following Waterloo.

[42] A. C. de Villepreux, D2, 18 Pluviôse IX.
[43] The phrase belongs to Louis Bergeron, 'Political Culture of the French Revolution' (conference held at Balliol College, Oxford, September 1987), session 6, debates.

The fact that Napoleon had given orders to reactivate the rhetoric of the 'Nation-in-Arms' even as the Empire entered what proved to be its death-throes suggests that the Republic was not completely dead and buried in the village. On 18 March 1814, as the Comte d'Artois (future Charles X) passed through Roville and Neuviller en route for Nancy and a potential Bourbon Restoration, he was accosted by Antoine Bertier – the local landowner – who left him in no doubt as to the republican sentiments of a large proportion of the population. Bertier, an old revolutionary rallied to the Empire *faute de mieux*, earned a spell under house arrest for his impudence. However, it was the episode of the Hundred Days that demonstrated most clearly the survival of relict communities of village Jacobins. Even before he reached Paris, Napoleon had started to beat the war drums against noble and clerical privilege in a bid to attract left-wing (i.e. republican) support for a rehabilitated Empire. This attempt to rekindle the *élan* of the Revolution stirred powerful emotions – among old soldiers in particular. The mayor of Allan, Jacques-Michel Ferrent, was one such. A revolutionary of 1790 vintage, his installation in the place of Gouteron (1793 vintage) demonstrates just how little room for manoeuvre the Restoration prefects possessed in villages such as Allan. When on 10 March 1815 Ferrent got wind of Napoleon's disembarkation he rushed to join his old leader in the hope of finding him in Grenoble.

In fact the Hundred Days coaxed former revolutionaries out of the closet in four out of our six villages, or five out of seven if we include the hamlet of Roville. Only in Châtelaudren and Villepreux was there no immediate change of municipal personnel, and for two reasons. In both villages the Restoration prefects had allowed the power elite of the Empire to remain in office, thus removing the need for a political purge following Napoleon's return from exile; and secondly the municipal elections prescribed in the Imperial decree of 30 April 1815 never took place in these localities. Elsewhere we find scenes of incoherence bordering on confusion as the contending regimes manoeuvred for advantage. Indeed, the villagers of Allan found themselves caught up in the fighting between local Bonapartists and the forces of the Duc d'Angoulême in late March. The tricolour did not replace the white flag of the Bourbons on the bell towers of Montélimar until 8 April. In the Lozère, meanwhile, the department seemed to be split-ting apart in the view of contemporaries, as the Calvinist population of the Cévennes rallied massively to the Empire, while the highland Catholic villages of the north clung to the monarchy. Each regime, moreover, rushed legislation onto the statute book in order to anathematise appointments made by its predecessor. In late March 1815 Bonapartist prefects were ordered to reinstate all mayors and *adjoints* who had been in post at the time of the Allied invasion of 1814, but on 7 July Louis XVIII issued an ordinance recalling to office all those who had been in post at the moment of Napoleon's landfall in the Golfe Juan.

Old revolutionaries, or revolutionary sympathisers, returned to power by two routes. Either they were appointed by Napoleonic prefects and subprefects, or by special envoys, or they were freely chosen by electoral assemblies of 'active' citizens on the model of 1790. In some instances both happened: a special envoy of the Emperor appointed Jean-Baptiste Biscarrat – the ex-seigneurial judge, ex-District administrator and ex-Dechristianiser – mayor of Allan on 5 May 1815, together with a multi-generational *conseil* consisting of fathers who had been prominent in 1793–4 and their sons. Just over a fortnight later, Biscarrat's appointment was sanctioned by an electoral assembly of the village. He would resign following Waterloo. In Roquelaure the restoration of the link with the Year Two came from below: via a municipal election held on 21 May. Jean-Baptiste Barrué, who was probably the son of Joseph-Marie Barrué, the most prominent republican of the village during the Directory, briefly became mayor. In Neuviller the electoral assembly of the village actually removed Maurice Jordy, who had become suspect as the chateau owner (see p. 144), and replaced him with a native-born individual with a track record in local government covering the period 1790–3.

The hardest cases to diagnose are those of Roville and Saint-Alban, but here we do at least catch a glimpse of the real forces at work in the village by this date. Far and away the largest landowner in Roville, Antoine Bertier also posed as the 'agronomic' successor to intendant Chaumont de La Galaizière *fils*, the last seigneur of the Comté de Neuviller. As such he fought a running battle with his fellow but less 'enlightened' villagers over enclosures and other improvements pioneered since 1791. But Bertier was a staunch revolutionary, indeed a republican by natural inclination, and the political stance adopted by the village community in order to combat his schemes can best be described as 'neo-Jacobin'. Bertier's *ralliement* to the Empire was crowned by his election to the Chamber on 10 May 1815; however, the inhabitants of Roville clung resolutely to the time warp of Jacobinism. Twice the electors were called out to choose their mayor and *adjoint* and twice they chose men of 1793, to the evident fury of the subprefect. The defence of the common land partition carried out in 1794 seems to have been the critical issue. Personalities coloured the events of 1815 in Saint-Alban, too. With the exception of Noé-Jean Atrasic, who had died during the First Restoration, all the actors in the bitter factional disputes of the 1790s remained on the scene, and Napoleon's return soon provided the means of resuming intracommunal score settling. Augustin Enjalvin, the long-serving mayor whose administrative skills seem to have made him indispensable to each succeeding regime, was toppled – probably by popular election – and replaced by his arch rival Vincens (son-in-law of the late Atrasic). Since Jean-Antoine Mathieu remained *adjoint*, this produced stalemate and the village was plunged into turbulence as a result. Before the new incumbent could be formally installed in office, however, the news of Waterloo came through and the Napoleonic prefect was forced to pack his bags. To his immense indignation, Vincens was then toppled in turn by the Bourbon ordinance requiring the reinstatement of all those who had been in office on 1 March 1815. Enjalvin returned, therefore, and he would remain mayor until 1826 when we finally lose sight of him. Whether any of these figures possessed genuine ideological allegiances remains an open question, and one to which the episode of the Hundred Days brings us no closer to an answer. By the summer of 1815 labels seem to have been reversed by comparison with 1793: Enjalvin is the 'good royalist'[44] and Vincens features as the dangerous subversive.

Village Jacobinism may have been in a time warp by 1815, then, and it was indubitably destined for biological extinction. On the evidence of our villages, however, it had not been 'eclipsed', 'put to sleep' or smothered, whether in 1795, 1800 or 1804. Yet the case of Saint-Alban, in 1815, serves to emphasise once again that villagers tended to exercise 'sovereignty' according to their own rules, rules whose purchase was generally local even though they might be capable of wider application. The view of village politics from within that this chapter has attempted to explore does not automatically replicate the view achieved from the outside, therefore. Yet neither is sufficient on its own if we are to understand fully how local political arenas functioned. The example of Châtelaudren will illustrate the point. Despite all our accumulated 'internal' knowledge, the dynamic of politics in the village between 1814 and 1816 eludes us. Why were mayor Cadiou and *adjoint* Verdun – both enthusiastic revolutionaries and Bonapartists – not dismissed at the time of the First Restoration? When dismissal finally occurred – on 1 September 1815 – why were they replaced by an ex-*chouan* who had participated in the assault on the village in 1795 and the former *agent national* of the commune from the days of the Terror? The appointment to the mayorship of the wealthy royalist proprietor and ex-*chouan* Geslin de Bourgogne is readily explicable, but the choice of Pierre-René

[44] A. D. de la Lozère, 2Z 12, 1 August 1815.

Le Rumeur as his running mate can only mean that the higher authorities were conscious of the need to perform a careful political balancing act. However, we need an 'outside' perspective in order to work this out.

The presence of a fifty-one-year-old Jacobin among those at the helm of this ardently patriotic village conferred credibility on the Bourbon regime while it was finding its feet. By 1821 Le Rumeur had outlived his usefulness and he was replaced by Louis Dubourblanc, a scion of one of the more moderate royalist families of the neighbourhood. Pragmatism also underscored the approach of the prefect of the Lozère. Despite unremitting pressure from local ultra-royalists to cashier all those who had held office between 1790 and 1815, he made no attempt to alter the status quo in Saint-Alban.[45] Jean-Antoine Mathieu died in office, in 1824, whereas Augustin Enjalvin relinquished the mayorship in 1826 having been active in local government for thirty-seven of his seventy years of age. Maurice Jordy of Neuviller also completed a remarkable thirty-year public career during which he had rarely been out of office for more than a few months at a time. He gave up the post of mayor just two years before his death in December 1823, and was buried as close as possible to the walls of the church that he had transformed into a Temple of Reason back in 1794. Unsurprisingly, Michel Gouteron, the long-standing Jacobin mayor of Allan, never regained office after the Second Restoration. With men like Gouteron and Biscarrat held at bay, the municipal council gradually edged its way towards a compromise with the heirs of the late and unlamented seigneur. As for Jean-Baptiste Barrué, he disappeared without trace after 1816 – the year in which he was removed from the *conseil municipal* of Roquelaure 'pour ses mauvaises opinions'.[46] He had already lost the mayorship to a more pliant member of the proprietorial elite who was too young to have participated in the struggles of the late *ancien régime* and the Revolution. Villepreux, as we know, was not a locality structured around continuity: following Waterloo Jean Brault resigned as mayor to be replaced by a figure entirely new to the village.

---

[45] See A. N., F^IC III Lozère 3, Barrot, president of the electoral college of the *arrondissement* of Mende to the Minister of the Interior, Mende, 20 August 1815.
[46] A. D. du Gers, 2M 44, Roquelaure.

CHAPTER 6

Church and state in miniature

When the deputies of the National Assembly voted to subject ministers of religion to a test of loyalty they crossed a divide and ensured that the debate on the merits of the Revolution would be conducted – quite literally – in churches and chapels across the land. It is for this reason that we have depicted the clerical oath of 1791 as the formative, or matrix, event of the decade. The clashes between church and state filtered the experiences of county dwellers during these years to a degree without parallel. But mere observation of the clashes as they were enacted at the level of the village will not take us very far. Parishioners were not robots all equipped with the same quantum of religious experience. Gender, geography and institutions, to mention only the most obvious variables, intervened to shape those religious cultures which in turn shaped villagers' responses to the forces taking charge of their daily lives. Pressures for change did not wait upon the events of 1789, either, as this study has frequently emphasised. The transition from a confessional state to one willing to countenance a free market in religious practice had already started: the *consuls* of Allan signalled as much when in May 1788 they set aside a portion of the Catholic cemetery for the burial of villagers adhering to the Calvinist faith.

To advance the proposition that the quantity – and quality – of religious experience differed from village to village is not the same as proving it, however. Institutions that function smoothly and uneventfully tend to leave few traces behind them, as we noted at the end of chapter 4. Few scholars of the village, in consequence, have managed to penetrate the opacity of spiritual life within the rural parish. Direct testimony such as the memoirs of the incumbent that Gérard Bouchard exploited in his remarkable study of the village of Senneley-en-Sologne is extremely rare and not, therefore, a resource available to the historian working with a comparative remit.[1] Indirect, if all too often imprecise, testimony is more plentiful, though,

[1] G. Bouchard, *Le Village immobile: Senneley-en-Sologne au XVIIIe siècle* (Paris, 1972).

and it should enable us to draw out some of the contrasts and similarities between our sites of study. For a start, all six villages, and even the two satellite hamlets of Roville and Rennemoulin, were seats of parishes and therefore by definition endowed with at least one church providing facilities for regular worship. However, some were in more secure possession of their spiritual 'territory' than were others. Despite their best endeavours, the clergy of Saint-Alban were never able to assemble – and police – the entire population of their far-flung parish. In any case, the parish church was too small and too cluttered with private stalls to perform its allotted role, and the inhabitants of outlying hamlets tended to worship elsewhere, or not at all. The bishop of Mende acknowledged the difficulty – and the attendant risk of heterodoxy – when he allowed a chapel-of-ease to be built in Lajo, the most distant hamlet, with a part-time celebrant who was also empowered to record births, marriages and deaths. By contrast, the narrow confines of Châtelaudren's parish enabled it to suck in worshippers from surrounding parishes whose size and semi-*bocage* landscape tended to strain loyalties to the mother church.

True, Châtelaudren possessed two spacious edifices (Saint-Magloire and Notre-Dame-du-Tertre) offering Sunday services in rotation, not to mention an array of taverns and artisans' boutiques. This promiscuity of town and country at the spiritual level would be redirected once the oath of legislation took effect and prompted Catholics to rethink their community allegiances. In Neuviller a priory church adequately accommodated parishioners, notwithstanding the construction of a seigneurial side-chapel in 1768. The only other consecrated building in the village was a domestic chapel located within the precinct of the chateau. Likewise Roville, where the parish church had been rebuilt in the heart of the hamlet in 1756–7 and easily managed to contain a population of a little under 200 inhabitants. In Villepreux, too, the parish church was centrally located and sufficient in size to meet the needs of the local population. Several beneficed chapels and a ruined priory occupied by three Cordelier friars also existed at the time of the Revolution, but they scarcely impinged on the spiritual life of the parishioners. As the owners of the large farm of Les Bordes, the friars were perceived mainly as landlords. In the south, by contrast, the institutional underpinnings of village Catholicism appeared more complex. Religious, or quasi-religious, confraternities of Pénitents Blancs maintained chapels in both Saint-Alban and Allan. Moreover, in Saint-Alban beneficed parish clergy and Pénitents coexisted alongside a late medieval exemplar of Catholic piety in the shape of *prêtres habitués*, that is to say unbeneficed clerics living communally. Unsurprisingly, Béraud, the venerable *curé* of

Saint-Alban, did not get on with these clerical auxiliaries even though they helped him to service the parish during his declining years. On the other hand the ubiquity of *prêtres habitués* ensured that the Lozère would never experience the dearth of ordained men that afflicted other parts of the country in the decade following the implementation of the Napoleonic Concordat.

The parish church of Allan was both too small and too inaccessible for a population that by the late eighteenth century manifestly preferred to live in the expanding hamlets of the plain rather than the *castrum*. Although there existed a chapel that had once formed part of a Benedictine monastery in the southeastern corner of the parish, it is probable that the inhabitants of the more distant farmsteads did not routinely attend the Sunday services in the *chef-lieu*. This, at any rate, was one of the reasons put forward when the proposal to relocate the church was first aired in the 1820s. Some allowance must also be made for the fact that the parish of Allan was not homogeneously Catholic. In the period covered by our study some thirty-two households (about 16 per cent of the total population) retained an ancestral adherence to the Calvinist faith. This Protestant nucleus added a unique tincture to the civil and ecclesiastical life of the village both during and after the Revolution. Elsewhere Protestants were oddities of no great religious or social consequence: the farmers of Neuviller were accustomed to the sight of Christophe Klein, the Anabaptist herdsman, taking their stock to pasture, whilst in Châtelaudren the discovery of lead and silver ore seams brought an influx of Lutheran miners from Alsace and further afield to the village in the 1760s and 1770s. They were shunned by the indigenous community and denied burial in the Catholic cemetery. When David Lauterbach of Sainte-Marie-aux-Mines (Alsace) sought the hand of a local girl, the marriage contract stipulated a public abjuration of 'l'hérésie de Luther'.[2] Allan's Calvinists, by contrast, were long-established and well-respected members of the community. All were directly descended from 140 individuals who had been compulsorily 'converted' in 1686, and while little if any intermarriage took place before the Revolution, it is likely that they had been practising their faith unhindered for several decades prior to the Edict of Toleration. The alacrity with which the *consuls* agreed to spend 273 *livres* 15 *sous* in order to reinstate their cemetery is a fair indication of the esteem in which they were held.

At Roquelaure the parish church was small, cramped and quite inade-quate for the needs of an expanding population. Most parishioners lived

[2] See Le Page, *Les Bleus du Châté*, p. 36.

outside the *chef-lieu*, as we have noted, and in the absence of outlying chapels such as those dotting the Breton countryside, they had to make a journey to the *bourg* for spiritual comforts or else do without. Only the seigneur was spared this tedious necessity since the chateau of Le Rieutort – his autumn residence – was equipped with a domestic chapel. The signs nevertheless suggest that parish services remained well frequented, at least until the time of the Revolution. In 1772 the *curé* obtained permission to demolish the iron railings that impeded access to the communion table and to substitute a stone balustrade instead. While the move may have signalled a shift in popular religious culture, it seems more likely that the priest simply wanted to create a larger space for the congregation. Religious life in the parish was dutiful and conformist rather than intense, in any case. Alone among our villages, the church of Roquelaure had no income to speak of, and therefore no functioning vestry council (*fabrique*). The fact that the incumbent earned little from the *casuel* and relied instead on a share of the tithe seems also to indicate a degree of spiritual detachment. By way of contrast, *curé* Béraud of Saint-Alban collected about 600 *livres* annually in rents for Foundation Masses.

Funds for the maintenance of the clergy, for the fabric of the church and for charitable purposes (including educational provision) would dwindle sharply after 1789 to produce consequences that few, in the first flush of enthusiasm for the Revolution, could have anticipated. It is therefore important to try to take some measure of the resources generated within the parish community at the end of the *ancien régime*. The clerical income declarations filed in 1790 are helpful in this regard, as are the accounts submitted by churchwardens (*fabriciens*). The best endowed parishes were those linked closely to the urban economy and with a long history of noble benefaction, namely Châtelaudren and Villepreux. The *fabrique* of Villepreux enjoyed a very comfortable income of 1,600 *livres* a year made up chiefly of rents from land and dwelling houses in the *bourg*. In addition, it was buttressed by a separately funded Charité des Pauvres, about which more will be said below. The ecclesiastical tithe in this region of high-yield arable farming was worth about 8,000 *livres* gross on average, but most of the proceeds went into the coffers of the priory. Nonetheless, *curé* Teissier had some land attached to his living and estimated his income from all sources at around 1,300 *livres*. In Châtelaudren the tithe was negligible, as we know, but the collegiate church of Notre-Dame-du-Tertre was well endowed with funds deriving from foundations, pew rentals and ground rents in the neighbouring parish of Plouagat. The revenue stream of the *fabrique* of Saint-Magloire – the parish church – had been depleted as a result of damage caused by the flood of

1773. In 1793 the constitutional priest Jean-Zacharie Bourgneuf would claim that the straitened circumstances of the *fabrique* had prevented him from renewing the altar plate, but the date makes this sound like special pleading. Apparently the flood had also washed away the *hôpital* of Châtelaudren, thereby curtailing facilities for the destitute poor. In 1786 the *général* decided to concentrate its resources on the provision of outdoor relief instead.

At Roquelaure, as we know, all parochial expenditure was pared to the bone since the tithe owners doggedly refused to contribute anything, and the laity seem not to have been interested in buying Masses for their souls. The churchwardens were lucky if they collected even 10 *livres* per annum towards the cost of candles. The *fabrique* of Saint-Alban was grossly underfunded, too. Béraud, the *curé*, deplored the fact and lamented that the poor of the parish were not catered for either, despite all of his efforts over twenty years to persuade the tithe owner (the bishop of Mende) to make provision. However, this situation arose in part because the considerable income from Foundation Masses went into the purse of the incumbent rather than the coffers of the *fabrique*. Lack of any formal provision for the poor was a feature endemic to the highland villages of the district of Saint-Chély-d'Apcher, as the evidence gathered in 1790 by the National Assembly's commission of enquiry would demonstrate. According to the Committee on Mendicity chaired by the Duc de La Rochefoucauld-Liancourt 'one third of the population' of Saint-Alban and Lajo lived in daily need of assistance.[3] The chronic lack of funds of the *fabrique* of Neuviller (income 69 *livres* 15 *sous*) left the church in this locality in a similarly parlous state. As a building, indeed, it was close to collapse by the century's end. But at least the poor enjoyed access to a regular source of charitable relief in the years before 1789. The *économat* or hospital founded by testament of prior Rosselange in 1745 was producing an income of 728 *livres* per annum when the Revolution struck. The poor of Allan likewise benefited from the proceeds of a number of bequests. Each year the *conseil politique* appointed a 'recteur des pauvres' who, under the guidance of the *curé*, dispensed 112 *livres* 4 *sous* in the form of small cash sums, plus whatever had been collected in kind from private donors. Whether the *fabrique* had resources of its own is not recorded; indeed, it is far from certain that a body existed outside the *conseil politique* for the purpose of receiving and administering income earmarked for ecclesiastical purposes.

Allan's poor relief system began to creak almost as soon as the Revolution got under way. Most of the capital had been placed with 'le ci-devant

[3] A. N., F^{16}970.

Clergé de France' and arrears of interest payments soon started to build up. Meanwhile laymen whose ancestors had made pious bequests for the good of their souls somehow 'forgot' to keep up with the payments. This erosion of charitable provision does not appear to have affected the parishioners of Villepreux, however. Of all our villages Villepreux boasted the most intricate and lavishly resourced mechanism for outdoor relief, a consequence very largely of the efforts of Vincent Depaul in the early part of the seventeenth century. With the financial backing of his patron and one-time seigneur of Villepreux, Philippe-Emmanuel de Gondi, Depaul founded the Congregation of the Mission which swiftly developed a charitable arm. By 1658 the Charité des Pauvres of Villepreux had come into being, and over the following century this body attracted and then absorbed many other charitable foundations and bequests. The Dames de Charité as they were known locally proved capable of laying out sums of 300 *livres* and more at one go: during the harsh winter of 1784, for example. They came to the rescue of the village poor again in 1789–90, feeding large numbers employed on public works schemes, and once more in the early months of 1793.

Buoyant church revenues and schooling tended to march hand in hand at the end of the *ancien régime*. Where resources were scarce, it was usually the case that primary instruction was also poorly developed. The monarchy acknowledged, intermittently, that the secular power also had a role to play in this domain, but royal agents on the spot brought a mixture of pragmatism and prejudice to the question of educating the masses. Some intendants could see merit in allowing villages to add the salary of a schoolmaster to their tax rolls when clerical provision proved insufficient; others could not. Roquelaure, unsurprisingly, had no one to teach the sons and daughters of the village, a situation not untypical to judge from the wretchedly low literacy rates prevailing throughout the southwest. Those who needed the skills of reading and writing – the tight knot of families supplying the *consuls* and *jurats* – made use of the royal colleges of Auch and Toulouse instead. All the other villages found the wherewithal to employ someone to provide basic instruction for boys and, on occasion, girls. At Saint-Alban one of the *prêtres habitués* performed the role of schoolmaster, and Noé-Jean Atrasic contrived to add his unmarried sister Marguerite to the pay roll as schoolmistress whilst holding office as first *consul*. The bishop, however, did not approve. Spinsters closely supervised by the *curé* also provided schooling for girls in Châtelaudren, if their parents could afford to pay. The resources of a foundation dating back to the time of the Gondi met the wages of the schoolmaster of Villepreux, François Hersant, although this would not prevent him from becoming an enthusiastic Jacobin following the change of regime. Only in the case of Allan is there clear evidence of a communal decision to employ a 'percepteur de la petite jeunesse' who was not financially beholden to the church. Of course we cannot know whether he was under the thumb of the *curé* notwithstanding, but it appears unlikely since he seems to have received children of Protestant families for instruction as well as those of Catholics.

RELIGIOUS EXPERIENCE BEFORE 1789

It would be useful if this oblique and rather fragmentary evidence could be supplemented with data gleaned from episcopal visitation records in order to help us reach general conclusions about the quality of religious experience in our six villages. Unfortunately data of this sort barely exist for the period in question. Of course, we could project back, a procedure which most church historians consider to be legitimate. 'It is not possible to draw up a map of religious fervour for the France of the eighteenth century,' comments Ralph Gibson, 'but there is no doubt that such a map would strongly resemble the map drawn up in 1947 by Canon Boulard.'[4] What does this map show? That Villepreux was situated in a zone of low and ebbing levels of religious commitment, whereas Saint-Alban formed part of a southern bastion in which rural Catholics lived their faith seemingly immune to the secularising pressures of the modern world. To take but one index of piety, the vast majority of the adult males of Saint-Alban completed their Easter duties in 1829,[5] a situation that is not likely to have changed very much before the century's end since episcopal investigators recorded an average Easter turnout of 97.2 per cent in the mountain sector of the diocese of Mende in 1909.[6] By contrast fewer than 7 per cent of the Catholics of the diocese of Versailles bothered to fulfil the Easter obligations of their faith in 1834, although that proportion would rise to 15 per cent in 1859–61 before settling at 11 per cent towards the end of the century.[7] What of the other villages? Here the procedure is more questionable because they tend to fall in the middle. While Gérard Cholvy agrees that dioceses such as Mende and Versailles can be located at opposite ends of a spectrum of 'religious vitality'[8] in 1880 or thereabouts, Châtelaudren and Roquelaure

[4] R. Gibson, *A Social History of French Catholicism, 1789–1914* (London and New York, 1989), p. 9.
[5] Archives de l'Evêché de Mende, Diocèse de Mende, registre, 1825–30.
[6] Gibson, *A Social History of French Catholicism*, table 6.5.
[7] *Ibid*.
[8] G. Cholvy and Y.-M. Hilaire, *Histoire religieuse de la France contemporaine* (3 vols., Toulouse, 1985–8), I, p. 260.

fall within zones where the rural population accepted the disciplines of Catholic devotion while remaining aloof from the clergy. As for the regions in which Allan and Neuviller can be found, they were judged to be only 'middling' in their commitment, that is to say partially detached from the formal practices of Roman Catholicism. In the diocese of Nancy, to be sure, only 47 per cent of the adult population attended Easter communion in the years before the First World War.[9]

How much trust can be placed in broad generalisations of uncertain chronological relevance? Not very much unless they confirm what we already know, or suspect. The problem with 'projecting back' when applied to an exercise in micro-history is that the procedure smooths away the texturing of events, and attributes a linear pattern to shifts within the mental sphere. In fact it is more than likely that the intensity of religious experience within the village fluctuated, just like the intensity of political experience. Generalisations rooted in quantitative analysis of the extent to which the formal requirements of post-Tridentine Catholicism were adhered to also fail to take into account the popular dimensions of piety which villagers may well have regarded as the most meaningful aspects of their religious existence. In all of the villages and hamlets we have studied, for instance, the cult of the dead is much in evidence. Burial in church was only abandoned with the greatest reluctance in the 1770s. As late as 1783 the *général* of Châtelaudren was reminded that it should not allow corpses to be brought into the church, whatever the ostensible justification. Nothing in daily life, moreover, caused greater consternation than a proposal to close or relocate a burial ground. Villagers were generally prepared to run the risk of death from infectious disease rather than be separated from their ancestors. A scheme to remove the cemetery from the centre of the village of Saint-Alban was first discussed by the *consuls* in 1781, but more than forty years later the municipal council remained implacably opposed, observing that as matters stood worshippers could pass directly from the church doorway to the burial mounds of their forbears ('se recueillir sur la tombe et la cendre de ces pères, d'y pouvoir prier pour eux et les faire participer aux prières de l'église').[10] An alternative solution which the civil and ecclesiastical authorities occasionally agreed to was the physical transfer of human remains. Following the re-siting of the parish church of Roville, the inhabitants successfully petitioned to have the bones of their kith and kin dug out of the old graveyard and reburied in the new cemetery.

---

[9] Gibson, *A Social History of French Catholicism*, table 6.5.
[10] A. D. de la Lozère, E Dépôt St-Alban: 132 (D2), 18 March 1823.

The necrological emphasis of village piety appears most tellingly in the case of Saint-Alban. Yet even here it would be wrong to depict popular religious culture as somehow fixed for all time. Nearly all of the Masses for the dead from which *curé* Béraud derived such a handsome supplementary income at the end of the *ancien régime* had been endowed before 1674. Only eight out of seventy-six had been founded after that date. The rather low-key religiosity of the inhabitants of Neuviller placed much less emphasis on the community of the living and the dead. The village dutifully celebrated the prescribed feast days of the diocese, but reserved its greatest animation for the feast of Saint Liboire, the local patron, whose remains had been donated to the church by the Princes de Salm, one-time seigneurs of the parish. The display of the relics in a solemn procession to the chateau was the high point of the year, not least because it had become the occasion for a fair that attracted the population of surrounding parishes. On the other hand the ritual of the occasion exposed the alliance of church and chateau for all to see, and helped to fuel a current of anticlericalism among the villagers. The church of Villepreux also housed relics: those of Saint Nom. But they had been 'sanitised' in 1735 and no longer attracted attention as an object of popular veneration. There was little trace, too, of Vincent Depaul's missionary activity, unless it can be held responsible for converting the parish into a rather chilly example of reformed Catholic piety on the Tridentine model. It is a model recognisable in the accounts of the agents sent out at the time of the Consulate who would paint a bleak picture of superficial conformism in the villages around Paris. 'Dans les campagnes,' reported one observer in 1801, 'on aimerait mieux des cloches sans prêtres, que les prêtres sans cloches.'[11]

But was it necessary to choose between bells and priests? Southern villagers, in particular, enlisted both in their efforts to come to terms with a natural world whose elements threatened more than they succoured. Bells were routinely rung (in Roquelaure and elsewhere) in order to ward off thunder, and priests were expected to make available their supposed powers of intercession for virtually any community undertaking, no matter how remote from conventional Catholic belief or practice. Every few summers the incumbent of Allan accompanied his parishioners to local shrines in order to pray for rain; he was also expected to carry out 'des exorcismes des incettes [*sic*]'[12] if the situation so required. Apparently the bishop of

---

[11] 'Mission en l'an IX du Général Lacuée dans la 1ère division militaire', in F. Rocquain, *L'Etat de la France au 18 Brumaire* (Paris, 1874), p. 254.

[12] See *Archives départementales de la Drôme: inventaire de la série E (supplément)* (n.p., n.d.), commune d'Allan, E6609.

Saint-Paul-Trois-Châteaux found nothing untoward in the behaviour of either the priest or the parishioners. Practices of this sort were probably widespread and are easier to chronicle than to decode. If bishops were not prepared to condemn such 'indecencies', the task devolved upon the civil authorities instead. Secular hygiene demanded the closure of overfull cemeteries even if spiritual hygiene did not. In 1800 the mayor of Roquelaure would take it upon himself to upbraid the celebrant at Vespers one Sunday evening 'for having publicly blessed cattle'.[13] As we shall see, the village had moved from a situation in which both bells and priests were outlawed (the Terror) to one of ecclesiastical free enterprise (the Directory) in which a priest could be recruited to cater for the laity's every taste.

TOWARDS SEPARATION

The Gallican church had been one of the few institutions of absolute monarchy whose structures had not crumbled in 1789–90. This partial immunity to the ideological fall-out of the Revolution would not endure, however. Most of the non-juring clergy had been ousted from their villages by the spring of 1792; by the end of the summer of that year they would be faced with the stark choice of quitting the country or remaining as fugitives and outlaws under constant threat of arrest. Le Corvaisier of Châtelaudren fled to Jersey, Roux of Roquelaure to Spain and Seignelay of Neuviller to Mannheim, from where he wrote a letter to his father requesting that his winter clothes and a breviary be put in the post. Raynaud of Allan and Teissier of Villepreux disappeared without trace, and it seems unlikely that they remained in the country. Béraud of Saint-Alban died not long after retracting his oath. Yet within a year the first of their successors would be stepping down from the pulpit as the phenomenon known as 'déprêtrisation' threatened to bring the experiment with a constitutional church to an ignominious conclusion. Both Chapoteau of Roquelaure and Serpeille of Allan were put under arrest, while the others were banished to the margins of public life.

Historians have labelled this episode Dechristianisation. The label is not particularly helpful to us since it was coined in the 1840s in order to capture the process of secular drift from the institutions, practices and beliefs of Roman Catholicism. The sudden pressure to retire the constitutional clergy and to close down churches as places of Catholic worship in late 1793 cannot

---

[13] See E. Aubas, 'Monographie de la commune de Roquelaure', *Bulletin de la Société archéologique du Gers*, 34 (1933), 284–5.

be described as a process. Nor does it seem likely that rural people were 'dechristianised' in any meaningful sense as a result of their experiences. *Déprêtrisation* and church closure came in waves or spasms from the outside. In none of our villages is there much direct evidence that it was desired from within; on the contrary, there is quite a lot of testimony to indicate dismay, even hostility. The vagaries of village-level 'dechristianisation' depended most on the calibre, temper and peregrinations of the *représentants-en-mission*. Much of Brittany remained unscathed because the few *représentants* who penetrated the region were preoccupied with logistical matters and confined their attention to those localities situated on military highways. The Jacobin nucleus of Châtelaudren knew better than to destabilise the Republic's precarious hold in the district: only after the intervention of an emissary of General Sabatier did François Flahec the curate agree to stop celebrating Mass in the parish church of Saint-Magloire, that is to say on 17 Germinal II (6 April 1794). Four days later Saint-Magloire was turned over for use as a wood store and saltpetre manufactory.

By this date public worship had long since lapsed in the villages of Roquelaure, Villepreux and Neuviller, however. Their church buildings had been commandeered for use by *sociétés populaires* instead. At the instigation of *représentant* Dartigoeyte, the Gers became one of the bastions of anticlericalism and ostensible atheism in the southwest, and on 1 Frimaire II (21 November 1793) Chapoteau of Roquelaure duly declared 'au pied de l'arbre de la liberté qu'il ne vouloit avoir à l'avenir que le titre de bon républicain et bon montagnard'.[14] The vault containing the remains of the dukes of Roquelaure was ransacked – again in response to outside pressure – a few weeks later. Chapdelaine of Villepreux, meanwhile, would abdicate on 6 Frimaire and Brocard of Neuviller at about the same time as far as we can determine. In the absence of municipal records for the relevant period in Saint-Alban, the precise chronology is again difficult to ascertain. But the Lozère was very thoroughly *déprêtrisé*, first by *représentant* Châteauneuf-Randon and secondly by his colleague Jean Borie, and it seems likely that public worship had ceased in the *bourg* either by the end of Frimaire or by the first *décade* of Nivôse (late December 1793). At about this time orders were given for all wayside crosses to be removed, and for the chapel of the Pénitents Blancs to be fitted out for the manufacture of saltpetre. What of the villagers of Allan, whose circumspect attitude towards official Catholicism has already been noted? Only in retrospect (10 Ventôse II/28 February 1794) do we learn from the municipal minutes that the church had

[14] A. D. du Gers, L 699*.

been closed down. The Calvinist minority would have had no temple of their own until after the Concordat. We learn from other sources, however, that a carnival parodying Christian beliefs had paraded through the narrow alleyways of the *castrum*, and that its instigator had been Jean-Baptiste Biscarrat. Although no longer resident in Allan, Biscarrat remained an influential local figure whose public career impinged repeatedly on the life of the village. The inhabitants of Allan may have responded sympathetically to *déprêtrisation* and the inauguration of the Cult of Reason, then, but if they did, they were the only ones to do so.

Within days of the forced closure of the church at Roquelaure and the desecration of the tombs of the dukes, a clamour led by women demanded the restoration of public worship. The Convention's decree reaffirming freedom of worship had undoubtedly reached the village. Local militants grew anxious lest they be accused of excessive zeal, not least because Dartigoeyte had also been sniffing the political wind and speaking out against the initiatives of so-called 'faux patriotes'.[15] Signs of resistance, or division, can be detected in Villepreux and Neuviller as well. In neither locality is it absolutely certain that villagers were prevented from re-entering church buildings (and ringing the bells) at times when they were not being used either for the Cult of Reason or for meetings of the *société populaire*. On 1 Nivôse II (21 December 1793) the municipality of Villepreux was drawn into a dispute 'relativement aux rivalités des differens cultes'.[16] The minute conjures up an image of *de facto* religious pluralism more usually associated with the post-Separation regime of the Directory. This defiance is even more noticeable in the case of Châtelaudren – a late convert to the politics of *déprêtrisation*, as we have seen. Perhaps Jean-Zacharie Bourgneuf, the constitutional priest, and Flahec, the curate, were taking a cue from their constitutional bishop who had refused to abjure; at any rate, they continued to participate fully in the civil life of the community. A solemn Mass and *Te Deum* was organised on 20 Nivôse II (9 January 1794) in order to celebrate the recovery of Toulon, and civil assemblies continued to be announced from the pulpit as in the days of the *général*. When in Germinal 'la révolution sacerdotale'[17] finally caught up with the villagers, Flahec demanded to know what law had been enacted that actually disqualified him from saying Mass.

The church of Allan remained closed, however. Here Jacobinism accommodated the move towards the 'dechristianisation' of everyday life with

---

[15] Aulard (ed.), *Recueil des Actes du Comité de Salut Public*, IX, Dartigoeyte to CSP, Auch, 23 Frimaire II.
[16] A. C. de Villepreux, D2.   [17] The phrase belongs to Dartigoeyte; see note 15.

no obvious signs of tension, almost the reverse in fact. Courting couples contracted marriage as in years past, but now the ceremony took place in 'la salle de la Société populaire' with municipal officers presiding. More tellingly, perhaps, villagers did not hesitate to make use of the facilities for civil divorce put in place by the law of 20 September 1792. Again the club provided the forum and the municipality the conciliation tribunal. In fact many old taboos seem to have broken down for a time in the face of the secularising impulses of the Year Two. Over fifty years later the parish priest would recount how he had been asked to bless a number of these marriages, notably one contracted by Jean-Baptiste Magnet who had taken Elizabeth Galien, 'calviniste entêtée',[18] for his wife. At the priest's insistence the children of the marriage had been raised in the Catholic faith, but now, in 1849, their elderly and widowed mother was anxious to convert. Was Calvinism the only vector of 'dechristianisation' in Allan? It seems unlikely, for the *état-civil* of Villepreux also yields instances of civil marriage and divorce in 1795. On the other hand, the presence of Calvinists had helped to nurture an ecumenical climate within the village; and once both Calvinist and Catholic notables had discovered a new identity in Jacobinism few barriers to the permeation of secular culture remained. Jean-Joseph Sauvayre, one of the first priests to be appointed to Allan after the Concordat, faced an unenviable prospect in consequence. There was no presbytery and the church had been stripped bare. His first task on arrival was to make a wooden box so that the Holy Viaticum could be safely transported outside the village.

If the phenomenon that historians have dubbed Dechristianisation was intended to clear the way for a new, post-religion, landscape, then it failed. Anticlericalism did not unleash a cultural revolution in the village. Indeed, the intermittent absence of the clergy during the years after 1794 may have reinforced the mongrelisation of popular religious experience. Departing priests encouraged their flocks to remain united, thereby empowering the laity in a reversal of *ancien-régime* trends. When, after 1802, a religious settlement was finally achieved, the frontier between the sacred and the profane had to be renegotiated. These unanticipated consequences of the policy of repression only became apparent once the deputies of the Thermidorian Convention had resolved to curtail the experiment with a single constitutional church, however. On 3 Ventôse III (21 February 1795) they voted to bring the virulent anticlericalism of the previous eighteen months to an end and to adopt a policy of 'live and let live'. The Civil Constitution of the Clergy and the contentious oath that had buttressed it

---

[18] A. D. de la Drôme, 51V 66.

were repudiated to all intents and purposes, and a regime of religious freedom proclaimed. The formal separation of church and state was re-enacted in the Constitution of the Year Three (article 354), and it would remain the cornerstone of religious policy under both the Directory and the Consulate until Napoleon's Concordat with the Papacy was implemented in 1802.

This 'freedom' was a pretty fragile construct, however. Catholics (and for that matter Protestants) could practise whatever form of religious worship they pleased, but with no help from the Republic, whose officials were expected to devote their time and energy to elaboration of the civic landscape of festival and ceremony outlined in chapter 4. No external display of religious identity (processions, the ringing of bells, singing, etc.) was permitted, priests could not wear ecclesiastical garb in public and were enjoined to respect the *décadi* as the day of repose, and in many instances churches remained out of bounds. Some had been sold, others converted into storehouses or rendered uninhabitable. Moreover, those wishing to pray together were prevented from collectively purchasing, or renting, alternative buildings for the purpose. Also, many deputies had a real struggle to remain true to the decisions rather surprisingly agreed on 3 Ventôse. In an area where no real conviction existed, legislators found it hard to display courage in the face of political challenges whose resolution appeared to lie in a return to the policy of anticlericalism. A decree of 11 Prairial III (30 May 1795) enabled priests of whatever coloration to resume office in return for little more than a statement of submission to the laws of the Republic; would-be worshippers even regained (shared) access to their former churches. But as royalists prepared to dispute the forthcoming elections with a real likelihood of success in many parts of the country, the deputies took fright. Measures passed in Fructidor of the Year Three and Vendémiaire and Brumaire of the Year Four put the policy of religious conciliation into partial reverse. Deported priests who had returned from abroad once again faced the prospect of arrest, and the stealthy move towards the reinstatement of public worship that had been in progress since the summer was brought to a halt.

Lay activism in order to preserve the outward forms of religious life had probably been taking place in some of our parishes since Thermidor, but it only becomes detectable in the aftermath of the Separation. On 29 Germinal III (18 April 1795) a joiner, Jean-Louis Lepine, informed the municipality of Villepreux 'qu'il étoit dans l'intention d'exercer le culte catholique conjointement avec plusieurs citoyens qui doivent se rassembler chez lui à cet effet'.[19] Lepine was the front man for a group of five

---

[19] A. C. de Villepreux, D2.

male villagers comprising a near indigent stonecutter, a market gardener and two landless labourers. Emboldened by the law of 11 Prairial III, they returned on 1 Thermidor in order to request that 'le batiment servant d'église précédemment soit mise à leur disposition à l'effet d'y rassembler les citoyens de cette commune qui désirent exercer le culte catholique'.[20] Not until a week after this initiative, however, did a priest signal his willingness to make the requisite declaration of submission. News of the change of policy reached the villagers of Neuviller and Roville more swiftly, largely because *représentant-en-mission* Mazade was passing through Vézelise – the district *chef-lieu* – and made it the subject of a printed address on 10 Ventôse III (28 February 1795). The news was joyfully received and wilfully misinterpreted: the inhabitants of Roville, for example, burst into the church and rang the bells. In Roquelaure the parish church remained off limits thanks to the vigilance of the municipality. Instead the resumption of collective worship took place within a domestic setting: after a careful inspection carried out in Germinal IV (March–April 1796) the *agent municipal* was able to report that an outbuilding of the chateau had been used for occasional Masses, and that he had found people praying in an 'oratoire'[21] rigged up in the house of widow Serres. No priests and no bell ringing were in evidence, however. In fact it was not until the following year that a priest reappeared in order to reinstate church-based worship. Mazérat, who seems to have been the constitutional successor to Chapoteau, transferred his ministry from private houses and, no doubt, cowsheds to the church. He would be criticised by the mayor for his willingness to bless cattle as we have noted, and would never manage to secure the allegiances of more than a fraction of the villagers. Just as soon as the old (non-juring) *curé*, Jean-Frix Roux, returned from Spain two-thirds of the parish appear to have switched to his services instead.

In the Lozère and also in Brittany, by contrast, village populations seem rarely to have been separated from their priests for any length of time. *Représentant* Borie had threatened with death anyone who gave refuge to a refractory, but 'ex-priests' in full habit could be seen on the streets of Saint-Chély-d'Apcher and Mende even before Thermidor intervened. The municipality of Saint-Alban habitually left the parish church unlocked and scarcely bothered to enforce the legislation requiring ecclesiastics to make a token declaration of submission. In these highlands refractory priests came and went more or less as they pleased, until the Year Six at any rate. As for the constitutional church, it scarcely existed as a viable alternative. When

[20] *Ibid.*
[21] A. D. du Gers, L 650, Administation municipale, séance extraordinaire, 18 Germinal IV.

Guillaume Pie, one of the rare jurors of the neighbourhood, died in 1799 his corpse was dug up and dragged along the public highway with a rope around its neck. In Châtelaudren, as we have seen, *déprêtrisation* arrived late in the day and made only a fleeting impact. Both the *curé* Bourgneuf and the *vicaire* Flahec remained on hand, taking care to keep their residence certificates up to date. In this corner of the Republic pacification of the *chouannerie* drove forward the policy of religious reconciliation in any case. Flahec contrived to resume his ministry in July 1795 and it is likely that Le Corvaisier, the former *recteur*, could have done the same had he not been reluctant to return. On the other hand, the municipality and, subsequently, the Cantonal Administration doggedly refused to give up the church of Notre-Dame-du-Tertre which had become a military storehouse.

One casualty of the 'forgive and forget' policy practised during the spring and summer of 1795 was republican schooling. After many false starts the deputies had endorsed Lakanal's scheme for secular elementary schools on 27 Brumaire III (17 November 1794), but the legislation did not forbid the setting up of potentially rival private (i.e. religious) schools. Separation and the ending of institutionalised anticlericalism put the Republic's rather meagre educational provision in jeopardy, therefore. Quite a lot of village schools had survived the dislocation of the early years of the Revolution in the Meurthe department: about one-third of communes still funded a schoolmaster or mistress by one means or another, including Neuviller, Roville and Laneuveville. These schools rapidly emptied, however, as the implications of Separation sank home. As one schoolmaster whose pupils dwindled to three observed, 'la cause en est que depuis deux décades que l'on chante la messe au temple',[22] adding cynically that before the summer was out municipalities would be requiring masters to include the catechism in their teaching. In Neuviller where François François had just been appointed and negotiations were under way to fit out the ex-presbytery as a schoolhouse, secular instruction came close to collapse for want of takers. Attempts were made to retrieve this situation the following year (spurred on by the Daunou law of 3 Brumaire IV/25 October 1795), but it was an uphill struggle. Acknowledging the neglected state of public education in the canton, commissaire Jordy recorded that 'le principal motif étoit que les parents vouloient que leurs enfants furent instruits comme sous l'ancien régime'.[23] In Saint-Alban there had been no village schooling available for over four years, according to an entry in the minute book of the Cantonal

[22] See A. de Rohan-Chabot, *Les Ecoles de campagne en Lorraine au XVIII ͤ siècle* (Paris, 1967), p. 214.

[23] A. D. de Meurthe-et-Moselle, L 2943bis, 23 Ventôse IV.

Administration dated 18 July 1796. The young of Villepreux, by contrast, never lacked opportunities for instruction, thanks largely to the determinedly republican efforts of François Hersant. Indeed, he would be rapped over the knuckles in 1798 following a school inspection that uncovered 'quelques livres intitulés Catéchismes et rédigés d'après la Constitution de 1793'.[24] Yet even he had to accept that parents often wanted more than a diet of republican morality and good citizenship for their children. Three months after the Separation law he was providing instruction to fifty-six children aged between five and thirteen, but thirty-two others – including most of the sons of the better-off – had defected to classes being offered by a priest and also by a former monk.

The interruption of schooling in Saint-Alban was a by-product of the collapse of charitable provision after 1792 since the schoolmaster's keep had been met from endowment income. Revolutionary *bienfaisance*, unlike *ancien-régime* bequests and alms giving, would not be designed to meet educational needs. The decree of 18 August 1792 which abolished orders and confraternities also struck down charitable bodies that had been engaged in educational activities. Their property was to be sold off as *biens nationaux*, a move that was extended to all charitable institutions and foundations on 23 Messidor II (11 July 1794). The consequences of this policy are not easy to disentangle at the village level, but they may not have been as serious as is sometimes supposed. None of our villages was reliant on the resources of a large abbatial foundation. The closure of the Benedictine abbey (Domerie) of Aubrac on the confines of the Aveyron and the Lozère, for instance, would dramatically worsen the plight of the poor throughout the neighbourhood. However, the indigent of Saint-Alban did not number among the recipients of its largesse. The loss of the Charité des Pauvres of Villepreux would have been a grievous blow, to be sure, but a takeover by the municipality seems to have preserved its activities. While the endowments succumbed, as far as we can tell the Charité's landed assets survived pretty much intact. Right through the Revolution it continued to supply outdoor relief to the poor and would declare a healthy income of 1,673 *livres* 16 *centimes* in the year ending 21 Brumaire VI (11 November 1797). The lands of the *économat* (hospital) of Neuviller *were* sold off, however, while the village elders of Allan experienced increasing difficulty in collecting monies owing to the poor as previously noted.

The disposal of property belonging to charitable institutions was halted towards the end of 1796. In Neuviller the Cantonal Administration moved

---

[24] See E. Tambour, *Etudes sur la Révolution dans le département de Seine-et-Oise* (Paris, 1913), p. 149.

speedily to see what – if anything – could be retrieved from the wreckage and with some success it would seem. As for the revolutionaries' own secular experiments in the realm of public assistance, few traces survive. Funds for the relief of dependents of serving soldiers (*défenseurs de la patrie*) certainly materialised in Allan and also in Châtelaudren, and on a fairly regular basis. But the idea for a Grand Livre de la Bienfaisance Nationale which Barère had formulated on 22 Floréal II (11 May 1794) seems chiefly to have provided rhetorical rather than material comforts. Only in the instance of the hamlet of Rennemoulin do we have clear evidence of monies being paid out to qualifying country dwellers: twelve indigent inhabitants, including *veuve* Vaast, who had remonstrated about the burden of National Guard duty back in 1790, received 8 *livres* apiece.[25] If any of our elderly villagers were enrolled for pensions, the benefit would have been wiped out by inflation within two or three years. Most of the Convention's initiatives in the field of *bienfaisance* had been discontinued by 1798 in any case.

In espousing a policy of religious pacification during the spring of 1795, the deputies gambled that the refractory clergy, together with their adherents in the parishes, could be rallied to the institutions of the Republic. To many the gamble had never looked attractive; it simply gave back to refractories the freedom to subvert the regime and to work towards a Counter-Revolution. They pointed to the studied refusal of many clerics even to make the anodyne declaration of submission, and to the ingenuity of those seeking to reinstate Catholicism as the dominant and ostentatiously public form of worship. The success of neo-royalist candidates, often with refractory priests acting as muster-agents, in the elections of Germinal V (March 1797) gave impetus to the reaction and brought on the crisis. The *coup* of 18 Fructidor V (4 September 1797) has been likened to a second religious Terror, which is certainly an exaggeration.[26] Nevertheless, there can be no doubt that the consequential repression substantially compromised the policy of reconciliation, if only for a time. It also curtailed the free market in religious opinion and practice that had begun to take root in the parishes from 1795 onwards.

With the repeal of the deportation laws seemingly a certainty by the late summer of 1797, Gilles Le Corvaisier finally ventured back to Châtelaudren.

---

[25] A. Defresne, 'Les Registres municipaux de Rennemoulin jugés au point de vue économique', in *Recherche et publication des documents relatifs à la vie municipale de la Révolution: Comité départemental de Seine-et-Oise: bulletin de 1912–1913* (Versailles, 1913), pp. 53–4.

[26] See N. Aston, *Religion and Revolution in France, 1780–1804* (Basingstoke, 2000), p. 312, and S. Desan, *Reclaiming the Sacred: Lay Religion and Popular Politics in Revolutionary France* (Ithaca and London, 1990), pp. 11–12, 176.

But too late! Despite declaring his desire to reside peaceably 'en vertu de la loi du 7 Fructidor dernier',[27] it was pointed out to him that the law of 19 Fructidor V (5 September 1797) required his departure from the Republic within fifteen days. All the electoral operations of the Côtes-du-Nord had been annulled, like those of the Lozère (see p. 192). 'Depuis la publication de la loi du 19 Fructidor les prêtres réfractaires ont cessé d'officier dans les églises,' announced *commissaire du Directoire-Exécutif* Servière from Mende, but this was wishful thinking. The Cantonal Administration of Saint-Alban may have claimed (on 1 Vendémiaire VI/22 September 1797) that there were no refractories in the neighbourhood and that the church was kept under permanent lock and key, yet well-founded reports to the effect that refractory clergy had held a public Mass in the parish church on 15 Brumaire VI (5 November 1797) reached the ears of the authorities.[28] All members of the Administration save for Félix-Trophime Vincens were suspended. The *agent* and *adjoint* of Allan needed no prompting, by contrast. On receipt of news of the *coup* they nailed a proclamation giving details of the 'royalist conspiracy'[29] to the door of the ex-church and posted a sentry to keep an eye on it. A visit to the ex-presbytery followed – no doubt timed in order to give Charles Reynaud, the former *curé*, a chance to pack his bags and go. His servant reported, on 29 Vendémiaire VI (20 October 1797), that he was no longer at home. Since the narrative record of events in Neuviller and Roquelaure is incomplete it is not possible to explore the impact of the *coup* in these villages, but there is little reason to suppose any reluctance or foot dragging by the local authorities. In Villepreux, where differences of religion had rarely excited much debate, Jacques Chupin speedily presented himself in order to take the 'hatred' oath. This secular-minded Cordelier monk had signed the *cahier de doléances* in 1789, adhered to the Civil Constitution of the Clergy in 1791 and, following a period of obscurity, reappeared to declare his submission to the laws of the Republic in 1795. He was still providing Masses to a congregation in the village on the eve of the Concordat.

TOWARDS COMPROMISE

Priests in flight, villagers prevented from celebrating Christmas in their churches, renewed pressure to respect the *décadi*, regimented observance of civic festivals, Jacobin-style oaths and oratory; these were the most visible

[27] A. C. de Châtelaudren, Municipalité, délibérations, an II–an VII, 4 Vendémiaire VI.
[28] See Delon, *La Révolution en Lozère*, p. 751.
[29] A. C. d'Allan, RV 2, Délibérations communales, 3 Vendémiaire VI.

traits of the Year Six (1797–8). But they should not be allowed to deflect attention from the deeper shifts in attitude that were taking place. Since the spring of 1795 villagers had grown accustomed to having their own way in matters of religion as in so much else. For a few, lay empowerment meant dispensing with religion as traditionally revealed by the Catholic (or indeed the Protestant) church altogether; but for the majority it meant picking and choosing between celebrants, between liturgies and, we suspect, between devotional practices that had always formed a package hitherto. To judge from the evidence of the surveys commissioned by Napoleon Bonaparte on the eve of the Concordat, country dwellers no longer automatically accepted that the social discipline of regular church attendance also demanded the spiritual discipline of confession, absolution, communion, fasting and so on. As has been remarked, this attitude of partial detachment was particularly noticeable in the villages encircling Paris and Versailles.[30]

The so-called Terror of the Year Six did not arrest the overall trend, then. Villagers yielded in response to the renewal of persecutory pressures, as they had done repeatedly since 1792, but in the knowledge that the second Directory had no real desire to overturn the *modus vivendi* established in 1795. By Floréal VI (May 1798) public dancing on Sundays had resumed in the localities forming the canton of Marly: the authorities were informed, but they decided to look the other way. The villagers of Villepreux quietly drew the appropriate conclusion and resumed agricultural work on the *décadis*. After the elections of the Year Seven (March 1799) the regime visibly relaxed in any case. The 'hatred' oath was replaced with a more accommodating formula and, from that autumn, deportees began to trickle back to their villages. The old priest of Laneuveville, the hamlet on the plateau above Neuviller, returned on 1 Brumaire VIII (23 October 1799) and duly swore 'de m'opposer de tout mon pouvoir au rétablissement de la Royauté en France et à celui de toute espèce de tyrannie'.[31] His 'temple' as it was now called was in a ruinous state, like that of Neuviller. Nevertheless, his example was followed by several other refractories from the neighbourhood. But not Seignelay, whose sojourn abroad seems to have ended with his death.

The Directory was therefore in the process of returning to a policy of reconciliation when it was overthrown by General Bonaparte and his co-conspirators. To be sure, the *coup* of Brumaire sent out a signal to diaspora communities of clerics all over Europe that it was now safe to re-enter France; but, again, the initial running was made in rural parishes up and down the land. Faced with the energy of the laity and the freelance activities

<hr/>

[30] See note 11.   [31] A. D. de Meurthe-et-Moselle, L 2945.

of large numbers of frequently quarrelsome priests, the government found itself in danger of being pushed along by events. The oath requirement was diluted, yet again, to the point where it amounted to little more than a declaration of adhesion to the new constitution, and the prospect of the restitution of unsold church buildings was dangled enticingly. Catholics could now gather for church-based worship on Sundays, or for that matter on any other day excluding the *décadi*. Never had the free market in denominational, or even non-denominational, worship seemed more real. On Sundays the church-going population of Villepreux could choose between Mass celebrated by Jacques Chupin, the ex-Franciscan, at 7.00 am; Mass celebrated by Jacques Cochard, one-time priest, schoolmaster and *adjoint* of the commune, at 9.00 am; and Mass celebrated by Louis Teissier, ex-*curé* and refractory cleric, at 10.00 am. Moreover, for those still attached to the cults of the Revolution, the church metamorphosed into a 'temple' on the tenth day.

Matters were not nearly as straightforward from an administrative point of view, however. Furthermore it is likely that some of the Cantonal Administrations were taken aback by the turn of events. That of Marly clothed its dismay in a coded lament that the newly approved Constitution of the Year Eight was being used by certain individuals in order to 'troubler le bon ordre'.[32] The instruction to reopen churches on non-*décadi* days seems to have caused widespread grumbling throughout the Seine-et-Oise. In Saint-Alban, by contrast, it occasioned a huge sigh of collective relief. Yet tensions remained, if not with the laity then with the clergy. The administrators of the Gers sought clarification from the Minister of Police as to whether they should administer the oath of fidelity to the new constitution to priests. Fouché's reply revealed not only considerable confusion but a deep-seated fund of anticlericalism, fuelled, perhaps, by doubts as to the sustainability of Bonaparte's regime. Returned priests who had fallen foul of the deportation and detention legislation, whether in 1792, 1793 or 1797, *were* required to swear the oath. Those who had not, or who had refused, could not remain on the territory of the Republic, he advised the prefects on 1 Thermidor IX (20 July 1801). Pierre-Nicolas Dumaire, one-time constitutional incumbent of Roville, willingly subscribed to the new oath on 5 Pluviôse VIII (25 January 1800), but that was only to be expected. It was the haughty and triumphalist demeanour of the refractory clergy that alarmed ministers. Prefect Jerphanion of the Lozère tried to nudge the overwhelmingly hostile clergy of his department towards

[32] A. D. des Yvelines, 23 L2, 25 Nivôse VIII.

acceptance – with some success it seems. Although we cannot be certain, it is probable that the refractories who had resumed control of the parish of Saint-Alban did agree to compromise some time in Pluviôse.

The Breton departments caused Fouché and Portalis, the future Minister for Religious Affairs, the greatest anxiety, however, for many of the returning refractory clergy showed no desire for reconciliation either with their constitutional brethren or with the government. The old bishop of Tréguier whose pre-1789 diocese had embraced Châtelaudren resumed the offensive against the constitutional church with a catechism printed in London warning Catholics of the dangers of consorting with juring clerics. Bishop Jacob, his constitutional replacement, did his best to counter such propaganda, but tensions among the clergy escalated in Châtelaudren as elsewhere. Both Le Corvaisier and his non-juring curate de Keruzec had now returned, and they and their supporters appear to have secured control of Notre-Dame-du-Tertre. Ignoring the legislation banning external manifestations of religious worship, they started to ring the bells again, which prompted the local authorities to remove the bell clappers. This was in April and May of 1800, when everyone knew that the mandate of the Cantonal Administration was about to expire. The *décadi* cult in the village's other church was already on its last legs, although the services offered by the constitutional priest showed greater signs of life. Did Le Corvaisier and de Keruzec sign their adhesion to the Constitution of the Year Eight? We know that Le Corvaisier did, since he was offered preferment in a neighbouring parish once the Concordat had been ratified and made public.

Lay responses to the confusions and opportunities of these years are difficult to fathom in any detail. Certainly, we hear little of the *décadi* and its attendant ritual practices in any of our villages after Brumaire. Roville may have replanted its Liberty Tree (see p. 150), but Altars to the Fatherland and the elaborate calendar of civic festivals perfected during the Second Directory were rapidly consigned to oblivion. Fouché, the Minister of Police, grumbled to the prefect of the Côtes-du-Nord that the refractory clergy were monopolising churches and forcing the local authorities to use taverns for their *décadi* assemblies, but if this was true nobody at village level seemed to mind.[33] Was the constitutional church also being consigned to oblivion? Here we need to be cautious, and for two reasons. In Roquelaure, Villepreux and perhaps also in Allan, the climate of religious freedom – albeit uneasy – had allowed adherents of the constitutional church to regroup

[33] See R. Durand, *Le Département des Côtes-du-Nord sous le Consulat et l'Empire, 1800–1815: essai d'histoire administratif* (2 vols., Paris, 1926), I, p. 380.

and to fashion forms of religious practice that addressed their needs. The return of the refractories did not, of necessity, work a realignment, therefore. Neither Raynaud's Masses in Allan nor those of Teissier in Villepreux appear to have attracted majority support and, after a short while, they both gave up the attempt to coax their flocks back into the fold. The second reason for caution concerns the demeanour of the exiles as they flowed back into France during the winter of 1799–1800. Strong-minded priests breathing fire and brimstone against young couples who had contracted civil marriages, parents who had withdrawn their children from catechism classes, and adults who had participated in the sales of church property were not well equipped for the struggle to win back hearts and minds. As Napoleon would come to realise ahead of many of his councillors, the constitutional church was not simply a second-best church that could be discarded without penalty.

The compromise or Concordat that brought an end to the separation of church and state was formally signed on 27 Messidor IX (16 July 1801) and ratified both in Rome and in Paris by the end of that summer. The agreement was made public the following year – on 18 Germinal X (8 April 1802) – by which time Napoleon had done what he could to secure the position of the constitutional clergy and had added, without much consultation, restricting clauses known as the Organic Articles. Since the First Consul's remodelling of local government machinery (see p. 194) had reduced the powers of deliberation vested in municipal councils we do not know exactly how and when the news was announced in our villages, but it is likely that whatever bells remained were tolled in a chorus of approval. Indeed, the question of bells and of repairs to the fabric lay uppermost in many parishioners' minds. Caffarelli, the new bishop of Saint-Brieuc, was able to retrieve between two and three thousand serviceable bells that had been stockpiled in a depot in Rostrenen. As for church buildings, they were in a dilapidated, even ruinous state everywhere: that of Roquelaure had been closed by prefectoral order on grounds of safety, Neuviller's church was also highly dangerous, and the chapel in Rennemoulin teetered on the brink of collapse. Ornaments and sacred vessels were in short supply, too, as we have noted in the case of Allan; and the presbyteries had all been sold off, of course. Not until 1829 would the parishioners of Allan raise sufficient funds to build a replacement, whereas their counterparts in Villepreux and Roquelaure managed to buy back the original buildings in 1819 and 1823 respectively.

The Concordat provided no miracle cure to reunite shattered congregations; time was the only real healer in this area. It quickly realigned church and state, however, and on a basis that the Organic Articles made certain would be very much to the advantage of the latter. A demonstration can be found in the question of access to and control over space. Prior to 1789 there had been a fairly clear understanding that the interior of the church was sacred space. True, well-to-do or high-status members of the laity tried constantly to privatise a portion of that sacred space, either by maintaining family stalls in the nave or by securing the right to burial in church. But the secular power trod with care in this area. Intendants merely requested that incumbents make announcements from the pulpit, and when in March 1774 the seigneurial bailiff of the barony of Saint-Alban wished to inform the inhabitants that tendering for the collection of taxes was about to begin, he went to the church door 'as Mass was ending'.[34] Only in Châtelaudren did a significant blurring of the sacred and the profane take place; even so the *général* never met in the body of the church.

After 1789 this understanding broke down, unsurprisingly. The clergy had become salaried employees of the state and control of the church and of its space gradually slipped out of the hands of the churchwardens altogether. After 1792, in fact, the role of the *fabrique*, or church management committee, becomes difficult to separate from that of the municipality. Dechristianisation, or rather *déprêtrisation*, completed the process, not least because churches were stripped of the accumulated junk of centuries and added unequivocally to the village stock of public space. Although the sale of some church buildings threatened to put the process into reverse, so to speak, Napoleon used the opportunity afforded by the Concordat to consolidate the advances made by the secular power. The prefects expected government instructions and circulars to be communicated to the laity in the reopened churches as a matter of course. A number of bishops disapproved, notably Caffarelli, the spiritual superior of the *curé* of Châtelaudren. Some clergy such as Le Corvaisier were willing to play the role allotted to them; after all, they had been deeply involved in the secular life of their communities during the *ancien régime*. Others were less willing to act as agents of government and saw no reason why village mayors should be allowed to make announcements in church. The porch of the parish church might be construed as public space, they conceded, but not the interior.

A further illustration of the straitjacket within which the Napoleonic regime sought to confine the post-Concordat church can be found in the legislation relating to *fabriques*. As foreshadowed in the Organic Articles, these vestry councils were restored on 7 Thermidor XI (26 July 1803) with the promise that any unsold assets would be returned. But it was inherently

---

[34] A. D. de la Lozère, C 1247.

unlikely that any body possessing financial resources at the communal level would remain unsupervised, and so it transpired. Both the village mayor and the parish incumbent were to put forward candidates, and the prefect would make the final choice. In the Côtes-du-Nord, where bishop Caffarelli never hesitated to combat the encroachments of the secular power, this smacked of interference in the ecclesiastical domain and he instructed his clergy to set up an alternative system of *fabriques* over which officials of the state could have no control. The prefect was advised to avoid a confrontation on the issue with the result that a parallel provision seems to have come into being, although this cannot be verified in the case of Châtelaudren. A compromise was eventually reached, in 1810, but it still blurred responsibilities to the advantage of the secular power inasmuch as the mayor became an *ex officio* member of the *fabrique*.

If the Concordat put an end to the religious experimentation of the 1790s, it did not mark a return to the *status quo ante*. A huge turnover of institutions and personnel had taken place, resulting in a significant desacralisation of the countryside. Nationwide it is estimated that between a fifth and a quarter of the parish network was amputated between 1790 and 1815, little or any of which would be reconstituted in the course of the nineteenth century. Translated into local and human terms, this meant that the villagers of Rennemoulin had to choose whether to worship at Villepreux or Noisy from 1804. From 1806 their graveyard was closed as well. The parish of Crévéchamp three or four kilometres to the northwest of Neuviller also succumbed. The inhabitants were aghast to learn in 1811 that they would be expected to contribute towards the cost of repairs to the mother church 'étant annexé à Neuviller'.[35] There were winners as well as losers, however. The thinning of the Breton countryside, particularly in the Côtes-du-Nord where subdivisions of parishes known as *trèves* were commonplace, worked to the advantage of the more important ecclesiastical nuclei. Châtelaudren's churches benefited from an influx of rural worshippers once civil peace had been restored. By 1809 de Keruzec, the auxiliary priest or curate, was petitioning for a salary increase to reflect his additional workload. The inhabitants of Lajo and surrounding hamlets located in the most distant corner of the parish of Saint-Alban likewise profited. In 1803 they managed to persuade the Concordat bishop of Mende to grant them *succursale* status – effectively a parish of their own.

Some justification for these wrenching alterations to the fabric of religious life can be found in the shortage of personnel. Even though

---

[35] A. D. de Meurthe-et-Moselle, N[on] C[oté] G3 94/1/1, 10 May 1811.

new diocesan seminaries began to address the deficit from 1806, the secular clergy had recovered only 60 per cent of their late *ancien-régime* numerical strength by the end of the Empire. Auxiliary priests (*vicaires*) were in particularly short supply, and the Bourbons would return to a country whose truncated parish structure still could not guarantee access to a clergyman. In 1816 around 15 per cent of parishes had no regular incumbent. Although none of our villages went short of spiritual services for reasons beyond their control after 1802, it is clear that the Concordat bishops and their vicars-general possessed less freedom of manoeuvre than they would have liked. The new incumbent of Villepreux was a priest hailing from the diocese of Gap, Jacques Brochier; but clerical recruitment had been faltering in this region for decades. Teissier himself had originally come from Provence. In Allan and Roquelaure, which were probably the most detached parishes after Villepreux, outsiders also had to be brought in. Jean-Frix Roux, the old *curé* of Roquelaure, had indeed returned (from Spain), but was soon called to Auch in order to become a vicar-general. Mazérat and the other constitutional priests who had provided intermittent services in and around the village scarcely proved acceptable – at least to the bishop. Instead it fell to an outsider to reconcile the fragmented congregation, a task that he appears to have achieved by 1807. Neither Raynaud nor his constitutional successor was appointed to the *succursale* of Allan, and reading between the lines it seems that the new bishop of Valence had difficulty finding *any* priest willing to take on the task of restoring orthodox forms of Catholic worship in this village. Separate arrangements had been made for the small Calvinist community, of course, including their own place of worship. One of the many problems facing the eventual incumbent of Allan was the dispersion of the population outside the *castrum*, which made the purchase of a horse an unavoidable necessity.

Bonaparte had intended that the constitutional church form part of the new religious landscape with perhaps one-third of parishes being allocated to the jurors of 1791. But that never seemed likely to happen, and least of all in the diocese of Saint-Brieuc where Caffarelli made little attempt to conceal his preference for royalists and former refractories. Notwithstanding its well earned reputation as a bastion of the Republic, Châtelaudren's religious landscape on the morrow of the Consulate had a familiar feel, therefore. Le Corvaisier and de Keruzec were both in residence again and providing spiritual services. Death would separate Gilles Le Corvaisier from his old parish in 1804, but de Keruzec continued to work alongside his replacement – an ex-juror priest from nearby Plélo whose brother carried on a hat-making business in Châtelaudren. During the critical transition years between 1799 and 1804 Le Corvaisier's close kin ties with the local bourgeoisie and his earlier career as a reform-minded cleric helped to create a space for compromise. In none of our villages, as it turns out, was the *ancien-régime* incumbent reinstated, but this is not to imply that their successors were all drawn from the ranks of the constitutional church. They almost certainly were not, with the possible exception of Brochier of Villepreux. At Saint-Alban Béraud's former curate, Vital-Urbain Cros – a refractory who had gone into hiding during the Terror – took over the parish.

The revival of lay teaching orders, which had not been envisaged in the Concordat, raises the possibility that the provision of elementary instruction also recovered during the Empire. On the evidence of this study, however, it cannot be said that the change of regime made much difference. Village schools – where they existed – continued to function, but under the more or less declared authority of the parish priest. Where the female teaching orders had regrouped, as in Châtelaudren, the civil authorities were torn between the desire to regulate and the inclination to turn a blind eye in the knowledge that initiatives of this sort helped to relieve the burden on the public purse. The Imperial University made scarcely any impact at elementary level. However, there is some evidence that village elites were not quite so willing to scrap the experiments of the 1790s. In Lorraine a long tradition of providing basic schooling for all and sundry existed, with the result that villages such as Neuviller and Roville had never been without a schoolmaster. Moreover, the ethic of public and secular primary education had left a deeper imprint here than almost anywhere else. The village bigwigs of Neuviller therefore frowned at the prospect of ecclesiastical supervision of their schoolmaster. On the morrow of the Brumaire *coup* the Cantonal Administration appointed Maurice Jordy and Antoine Bertier to inspect the schools of the canton on a suspicion that attempts were being made to restrict the syllabus of instruction.

The choice of commissioners was not accidental, since both men had been deeply committed to all forms of civic expression throughout the 1790s. Bertier would take up the cudgels again at the time of the Restoration, when the spectre of clerical control began to cause serious alarm. An enthusiast for new ideas, particularly ideas with a liberal hue, he canvassed support in the two villages for the establishment of a 'mutual' school; that is to say an establishment dedicated to the Lancastrian system. He even persuaded Nicolas Pierron, Neuviller's long-serving schoolmaster, to travel to Metz in order to receive training in the monitorial method. The proposal assumed, however, that the municipal council of Neuviller would vote funds or, at the very least, supply construction timber from its communal woods. In 1818, after two occupations, repeated requisitions and three lost harvests in a row, the vine growers of the larger village were distinctly lukewarm. Bertier pressed ahead with his project notwithstanding, but Forbin-Janson, the new bishop of Nancy, was implacably opposed and the school would close its doors in 1827.

The grinding poverty of the post-Concordat Catholic church was felt acutely by the poor. The reconstituted *fabriques* tapped into the social pretensions of the well-to-do by resuming the practice of renting out pews and stalls; that of Neuviller even introduced fees for burials outside the usual grave line in 1809. Yet the monies generated were spent on re-equipping church buildings and not on charitable relief. Even so, rental income and the proceeds of collections fell far below the needs of the moment. The accounts of the *fabrique* of Allan for 1816 record an income of 30 *francs* and expenditure of 166 *francs* 50 *centimes*. The position improved marginally the following year with a declared income of 65 *francs*, but liabilities remained the same and the accumulated debt rose to 343 *francs*. In Saint-Alban the *fabrique* spent 540 *francs* during the second half of 1819 despite an income of only 69 *francs*. It is true that church buildings were often in a deplorable state. The *desservant* of Allan complained to his bishop in 1822 that rural parishes were functioning in conditions of total penury, particularly in cases where the churches had been commandeered by village Jacobins. 'Celle d'Alan,' he continued, 'a subi ces cruelles chances, elle a été entièrement démeublée; le peuple ayant partagé le système des chefs dont la commune a fourni un des principaux coryphées [Jean-Baptiste Biscarrat] n'a laissé que les pierres qui ont été encore tant de fois polluées par les chansons honteuses ou les actions les plus révoltantes suivi[e]s des discours les plus désorganisateurs.'[36]

Secular provision for the poor certainly had some impact, but only in the villages of Villepreux and Châtelaudren. The municipality of Villepreux managed to protect the physical property of the Charité des Pauvres, as we have seen, but in Châtelaudren the resources of the *fabrique* of Notre-Dame-du-Tertre had dwindled away as a result of sales and *rente* extinctions. By the time the policy of selling off the property of the parishes had been rescinded (7 Thermidor XI/26 July 1803), the total regular income of *all* the *fabriques* of the district of Saint-Brieuc only amounted to 486 *francs* per annum. By this date the churchwardens of Châtelaudren were reliant on the proceeds of door-to-door collections and pew rentals for the bulk of their income. The establishment of *octroi* toll booths around the village came to

---

[36] A. D. de la Drôme, 51V 66, Robert to Monseigneur l'Evêque, Allan, 2 July 1822.

the rescue, however. In 1804 the municipal council allocated 400 *francs* to the *bureau de bienfaisance* for the relief of poverty, and the following year 600 *francs*. By 1807, in fact, the *octroi* would turn out to be a real money-spinner, these subsidies (now 900 *francs*) having become routine. While all of the other villages were struggling to restore the fabric and to meet the running costs of the post-Concordat church, Châtelaudren could comfortably afford to increase the curate's stipend from 350 *francs* to 500 *francs* in 1809.

For all the material penury the Concordat had at least stabilised relations between the clergy and the laity, and between the church and the state. Napoleon's battles with the Holy See would not cease in 1802, of course, and as late as 1815 royalists would cause alarm in Châtelaudren by circulating rumours that the restored Empire planned to demolish all of the churches. In practice, however, the religious landscape of the village had taken on a settled outline by the end of the Consulate, and would retain that outline throughout the nineteenth century. Although many village churches still bore physical and visual reminders of the attempt to uproot religious practice in 1793 and 1794, the period of revolutionary experimentation had come to a close. Catholicism once again featured officially as the religion espoused by the great mass of the population. The rights of non-Catholics (Allan's Calvinists, for instance) were now vindicated, however, both in law and in practice, and (in theory at least) no one could be forced to contribute towards the costs of public worship. The material possessions of the old Gallican church had gone for ever, and so had the ecclesiastical tithe. A pragmatic and historic compromise had indeed been reached. Napoleon would acknowledge as much when he remarked that 'in religion I do not see the mystery of the incarnation, but the mystery of the social order'.[37]

Yet church and state had been bound together very tightly – perhaps too tightly – and in ways that ordinary villagers could not fail to notice. Parish priests were now public servants owing conspicuous loyalty to the regime. When the bureaucrats of the Ministry of Religious Affairs sought to introduce a new catechism or a feast day in honour of 'Saint Napoleon', they had little choice but to incline gracefully. The security of tenure that had enabled *abbé* Béraud to launch lawsuits against the bishop of Mende, among others, no longer existed as far as the great majority of the clergy were concerned. They were pawns of the bishops, who in turn were pawns of the prefects by and large. Awkward priests, or priests who failed to toe the line, did not remain long in their parishes. And toeing the line increasingly

[37] Quoted in G. Ellis, 'Religion according to Napoleon: The Limitations of Pragmatism', in N. Aston (ed.), *Religious Change in Europe, 1650–1914* (Oxford, 1997), p. 235.

meant sharing responsibility for a whole range of religious practices with the village mayor in a manner that would have been unthinkable prior to 1789. State power had advanced from the porch and the vestry into the nave of the church and into the belfry. On the other hand, bishops were no longer hindered by the vested interests of lay benefactors.

But what of the quantity – and quality – of religious experience after twenty-five years of civil upsets? If judged in terms of its physical presence, our villagers could be forgiven for concluding that organised religion had beaten a rapid retreat. By comparison with 1789, the countryside through which the Comte d'Artois travelled in March 1814 on his way to assert the claims of the Bourbons had been significantly emptied of religious institutions, be they abbeys and monasteries, chapels and oratories, wayside shrines and crosses, or bell towers. Even priests were thin on the ground in some localities, and they certainly did not enjoy the degree of respect that had been accorded to members of the First Estate at the end of the *ancien régime*. In 1806 Caffarelli, the bishop of Saint-Brieuc, reported that he had lost nearly 250 ordained clergy and trained only 25 replacements in the four years since the application of the Concordat. As late as 1818 the bishop of Valence was still struggling to overcome a shortfall of 236 priests across his diocese. Yet we must refrain from drawing simplistic conclusions from this largely irreversible process that had accomplished the secularisation of physical space. The damage sustained to the spiritual fabric of the communities we have studied *was* reparable by and large. Even the villagers of Allan, whose detachment, even disenchantment, on the morrow of the Concordat seems to have owed most to the ideological contamination of the Revolution, would rediscover the church-going habit. In 1849 *curé* Permingent described his parish as 'toujours animée de la foi la plus vive et la plus généreuse'.[38]

---

[38] A. D. de la Drôme, 51V 66, Permingent to Monseigneur l'Evêque de Valence, Allan, 10 January 1849.

CHAPTER 7

Land of liberty?

In 1750 Victor de Riquetti, Marquis de Mirabeau, purchased the seigneurie of Roquelaure from the Duc de Rohan-Chabot, attracted, so it was said, by the ducal title included in the purchase price. Be that as it may, the future 'ami des hommes' spent the next ten years prodding an unenthusiastic Gascon peasantry into the roles envisaged by the Physiocrats in their blueprint for agrarian reform. Nearly simultaneously, government ministers also turned their minds to the supposedly untapped potential of the soil. Voltaire noticed the sea change in conversations with his contemporaries: discourse on agricultural topics had replaced drama and theology. Everyone was familiar with the techniques of enlightened farming, he suggested mischievously, save for the farmers.[1] In the 1760s and early 1770s measures to encourage the ploughing up of wasteland (*défrichement*), to facilitate the subdivision and enclosure of common pastures and to relax controls over the grain trade flowed thick and fast. Bourbon ministers were acutely aware of concurrent developments in England and the north German lands, and not a little anxious at their own rather piecemeal progress in eroding rural 'ignorance'. Behind nearly every attempted agrarian reform lay fiscal imperatives which betrayed, in turn, a nagging preoccupation with Great Power rivalries. This anxiety – tinged with exasperation at the seemingly incorrigible risk aversion of ordinary country dwellers – provides a link between the royal intendants, revolutionary legislators and Napoleonic prefects.

The broad pattern of land use and ownership in each of the six villages has been described in chapter 1. It is now time to add to this information and to place it in a dynamic context. With the one notable exception of Neuviller, the physical environments in which our villagers spent their lives altered only gradually. Even in Neuviller, the reorganisation undertaken by

---

[1] See P. M. Jones, 'Agricultural Modernization and the French Revolution', *Journal of Historical Geography*, 16 (1990), 38.

Chaumont de La Galaizière in 1771–2 (see pp. 238–45) simply replaced one open-field landscape with another. An open-field landscape of strips and elongated fields would have been familiar to the villagers of Villepreux, too. Although ownership of the soil surface changed significantly in the course of the Revolution, as we shall see, the use to which the land was put, and the manner in which holdings were organised, changed scarcely at all. The Châtelaudrinais, by contrast, did not live in an agricultural landscape in any proximate sense. The arable occupied just nineteen hectares and could be expected to yield no more than 3 per cent of the villagers' annual cereal requirement.[2] When travelling beyond the confines of their diminutive parish they might have noticed that the open fields of neighbouring villages were increasingly dotted with enclosures to produce a semi-*bocage* landscape, but that is all. They would certainly have been aware that the tenanted farms and *convenants* were owned almost exclusively by resident noble families. Before 1789 the bourgeoisie of Châtelaudren showed little interest in owning land.

All changed towards the south, however. The villagers of Allan inhabited a visibly Mediterranean landscape of scrub pine and evergreen oak, dry and stony sheep pastures and patchwork fields divided by drainage ditches. Biennial rotation of the arable placed few demands on collective energies, not least because landowners could remove their fields from stubble grazing more or less at will. The arable and even the pastures were giving way to plantations of vines and also mulberry orchards in any case. Flock owners were forced to turn to the forests, instead, where the respective rights of the seigneur and the inhabitants remained ill defined. Forest and thin, boulder-strewn pastures also marked out the physical environment of the Margeride villages, of which Saint-Alban was a prime example. On the *limagne* soils adjacent to the village regular biennial crop rotation (rye/fallow) could be practised, but in the higher-altitude hamlets grain production relied heavily on slash-and-burn techniques (*écobuage*), that is to say a rotation of fields cut at irregular intervals from the surrounding heath and pasture. In this low-density human setting, access to land was not a major problem during the period under study. About one-third of the soil surface was given over to common pastures and forest. In the hamlet of Sainte-Eulalie, whose territory straddled the 1,400-metre contour, over 1,000 hectares were available for collective use.[3] The problem was rather one of soil fertility, a difficulty that villagers sought to overcome by inviting transhumant shepherds to

---

[2] A. D. des Côtes-d'Armor, 2E Dépôt 19, circular letter of the prefect of the Côtes-du-Nord to mayors, Port-Brieuc, 19 Thermidor VIII.
[3] See *La Margeride: la montagne, les hommes*, p. 108.

make use of their highland pastures in return for the precious animal dung deposited by their flocks. The inhabitants of Roquelaure possessed scarcely any common pasture, by contrast, and nearly all of the woodland belonged to the seigneur. Viewed from the vantage point of their hilltop village the lie of the land appeared open and ordered, but appearances were deceptive. Fields were grouped by *métairie* and bounded either by ditches or by hedges to produce a segmented if not strictly enclosed landscape. These *métairies* were geared to wheat production in a biennial rotation and each possessed its own access roads and paths and could therefore function with a large degree of independence from its neighbours. The modern topographical map of the commune records this agrarian history in faithful detail: at least fourteen such farms, containing between fifteen and forty hectares of arable apiece, can be identified.

We encounter the term *métairie* in Allan, in Saint-Alban and in the hinterland of Châtelaudren, where it was often employed in lease documents even though the transaction plainly refers to cash tenancy of fixed duration. But in Roquelaure it was no misnomer: *métairies* were sharecrop farms owned by non-resident landlords and put out to precarious tenure. They formed part and parcel of the *rentier* mentality and lifestyle that agricultural theorists construed as one of the main obstacles to reform in the countryside. In the future department of the Gers some 18,500 farms (between 80 and 85 per cent of the total) were held on this basis, and it is probably true to say that *métayage* was endemic throughout the southwest.[4] Not surprisingly, therefore, Mirabeau identified sharecropping as a prime target for his reforming zeal on taking possession of the duchy of Roquelaure. Unable to reside in Gascony for more than a few months at a time, he bombarded his agent with a steady stream of epistolary advice that included instalments of *L'Ami des hommes* fresh from the press. To judge from a fragment of this correspondence that has been published, Mirabeau set out both to reinstate the ethical basis of seigneurial authority in the neighbourhood and to exploit commercially the assets of an extensive seigneurial *réserve*. After some hard swallowing ('il seroit déshonorant pour moi de paroître agir si contradictoirement à mes principes'),[5] he instructed his officials to take responsibility for foundlings, but only if the parents made themselves publicly known. However, instructions were also issued to collect feudal

[4] See *Annuaire pour l'an XII contenant des notices pour la description et la statistique du département du Gers publié par ordre du préfet* (Auch, an XII), p. 176. Also *Plan détaillé de topographie, suivi de la topographie du département du Gers (par le citoyen Dralet)* (Paris, an IX), p. 272.
[5] See S. Daugé, 'Un Physiocrate, seigneur de Roquelaure', *Bulletin de la Société archéologique du Gers*, 1905, 202.

dues more diligently and to place the much degraded forest assets of the seigneurie under scientific management.

The croppers were his main bugbear, though, for they held the key to the economic future of the seigneurie through their control over the production of wheat. In acquiring the duchy, Mirabeau had acquired a *réserve* parcelled out into eighteen *métairies* (eight or nine of which were located on the territory of the parish of Roquelaure). With easy access to the flour mills of the Garonne and to lucrative markets (Canada, Martinique) across the ocean, wheat had become an eminently tradable commodity. But *métayage* – in the judgement of the Physiocrats at least – was structurally incapable of responding to these opportunities. Waste no tears on the plight of the sharecroppers, he admonished his agent, but rather read the fifth part of *L'Ami des hommes*: 'quand vous aurez lu cela et les autres instructions de détail que vous me demanderés, vous verrés que vous renverrés bien loin dans votre idée les malheureux métayers, la charrue à boeufs, la petite culture; et Dieu nous donnera peut-être la joye de fonder de bons gras laboureurs dans tous nos domaines'.[6] Did Mirabeau accomplish the tenurial transformation that he had in mind? We know that two of the *métairies* were switched to fixed rentals (expressed primarily in wheat) in 1754, but the majority survived unscathed. Mirabeau had no talent for practical matters, as he readily admitted, and in 1761 he sold the duchy on.

Nowhere else did physiocracy make even a fleeting impact. Its legacy is to be found rather in the harnessing of government support for private initiatives. In this respect the land clearance edicts introduced and perfected between 1764 and 1770 continued the work of Mirabeau and his disciples. By dangling the prospect of a fifteen-year exemption from the *taille* and the tithe, the monarchy hit on an eminently practical way of converting the nostrums of the reformers into action on the ground. None of the other stimuli applied by government to the workings of the rural economy produced even remotely comparable results in the years before 1789. In our southern villages even quite modest individuals scrambled to take advantage of this temporary relaxation of the fiscal regime. The switch to vine cultivation drove the process in Allan, whereas high grain prices and the chance to escape a punishing tithe impost provided more than adequate incentive in Roquelaure. The seigneur numbered among the most active clearers, and by 1789 there was very little wasteland left in the village. On the other hand, the extension of the fiscal net to the cleared land from the mid-1780s caused real resentment. At Roquelaure it stoked up a systemic

---

[6] *Ibid.*, p. 206.

resistance to the tithe that had been building since the proctors had hauled the community through the courts in 1781.

Land clearance succeeded because there were no losers. Every proprietor and resident villager, with the possible exception of the parish priest, had something to gain. Never again would a government measure to mobilise the resources of the soil enjoy such a fair wind, however. Enclosure, the break-up of the commons, the restriction of collective use-rights, strip consolidation and so forth, all divided villagers. But these issues would set villager against villager in complex and unpredictable ways, if only for the reason that rural landscapes differed, and so did the social forces in play within each locality. Ministers and their executive officers in the field also had to contend with a differential jurisprudence in matters relating to the exploitation of the land. As our case study of Neuviller and Roville will shortly demonstrate, Custom could not easily be overturned when endorsed by *parlementaires* imbued with a deep distrust of the motives and practices of reforming absolutism.

In Allan, as we have noted, few restraints could be brought to bear on owners of land who felt disinclined to share it with other members of the community, or neighbouring communities, once crops had been removed. Invoking the jurisprudence of the Parlement of Aix, the intendant of Provence asserted, in 1768, that a generalised 'right' of *vaine pâture* and *parcours* did not exist. And if the arable was not automatically subject to collective grazing, it can be taken as read that neither were vineyards or the meadows. Logically, therefore, proprietors were free to enclose their land as and when they pleased. His counterpart in Brittany agreed – not that it made much difference to the villagers of Châtelaudren. 'Dans aucune province,' he reported in 1769, 'la liberté de clore les héritages au gré du propriétaire n'a été plus autorisée et plus protégée. La Coutume générale du pays le permet expressément.'[7] The jurisprudence of the Parlement of Toulouse was altogether more pragmatic. Nevertheless, in localities such as Roquelaure, where the structure of land holding militated against the exercise of communal grazing, such practices were strongly discouraged. Writing in the Year Nine (1800–1) an official of the prefecture of the Gers asserted that 'jamais le droit de parcours ni celui de vaine pâture n'y ont été établis',[8] and the compilers of the Statistique Agricole of 1814 agreed: 'le parcours n'est point en usage. Chaque propriétaire demeure maître de sa propriété.'[9] In reality it is unlikely that matters were quite so clear cut.

---

[7] A. N., H1486, d'Agay, intendant, to Controller-General, Rennes, 10 April 1769.
[8] *Plan détaillé de topographie*, p. 130.   [9] *La Statistique agricole de 1814: Gers* (Paris, 1914), p. 272.

Gleaning was almost certainly tolerated in the village and no one could prevent rough grazing on roadside verges and along hedge boundaries. But the lack of commons and the inaccessibility of the (seigneurial) forests meant that there was no village flock. Owners of animals who were not at the same time tenants of *métairies* had to make do with whatever grazing they could find.

Yet in Saint-Alban, which was also subject to the jurisprudence of the Parlement of Toulouse, collective practices were long established and stoutly defended. In view of the lengthy growing cycle of highland rye (resulting in nearly simultaneous harvesting and replanting on *écobuage* plots), gleaning and stubble grazing tended to be rather truncated, but the *chef-lieu* village appears to have possessed two common herds (one for sheep and one for pigs and cattle) that were turned out each morning during the fine season. Each constituent village and hamlet of the canton did likewise; in fact the 'berger commun' remained a familiar feature of rural life in the mountains of the Lozère until well into the twentieth century. But conditions in Saint-Alban were exceptional, in the sense that individual and collective exploitation of the land could be pursued as largely separate activities owing to the availability of extensive common pastures and forests. Enclosure was simply not an issue, although the debate over conditions of access to the commons and the 'right' of larger stock owners to maintain a 'troupeau à part' would quicken under the impact of Revolutionary and Napoleonic legislation.

Enclosure became an issue when inserted into an open-field landscape whose *sine qua non* was collective discipline; that is to say when individual farmers decided that they could profitably dispense with the obligatory crop rotation upon which the majority depended for their wellbeing. In Villepreux the principal enclosed spaces were the chateaux gardens and parks, and the game warrens of the Royal Domain. Open-field enclosure was frowned upon and, as far as we can tell, the 'gros fermiers' whose leases accounted for nearly all of the village arable showed no inclination to close off their fields. Strips, even strips sown with fodder crops such as clover and lucerne, were marked with stone boundary posts. In a fertile and high-yield cereal landscape this was eminently sensible, but it also implies that the limits of customary practice were understood and generally respected. Significantly the village possessed no common flock, even though a census of stock enumerated 68 horses, 148 cows and 844 sheep in 1784. In all probability the bulk of the stock belonged to the 'gros fermiers' who had little need of *parcours* and *vaine pâture* outside their own holdings. In the absence of evidence of complaint or recrimination, it is likely that stubble grazing (and gleaning) by consent were practised. *Parcours* is another matter, for in June 1790 the municipal officers of the adjacent village of Les Clayes complained that the inhabitants of Villepreux were invading their forest, not to pasture stock but in order to collect dead wood. However, the date suggests that this inappropriately labelled activity may have been a recently discovered 'right' linked to the outbreak of the Revolution rather than a relic of customary practice. In any case, the main challenge to freehold property right in the eyes of the Villepreussiens was 'le régime arbitraire des chasses'.[10]

Only in the east could it be said that land enclosure was prohibited both formally and informally. And, by extension, that common rights enjoyed the protection of legal instruments, or what passed for legal instruments in the context of the *ancien régime*. Whether separately or in combination, judgements of the Parlement of Nancy and prescriptions of the Custom of the duchy of Lorraine forbad farmers from altering the cropping cycle and upheld as a 'right' stubble and fallow grazing and second haying in fields and meadows belonging to others, not to mention the practice of intercommoning. In Lorraine and the Barrois, therefore, the edifice of 'custom in common' could be presumed in the absence of local agreements to the contrary. The ministers' decision to inaugurate the next stage in their programme of agrarian reform with a frontal attack on 'routine' and 'ignorance' in the newly annexed province of Lorraine was not taken idly, then. The presence in Nancy of an able and determined general in the person of Antoine Chaumont de La Galaizière also weighed in the balance. If Lorraine villagers could be induced to abandon their agricultural 'prejudices', it suggested that progress throughout the rest of the country would not be slow in coming. La Galaizière *fils* had good reason to appreciate the shortcomings of open-field agriculture as practised in Lorraine. Stanislas I had granted his father, the chancellor, the seigneurie of Neuviller (see p. 64) – a territory of some 440 hectares that a verification of 1751 showed to be composed of about 2,000 individually owned parcels. By comparison the much larger territory of Villepreux was divided into a mere 754 land holdings in 1736. With the absorption of the adjacent hamlet of Roville into the Comté de Neuviller in 1754, La Galaizière *père* began to think seriously about reform, but the task of refashioning the landscape – the conclusion towards which agronomists in Lorraine were inescapably drawn – would fall to his son.

The Edict of Enclosure for the duchies of Lorraine and Bar was promulgated at the behest of La Galaizière *fils* in March 1767. It was accepted

---

[10] Thénard, *Bailliages de Versailles et de Meudon*, p. 91.

with reluctance and misgivings by the Parlement in Nancy on 11 June of the same year. Both parties acknowledged that it was likely to be resisted by the landless or semi-landless poor who relied on free grazing to maintain a few head of stock, a practice that otherwise would have been quite beyond their resources. Nevertheless, La Galaizière *fils* predicted that 'dans quatre ou cinq ans tous les héritages susceptibles de clôtures seront renfermés'.[11] This conviction was misplaced on at least three counts. For a start, it presupposed that a heavily divided landscape *could* be enclosed. On the evidence of his own holdings in and around Neuviller La Galaizère *fils* was beginning to grasp that the real source of agricultural 'backwardness' lay elsewhere. Second, it underestimated the strength of community feeling on the issue. In 1789 almost every village of the future canton of Neuviller would explicitly reject the Edict of Enclosure in its *cahier de doléances*. Finally, enclosure meant different things to different people. In the minds of La Galaizière *fils* and the officials of the Contrôle Général it meant an end to *vaine pâture* and *parcours*, but this was not necessarily the conclusion drawn by *parlementaires* in Nancy or by tens of thousands of Lorraine villagers. The *parlementaires*, indeed, would flatly refuse to register a concomitant edict that outlawed the 'droit de parcours'.

We cannot be certain when Antoine Chaumont de La Galaizière resolved to cut the Gordian knot and totally transform the agricultural territory of the villages which he controlled along the banks of the Moselle river. Radical surgery to cure the problem of property subdivision and dispersion had rarely been tried before, not least because it demanded surveying skills of a very high order. On the other hand, La Galaizière *fils* knew that he enjoyed the support of Bertin and other enthusiasts for agrarian reform grouped around the Contrôle Général, and he could be confident of getting his own way on the ground. The fearsome reputation of his father (see pp. 80–1) would see to that. In the early 1760s he tried to consolidate his own holdings within the territory of Neuviller by means of strip exchanges with his neighbours, and it is possible that the idea for a full-scale remodelling operation germinated at this point. Or perhaps a recognition of the futility of engineering change by such a piecemeal route was what drove him on. Be that as it may, the acceptance of the enclosure edict by the Parlement of Lorraine undoubtedly marked a turning-point. Thereafter events moved swiftly. In December 1768 his agents obtained the 'consent' of the inhabitants of Neuviller and Roville in general assemblies, and Joseph Mougeot – a talented surveyor from Nancy – was put in charge of the exercise. It was

[11] A.-J. Bourde, *Agronomie et agronomes en France au XVIIIe siècle* (3 vols., Paris, 1967), II, p. 1155.

also 'agreed' that the common pastures of each village would be partitioned in a concurrent operation. As the landscape was about to be redesigned, they would have to be re-sited in any case. Mougeot drew up two large-scale plans in order to demonstrate the feasibility of a strip consolidation which simultaneously furnished each landowner with a means of accessing his property without trespassing on that of his neighbours (see maps 9 and 10). La Galaizière's scheme therefore offered an escape route from compulsory crop rotation, and an incentive to enclose for those willing to take it. A standard strip width of 3 *toises de Lorraine* (8.58 metres) was laid down and the inhabitants undertook never to subdivide their holdings in the future.

All of this remained largely a paper exercise until the recognition of the new distribution of land holdings and *chemins de division* (wagon ways) was completed in December 1770, however. Since crops had already been sown, the villagers agreed (probably genuinely on this occasion) to harvest within their old limits and to compensate one another as necessary. The major work of ploughing out the old strips and redesignating the pastures was therefore suspended until the harvest of 1771 had been lifted. In the meantime various sales, purchases and exchanges took place as the reality of the new landscape began to dawn on all concerned. La Galaizière's officers had to intervene and buy out several individuals whose opposition might otherwise have jeopardised the operation, and squabbles arose over harvest compensation and ownership of field trees. Pierre Dieudonné, the *greffier* of the seigneurial court and future commander of the National Guard of Chaumont/Neuviller, emerged with his property concentrated into two blocks of 7.68 and 4.6 hectares, but he grumbled that he was being denied ownership of a large pear tree situated in the more substantial of the two fields. Institutional owners needed to be placated, too. The Tiercelins, a male religious order based in Bayon, possessed considerable holdings in Neuviller, Roville and surrounding villages, and they were nervous about costs. On the other hand, the reshaping of their holdings that could now be carried out amply demonstrated the potential of the operation. In 1751 the Tiercelins' farm at Neuviller comprised 140 parcels of arable plus some portions of meadow, a small quantity of vines and a hemp field. The plough-land was scattered across all three 'saisons', of necessity, and varied from strips no more than 3 metres wide and 328 metres long to elongated rect-angles 100 metres by 40 metres. Around 15 per cent of the plots contained 4 *hommées* (0.08 hectares) or less – scarcely room in which to manoeuvre a plough-team. Grossed up this holding represented about 33 hectares, which is more or less what the monks retained after 1771, but in eleven blocks.

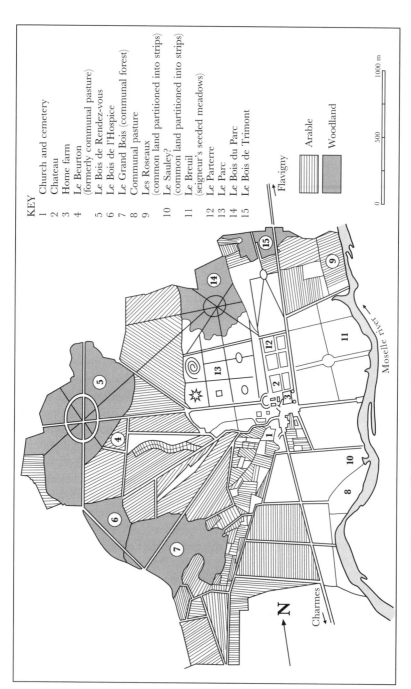

KEY

1 Church and cemetery
2 Chateau
3 Home farm
4 Le Beurton
   (formerly communal pasture)
5 Le Bois de Rendez-vous
6 Le Bois de l'Hospice
7 Le Grand Bois (communal forest)
8 Communal pasture
9 Les Roseaux
   (common land partitioned into strips)
10 Le Sauley?
   (common land partitioned into strips)
11 Le Breuil
   (seigneur's seeded meadows)
12 Le Parterre
13 Le Parc
14 Le Bois du Parc
15 Le Bois de Trimont

Arable

Woodland

0   500   1000 m

Moselle river

Flavigny

Charmes

N

Map 9. Neuviller [Chaumont]-sur-Moselle (after the strip consolidation of 1770–1)

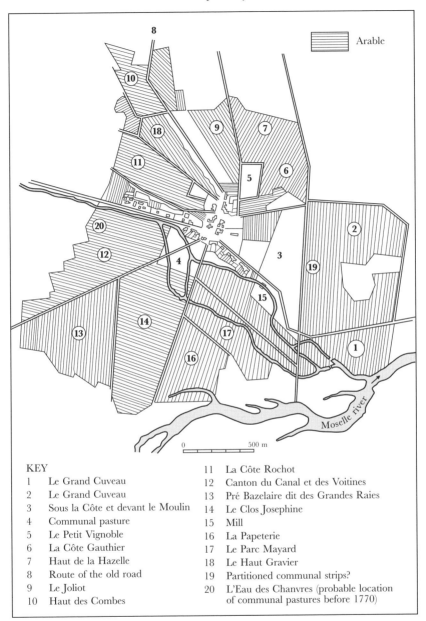

Arable

KEY
1 Le Grand Cuveau
2 Le Grand Cuveau
3 Sous la Côte et devant le Moulin
4 Communal pasture
5 Le Petit Vignoble
6 La Côte Gauthier
7 Haut de la Hazelle
8 Route of the old road
9 Le Joliot
10 Haut des Combes
11 La Côte Rochot
12 Canton du Canal et des Voitines
13 Pré Bazelaire dit des Grandes Raies
14 Le Clos Josephine
15 Mill
16 La Papeterie
17 Le Parc Mayard
18 Le Haut Gravier
19 Partitioned communal strips?
20 L'Eau des Chanvres (probable location of communal pastures before 1770)

Map 10. Roville-devant-Bayon (after the strip consolidation of 1770–1)

The recasting of the landscape of Neuviller and that of its contiguous hamlet Roville caused a 'sensation'[12] in Lorraine on La Galaizière's own admission, and it is worth pausing to consider what he was trying to achieve. Was he hoping to kick-start a land reorganisation programme throughout Lorraine? Was he acting under instruction from Ministers and Councillors-of-State in Paris? Was he simply pursuing the productivity option to its logical conclusion in the manner of Mirabeau and the Physiocrats? Or perhaps the landscaping exercise formed part and parcel of a utopian project to transform an unremarkable locality into a model seigneurial village and estate? None of these ambitions would be strictly incompatible, of course, and such evidence as we possess hints at overlapping motivations. Certainly La Galaizière *fils* appears to have had larger aims, for the Tiercelins of Bayon began to compute the probable cost to themselves of the exercise should it be extended to the neighbouring localities of Lorey and Saint-Remimont. Moreover, La Galaizière managed to persuade the Princesse de Craon to initiate a very similar operation in Laneuveville, the settlement on the plateau above Neuviller. It was carried through by the same surveyor between 1771 and 1775, but only after a number of setbacks. Whether La Galaizière *fils* was acting on instructions is unclear, but Ministers knew and approved of what he was doing and he was reimbursed his costs (a total of 32,641 *livres*). In return he despatched to Paris a huge and colourful map recording his achievements on the banks of the Moselle. Two smaller but still very impressive cadastral maps of Neuviller and Roville were drawn up by Mougeot to serve as title documents, and they were kept in a cupboard in the chateau. The one of Roville disappeared from view in the late nineteenth century, but the 'Carte Générale d'une Nouvelle Division et Distribution du ban de Neuviller' provides what are probably the best clues as to what La Galaizière was about. It reveals an operation to regroup and concentrate the seigneur's *réserve* at the northern end of the *ban* with the remainder of the village *finage* laid out rather as an extension of La Galaizière's park. As soon as it was safe to do so, the inhabitants repudiated what had been done in their names. They would even claim that Antoine Chaumont de La Galaizière exploited the remodelling exercise so as to discreetly and fraudulently extend his property holding in the village.

Be that as it may, the fact remains that others benefited, too, and some of them responded in textbook fashion by enclosing a portion of their new holdings. Pierre Dieudonné, for example, immediately enclosed the smaller of his two fields. But most owners of land made no move in this direction.

---

[12] A. N., H1486, de La Galaizière to Controller-General, Paris, 17 March 1771.

La Galaizière *fils* betrayed his own ambivalence towards the seigneurie as an economic enterprise by ordering thousands of ornamental Italian poplar saplings which he then proceeded to plant at intervals along the *chemins de division*. These trees sucked the moisture from the soil and soon started to cast a shadow over the crops: by 1792 most had been 'accidentally' knocked over by peasant cultivators' plough teams, or deliberately felled. Even Pierre Dieudonné's enclosure would get him into trouble. In 1794 his neighbour, widow Fresée, complained that the hedge had grown two feet beyond the marker stones and was drying out her arable.

As an exercise in practical agronomy the land reorganisation was flawed in another way, too. La Galaizière plainly supposed that his scheme would make practices such as *vaine pâture* unnecessary, resulting in redundancy for the common herd of both Neuviller and Roville. Yet the formal texts whereby he secured the consent of the population were insufficiently explicit on this score, and, in any case, the mass of landless and semi-landless inhabitants, not to mention some larger tenant farmers, begged to differ. Even the abandonment of compulsory crop rotations had required a special dispensation from the Royal Council in order to make it legal, and, as we have noted, the 'droit de parcours' also remained an obstacle. When the common pastures of Neuviller and Roville were divided up in 1771 La Galaizière took the precaution of spelling out that the beneficiaries would no longer be liable to *vaine pâture*, but he was forced to acknowledge that the plots remained subject to the *parcours* of stock belonging to neighbouring villages.

Had the land reorganisation operation been followed by systematic enclosure, the ambiguity over customary practices might have been speedily resolved. On the other hand, the cultural resistance to enclosure in Lorraine was considerable, and there were instances in both villages of (rather inadequate) enclosures being broken down by cattle and horses as the herdsman looked on. Larger tenant farmers adopted a paradoxical attitude in this respect. They made selective use of the freedom to enclose, while turning a blind eye to the depredations of their stock on the lands of others in the name of *vaine pâture*. In the autumn of 1792 Joseph Antoine, the tenant of the Tiercelins in Neuviller, allowed his farm servant to drive his stock into one of the enclosures belonging to Pierre Dieudonné. In his defence before the Justice of the Peace, Antoine retorted that the spot where his cattle had been grazing 'n'est ny clôs ny ruralle, et n'a été reconnus clôs en nulle manière'.[13] There is evidence, moreover, to indicate that the common herd,

---

[13] A. D. de Meurthe-et-Moselle, L 4194, 5 November 1792.

an institution chiefly serving the needs of the poor, survived in both local-ities. After a pause of several years, it was reconstituted in Roville around 1781 – probably as a weapon of war against La Galaizière *fils*, whose *triage* of the communal pastures had bred resentment. No longer intendant of Lorraine, La Galaizière ordered his seigneurial officers to prosecute the com-munity's herdsman. It made no sense to ban *vaine pâture* on the divided commons, he complained, whilst simultaneously allowing it to subsist in the reorganised arable territory of the village. The case went back and forth in the courts with the Parlement of Nancy providing succour to the inhabitants and the officials of the Contrôle Général in Paris rallying to the defence of their embattled *commissaire* in the provinces. *Force majeure* decided the outcome, in the shape of the Revolution and the sequestration of the La Galaizière family properties. In 1793 the inhabitants of Roville still had their 'troupeau commun' and were well on the way to recovering the *triage* portion of their communal pastures as well.

If *vaine pâture* and the common herd survived in Roville (the case of Neuviller is less clear cut), what final verdict can be offered as to the pro-ductivity 'pay off' of the exercise carried out between 1768 and 1771? For Antoine Chaumont de La Galaizière personally, the operation proved bruis-ing, possibly disillusioning, but not unrewarding. He gave up none of his seigneurial prerogatives, and yet emerged with a largely consolidated block of vines, arable and forest, augmented by approximately thirteen hectares deriving from the exercise of his right of *triage* over the commons. The vil-lagers suspected him of other forms of profiteering, of course. They would point out that his 'generosity' in allowing the *chemins de division* to be taken from his land holding overlooked the fact that the areas previously occupied by the old pathways had disappeared without trace. The parish priest also had good reason to be satisfied with the compact post-1771 align-ment of the lands of the *cure*. However, the benefit to individual farmers, whether owner-exploiters or tenants, is harder to determine. Phil Hoffman has pointed out that the Tiercelins of Bayon were able to lease out their Neuviller farm for 620 *livres de Lorraine* in 1788 compared with 400 *livres de Lorraine* in 1765 – a real rent increase of 32 per cent.[14] This provides a useful clue as to the scale of the potential 'pay off'; but in order to be certain we need to know whether the Tiercelins' farm remained geared to cereal production, or whether the tenant exploited the post-1771 freedom of manoeuvre to move into viticulture. We also need more lease series for

---

[14] P. T. Hoffman, *Growth in a Traditional Society: The French Countryside, 1450–1815* (Princeton, N.J., 1996), pp. 29–33 and note 27.

comparison. Contemporaries, or near contemporaries, would claim that the operation succeeded as an economic exercise, but not as well as it might have done had *vaine pâture* and *parcours* been repudiated from the outset. Antoine Bertier, La Galaizière's agronomic heir-apparent in Roville, battled against 'custom' throughout the 1800s and 1810s, and *vaine pâture* was still being practised in Neuviller at the end of the nineteenth century.

FROM FREEDOM TO *LIBERTÉ*

It will be apparent, then, that there was no such thing as a consensual language of 'rights' and 'freedoms' in the agrarian sphere at the end of the *ancien régime*. Far from clarifying the issues, the interventionism of Physiocrat-influenced seigneurs and of ministerial devotees of streamlined administrative monarchy had succeeded mainly in aggravating misunderstandings at the village level. Would the revolutionaries fare any better? The problem they faced in the early 1790s was that the agendas had not really changed. Powerful voices continued to call for the liberalisation of the rural economy, whereas the evidence of the *cahiers de doléances* tended to point in a different, even an opposite, direction. In Lorraine, for example, 43 per cent of the parish *cahiers* mentioned the Edict of Enclosure, in nearly every case to condemn it.[15] The revolutionaries' own attempts to find a solution lacked conviction, therefore. The law of 28 September–6 October 1791 was the nearest they ever came to a 'rural code' applicable to the whole of the country, and it endorsed the substance of peasant 'customary law' while simultaneously proclaiming that owners were at liberty to enclose their land if they so wished. But which of these 'freedoms' carried priority? The freedom to withdraw land from *vaine pâture*, the freedom to keep a flock on the pastures independently of the 'troupeau commun', or the freedom to drive one's beasts into fields and meadows belonging to others?

At least villagers were clear in their own minds, and until 1795, or thereabouts, it was the views of the numerical majority that tended to prevail. Within a matter of days of its election the new municipality of Saint-Alban reaffirmed its determination to remain loyal to the practice of the single flock or herd – presumably in the face of individuals who were planning to buy in stock and put them out to pasture on the extensive commons as soon as the grass began to grow. Right through the Revolution they defended what were termed the 'anciens usages'[16] albeit in the face of some resistance.

---

[15] M. Lacoste, 'La Crise agricole dans le département de la Meurthe à la fin de l'Ancien Régime et au début de la Révolution' (dissertation, University of Paris, 1951), pp. 480–7.

[16] A. D. de la Lozère, L 418, 10 Germinal IV.

In March 1796 the annual ritual of signing up the village herdsman was
re-enacted ('attendu que dans la présente commune le parcours et vaine
pâture se trouve en ûsage depuis un Tems immémorial'),[17] but with an
oblique concession. Anyone who wished to make alternative arrangements
could do so, on condition that he or she continued to contribute to the
maintenance costs of the common herdsman. This was the thin end of
the wedge of *liberté*: a few months later widow Chauvet was cited before
the Justice of the Peace for having refused 'de prendre à son tour le vacher
commun'.[18] The villagers of the Moselle valley scrutinised the messages
coming out of Paris on the subject of *troupeau à part*, too. In Lorraine
and the Trois Evêchés *troupeau à part* was a seigneurial privilege that had
been vigorously exploited prior to 1789. The inhabitants of Laneuveville
complained in April 1789 that Maréchal Beauvau's steward had swamped
the pastures with a flock of sheep some 200 strong. Seigneurial privilege
or no, the National Assembly refused to trade one man's *liberté* against
another's in a knee-jerk reaction, however. On 9 May 1790 it announced
that it was reserving its position – to the satisfaction of the *fermiers* and
the dismay of ordinary country dwellers across the region. That first year
of Revolution brought all the latent agrarian resentments to the surface. In
Allan and Roquelaure villagers challenged the 'foins et pailles' rule that reg-
ulated ownership of stock by those who did not also own property. Still in
a state of euphoria following the victory against their seigneur in the courts
of Aix a fortnight earlier (see p. 99), the consuls of Allan announced that
anyone who pleased might henceforth keep a goat. As for the transhumant
flocks heading for the Alpine pastures, their shepherds would now have to
pay if they wished to make use of the community's scrubland grazing.

It would be a mistake to suppose that villagers were interested only in
shoring up the edifice of collective rights, however. Just as the powerful
felt no compunction about profiteering from *vaine pâture* whilst closing
off their own holdings if circumstances dictated, the poor and dispossessed
made no secret of their desire to acquire individualised access to land whilst
retaining a customary and collectivist vision of the landscape in general.
Among the most persistent criticisms of La Galaizière's remodelling operation in Neuviller was the charge that villagers could no longer recognise and
relate to their own landscape. Unfamiliar subdivisions called 'cantons' or
'quartiers' had replaced the old three-field configuration, and it would take
many years before the nomenclature of these cantons became meaningful.
The removal (and relabelling) of the much depleted common pastures to

[17] *Ibid.*   [18] *Ibid.*, 10 Thermidor IV.

another part of the *finage* caused particular upset. The old location – known as 'le Beurton' – had been retained in part by La Galaizière as his *triage* portion and redesignated 'la Grande Raye'. Resentment over the *triage* mingled with resentment over the disfiguration, and in December 1792 it was reported to the Justice of the Peace that 172 poplars, 14 elms and one willow tree had been discovered in the canton of 'la Grande Raye' (alias 'le Beurton'), felled by persons unknown. Such shifts in the familiar, even the physical, would not be confined to Neuviller, though.

In all six of our core villages, the decisions taken by the revolutionary legislators to sell off large quantities of corporately owned property (ecclesiastical, charitable, *émigré*, etc.) induced a quickening in the land market. These decisions would also nurture the property-owning ambition of the rural poor, particularly during the climactic years of the Revolution when economic and political imperatives combined to produce a widespread expectation of land reform. In the first instance, however, we need to reach a judgement about the quantities of property coming onto the market in 1791 and years beyond. Modern research has tended to play down the significance of the sales of *biens nationaux*. Unusual were the localities in which even 10 per cent of the soil surface changed hands as a direct consequence of government interventionism in the land market between 1791 and 1814. On current best estimates, the taking into public ownership of ecclesiastical property affected between 5 and 6 per cent of the soil surface on average, and the seizure of lands belonging to *émigrés* and outlaws a further 3 or 4 per cent.[19] While much depended on the incidence of church property even more depended on chance, or perhaps we should say on political fortune. For instance, only in Villepreux and Neuviller were there ecclesiastical institutions in possession of significant landed assets. When the lands of the *cure* of Villepreux, those of the *fabrique*, and the priory's farm of Les Bordes were put up for sale in 1796, roughly 8 per cent of the village arable changed hands, not to mention nine dwelling-houses. In Neuviller, by contrast, this figure can be doubled. Elsewhere, however, little more than remnants (Châtelaudren 3 per cent, Roquelaure 1 per cent) became available for purchase.

Chance entered the picture because the major landowners in each village were nobles or, in the case of Villepreux, the Civil List. Noble property was seized by the state only where it could be shown that the legal owner had emigrated, or was subject to the penalty of confiscation following a death

---

[19] See B. Bodinier, 'La Vente des biens nationaux: essai de synthèse', *Annales historiques de la Révolution française*, 315 (1999), 7–14; also G. Béaur and P. Minard, *Atlas de la Révolution française*, X: *Economie* (Paris, 1997), pp. 11, 42–5.

sentence ordered by the Revolutionary Tribunal. Nobles, unlike the clergy, possessed considerable room for manoeuvre, then, and they made the most of the fact. Madame Lériget de La Faye, the ex-seigneur of Allan, owned six substantial tenanted farms in the agricultural plain below the village, as we have noted. All attempts by the local Jacobin elite to get their hands on this bounty failed. Although Lériget was a ward of court, she remained domiciled in the Republic (under the close supervision of her guardians and heirs no doubt). The presumed emigration of her husband provided insufficient grounds for confiscation since their possessions had always been held legally separate. The 'Jacobins' of Allan had to make do with eighteen hectares of arable and vines (0.62 per cent of the territory) emanating from a deported priest; but at least they managed to deter other bidders and secured nearly all of this property when it was sent for auction. The disreputable and quarrelsome Molette-de-Morangiès brothers of Saint-Alban also took good care not to emigrate, or to become identifiably involved in any of the royalist conspiracies punctuating political life in the Lozère during the 1790s. Although an attempt was made to declare the older sibling, Jean-François-Charles, an *émigré*, the District authorities could not be persuaded to advance beyond the stage of sequestration in view of the abundant evidence of prolonged residence. The family's possessions were mortgaged to the hilt in any case, and the local bourgeoisie had to make do with the slender pickings of the *cure* and various ecclesiastical foundations.

Proof of residence also stymied any prospect of a substantial change in the patterns of land holding in Roquelaure. A *parlementaire* noble from Toulouse, Pierre-Emmanuel de Reversac de Celès de Marsac, had acquired the seigneurie in 1781. Its resources, as we know, took the form of ground rents for the most part. With at least eight *métairies* and dozens of scattered plots of arable and vines, de Marsac appears to have owned about a quarter of the soil surface of the parish. The question of residence therefore took on huge significance; and no doubt the ex-seigneur felt some considerable relief when the municipality of Toulouse issued him with a signed attestation on 7 January 1792. However, political 'sins' dating from 1789 were about to catch up with him, for in the spring of 1794 the *parlementaires* of Toulouse were collectively indicted for having uttered 'treasonous' protests against the will of the National Assembly. Transferred to Paris, de Marsac would expire on the guillotine a few months later – his property forfeit. Yet for reasons that are unclear the lands were never put up for sale, although the Nation proceeded to dispose of the contents of the two chateaux of Roquelaure and Le Rieutort the following year. In all probability legal title to the real estate of the former seigneurie had been passed over to his wife and son.

As a result the sales of *biens nationaux* in Roquelaure were confined to ecclesiastical property of no great consequence, plus a meadow belonging to the Marquis d'Astorg whose principal land holding lay in a neighbouring commune. Prosper Celès de Marsac and his widowed mother still owned around 19 per cent of the village territory in 1823.[20]

Only in the cases of Neuviller and Villepreux is there substantial evidence to indicate that the sales of *biens nationaux* made a difference. The manoeuvres of the Chaumont de La Galaizière family failed to prevent the confiscation of their holdings in Lorraine. Everything they owned, whether in Neuviller and Roville, or Bayon, Crévéchamp and Mangonville, was eventually put up for sale. In addition the substantial assets of the Tiercelins of Bayon, the priory of Flavigny and other ecclesiastical institutions were offered on the market. The immediate beneficiary in Roville was Antoine Bertier – an outsider from Nancy who was able to acquire the ex-seigneur's holding more or less intact. He would build it into a 190-hectare farm and lay the foundations that turned Roville into a site of agricultural innovation in the nineteenth century. In Neuviller, the larger village, the transition was more prolonged and confused. Since the 1770–1 land reorganisation had left La Galaizière *fils* in possession of 1,190 *jours* (238 hectares) and ecclesiastical bodies of another 364 *jours* 9 *hommées* (73 hectares), we can determine with a fair degree of confidence that at least two-thirds of the territory of the village (including woodland) must have changed hands. But the purchasers were no more men of the village than was Bertier in Roville. The home farm (around sixty-five hectares), whose buildings and courtyard are still visible below the chateau, was sold to Joseph Beutz, a wealthy innkeeper and trader from Vézelise, for 2,010,000 *livres*. Local inhabitants did compete for the vines and some of the more easily dismembered strips of arable, but without much success. The chateau, park and ex-seigneurial forest would eventually fall to Maurice Jordy who was not a local either, although he would make his home in the village.

The inhabitants of Villepreux and the adjacent hamlet of Rennemoulin likewise witnessed a significant turnover in the composition of the possessing class as a result of the sales of national property. Until 1794, moreover, it appeared that they would play the role of passive bystanders in common with their counterparts in Neuviller and Roville. The critical factor in the land ownership equation in these localities, of course, was the confiscation and sale of the Civil List farms. When their acreage is added to the ecclesiastical property coming onto the market, a simple calculation shows

[20] A. D. du Gers, 3P 1386.

that about 58 per cent of the surface of the parish of Villepreux changed hands, and 36 per cent of that of Rennemoulin.[21] Neither parish contained any *émigré* possessions, although the denunciation and subsequent execution of Henri-Anne Mecquenem d'Artaize, proprietor of the Gondi chateau in Villepreux, would normally have been followed by seizure. As in Roquelaure, the widow managed to preserve both the chateau and the thirty-seven hectares of land attached to it. There was no *laboureur* class in Villepreux, as we have noted, and all six of the big tenanted farms that came onto the market were knocked down to wealthy bourgeois hailing either from Paris or from Versailles. The resident 'gros fermiers' did not bid for them. Jean-Germain Prissette, the *agent municipal* and a fixture in most of the power combinations of the revolutionary decade, managed nearly to double his possessions with a judicious purchase of four hectares of church land, and one or two local traders made purchases of a similar nature. But the rank and file of Villepreux (artisans, agricultural day labourers) lacked the means to buy at auction in keeping with the proletarianised populations of most of the other villages of the district. As we shall see, they would look to Paris and Versailles for a political solution.

Much land changed hands in Neuviller and Villepreux (not to mention Roville and Rennemoulin), then. Paradoxically, though, little else changed. The fundamental patterning of the landscape remained intact in both villages, as did the dominant characteristics of the rural economy. The new owners continued old tenurial practices in Villepreux, allowing the trajectory of large-scale cereal farming to continue pretty much undisturbed. Their farms did not get any bigger – engrossment pressures had eased well before the onset of the Revolution in any case – but they did not get any smaller either. In Neuviller, the likes of Jordy and Bertier ensured that the dislocation caused by the dispersal of the holdings of Chaumont de La Galaizière would be a purely temporary phenomenon. Both men proceeded patiently to buy up the properties that had eluded them in the early 1790s. With the acquisition of the chateau, park and ex-seigneurial woodland of Neuviller in 1802 Jordy found himself in control of about one-half of the territory of the commune – not far short of Antoine Chaumont de La Galaizière's presence in the village on the eve of the Revolution.

FROM *LIBERTÉ* TO *ÉGALITÉ*

Most villagers were not at liberty to buy land at auction, as we have said, and from the summer of 1792 legislators began to discuss redistributive measures

---

[21] A. D. des Yvelines, 2 Q55.

that would not depend for their operation on the laws of the marketplace. The timing was no accident: harnessing the masses to the Revolution was a matter of urgent priority as France terminated the experiment with constitutional monarchy and prepared for all-out war against her neighbours. The debates and policy decisions of these years help us, therefore, to uncover the thoughts that were uppermost in country dwellers' minds. They serve to remind us that an unassuaged hunger for land – not simply access to the land of others – had become one of the most powerful driving forces of the rural Revolution. The Jacobin mentality of 'fair shares for all'[22] fed upon this preoccupation. It presupposed, at the very least, that consideration be given to the feasibility of selling off *biens nationaux* in small and financially affordable parcels, and that the long-running debate about how best to extract value from the commons be settled on humanitarian rather than physiocratic terms; that is to say on the basis of subdivision into equal portions. But more far-reaching proposals were tabled for discussion, too, such as lease reform, limits on farm size and mechanisms for endowing the rural poor with land.

Lease reform was ardently supported by the sharecroppers of the Gers, those of Roquelaure included. However, the deputies showed themselves to be reluctant to intervene in matters of private contract unless there was a suspicion of seigneurial duress. The substance of cropper petitions mostly went unanswered, in consequence, although palliatives were offered on the issue of the tithe. In the hinterland of Châtelaudren, however, noble control of the soil surface was exercised through the institution of *domaine congéable* for the most part. *Domaniers*, like sharecroppers, lived in permanent fear of expulsion even though the terms of the contract gave them possession of the 'édifices et superficies' of their *convenants*. Yet since they were usually in debt to the landlord, part-ownership provided precious little protection in reality. The seigneurial character of such a mode of tenure seemed undeniable to the many thousands of *domaniers* who petitioned the National Assembly for redress in 1790 and 1791, but the deputies initially responded with a decree prescribing reform rather than abolition. Within days of the Paris insurrection of 1792 against the king the legislative pendulum swung in favour of the *domaniers*, however. They were granted full ownership of the soil surface of the holdings that they occupied. None of these changes directly affected the ordinary inhabitants of Châtelaudren, of course, although the victory of the *domaniers* caused the supply of *biens nationaux* to dry up. Since emigrant nobles had lost the legal title to large tracts of land in the parishes of Plélo, Boqueho and

---

[22] See J.-P. Gross, *Fair Shares for All: Jacobin Egalitarianism in Practice* (Cambridge, 1997).

elsewhere, these farms could no longer be put up for sale by the Nation. Not until 1797 when the reformed version of *domaine congéable* was reinstated could the sales of *biens nationaux* resume in earnest. It was at this point that Jean-Marie Suant, François Artur and Joseph Prodhomme, all men who had made their fortunes out of Châtelaudren's passing trade, decided to invest in farmland.

In none of the other villages was lease reform a major issue. The poor of Villepreux attributed their woes to a lack of employment and a lack of land – as well they might. The 'gros fermiers', having monopolised the productive surface of the village, were now in a position to exert a stranglehold over the supply of foodstuffs. It was certainly true that several of the Royal Domain farms had grown significantly in size: that of Le Trou Moreau had expanded from 88 to 154 hectares between 1719 and 1778, whereas Les Grand' Maisons had increased from 74 to 108 hectares over a similar period.[23] Public anger at these overmighty tenants broke loose in the autumn of 1793 when a grain census in the village disclosed that they were holding large quantities of unthreshed wheat in their barns. Not only were they failing to stock the markets, they were failing also in their duty to provide (threshing) work for underemployed Villepreussiens. One of the 'gros fermiers' was rounded up for detention under the Law of Suspects, and the others hastened to take on labour and to practise ostentatious obedience to the law for the remainder of the Year Two (1793–4). The sharp escalation in class tensions consequent upon the 'second' Revolution of the summer of 1792 also focused attention on the behaviour of the big tenant farmers of Neuviller. A new municipality had been elected to office and under the guidance of its *procureur* Joseph Cardot – a veteran of the 1790 struggle against the puppet municipality installed by the *curé* – Joseph Antoine, the tenant of the Tiercelins, and Benoît Gérard, tenant of the twenty-eight-hectare holding belonging to the *économat* or hospital, became targets. Their cattle and horses were repeatedly impounded on the specious pretext that they had infringed community grazing practices. Clearly, in the distorting atmosphere of the Year Two, it was acceptable for some citizens to make use of *vaine pâture*, but not others.

Endowing the deserving poor with land was no easy task, and since the poor were all too often the elderly, the infirm and the widowed, the task would become confused with the revolutionaries' charitable designs. The partitioning of communal pastures had long been touted as a solution to

---

[23] See O. Grandmottet, 'Histoire rurale de la seigneurie de Villepreux au XVIIIe siècle' (dissertation, Ecole des Chartes, 1951), pp. 23, 44 and *passim*.

rural poverty, and one that was relatively cost free in the legal sense. The same applied to *biens nationaux*. Until such time as their final destination had been determined, they existed in a kind of legal and administrative limbo. Perhaps the poor could be endowed with plots or allotments carved from *émigré* estates both as a gesture towards self-sufficiency and as a recompense for political loyalty. Similar thinking was applied to the property of Suspects – another potential land bank that many felt should be exploited in order to meet the socio-economic objectives of the Montagnard dictatorship. More radical proposals for a total recasting of property relationships in the countryside were also voiced from time to time, although the ban placed on the discussion of the so-called Agrarian Law ensured that few traces have survived.[24] Such ideas had certainly occurred to the administrators of the District of Versailles, who were readying themselves for an effort to abolish the rural proletariat when Thermidor struck. In Lorraine, too, a refracted memory of Antoine Chaumont de La Galaizière's achievement lived on. The radical emissary of the Conseil-Exécutif, Pierre-Auguste Mauger, urged 'une nouvelle distribution de terres qui fonderait la société sur un plan nouveau, remédierait à l'accaparement et contribuerait à dépeupler les villes, à condition que la mesure s'effectuât partout simultanément et sous l'énergique impulsion de commissaires spéciaux'.[25] Mauger's unbridled ambitions and behaviour whilst resident in Nancy placed him beyond the pale of orthodox Montagnard opinion, however, and he would finish his days in prison.

The first practical steps to compensate the poor with property of their own can be linked to the Paris insurrection of 31 May–2 June 1793. A long-awaited decree to expedite the egalitarian division of common lands was promulgated, and arrangements put in place to endow landless non-taxpayers with one-*arpent* plots sectioned from *émigré* estates. These arrangements were subsequently altered – in September – to furnish the poor with a 500-*livres* credit facility so that they could buy at auction instead. The repercussions of the legislation were considerable, if varied. Nearly all of the villages examined in this study received the news of the 'bons de 500 *livres*'[26] with enthusiasm. After all, in localities with no common land and no *émigré* farms in the vicinity the scheme appeared to offer greater flexibility. However, while some municipalities adhered rigorously to the

[24] See P. M. Jones, 'The "Agrarian Law": Schemes for Land Redistribution during the French Revolution', *Past and Present*, 133 (1991), 96–133.
[25] See A. Troux, *La Vie politique dans le département de la Meurthe d'août 1792 à octobre 1795* (2 vols., Nancy, 1936), II, p. 152.
[26] For a discussion of this law, see Jones, 'The "Agrarian Law" ', 109–15; 120–6.

law, others adapted it to local conditions. Châtelaudren decided that only non-owning and non-taxpaying households headed by widows, or widowers, should be listed as potential beneficiaries, whereas the Jacobins of Roquelaure clearly felt that it would be unfair to exclude micro-proprietors possessing just a hut and a garden. They encouraged all those 'qui n'ont pas un sac [0.39 hectares] de terre labourable'[27] to apply to the District. There is little evidence to suggest that any of these 'bons' were ever used, though. In most cases they were not even applied for. The administrators of the District of Montélimar issued about forty, although none to the inhabitants of Allan whose communal forest and scrubland precluded any possibility of benefit. And besides, it became painfully evident that productive land rarely changed hands for as little as 500 *livres* per *arpent* (between 0.52 and 0.34 hectares).

What the poor needed was a means of vindicating their 'rights' *before* land entered the marketplace. The welcome extended to Saint-Just's speech of 8 Ventôse II (26 February 1794) proposing that Suspects' property should be next in line for distribution was undoubtedly predicated on the belief that 'indigent patriots'[28] were about to receive a direct handout. Pierre-René Le Rumeur, the *agent national* of Châtelaudren, was conversant with the nature of Saint-Just's proposals only a matter of days after he had presented them to the Convention, and work began on drawing up the list of beneficiaries within the month. The same alacrity was displayed in Roquelaure and Villepreux, whereas the *comité de surveillance* of Saint-Alban received a garbled account that confused the act of political justice intrinsic to Saint-Just's scheme with on-going efforts to alleviate suffering through the practice of *bienfaisance*. Galvanised by the District of Versailles, the *comité de surveillance* of Villepreux and the municipality assembled in joint session on 18 Germinal II (7 April 1794) in order to compile their list. With so many landless and impecunious inhabitants in this politically reliable village, it should not have been a difficult task. But the landless were not, by definition, indigent and, in any case, the landless had been catered for by a process that we must now examine. A tally of twenty-eight elderly or infirm persons and twelve beggars was submitted. Nearly half of those scheduled for relief at the expense of Suspects were widows.

It is worth recalling at this juncture three important facts about the village of Villepreux. They have been mentioned before, but now need to be brought together. First, the productive territory of the village was nearly all 'imprisoned' within six large farms whose holdings could be found on

---

[27] A. D. du Gers, L 699*, 30 Ventôse II.   [28] Law of 13 Ventôse II.

either side of the wall enclosing the Grand Parc of the chateau of Versailles. The unproductive territory of the village (woodland, game covers) was likewise enclosed within the Parc for the most part. The second point follows from the first. A large proportion of households were either landless or semi-landless, and therefore dependent on the commercial activity engendered by close proximity to the palace, or on agricultural employment provided by the large tenant farmers of the neighbourhood. Day labourers alone numbered around 100 on the eve of the Revolution, but if shepherds, herdsmen, carters, farm servants and other vulnerable categories are included this figure rises by at least 50 per cent. Third, the villagers were exposed to the full blast of radical politics emanating from Paris and, after 1792, from Versailles. In few other localities is it likely that policies rooted in notions of redistributive justice would have produced a more sympathetic echo.

The pressures building up in the village have already been described in chapter 3 and chapter 5. Chronic land hunger had fused with indignation over the attempt to ban hunting in the Grand Parc to produce threats of mass trespass, occupation and clearance of grassland leased out to the 'gros fermiers'. Only the conviction that the authorities would shortly act of their own accord served to stay the hands, or rather the spades, of the village poor. In the summer of 1793 legislators acted with measures to facilitate the parcelling out of *émigré* estates, as we have noted. But land owned by, and now seized from, *émigrés* could never have alleviated the pressure in the Grand Parc villages on its own. The problem lay elsewhere – in the massive presence of Civil List properties – and the signal was finally given for a distribution of one-*arpent* (0.42-hectare) parcels drawn from this source to take place. In an operation carried out between November 1793 and May 1794 some 1,568 *arpents* (661 hectares) of cultivable land were parcelled out among 1,546 poor peasant or artisan households located in twenty-five of the eighty-four villages forming the district of Versailles.[29] This was not, of course, a solution to the socio-economic problems of the Paris grain belt. Yet it was a serious and quite possibly a unique attempt to embody the egalitarian principles of social Jacobinism in the agrarian sphere.

Of the 205 households residing in Villepreux in February 1794, a total of 103 were scheduled to receive one-*arpent* allotments worth approximately 600 *livres* apiece, and payable on hire-purchase (*arrentement*) terms over twenty years. Seventy-eight of the families listed owned no property

---

[29] See P. Jones, 'Agrarian Radicalism during the French Revolution', in A. Forrest and P. Jones (eds.), *Reshaping France: Town, Country and Region during the French Revolution* (Manchester, 1991), pp. 137–8.

whatsoever, not even the cottages or rooms in which they lived. Fifteen out of twenty-three households benefited in the adjacent hamlet of Rennemoulin. Casual talk in the village coupled the allotments with the campaign to limit farm size which had been pursued more vigorously on the Plain of France than anywhere else. The farms of La Tuilerie and Les Grand' Maisons were to be reduced to 200 *arpents*, it was said, and, indeed, many of the plots (known as 'les concessions des indigents')[30] were removed from the holding of the latter. They were sliced out of fields close to the Porte Saint-Vincent at a location described as 'La Beurrerie' – that is to say from territory enclosed within the Grand Parc (see map 3). The operation was scarcely an answer to the concentration of property in the district, however. Even reduced by 97 *arpents*, the Grand' Maisons farm was still well over 200 *arpents* in scale. Whether it answered the egalitarian objectives of the Jacobin Revolution and staunched the land hunger of the dispossessed we shall see in a moment. The administrators of the District of Versailles clearly regarded the exercise as a political down payment. Having finally completed the distribution, they reported to the Department authorities on 11 Prairial II (30 May 1794), 'nous sommes prêts à mettre en vente une grande quantité de petits lots de biens d'émigrés, et nous attendons les listes des chefs de famille non-propriétaires que les communes doivent nous envoyer'.[31]

More significant than any of the operations discussed so far, though, was the disposal of common lands. If we exclude collectively owned forest whose alienation not even the Jacobin deputies were prepared to countenance, commons (whether labelled pastures, heath, marsh, dry rocky wastes, or scrub) could be found within the territory of three out of our six villages. In all three (Allan, Neuviller, Saint-Alban), there was pressure from the poor to divide, and in two out of the three (Allan, Neuviller) that pressure was crowned with a measure of success. However, these are bald statements that cannot be allowed to pass without qualification. Only Châtelaudren possessed no common land whatsoever, whereas scraps of waste existed at Roquelaure and at Villepreux which by general consent were not considered worth sharing out. Pressure to divide, moreover, depended on a number of factors, not least perceptions of how the commons had been used, or abused, in the years prior to the Revolution. Specifically popular pressure in favour of partition depended, in turn, on the parameters attached to the exercise. The 'censitary' mode of division (in proportion to tax contribution or

---

[30] See A. de Saint-Seine, 'Histoire de la ferme de Grand'Maisons' (typescript, Villepreux, n.d.), p. 107.
[31] A. D. des Yvelines, 1Q 383.

land holding) attracted few takers among the poor, unsurprisingly, whereas the egalitarian ('par tête') solution, which the deputies eventually adopted and promulgated on 10 June 1793, evoked an enthusiastic response in many localities. Finally, it was unusual for villagers to vote to partition their entire stock of common land. For all the insistent demands of the moment, they were not unaware of ecological factors, or of the need to take decisions that would make sense in the longer term.

The perception of seigneurial abuse was rampant in Allan and Neuviller by the end of the *ancien régime*, as we have seen. Madame Lériget de La Faye's attempt to restrict grazing access to the scrub forest covering much of the territory of Allan had been fought off in 1789. However, the inhabitants of Neuviller (and Roville) had been soundly beaten by their seigneur. In return for a partition by household of what remained, they had been obliged to grant him one-third – and probably the best third – of their reconfigured communal pastures. The behaviour of La Galaizière *fils* in this regard was not abnormal, it should be said. Seigneurial *triage* was practised throughout Lorraine in the 1770s. Nevertheless, the 'droit de triage' featured alongside the Edict of Enclosure in the lists of grievances and anathemas formulated by country dwellers in 1789. The news that all *triages* had been abolished with a thirty-year retrospective application on 15–28 March 1790 caused rejoicing, therefore, and it set the scene for what was to follow. The struggle to recover the *triage* portion intruded upon village politics repeatedly for the next two years, as it did in nearby Roville and Laneuveville. Court action buttressed by the usual weapons of the weak (trespass, illicit tree-felling, etc.) was employed. However, it was not until May 1793, when the District court of Vézelise found in favour of the inhabitants of Roville and granted them permission to take back 131 *jours* (26 hectares) of pasture lost in 1771, that real progress was made. The arrival, a couple of months later, of the news that the National Convention had issued a decree positively encouraging a rigorously egalitarian division of the commons merely ratified what was about to happen in any case. The villagers of Neuviller voted to partition 46 *jours* (9.2 hectares) and to leave 64 *jours* (12.8 hectares) as open pasture; in Roville all of the newly acquired 131 *jours* were divided up, leaving just 26 *jours* (5.2 hectares) for communal use; while in Laneuveville, where the Princesse de Craon had been responsible for the *triage*, an overwhelming vote of the villagers resolved to parcel out every scrap of land (115 *jours*/23 hectares).

The southern Drôme and eastern Gard villages became an epicentre of common land agitation during the winter of 1792–3, and there can be no doubt that *partage* was high on the agenda of the Jacobin club of

Allan as well. But progress towards a land handout was hampered by two factors: a debt burden carried over from the liquidation of the Communes de Provence and augmented by the costs of litigation against their one-time seigneur, and the uncertain status of their collective assets. Forest and woodland was *not* to be divided according to both the law of 14 August 1792 and that of 10 June 1793, but what about terrain thinly covered with scrub oak and Mediterranean pine? The villagers would stand accused subsequently of ignoring this latter stipulation in their anxiety to parcel out their arid landscape, and when we look closely at the quantity and type of the land involved in the *partage* it is difficult to argue conclusively in their defence. On 20 Ventôse III (10 March 1795), after much hesitation and procrastination, a general assembly met and decided by overwhelming majority (although one-third of adults seem to have absented themselves) to divide seven extensive tracts of 'waste' among 714 qualifying members of the community. Some of this territory, such as 'le champ des Ebrachas',[32] had been wooded until 1790 and was now covered in heather. But the sheer quantity of the terrain in question (3,540 *sétérées*/787 hectares) argues that the villagers were simply turning a blind eye to the law. Balloting for the portions took place a few weeks later, but it seems unlikely that the operation went ahead on the scale originally envisaged. As the *procès-verbal* acknowledged, some of the territory would probably cost more than it was worth just to mark out.

In Saint-Alban the voice of the poor is hard to hear for reasons already mentioned. Virtually every constituent village and hamlet of this far-flung parish possessed extensive common pastures, and yet discussion of the law of 10 June 1793 remained low-key and inconsequential. Why? Three reasons can be adduced. First, the Margeride constituted a demographic low-pressure zone. If anything population densities were declining in the final decades of the eighteenth and first two decades of the nineteenth century. It would be a different story from the 1820s and 1830s, but these later developments fall beyond our remit. Second, mountain communities subsisting on thin, acidic soils rarely pushed for land clearance or partition, and Saint-Alban was no exception. The ecological consequences of loosening the soil did not need explaining to anyone. Third and by no means least, bourgeois landowners and peasant *ménagers* remained in virtually un-challenged political control throughout the period in question. We know that there was some discussion of, and enthusiasm for, the *partage* option,

---

[32] A. D. de la Drôme, 2 O 14, Mémoire sur la nécessité de transférer dans la plaine le centre communal d'Allan [1829]; also L 275, L 277, 1Mi 709.

however, because it was mentioned as a factor in the rivalry between Atrasic and Vincens, his son-in-law, and the Enjalvin brothers. Both parties owned property in the hamlet of Les Faux not far from Saint-Alban whose inhabitants enjoyed collective use of extensive pastures. But Atrasic had annexed to his own property a part of the pasture and the inhabitants enlisted Augustin Enjalvin in their defence. From the evidence of accusation and counter-accusation only one conclusion emerges clearly, however: that there was significant grass-roots support for the Convention '[qui] venoit d'assurer quelques propriétés au bon peuple en ordonnant le partage des communaux'.[33] Atrasic and Vincens appear to have resisted a partition, which would be logical. They were not even residents, and, as *forains*, could not hope to benefit. But it is far from certain that Augustin Enjalvin was in favour, either, even though he could expect to benefit alongside everybody else. Big landowners rarely stood to gain from the egalitarian option.

CONSOLIDATION

The undertaking given in September 1793 by the District of Versailles to the poor of Rennemoulin that the Convention would shortly decree their 'happiness'[34] begs an obvious question: how far were the legislative achievements of the early 1790s sustained and enshrined in post-revolutionary practice? The sales of *biens nationaux* proceeded by fits and starts right across the decade and into the next, and no serious attempt was made to reverse them, as is well known. But these sales need to be kept in perspective. They substantially by-passed our villagers, and it has been recently, and plausibly, argued that we would do better to concentrate on factors such as debt relief if we wish to find a measure of country dwellers' economic wellbeing in the years following the Terror.[35] Inflation, fuelled by the uncontrolled emission of paper money, was an unplanned and largely unanticipated by-product of revolutionary *liberté* that by 1795 no one could escape. Insofar as the poor tended to be borrowers rather than lenders, they stood to make an instant and very tangible gain by exploiting the depreciation of the *assignat* in order to pay off both short-term and consolidated debts (*rentes*). An examination of notarial records bears out this hypothesis to some degree.

---

[33] A. N., F⁷3681¹⁴, Aux citoyens délégués par le représentant-du-peuple Châteauneuf-Randon dans le district de Saint-Chély (n.d.).
[34] See p. 180, note 19.
[35] See G. Postel-Vinay, *La Terre et l'argent: l'agriculture et le crédit en France du XVIIIᵉ au début du XXᵉ siècle* (Paris, 1998), pp. 18, 41, 107, 132, 136–7; also Béaur and Minard, *Atlas de la Révolution française*, X: *Economie*, p. 11.

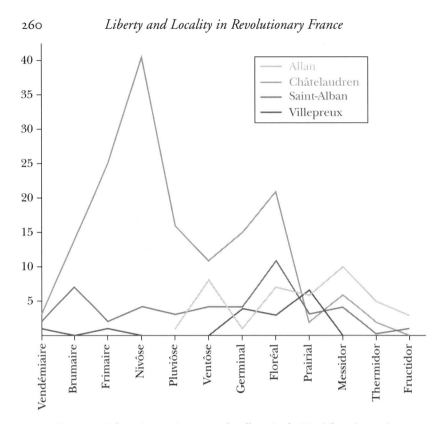

Figure 6. Debt extinction in case-study villages in the Year Three (1794–5)

In Allan, Châtelaudren, Roquelaure, Saint-Alban and Villepreux villagers hastened before the public notary in order to record the redemption of debt in greater numbers than ever before from the winter of 1795 onwards (see figure 6). Long-standing *rentes* weighing on the land were reimbursed (Châtelaudren, Roquelaure), but also debts linked to inheritance and the payment of dowries (Saint-Alban). In Neuviller, by contrast, it is harder to detect a collective effort to profit from the economic conjuncture, although this may simply reflect a paucity of notarial archives. Vulnerable villagers – most notably the day labourers of Villepreux – were liberating themselves, then, but debt readjustment between the relatively well off is what strikes the reader of notarial minutes most forcibly. On 24 Germinal III (13 April 1795) Jean-Baptiste Verdun, a retail trader of Châtelaudren, was indignant when the widow of Jean Rebourg, a peasant farmer of Treguidal parish, turned up with 344 *livres* in *assignats* in order to pay off a *rente* in kind of two bushels of wheat. He refused the proffered paper money and warned his debtor that the Convention would put a stop to such unseemly behaviour with retroactive legislation.[36]

Legislators had always regarded the 1791 compromise on collective rights as an unsatisfactory and therefore temporary measure, a holding operation until something more consonant with the new definition of freedom could be devised. Yet an improved statement of rights and responsibilities applicable to the rural economy proved very difficult to achieve in practice. Napoleonic attempts to promulgate a comprehensive 'rural code' comparable to the codifications of civil and criminal procedure foundered in 1808, and again in 1814. This was a serious setback for a regime that wished to place the land settlement of the Revolution – like so much else – within a secure framework of law. Viewed from the ramparts of Allan or the partly demolished towers of the chateau of Saint-Alban not a great deal had changed. The right to enclose and the right to grow what one pleased had been upheld but they were hard to enforce, particularly in those localities where such rights had been contested before the Revolution. With the definitive departure of La Galaizière *fils* all the old footpaths and bridle-ways across the land enclosed within his park were reinstated. The inhabitants of Villepreux knocked holes in the wall of the Grand Parc (wryly labelled 'portes de la liberté')[37] and resumed their peregrinations, too. Even though the Thermidorians managed to place a restriction on collective grazing in unenclosed meadows by means of a provisional measure that was renewed annually, the principle of *vaine pâture* was never directly challenged. It therefore remained in force where custom and practice so decreed. The institution of the common flock survived longest where the commons remained undivided. Thus the inhabitants of Saint-Alban again agreed terms with a village shepherd on 1 May 1820. The maximum size of the flock was limited to 500, and any farmer who insisted on grazing separately was warned to keep his animals on his own land.

The anxiety to consolidate the land transfers of the Revolutionary period on a basis of legality, albeit a compromise legality, is particularly evident in official attitudes towards those who had participated in the *partage* experiments carried out during the climactic phase of the Revolution. The beneficiaries of the one-*arpent* plots carved from the Civil List farms of the Versaillais did not have an easy time once the sun went down on the Year Two. In part this was due to cropping problems (the plots seem mainly to have been destined for subsistence use), and in part to the shock of paying rent and taxes in specie following the deflation and bumper

---

[36] A. D. des Côtes-d'Armor, 3E 30/341.   [37] A. C. de Villepreux, D2, 10 Prairial III.

harvests of 1797–8. But a suspicion of impropriety, even illegality, hung over the entire operation – mainly because the policy had been elaborated 'on the ground', so to speak, and had been only loosely covered by legislation. By 1805 the original 103 plotholders of Villepreux had been reduced to 78, often on specious pretexts. On the other hand, those who had put their land to work and kept up with the payments now enjoyed the guarantee that the Consuls had extended to all holders of *biens nationaux*. On 27 Thermidor VIII (15 August 1800) the Minister of Finances ruled that 'les arrentements dont il s'agit sont confirmés et recevront leur pleine et entière exécution'.[38] Yet this ruling was not sufficient on its own to clear away all of the legal ambiguities surrounding the one-*arpent* plots, for in some of the villages holders had fallen foul of the provisions of the law of 28 Ventôse IV (18 March 1796) which had launched a new form of paper currency – the *mandat territorial* – backed by the remaining unsold stock of national assets. An attempt would also be made to include the plots in the emperor's last-minute grab of leased-out communal property announced in the law of 20 March 1813. As far as we can tell, the beneficiaries in Villepreux overcame these pressures, however. They resisted, too, the harassment of the 'gros fermiers', or rather their successors, who thought nothing of ploughing the access paths leading to the holdings. The 'concessions Saint-Vincent' would be surveyed and recorded as such on the cadastral map of Villepreux in 1818, and these elongated strips remained an evocative feature of an otherwise enclosed landscape until the middle of the twentieth century.[39]

What of the common land partitions carried out in Neuviller, Roville and, ostensibly, in Allan? Here we detect a mingling of priorities in the administrative 'mind' during the Directory and post-Directory years: suspicious hostility towards a policy with dubious political credentials; irritation that an 'agronomic ' opportunity to make more efficient use of collectively owned property had been wasted; sober acceptance that egalitarian *partage* had happened for better or worse; and finally, as the shadows lengthened around the Empire, a grim readiness to throw compromise to the winds and to sacrifice the commons in the interests of the state, if not those of the individual. Political stabilisation appeared the most urgent priority on the morrow of Bonaparte's assumption of power, however, and this was achieved by the law of 9 Ventôse XII (29 February 1804) which provided a means of validating most of the *partages* inspired by the Jacobin decree of 10 June 1793. Nonetheless, officials disliked intensely the egalitarian 'par

[38] A. D. des Yvelines, 1Q 382, Observations (n.d.).
[39] A. D. des Yvelines, 2Mi 791 P; also Saint-Seine, 'Histoire de la ferme de Grand'Maisons', p. 107.

tête d'habitant'[40] principle, particularly officials such as the prefects and the subprefects who were vulnerable to pressure from landowners. No further *partages* would take place on this basis, and some would be converted into household partitions in which the usufruct status of the beneficiaries would be underlined by the payment of a small annual rental. Thus we find a hybrid regime in force in Neuviller by 1820. The 'pacquis du haut' (alias the seigneur's *triage* portion, alias the community's pre-1771 pasture formerly known as 'le Beurton') was held freehold because it had been divided in accordance with the decree of 10 June 1793, whereas the 'pacquis du bas' was now held in household portions 'à titre de jouissance usufruitière'.[41] Each strip of the 'pacquis du haut' contained 0.13 hectares and there were about 150 strips all together. However, the 'pacquis du haut' would face a threat from Maurice Jordy, on whom, it should be remembered, the legal rights of the La Galaizière family had devolved. Unblushingly, he began a court case in order to recover the *triage* portion for his own benefit.

In Roville, by comparison, the situation was more clear cut. Here, too, the *conseil municipal* secured the endorsement of the revolutionary *partage* in 1804, even though many of the beneficiaries had ceased to reside in the commune and had sold their plots (as was their right) to Antoine Bertier. But new arrivals to the village complained loudly about the injustice of this *de facto* alienation of the commons. According to a petition submitted in December 1814, nearly half of the population lacked access (not strictly true, since 16.35 hectares had never been divided). Be that as it may, the rights and wrongs of the 1794 *partage* remained a burning political issue, and probably help to explain the confrontation that took place in the village during the Hundred Days (see p. 198). The same is true of Allan, where the partition was subsumed into a much larger conflict pitting the Jacobin irreconcilables of the *conseil municipal* against Madame Lériget de La Faye and her heirs, as we have seen. Although we cannot be sure how much land was divided, a *partage* of sorts had certainly taken place, and it is equally certain that the operation was suspect in the eyes of the authorities. In 1808 the prefect of the Drôme would claim that the villagers had simply relabelled as wasteland 'un terrain d'environ deux cent hectares bien complanté'.[42] It seems unlikely that they ever received the endorsement of the law of 9 Ventôse XII.

---

[40] Law of 10 June 1793 'contenant le mode de partage des biens communaux', section II, article 1.
[41] A. D. de Meurthe-et-Moselle, WO 2594, mayor to prefect, Neuviller, 10 September 1825.
[42] A. D. de la Drôme, 2 Op 5, prefect [?] to subprefect of Montélimar, 3 May 1808.

Both Allan and Saint-Alban were vulnerable to the spoliatory legislation to which Napoleon resorted in 1813 in any case. All collectively owned property subject to any form of rental seems to have fallen within the scope of the law of 20 March 1813. Thus two meadows, a marshy field and a small quarry that the *consuls* and then the municipality of Allan had habitually leased out were appropriated by the government and listed for sale. Only the fact that Madame Lériget de La Faye also claimed ownership of these assets delayed what amounted to a late-in-the-day disposal *of biens nationaux*. No more than a passing comment in the surviving documentation confirms that the law of 20 March 1813 was also applied to Saint-Alban. Nevertheless, it is not too difficult to work out what must have happened. Most of the villages and hamlets of the parish controlled more pasture than they could make use of; consequently the highland sheep runs were often leased to transhumant shepherds. We know, too, that commons were occasionally leased out for fixed periods in order to raise funds for one-off expenses. From 1810, moreover, the prefecture promoted leasing as a solution to the swelling volume of complaint that the big stock-owners derived disproportionate benefit from commons left open to free grazing.

Victor Riquetti, the self-styled 'ami des hommes', died in the year that the Revolution broke out. But had he lived to witness the formidable authority that the principles of liberty and equality placed in the hands of reformers it is unlikely that he would have been impressed. The real revolution as opposed to the intellectualised 'revolution' envisaged by the various coteries of Enlightenment zealots turned out to be a defeat for the system builders. François de Neufchâteau, one of the few Physiocrat-influenced deputies to combine an economic vision of the Republic with a practical grasp of politics, acknowledged as much. 'In vain,' he concluded in 1806, 'has our Rural Code laid down the principle that the soil of France is as free as those who inhabit it, for today the French countryside still bears the traces of disorder and the marks of serfdom.'[43] On the other hand, a measure of legislative 'disorder' and the 'serfdom' of collective practices had been part of the price paid in order to persuade a participatory democracy to take root – a fact that he well understood.

To judge from the evidence of our village-based studies, then, land reform could never have followed the single path anticipated by the Physiocrats. For land was not only an economic resource waiting to be exploited; it was a political commodity, an unmistakable signifier of citizenship. Villagers

---

[43] See Jones, *The Peasantry in the French Revolution*, p. 136.

sought land of their own and the revolutionaries bestowed it – unevenly and sparingly – for complex reasons, therefore. The impoverished and illiterate day labourers of Villepreux (only seventeen out of seventy-five of whom could trace their signatures to a petition in 1798) wanted land in order to grow their own food, to be sure, but they also wanted it, one suspects, for reasons of self-respect. Land conferred independence, albeit in pitiable quantities. It also signalled to the 'gros fermiers' of the plain of Versailles that the rural proletariat could no longer be taken for granted. Yet the historian must refrain from requiring those whose citizenship had been vindicated by the acquisition of land to make an invidious choice. Unlike Antoine Chaumont de La Galaizière *fils*, poor country dwellers saw no logical reason why they should give up customary rights over the land of others just because they had been admitted to the ranks of property-owning republicans.

Conclusion

The challenge to compare the evolution of a discrete collection of villages over a sixty-year period has not been an easy one to overcome. There exists no generally approved methodology for the task, and the range of potential angles of approach is dismayingly large. It comes as no surprise, therefore, to discover that an influential handbook on methods for historians devotes little more than a page to the subject of comparative history.[1] Yet nearly everyone in the profession acknowledges that the comparative approach is capable of bringing new light to bear on the process of change over time and space. It does not replace conventional modes of analysis, but rather complements them to produce a richer understanding of the forces playing on events and conditioning individual lives. How, then, has this study enriched our understanding of the micro-history of the French countryside during the second half of the eighteenth century and the initial decades of the nineteenth?

A number of themes have been explored, but the one that stands out is bureaucratisation. The village, as observed in our case studies, was caught up in the power politics of reforming absolutism long before it was pressed into service by the revolutionaries as a building block of the new civic order. One by-product of this process was an altered self-image that prepared the way for the mental transformations that 1789 and the years beyond would usher in. Having become part of the System, village elites learned how to play that System to their own advantage. The most obvious losers were seigneurs, whose behaviour had been predicated on the assumption that their lordly powers and prerogatives could scarcely be challenged. The confidence and energy of resident village elites, as we have depicted them, make it rather hard to recognise – and endorse – Alexis de Tocqueville's schematic interpretation of the ills of French government, therefore. The

---

[1] A. Marwick, *The New Nature of History: Knowledge, Evidence, Language* (Basingstoke, 2001), pp. 213–14.

late *ancien-régime* monarchy was less a centralising than a bureaucratising force, a characteristic that would be shared with the administrations of the early years of the Revolution. Whether enlisted as subaltern agents of monarchy or answerable to Provincial Estates, village elites enjoyed a surprisingly large freedom of manoeuvre at the end of the old regime. Historians of the Revolution rightly draw attention to the 'autonomy'[2] of the village between 1789 and 1793, but they need also to recognise that this sense of freedom owed a good deal to trends observable during the closing decades of the *ancien régime*. After 1793 Tocqueville's thesis becomes more plausible, with a very real joining together of the forces of centralisation and bureaucratisation. Shorn of its Jacobin overtones, this coupling would find ultimate expression in the Napoleonic State.

But who were these village elites? In most of the cases where a firm identification has proved possible they were drawn from the tiny literate stratum of each village whose accumulated status and economic wellbeing can be linked to the seigneurie. Collectively speaking, we are dealing with court personnel (judges, investigating magistrates, clerks), attorneys, notaries and those under contract to gather in feudal dues and other perquisites of lordship. Village schoolmasters, whose traditional attachment lay with the church rather than the seigneurie, also moved into the limelight after 1789. Men such as Pierre Dieudonné, *greffier* of the assize court of Neuviller, Jean-Louis Rivot, the administrator of the Comté de Goello, or Jean-Baptiste Biscarrat, whose family had been hereditary holders of the office of *bailli-châtelain* of Allan since 1688, had to move smartly in order to make the transition to the new regime. To judge from the evidence at our disposal, ordinary villagers tolerated their careerism with reasonable good humour, however. At the village level there could be no genuine circulation of elites: certain individuals by reasons of birth, background or family connection were predestined to hold office whatever the power constellation, and that was that. Popular recruitment was tried by the Jacobin authorities and the Napoleonic prefects experimented with the appointment of *forains* to local office, but in each case the drawbacks outweighed the advantages of seeking to by-pass established hierarchies. Schoolmasters (Hersant in Villepreux, Hillion in Châtelaudren) were the only genuinely new recruits to village power elites. Such was the respect for tradition and continuity in the village of Saint-Alban that public opinion even allowed a former seigneur (suitably divested of his feudal privileges) to play a prominent role under the new regime. As the driving force behind the saltpetre

[2] The term belongs to Fournier, *Démocratie et vie municipale en Languedoc*, I, p. 339.

manufactory, Jean-Adam Molette-Morangiès would subsequently find himself accused of manic 'sans-culottisme'.[3]

The ideological affiliations of these micro-elites have been examined in detail, albeit with uncertain or ungeneralisable results. On the one hand, it is tempting to conclude that the clan- and kin-based politics whose rationale and mechanisms we have laid bare in the case of Saint-Alban was the norm. But even in a region noted for the strength of its household and lineage attachments, Saint-Alban seems to have been exceptional. And besides, the evidence of the survival – out of season – of tenacious neo-Jacobin allegiances points in another direction. Indeed, the next generation of villagers in Allan and Roquelaure would take part in the rural resistance to Louis-Napoléon Bonaparte's *coup d'état* of December 1851. The strange alloy of republicanism and popular Bonapartism would also leave a mark on the inhabitants of Roville, where the liberal-minded Antoine Bertier maintained a forceful presence in the locality throughout the Restoration and the July Monarchy. The residue of popular Bonapartism – manifested initially in a form of messianism – is evident in all of the villages studied, in fact. So widespread was a rumour that the emperor could be found living incognito in the chateau of Saint-Alban that, in 1822, the prefect of the Lozère sent out a party of gendarmes to investigate.

Yet this evidence, pointing to a sustained and enduring politicisation of a minority of villagers, must be set in a broader context. One advantage of close-focus analysis over a relatively long period of time is that it brings out the fine calibration of commitment to those rhetorical entities and ideals lying beyond the small world of the village. And the conclusion to which we are inexorably drawn is that villagers did not exit from one polity and attach themselves to another in steady incremental moves. Engagement ebbed and flowed across the span of an adult lifetime. Participation (in deliberative assemblies, in the National Guard, in clubs) brought with it a real sense of empowerment, and a strong incentive to commit to something more than the values enshrined in the parish pump. The mental refreshment stemming from the experience of electing a local official, attending the meetings of a *société populaire*, taking a turn at guard duty, wearing a cockade, chanting a republican hymn, signing a petition, or making a *don patriotique* should not be underestimated. Yet participation, or commitment, fluctuated over time, and fluctuated also in terms of its social purchase. There were moments between 1760 and 1820 when villagers responded *en masse* to issues lying

[3] See B. Bardy, 'Le Comte de Morangiès vit sa dernière heure', *Midi Libre*, 31 January 1993.

well outside their usual range of cognitive experience, but equally there were long moments of introspection and quiescence. One need only compare the frequency and vibrancy of the municipal council meetings of the early 1790s with their pallid counterparts of the Napoleonic Empire in order to grasp the point. Politicisation in the village was not a neat and linear process, then: roles were learned, forgotten (or abandoned) and relearned in a quasi-cyclical fashion.

A new civic order did eventually take shape, however, albeit not on the model envisaged by Laverdy in the 1760s, Brienne in the late 1780s, the Committees of the Convention in 1793–4, or even by François de Neufchâteau and his fellow Ministers and Directors in 1798–9. Notwithstanding all the back-sliding, some kind of cumulative process must have been in operation, and it is therefore not unreasonable to ask the question 'What enduring changes would villagers have acknowledged when looking back from the vantage point of 1820?' The answer falls into two parts – the concrete and the psychological – but since none of the villagers constituting the *dramatis personae* of this study committed such thoughts to paper we must try to answer on their behalf.

The concrete changes are fairly easy to specify, if not very revealing in themselves. From 1791, or thereabouts, all villagers enjoyed access to inexpensive and speedy judicial redress via the institution of the Justice of the Peace. This remained substantially the case even after the reduction in the number of cantons carried out at the time of the Consulate. Although we have no real reason to suppose that the seigneurial courts operating in our six villages dispensed arbitrary justice, there can be little doubt that first-instance judicial services became quicker and cheaper following their replacement. The freedom to track down and destroy game was highly prized, too. Indeed, in localities such as Villepreux or Rennemoulin it entered folklore as one of the mythic 'benefits' of the Revolution. Subsequent attempts during the later years of the Directory and during the Empire to confine the 'right' to hunt to landowners largely failed to achieve the desired effect. The easing of surplus extraction, whether in the form of the tithe or feudal dues, would have been commemorated in Roquelaure and Saint-Alban, and also in Allan. The issue of taxation, by contrast, elicited a more ambivalent reaction. All villagers would have saluted the moral victory scored by the revolutionaries in bringing former *privilégiés* into the tax net, but the achievement of fiscal equity was overshadowed by the fact that citizenship seemed to carry with it the responsibility to pay more tax not less. The Châtelaudrinais felt particularly aggrieved in this respect, as we have seen. The principle of equity also implied a policy of harmonisation between regions, and the Breton departments had, prior to 1789, enjoyed exemption from both the *taille* and the salt tax.

The most profound and enduring psychological shift to be consummated during these years was the revalorisation of the 'village'. After several false starts (Laverdy, the Calonne–Brienne reform), villagers were accorded administrative structures that rendered them indistinguishable from their urban brethren. The decision taken by the Convention in 1793 to abolish the label 'community of inhabitants' and to impose the all-purpose, egalitarian title of 'commune' thus brought to fruition a process that can be traced, distantly perhaps, to the edicts promulgated in 1764 and 1765 by Controller General Laverdy. The satisfaction of the inhabitants of Roquelaure and Châtelaudren was almost palpable; it brims from the documents recording the installation of the first municipalities in 1790 and helps us to understand how it became possible to put the new administrative regime in place so quickly and efficiently. All over the country peasant *élus* rushed off to buy ribbon for their sashes of office; deliberative bodies that had once fought shy of the most trifling expenditures now budgeted for considerable sums in order to sustain the embryonic Nation. By the end of the first full year of Revolution, the municipal councillors of Allan had incurred a bill of 1,441 *livres* solely for payments connected with the consolidation of the new order.

Villagers felt a part of the civic landscape that took shape, painfully, after 1787 from the very outset, then. The Revolution substantially remedied the rural inferiority complex. If Jacobin rhetoric hailing the 'citizen of the countryside' was taken with a pinch of salt, it remains a fact that country dwellers emerged from the Revolution and the Napoleonic experience with a sense that they were now living in a lawful society. Those who had grown to maturity and old age under the *ancien régime* would not have possessed this sense: seigneurs, intendants and assorted tax officials were all potentially malign forces to be propitiated, not treated as legal equals. However, a society full of laws presupposed a huge process of adjustment as well. The small world of the villager was an environment still largely structured by custom, precedent and private treaty at the end of the *ancien régime*: public law barely impinged on day-to-day life, and when it did so the declarations and edicts of the Royal Council were usually mediated through familiar institutions. After 1789 rural communities were confronted with an unremitting barrage of legislation: over 30,000 laws reached the statute book during the revolutionary decade alone.[4] Gone were the days when it was

---

[4] See *Plan détaillé de topographie*, p. 346.

possible to live in ignorance of legislation, or to practise partial compliance. On assuming office in 1800 the Consuls instructed that the *Bulletin des Lois* be transmitted to every village mayor throughout the length and breadth of the Republic. And lest there be any misunderstanding, municipal councils were ordered to include the subscription price in their communal budgets.

The late Directory years, moreover, had witnessed the growth of an enforcing bureaucracy – a development that would gain momentum throughout the Consulate and the Empire. The value of a bureaucracy that both obeyed and enforced the rule of law – by and large – should not be underestimated, despite Franz Kafka's damning verdict.[5] Leadership by men whose primary loyalty was directed towards the smooth running of an administrative system had been in short supply both before and during the Revolution. Yet the trend observable from the 1800s also tended to curtail the informalities of village life. The law turned out to be a double-edged weapon: it could be used to overturn custom and practice that was manifestly unjust, yet it also intruded upon relationships and arrangements that had worked well in the past and which scarcely required 'policing'. Why, asked several of our village *élus*, was it necessary to appoint (and pay for) *gardes-champêtres* (field constables) when customary harvest-time arrangements could be activated at a fraction of the cost? Napoleonic bureaucracy could be relied upon to deliver security, but at the price of a substantial disempowerment of villagers – a disempowerment that might even leave them with less freedom than they had enjoyed at the end of the *ancien régime*. It is noticeable, for instance, that the overhead costs of tax collection dropped significantly following Bonaparte's *coup d'état*, but Napoleonic stabilisation also resulted in villagers losing the power to draw up their own tax rolls and to appoint their own collectors. The responsibility for auditing accounts had been transferred as early as 1795, and it goes without saying that the new Direction des Impositions Directes established only days after the *coup* had no remit to return the power of oversight to village councils.

Equality in the eyes of the law formed the crucial ingredient of the civic landscape inhabited by villagers in 1820, then. All the other ingredients that had been mixed in over the years had lost their flavour by this date. Citizenship as a political concept had been driven out of the equation, or driven underground. The post-Revolution political culture of the village, such as it was, allowed no room for democracy. Having been sublimated into the person of the emperor, the doctrine of popular sovereignty was scarcely likely to resist the appeal of a 'legitimate' monarch who went to considerable lengths to emphasise that the rule of law as defined by Revolutionary legislators and Napoleonic officialdom was not at risk. Louis XVIII learned rather quicker than his supporters, in fact, some of whom persisted in the belief that the clock *could* be turned back. But the Châtelaudrinais did not want to become Bretons all over again. They subscribed just 25 *francs* when, in 1821, it was suggested that a monument be erected in honour of the 'Breton hero' Bertrand du Guesclin.[6] The inhabitants of Neuviller likewise drew strength and comfort from their new identity. By 1815 the name Chaumont could only recall to mind 'times that were better forgotten'.[7]

What of the seigneurs whose presence in the landscape of the village has turned out to be far more encompassing than was expected at the commencement of this study? Chancellor Antoine-Martin Chaumont de La Galaizière, the man who had conscripted *corvée* labour in order to demolish and rebuild the chateau of Neuviller, quit Lorraine in 1766 following the demise of Stanislas I. He would die in 1783 at the family seat of Mareil-le-Guyon in the Beauce. His son, Antoine, on whom the possessions in and around Neuviller had devolved, wisely chose to emigrate rather than seek rehabilitation under the new regime. An attempt to shelter the family assets by transferring ownership to his own son failed, and the Nation confiscated property with a total value of about 4 million *livres*. The unsold remnants (notably the chateau, park and woodland of Neuviller) were returned in the aftermath of Brumaire, but Antoine Chaumont de La Galaizière had no wish to be reminded of the Lorraine episode and sold what remained to Maurice Jordy, as we have seen. Like his father he lived quietly at Mareil-le-Guyon and would die there in 1812.

With the benefit of hindsight, it is possible to guess at the likely causes of the fragile mental health of 'la dame d'Allan'. Having lost her father at an early age, she was married whilst still a teenager into a branch of Dauphiné lineage nobility, the La Tour-du-Pin-Montaubans. Childless, the countess developed an obsession with Rousseau's sentimentalising novels and wrote the author adoring letters. They finally met in Paris in 1765, and there were probably other meetings, in the company of her husband, whilst visiting their properties in the Dauphiné. Rousseau was pressed to extend his botanising excursions to the neighbourhood of Montélimar and a room in the chateau of Allan was readied for his arrival. He never came, though. By 1770, indeed, Rousseau appears to have broken with the couple. Thereafter the count seems to have drifted apart from his wife, and in 1786

---

[6] A. C. de Châtelaudren, Municipalité, délibérations, an VII–1822, 15 December 1821.
[7] A. D. de Meurthe-et-Moselle, 1M 625, mayor [Jordy] of Neuviller to the prefect of the Meurthe, Neuviller, 28 September 1815. Also chapter 4, p. 119.

he left her in order to travel abroad. After he was accused (incorrectly) of emigration, the La Tour-du-Pin-Montauban estates were seized, but not the 'terre d'Allan', for reasons that we know. Monsieur de Montauban, as he preferred to be known, died, still childless, in 1806, but the unbalanced Madame de La Faye survived until 1814 thanks to the vigilance of her carers.

The seigneur of Roquelaure, Pierre-Emmanuel de Reversac de Celès de Marsac, can be considered unlucky to have lost his life on the guillotine for an 'offence' committed in 1789, and in good company. His predecessor the Comte Dubarry, by contrast, lived a charmed existence. While held in detention in Toulouse during the Terror, both his 'wife' (former mistress of Louis XV) and brother were sent for execution. Guillaume Dubarry managed to get back the estate near Toulouse that he had exchanged for Roquelaure, and devoted his declining years to botany. He would die peacefully, in his bed, in 1811. As for Jean-François-Charles de Molette, the eldest of the warring Molette de Morangiès brothers, he died violently in the chateau of Saint-Alban in 1801, apparently from injuries inflicted with a fire shovel. After a military career punctuated by accusations of fraud and immorality, a bigamous liaison and a spell of imprisonment, he had retired to the village in 1789. Tensions with his younger siblings, notably Jean-Adam Molette-Morangiès who would use the weapons of the Revolution against his errant brother just as he had used the *ancien-régime* courts, flared repeatedly. In 1798 Jean-François-Charles chased the ex-*sans-culotte* Jean-Adam from the Temple of Reason wielding an axe. Whether the elder brother finally met his end at the hands of a sibling or those of his mistress cannot be determined. Jean-Adam did not long survive him in any case. As for the property of the family, it had been held undivided and by now was weighed down with an accumulation of debt. In 1821 creditors forced the sale of the chateau together with all the remaining farms, and the history of seigneurial lordship in Saint-Alban finally came to an end.

Bibliography

MANUSCRIPT SOURCES

Archives Nationales, Paris

27AP 2   Papiers de François de Neufchâteau
27AP 4   Papiers de François de Neufchâteau
BII 11   Votes populaires: Gers
BII 17   Votes populaires: Lozère
BII 19   Votes populaires: Meurthe
B^{a}51   Elections aux Etats-Généraux: Mende
BB^{16}419   Correspondance générale de la Division civile: Lozère
DIII 138   Comité de Législation: Lozère
DIII 158   Comité de Législation: Meurthe
DIII 282   Comité de Législation: Seine-et-Oise
DIII 346   Comité de Législation: représentants-en-mission
DIV 43   Comité de Constitution: Meurthe
DIV^{bis} 27   Comité de Division du Territoire: Lozère
DXIV 3   Comité des Droits Féodaux: Côtes-du-Nord
DXIV 6   Comité des Droits Féodaux: Meurthe
DXIX 94   Comité Ecclésiastique: Gers
DXXIX^{bis}4   Comité des Recherches: Villepreux
F^{Ic}III Côtes-du-Nord 2   Esprit public, élections, 1790–an VIII
F^{Ic}III Côtes-du-Nord 5   Esprit public, élections, 1810–15
F^{Ic}III Gers 1   Esprit public, élections, 1790
F^{Ic}III Gers 2   Esprit public, élections, 1791–an V
F^{Ic}III Gers 3   Esprit public, élections, an VI–an XII
F^{Ic}III Gers 4   Esprit public, élections, an XIII–1811
F^{Ic}III Lozère 1   Esprit public, élections, 1790–an XI
F^{Ic}III Lozère 3   Esprit public, élections, 1812–15
F^{Ic}III Lozère 4   Esprit public, élections, 1816–70
F^{Ic}III Meurthe 1   Esprit public, élections, 1790–an X
F^{Ic}III Meurthe 2   Esprit public, élections, an IX–an X
F^{Ic}III Meurthe 3   Esprit public, élections, an XI–1810
F^{Ic}III Meurthe 4   Esprit public, élections, 1811–15

F³II Drôme 2   Administration communale
F³II Meurthe 28   Administration communale
F³II Meurthe 43   Administration communale
F⁷3681¹⁴   Police générale, Lozère, 1792–an III
F¹²557   Manufactures: série provinciale, Languedoc
F¹⁶970   Mendicité: Lozère
F¹⁶975   Mendicité: Gers
F¹⁷122   Inspection des écoles primaires, Lozère
F¹⁹1011   Lozère: correspondance adressée au Ministre de la Justice, Thermidor an IV
F²⁰212   Mémoires statistiques: Lozère
H1258   Provence: impositions des terres adjacentes, 1750–89
H1486   Droits et parcours, affaires générales, 1707–90
H1489²   Partage des communaux, 1644–1790, L–M
NN 96/2   Plan: projet de division du département du Gers, 9 Prairial II
T643   Séquestre des particuliers: sieur de Bruges
T1684   Séquestre des particuliers: Chaumont La Galaizière
W386   Tribunal Révolutionnaire, affaire Sénaux, Combette-Caumont et autres parlementaires de Paris et de Toulouse
Z¹ᴳ 461   Rôles de taille: Villepreux, 1790
Z¹ᴳ 549   Rôles de taille: Rennemoulin, 1790

Archives de l'Assistance Publique, Paris

Fonds Montyon, carton 5: Droit constitutionnel

Archives Départementales des Bouches-du-Rhône, Marseille

C 370   Communautés: capitation
C 995   Communautés: Allan
C 2577   Etat général des dettes des Communautés Terres Adjacentes de Provence, portées au 1ᵉʳ octobre 1774

Archives Départementales des Côtes-d'Armor, Saint-Brieuc

B2075   Juridiction de Châtelaudren, audiences, 1789–90
B2110   Juridiction de Châtelaudren, minutes, 1789–90
2E Dépôt 19/1–10   Archives administratives: Châtelaudren
3E 30/188   Notaires: Le Berne de Châtelaudren, minutes, an III
3E 30/216   Notaires: Jolivet de Châtelaudren, minutes, an III–an V
3E 30/289   Notaires: Hamon de Châtelaudren, minutes, an III
3E 30/318   Notaires: Le Rumeur de Châtelaudren, minutes, an III
3E 30/341   Notaires: Le Corvaisier de Châtelaudren, minutes, an III
3E 30/372   Notaires: Cocho de Châtelaudren, minutes, an II–an III

20G 20   Fonds des paroisses: Châtelaudren, procédures, 1775–85
20G 42   Fonds des paroisses: Châtelaudren, délibérations, 11 juillet 1756–24 janvier 1790
20G 46   Fonds des paroisses: Châtelaudren, impositions, 1706–87
20G 362   Fonds des paroisses: Plouagat-Châtelaudren, 1501–1790
20G 664   Fonds des paroisses: Tressignaux
75J   Fonds Geslin de Bourgogne
1L 406   Elections municipales, 1790–2
1L 583   Population, recensements, états nominatifs, par communes
1L 868   Statistique: mendicité, 1791
10L 86   District de Saint-Brieuc: population, états de citoyens actifs, etc., 1790–an II
10L 87   District de Saint-Brieuc: population, états de citoyens actifs, etc., 1793–an II
10L 89   District de Saint-Brieuc: population, états de citoyens actifs, etc., 1793
10L 106   District de Saint-Brieuc: Etats des charrues et demi-charrues, an II
10L 185   District de Saint-Brieuc: cultes décadaires, déclarations de revenus ecclésiastiques, par communes
18L 8   Administration cantonale, Châtelaudren, assemblées primaires, an IV–an VII
18L 10   Administration cantonale, Châtelaudren, état-civil et population, an IV–an VIII
100L 17   Fonds des comités de surveillance: Châtelaudren
100L 18   Fonds des comités de surveillance: Châtelaudren
101L 11   Fonds des sociétés populaires: Châtelaudren
5Mi 215   Registres paroissiaux, Châtelaudren, 1627–1706
2 O 37/11   Administration communale: Châtelaudren
1Q 2/6   Biens nationaux, 2ième origine, par communes
1Q 2/20   Biens nationaux, 2ième origine, par communes
1Q 2/62   Biens nationaux, 2ième origine, Plouagat
4U 7/2   Justice de paix: canton de Châtelaudren
V66   Cultes: circonscription des cures et succursales, an X
V68   Cultes: désignation des desservants, an XII
V380   Cultes: cures et succursales, états, an XII–an XIII
V382   Cultes: nominations aux cures, états, an XI–1840
V383   Cultes: nominations aux succursales, an XII–1819
V392   Cultes: états des décès, démissions, vacances, an XII–1841
V544   Cultes: prêtres
V577   Cultes: prêtres
V607   Cultes: prêtres
V1093   Cultes: Châtelaudren, an XI–1913
V1094   Cultes: Châtelaudren, 1807–18
V1095   Cultes: Châtelaudren, 1806–91

Archives Départementales de la Drôme, Valence

B 1340 Judicature d'Allan, cahiers, 1768–89

B 2446 Justice, Provence: Comté de Grignan et dépendances

2E 10728 Notaires: Alexandre Andrau d'Allan, actes, 18 janvier 1751–22 avril 1757

2E 10731 Notaires: Coustaury d'Allan, répertoire des actes, 23 février 1779–15 février 1791

2E 15783 Notaires: Jean Candy de Montélimar, répertoire des actes, 12 septembre 1793–10 Pluviôse IV

2E 21137 Notaires: Charles Raynaud de Châteauneuf-du-Rhône, répertoire des actes, 21 Fructidor II–3ᵉ Jour Compl. IV

2E 22557 Notaires: Louis Andrau de Montélimar, répertoire des actes, 27 janvier 1793–9 Pluviôse IV

2E 22562 Notaires: Félix Laurant de Montélimar, répertoire des actes, 24 Floréal II–2 Pluviôse V

2E 22698 Notaires: François Blanc de Montélimar, répertoire des actes, 28 Thermidor II–14 Ventôse III

2E 22699 Notaires: François Blanc de Montélimar, répertoire des actes, 14 Ventôse–15 Thermidor III

4E 51 Etat-civil, Allan, 1762–92

6E 16/1 Etat-civil, protestants, Allan, 1788

22G 4 Evêché de Saint-Paul, visites pastorales, 1643–4

L 147 Divisions administratives, 1790

L 156 Listes de citoyens actifs, canton de Donzère, 1790–1

L 159 Assemblées primaires, canton de Donzère, 1790

L 177 Personnel municipal, Albon–Loriol, 1792–an VIII

L 186 Voeux des communes sur les événements du 31 mai–2 juin 1793

L 186ᵇⁱˢ Sociétés populaires

L 187 Politique générale, acceptation de l'acte constitutionnel, 1793

L 188 Voeux des assemblées sur la Constitution de l'an III

L 204 Troubles et brigandages, canton de Donzère, an IV–an VIII

L 233 Population

L 234 Population, loi du 10 Vendémiaire IV

L 239 Agriculture

L 240 Produit des récoltes, 1791

L 242 Recensement général des grains de toute éspèce, 1792–3

L 244 Subsistances et approvisionnements, 1792–an II

L 275 Biens communaux, 1791–an II

L 276 Biens communaux, 1791–an II

L 277 Bois communaux, 1791–an III

L 283 Etats des dépenses communales et municipales pendant l'an IV

L 312 Contribution patriotique, 1790–1

L 321 Cadastre, 1790–1

L 353 Affaires militaires, tableaux par cantons

L 559 Traitements des curés

L 582   District de Montélimar, état nominatif des écclésiastiques qui ont abdiqué leur état, 28 Thermidor II

L 1151   Allan: comptes et correspondance, 1790, contestations de propriété, 1793

L 1783   Tribunal criminel, registre des jugements, 1 Vendémiaire–15 Ventôse XI

L 1791   Tribunal criminel, registre des jugements, 16 mars 1811

L 1956   Tribunal Criminel, dossiers

L 1964   Tribunal Criminel, dossiers

L 1997   Tribunal Criminel, dossiers

L 2119   Justice de paix, canton de Donzère, registre de jugements, 24 Floréal II–24 Floréal III

L 2120   Justice de paix, canton de Donzère, tutelle et curatelle, an II–an X

L 2367   Administration cantonale, Donzère, correspondance, an IV–an VIII

L 2368   Administration cantonale, Donzère, délibérations, 21 Brumaire IV–9 Floréal VIII

L 2369   Administration cantonale, Donzère, registres des Bulletins des lois, an IV–an VIII

L 2377   Société populaire d'Allan, délibérations, 5 jour Sans-Culottide II–20 Ventôse III

L 2378   Assemblées primaires, canton de Donzère, 1790–3

2M 99   Nominations: maires et adjoints, dossiers par communes, an VIII–1820

3M 7   Transferts de chefs-lieux de cantons, an IX–1881

3M 27   Elections: dossiers par communes, 1809

3M 41   Régime des Cent Jours: dossiers par communes, 1815

3M 193   Plébiscite des Cent Jours, relevés des votes par municipalités

1Mi 709   Allan: délibérations municipales, 21 février 1790–27 Ventôse III

5Mi 84   Allan, registres paroissiaux, 1700–20

2 O 14   Communes: Allan

2 O 15   Communes: Allan

2 O 17   Communes: Allan, biens communaux, an X–1894

2 Op 5   Biens communaux, généralités

2 Op 12   Cimetières, par communes

3P 2747   Cadastre: Allan, procès-verbal de vérification des plans, 1808

3P 2888   Cadastre: Allan, fixation des limites, 1807–11

Q 80   District de Montélimar, inventaire des ventes de biens nationaux de 1ère origine

Q 83   District de Montélimar, procès-verbaux d'enchères

Q 89   District de Montélimar, inventaire des ventes de biens nationaux de 2ième origine

Q 303   District de Montélimar, dossiers des émigrés, La Tour-du-Pin-Montauban

Q 305   District de Montélimar, dossiers des émigrés, Lériget

Q 418   Biens cédés à la Caisse d'amortissement, loi 20 mars 1813

Q 419   Biens cédés à la Caisse d'amortissement, rapports d'experts

Q 422   Caisse d'amortissement, dossiers communaux

10T 13/1   Enseignement

51V 52   Fonds de l'Evêché de Valence, nominations, Ventôse XI

51V 53 Fonds de l'Evêché de Valence, états généraux et statistiques diverses des paroisses et du personnel, an IX–an XII
51V 66 Fonds de l'Evêché de Valence: Allan
53V 1 Arrondissement de Montélimar, recensement des familles protestantes, 4 Thermidor X

Archives Départementales du Gard, Nîmes

L 430 Administrations et tribunaux révolutionnaires: révolte de la Lozère, 1793
L 431 Administrations et tribunaux révolutionnaires: révolte de la Lozère, 1793

Archives Départementales de la Haute-Garonne, Toulouse

B 1533 Parlement de Toulouse, actes, 2 mai 1744
1J 603 P.-M.-E. Reversac Celès, certificat de domicile, 7 janvier 1792

Archives Départementales du Gers, Auch

C 22 Population et état-civil, 1774–89
C 76 Etat général de la contenance de l'Election d'Armagnac en l'année 1741
C 639 Bureau intermédiaire d'Armagnac, registre de correspondance, 1787–8
C 648 Commission intermédiaire: administration communale, 1789–91
C 668 Bureau intermédiaire d'Armagnac
C 695 Correspondance du Marquis d'Arcamont au sujet de la convocation des Etats-Généraux
C 728 Bureau des finances de la généralité d'Auch, biens nobles
C 729 Bureau des finances de la généralité d'Auch, impositions communales pour 1760
C Supplément 723 Election d'Armagnac: état et département des paroisses, 1768
E 1215 Fonds Roquelaure, 1752–68
E 1216 Fonds Roquelaure, 1772–7
E 1226 Fonds Roquelaure, 1785
E 1229 Fonds Roquelaure, 1753
E 1230 Fonds Roquelaure, 1760–91
E 1248 Fonds Roquelaure, 1764–6
E 1252 Fonds Roquelaure, 1783–93
E 1554 Arcamont: délibérations, 1773–87
E 1557 Arcamont: rôles d'imposition, 1678–1789
E 1676 Roquelaure: divers, XVIe siècle–1792
E Supplément 1008 Roquelaure: cadastre, mutations
E Supplément 1010^1 Roquelaure: délibérations, 1766–74
E Supplément 1010^2 Roquelaure: délibérations, 1774–82
E Supplément 1010^3 Roquelaure: délibérations, 1784–90
E Supplément 1010^4 Roquelaure: registre d'inscription des décrets, 1789–93
3E 854 Notaires: Serres de Roquelaure, minutes, 1765–93

3E 3801   Notaires: Branet d'Auch, répertoire général des actes, 28 mai 1769–18 Floréal an VII

3E 8751   Notaires: Joseph Soubdès de Mirepoix, table

5E 552   Registres paroissiaux, Roquelaure, 1737–89

G 37   Chapitre métropolitain de Sainte-Marie d'Auch, baux à ferme, 1767–90

L 376   Garde nationale, 1790–9

L 401   Cultes: correspondance, circonscription des paroisses, 1791–2

L 420   Prêtres réfractaires, 1792–an VIII

L 474   District d'Auch, correspondance, an II–an IV

L 645   Canton d'Auch, correspondance, an IV–an VIII

L 646   Canton d'Auch, assemblées primaires, an IV–an VII

L 647   Canton d'Auch, contributions, an IV–an VIII

L 648   Canton d'Auch, guerre et recrutement, an IV

L 650   Canton d'Auch, culte, an IV–an V

L 699*   Société montagnarde de Roquelaure, délibérations, 19 mai 1793–10 Pluviôse III

2M 23   Personnel administratif, maires et adjoints, an VIII–1814

2M 37   Première Restauration: procès-verbaux de prestations de serment à Louis XVIII

2M 41   Cent Jours: élections des maires et des adjoints

2M 42   Cent Jours: élections des maires et des adjoints

2M 44   Deuxième Restauration: maires et adjoints, dossiers par communes

3M 352   Maires et adjoints, conseillers municipaux, démissions, suspensions, 1832–69

6M 33   Listes nominatives de population: Roquelaure, 1836

6M 625   Etat-civil, arrondissement d'Auch, tables, 1821

6M 885   Agriculture, enquêtes annuelles

6M 888   Agriculture, 1817–19

6M 977   Canton d'Auch nord, renseignements administratifs, 1854

O   Canton d'Auch nord: Roquelaure

3P 42   Tableaux d'expertise, Auch nord

3P 1385   Roquelaure: cadastre dit Napoléonien

3P 1386   Roquelaure: cadastre dit Napoléonien

Q 74*   District d'Auch: vente des biens nationaux, an II–an IV

Q 86   District d'Auch: procès-verbaux d'estimation des biens de 1ère origine, 1790–an II

Q 87   District d'Auch: procès-verbaux d'estimation des biens de 2ième origine, an II

Q 111*   District d'Auch: procès-verbaux d'adjudication des biens de 1ère origine, 23 décembre 1790–31 mai 1791

Q 112*   District d'Auch: procès-verbaux d'adjudication des biens de 1ère origine, 18 mai–25 mai 1791

Q 122*   District d'Auch: procès-verbaux d'adjudication des biens nationaux provenant d'émigrés, 12 Nivôse II–15 Germinal II

Q 123*   District d'Auch: procès-verbaux d'adjudication des biens nationaux provenant d'émigrés, 6 Prairial II

N[on] C[oté]   Commune de Roquelaure: procès-verbal de délimitation du territoire de la commune de Roquelaure

Archives Départementales de la Lozère, Mende

475B (1)   Cours et juridictions de l'Ancien Régime, Saint-Alban

475B (2)   Cours et juridictions de l'Ancien Régime, Saint-Alban

475B (7)   Cours et juridictions de l'Ancien Régime, Saint-Alban

475B (8)   Cours et juridictions de l'Ancien Régime, Saint-Alban

C 62   Recensement de population, 1736

C 100   Saint-Alban: rôles de la capitation et de l'industrie, 1761–88

C 481   Dénombrement des bêtes à laine qui existent dans le Gévaudan

C 866   Saint-Alban, taille, 1786

C 943   Biens nobles du Gévaudan, familles

C 1086   Rôle des impositions des communautés du diocèse, 1780

C 1247   Saint-Alban: comptes-rendus par les collecteurs, 1745–85

E 557   Saint-Alban, transaction de 23 décembre 1734

E 915   Archives civiles, Saint-Alban, 1672–1779

E Dépôt Saint-Alban: 132 (D1)   Cahier des délibérations du Conseil municipal de la commune de Saint-Alban, 1 septembre 1815–21 août 1822

E Dépôt Saint-Alban: 132 (D2)   Cahier des délibérations du Conseil municipal de la commune de Saint-Alban, 3 décembre 1822–17 février 1829

E Dépôt Saint-Alban: 132 (D3)   Délibérations du Conseil municipal du 22 janvier 1833 au 1er avril 1838

E Dépôt Saint-Alban: 132 (GG1)   Registre paroissial, 1700–24

E Dépôt Saint-Alban: 132 (GG7)   Registre paroissial, 1773–an VII

3E 2147   Notaires: Pierre Mathieu, 1695–1732

3E 5735   Notaires: Pierre Fontibus, 1773–4

3E 5740   Notaires: Pierre Fontibus, 1779–80

3E 5741   Notaires: Pierre Fontibus, 1780–1

3E 5743   Notaires: Pierre Fontibus, 1786–8

3E 14832   Notaires: Félix Boyer, 1780–3

3E 14833   Notaires: registre des actes reçus par Me Félix Boyer, 1783–93

3E 14834   Notaires: registre des actes reçus par Me Félix Boyer, 1793–1er Compl. III

F 572   Fonds divers: Marlet, François, médecin de Saint-Alban, 1787–9

G 1987   Saint-Alban, presbytère, 1781–6

G 2090   Etats des revenus des curés

1J 29   Certificats de résidence et laisser passer, J.-A. de Molette de Morangiès, 1792–an IV

1J 55   Registre de copies de lettres de Boissier fils et Cie, drapiers de Marvejols, 1812–25

1J 150   Documents intéressant Joseph Bruel, négociant en draps à Marvejols, 1769–1818

4J 25   Extraits d'actes concernant les terres de la famille Morangiès, 1619–1774

4J 37   Comptes entre J.-A. de Morangiès et J. Allier, fermier du domaine de Saint-Alban, 1793–8

4J 64   Famille Moré de Charaix

4J 74   Famille Moré de Charaix

4J 75   Famille Moré de Charaix

13J 15   Saint-Alban, Grazières-Mages

16J 1   Saint-Alban

17J 8   Famille Ayrald-Ollier de Saint-Alban, 1761–an II

17J 40   Titres des familles: Brugeroles de Saint-Alban, 1816–24

17J 81   Titres des familles: Marlet de la Chaumette

17J 104   Famille Salleix

23J 2   Fonds abbé de Sirven

L III   Extraits des délibérations de l'Administration municipale du canton de Saint-Alban, an III–an VI

L 146   Inventaire des pièces et procès-verbaux relatifs à l'exécution de l'arrêté du département du 18 avril 1793

L 190   Clergé, déclarations de revenus, 1790

L 191   Clergé, déclarations de revenus, 1790

L 319   Clergé, déclarations de revenus, 1789–90

L 333*   District de Saint-Chély-d'Apcher, registre général des arrêtés, 21 Germinal III–27 Brumaire IV

L 334   District de Saint-Chély-d'Apcher, politique générale, 1790–an II

L 339   District de Saint-Chély-d'Apcher, fêtes, 1790–an III

L 341   District de Saint-Chély-d'Apcher, secours pour pertes agricoles, 1791–an III

L 348   District de Saint-Chély-d'Apcher, Garde nationale

L 350   District de Saint-Chély-d'Apcher, levée des 300,000 hommes, 1793

L 351   District de Saint-Chély-d'Apcher, levée-en-masse, 1793

L 361   District de Saint-Chély-d'Apcher, déclarations des revenus du clergé, 1790

L 418   Administration cantonale, Saint-Alban, délibérations, 20 Pluviôse IV–10 Thermidor IV

L 419   Administration cantonale, Saint-Alban, délibérations, 10 Frimaire IV–27 Brumaire V

L 420   Administration cantonale, Saint-Alban, délibérations, 26 Nivôse VI–12 Nivôse VI

L 421   Administration cantonale, Saint-Alban, délibérations, 11 Frimaire VII–11 Ventôse VII

L 422   Administration cantonale, Saint-Alban, pétitions, 20 Frimaire IV–4 Pluviôse IV

L 423   Administration cantonale, Saint-Alban, pétitions, 1 Pluviôse IV–1 Frimaire V

L 424   Procès-verbal de l'assemblée primaire du canton de Saint-Alban, 2 Germinal VI

L 427   Administration cantonale de Saint-Chély-d'Apcher, emprunt forcé, an IV

L 520*   Comité de surveillance de Saint-Alban, délibérations, 20 octobre 1793–5 Germinal II

L 521   Comité de surveillance de Saint-Alban, délibérations, 10 Germinal II–30 Thermidor II

L 522   Comité de surveillance de Saint-Chély-d'Apcher, délibérations, 8 octobre 1793–20 octobre 1793

L 524   Comité de surveillance de Saint-Chély-d'Apcher, délibérations, 12 Germinal II–24 Messidor II

L 525   Comité de surveillance de Saint-Chély-d'Apcher, délibérations, 25 Messidor II–29 Brumaire III

L 527   Comité de surveillance de Saint-Chély-d'Apcher, délibérations, 12 Frimaire III–23 Ventôse III

L 528   Comité de surveillance de Saint-Chély-d'Apcher, pièces diverses

L 866   Correspondance, 1789–90

L 867   Fonds divers: assemblée primaire du canton de Saint-Alban, cahier des délibérations, 19 mai 1790–26 août 1792

L 868   Fonds divers: assemblée primaire du canton de Saint-Alban, cahier des délibérations, 2 décembre 1792–13 Brumaire IV

L 869   Fonds divers: assemblée primaire du canton de Saint-Alban, cahier des délibérations, 10 Brumaire IV–1 Germinal VI

L 870   Fonds divers: assemblée primaire du canton de Saint-Alban, cahier des délibérations, 2 Germinal VI

2L 307   Répertoire des actes reçus par le citoyen Mathieu, notaire, an VIII

2L 308   Répertoire des actes reçus par le citoyen Vincens, notaire, an VIII

1142L 1   Tribunal Civil du Département de la Lozère

M 11853   Recensements, population

M 12442   Délimitations de communes

M 12586   Maires

M 12793   Imprimés

M 13204   Propositions pour l'organisation des mairies, Saint-Alban, 1837–86

3P 487   Lajo, cadastre

3P 842   Saint-Alban, cadastre

3P 1268   Lajo, cadastre

3P 1302   Saint-Alban, cadastre

3P 1552   Saint-Alban, cadastre

2 O 1291   Saint-Alban: biens, section du chef-lieu, 1887–1940

2 O 1292   Saint-Alban: biens, section du chef-lieu, 1855–1940

2 O 1293   Saint-Alban: biens, sections de Grazières Mages, Le Rouget etc, 1888–1940

Q 110   District de Saint-Chély-d'Apcher, biens nationaux

Q 111   District de Saint-Chély-d'Apcher, biens nationaux

Q 112   District de Saint-Chély-d'Apcher, biens nationaux

Q 113   District de Saint-Chély-d'Apcher, biens nationaux

Q 168   District de Saint-Chély-d'Apcher, déclarations des acquéreurs des biens nationaux ouvertes en exécution de... la loi du 11 Frimaire VIII
Q 225   District de Saint-Chély-d'Apcher, sommier des baux, 1791–1810
Q 226   Bureau du Malzieu, sommier des biens des suspects, an II
R 7632   Affaires militaires, Garde nationale, an XII–1871
R 7720   Affaires militaires, déserteurs, 1801–16
R 7736   Affaires militaires, occupation, 1815
R 7814   Affaires militaires, lettres de soldats, 1805–11
1T 682   Monographies communales, 1862–74: Saint-Alban
162 II U   Saint-Alban: Félix Vincent, répertoire de notaire, an IX–1825
59V 1   Circonscriptions paroissiales, an X–1887
59V 2   Circonscriptions paroissiales, 1843
94V 5   Fabriques, Noalhac–Saint-Alban, 1826–1908
2Z 1   Sous-préfet de Marvejols, registre de correspondance active, 1 Floréal VIII–3 Germinal X
2Z 2   Sous-préfet de Marvejols, registre de correspondance passive, 25 Germinal VIII–2 Messidor XI
2Z 3   Sous-préfet de Marvejols, registre de correspondance active, 5 Germinal X–20 Germinal XII
2Z 5   Sous-préfet de Marvejols, registre de correspondance active, 20 Germinal XII–23 septembre 1806
2Z 6   Sous-préfet de Marvejols, registre de correspondance active, 23 septembre 1806–22 janvier 1808
2Z 10   Sous-préfet de Marvejols, registre de correspondance active, 26 janvier 1813–29 juillet 1814
2Z 12   Sous-préfet de Marvejols, registre de correspondance active, 1 août 1814–7 mai 1816

Archives Départementales de Meurthe-et-Moselle, Nancy

AC 398 1   Registre: 'Naissances, mariages et décès depuis 1692 jusque 1730 au 15 février inclusivement'
AC 398 2   Registre: 'Naissances, mariages et décès depuis le 16 janvier jusque au 7 décembre 1784'
AC 398 3   Registre: 'Naissances, mariages et décès depuis le 30 décembre 1784 jusque au 24 décembre 1789'
B 1947   Chambre des comptes de Lorraine, terre de Roville, 1770
B 10494   Recette de Nancy, biens ecclésiastiques, 1790
B 11435   Chambre des Comptes de Lorraine, arrêts sur requêtes, 1790
B 11736   Ban de Neuviller-sur-Moselle, 1738
B 11928   Distribution des terres composant le ban de Neuviller entre les habitants dudit lieu, 1771
B 12306   Affouages, procès-verbaux de délivrance, 1776–80
B 12310   Maîtrise de Nancy, affouages, 1789–91
BJ 9925   Prévôté-bailliagère de Neuviller-sur-Moselle, procès-verbaux, 1776–90

BJ 10216   Prévôté-bailliagère de Neuviller-sur-Moselle, feuilles d'audience, 1771–2

BJ 10264   Justice de Neuviller-sur-Moselle, 1735–51

BJ 10265   Prévôté-bailliagère de Neuviller-sur-Moselle, registre d'audiences, 1766–71

BJ 10500   Prévôté-bailliagère de Neuviller-sur-Moselle, feuilles d'audience, 1789–90

C 440   Subdélégation de Nancy, requêtes

C 478   Subdélégation de Vézelise, affaires communales, 1754–89

C 479   Subdélégation de Vézelise, Roville–Sauxerotte

C 489   Subdélégation de Vézelise, Gélocourt–Gemonville

C 491   Subdélégation de Vézelise, Jevoncourt–Oguéville

C 560   Assemblées municipales, 1787–8

E 19   Pied terrier, 1719

E Supplément 2955   Crévéchamps, délibérations de l'assemblée municipale, 1788–90

E Supplément 3065   Laneuveville-devant-Bayon, délibérations de l'assemblée municipale, 1788–90

E Supplément 3121–30   Neuviller-sur-Moselle, 1770–91

E Supplément 3141   Roville, délibérations de la municipalité de Roville-devant-Bayon, 1788–91

E Supplément 3144   Roville, translation des ossements de l'ancien cimetière dans le nouveau, 11 septembre 1764

31E 129   Notaires: Auguste Landry, notaire public à Haroué, an III

31E 130   Notaires: Auguste Landry, notaire public à Haroué, an IV–V

31E 201   Notaires: Maurice Jordy, notaire au marquisat de Craon, 1788

31E 202   Notaires: Maurice Jordy, notaire au marquisat de Craon, 1789

1F 8   Don de M. Malglaive, 1905

1F 9   Terrier général du Comté de Neuviller, 1751

1F 10   Remembrement du Comté de Neuviller, 1770–1

1F 11   Inventaire général des titres et papiers concernant le Comté de Neuviller et dépendances, 1752

1F 12   Extrait tiré sur l'original de la nouvelle division et distribution du ban de Roville, 1 octobre 1770

1F 13   Livre contenant le dépouillement des droits, rentes, et revenus des baronnies d'Orme et d'Haroué unies et érigées en marquisat sous le titre d'Haroué [n.d.]

1F 187   Documents relatifs à Neuviller-sur-Moselle, 1792

1F 317   Neuviller-sur-Moselle: plainte contre le détournement qu'a fait l'intendant de La Galaizière à la chaussée en cours de construction de Flavigny à Neuviller [n.d.]

1F 324   Roville: baux à ferme par Antoine de Chaumont de La Galaizière, 1791–3

G 818   Eglises paroissiales: Roville-devant-Bayon, comptes, 1759–60

G 1105   Eglises paroissiales: Neuviller-sur-Moselle

G 1179   Eglises paroissiales: Laneuveville-devant Bayon; Roville-devant-Bayon

H 387   Clergé regulier avant 1790

H 851   Clergé regulier avant 1790
H 852   Clergé regulier avant 1790
H 853   Clergé regulier avant 1790
1J 186   Ferme-expérimentale de Roville, 1819–24
1J 436   Dons de M. Paul Montigny de Neuviller-sur-Moselle
L 233   Population
L 306   Impositions
L 308   Impositions, District de Vézelise
L 316   Contribution patriotique
L 318   Contribution patriotique
L 2552   Elections, District de Vézelise
L 2554   Elections municipales, District de Vézelise, 1790–1
L 2590   Partage des biens communaux, 1790–3
L 2718   Garde nationale, District de Vézelise
L 2746   Etats nominatifs des prêtres, District de Vézelise
L 2943bis Administration cantonale, Neuviller-sur-Moselle, délibérations, 14 Nivôse IV–27 Thermidor IV
L 2944   Administration cantonale, Neuviller-sur-Moselle, délibérations, 1 Vendémiaire V–3e Jour Complémentaire V
L 2945   Administration cantonale, Neuviller-sur-Moselle, délibérations, 10 Vendémiaire VIII–18 Floréal VIII
L 2947   Canton de Neuviller-sur-Moselle: comptes communaux, 1791–an III
L 2948   Administration cantonale, Neuviller-sur-Moselle, registre de l'enregistrement des patentes délivrées pendant l'an V
L 2949   Administration cantonale, Neuviller-sur-Moselle, quittances pour droit de patentes
L 3143   Société populaire républicaine, Vézelise
L 3401   Comité de surveillance, Roville
L 3448   Comite révolutionnaire de Vézelise, délibérations, 24 Vendémiaire III–14 Frimaire III
L 3449   Comité révolutionnaire de Vézelise, délibérations, 14 Frimaire III–24 Pluviôse III
L 4193   Justice de paix, canton de Neuviller-sur-Moselle, enregistrement des affaires, 2 Germinal III–12 Ventôse VI
L 4194   Justice de paix, canton de Neuviller-sur-Moselle, audiences, 27 December 1790–30 August 1792
L 4195   Justice de paix, canton de Neuviller-sur-Moselle, jugements et actes, 1793–an II
L 4196   Justice de paix, canton de Neuviller-sur-Moselle, jugements et actes, an III
L 4197   Justice de paix, canton de Neuviller-sur-Moselle, jugements et actes, an IV
1M 625   Communes, changements/modifications de noms
2M 28   Maires et adjoints, arrondissement de Lunéville
2M 29   Mutations dans les conseils municipaux, arrondissement de Lunéville

2M 33   Etat nominatif des maires, adjoints et membres des conseils municipaux, 1814

2M 36   Cent Jours: annulations par le sous-préfet de Lunéville

7M 116   Agriculture

7M 122*   Agriculture

1Q 55   Emigrés, indemnisation, A–F, 1824–8

1Q 173   Biens nationaux, mobiliers, District de Vézelise

1Q 258   Biens nationaux, état général des acquéreurs, District de Vézelise

1Q 466^{1} Vente de biens nationaux, 2ième origine, District de Vézelise

1Q 564^{1} Vente de biens nationaux, 2ième origine, District de Vézelise

1Q 567   Vente de biens nationaux, 2ième origine, District de Vézelise

1Q 596   Vente de biens nationaux, 2ième origine, District de Vézelise

1Q 722   Vente de biens nationaux, 2ième origine, District de Vézelise

1Q Supplément 170   Neuviller-sur-Moselle, mémoire sur la mouvance des terrains attachés à la cure, 1791

2Q 121   Neuviller-sur-Moselle

V 9   Personnel ecclésiastique, par communes, 1825–93

V 150   Fondations, constitutions de rentes, legs, par communes, 1811–1906

WO 2593   Administration communale, Neuviller-sur-Moselle, service vicinal

WO 2594   Administration communale, Neuviller-sur-Moselle, biens communaux

WO 2595   Administration communale, Neuviller-sur-Moselle, travaux communaux

N[on] C[oté] AC 398   Neuviller-sur-Moselle, plan cadastral

N[on] C[oté] AC 398/1   Neuviller-sur-Moselle, cahier des délibérations, 29 septembre 1820–20 août 1826

N[on] C[oté] AC 398/2   Neuviller-sur-Moselle, cahier des délibérations, 3 septembre 1826–4 mai 1835

N[on] C[oté] G3 94/1/1 Neuviller-sur-Moselle, cahier des délibérations, 18 mars 1809–2 février 1812

N[on] C[oté] G3 94/1/2   Neuviller-sur-Moselle, cahier des délibérations, 6 mai 1812–1 mai 1820

Archives Départementales des Yvelines, Versailles

B4365   Justice: prévôté de Villepreux, 1503–1790

B4383   Justice: prévôté de Villepreux, pièces de greffe, 1756–67

B4384   Justice: prévôté de Villepreux, pièces de greffe, 1768–74

B4385   Justice: prévôté de Villepreux, pièces de greffe, 1775–90

C6   Villepreux: procès-verbal d'arpentage, 1787

C6   Rennemoulin: procès-verbal d'arpentage, 1787

3E Villepreux 94   Notaires: J.-G. Prissette, 22 septembre 1794–22 septembre 1795

3E Villepreux 95   Notaires: J.-G. Prissette, 23 septembre 1795–21 septembre 1796

3E Villepreux 96   Notaires: J.-G. Prissette, 22 septembre 1796–21 septembre 1797

5F 16   Note sur Villepreux par Amédée Brocard

J3096   Villepreux: la Révolution de 1789

J3405 Terrier de la seigneurie de Villepreux, 1744

2J 26 Archives du château de Mareil-le-Guyon, papiers Chaumont de La Galaizière

2J 27 Archives du château de Mareil-le-Guyon, papiers Chaumont de La Galaizière

2J 32 Archives du château de Mareil-le-Guyon, papiers Chaumont de La Galaizière

2J 33 Archives du château de Mareil-le-Guyon, papiers Chaumont de La Galaizière

2J 34 Archives du château de Mareil-le-Guyon, papiers Chaumont de La Galaizière

1LM 366 Assemblées primaires, élections, 1790

1LM 367 Assemblées primaires, élections, 1791–an V

1LM 371 Elections, canton de Marly-la-Machine, an VI

1LM 374 Administrations municipales, 1790–1

1LM 424 Fêtes et cérémonies publiques

1LM 464 Agriculture, 1793–an VIII

1LM 501 Administration et comptabilité communale, Villepreux, 1790–an VIII

2LM 46 District de Versailles: organisation des autorités constituées, an III–an IV

2LM 51 District de Versailles: comité révolutionnaire du district de Versailles, 1793–an II

2LM 54 District de Versailles: sociétés populaires du district, an II

2LM 63 District de Versailles: correspondance envers des municipalités, an II–an III

2LM 69 District de Versailles: divisions administratives, 1790–an II

2LM 74 District de Versailles: délits de chasse, Grand Parc, 1790–an II

2LM 82 District de Versailles: agriculture, 1790–an III

2LO 92 District de Versailles: Comités de surveillance, Villepreux, rapports, 23 Nivôse II–9 Fructidor II

2LR 111 District de Versailles: recrutement

2LX 179 Etats des indigents du district, an II

2LX 183 Tableaux de mendicité, District de Versailles, 1791

23L 1 Administration cantonale, Marly-la-Machine, délibérations, 1 Frimaire IV–10 Floréal V

23L 2 Administration cantonale, Marly-la-Machine, délibérations, 20 Floréal V–14 Germinal VIII

23L 4 Administration cantonale, Marly-la-Machine, assemblées électorales

23L 5 Administration cantonale, Marly-la-Machine, personnel administratif

23L 7 Administration cantonale, Marly-la-Machine, police générale

23L 8 Administration cantonale, Marly-la-Machine, fêtes, décadis, arbres de la liberté

23L 16 Administration cantonale, Marly-la-Machine, population

23L 17 Administration cantonale, Marly-la-Machine, état-civil

23L 18 Administration cantonale, Marly-la-Machine, agriculture

23L 19 Administration cantonale, Marly-la-Machine, comptabilité

23L 20 Administration cantonale, Marly-la-Machine, agents, gardes champêtres

23L 21   Administration cantonale, Marly-la-Machine, emprunt forcé, an IV
23L 31   Administration cantonale, Marly-la-Machine, patentes
23L 46   Administration cantonale, Marly-la-Machine, travaux publics
23L 47   Administration cantonale, Marly-la-Machine, instruction publique
47L 83   Tribunal du District de Versailles, Teissier, ci-devant curé de Villepreux
2Mi 115 T   Monographies d'instituteurs: Villepreux, 1899
2Mi 791 P   Villepreux: cadastre napoléonien, plans [on microfilm]
9M 984   Villepreux: état nominatif des habitants, 1817
13M 8   Enquêtes statistiques, 1816–30
2 O 261/4   Villepreux: affaires communales, 1812–1938
2 O 261/5   Villepreux: biens communaux, 1812–1938
1Q 380   Biens nationaux, Rennemoulin, concessions
1Q 381   Biens nationaux, état des citoyens de la commune de Villepreux qui n'ont aucune propriété
1Q 382   Biens nationaux, Villepreux
1Q 383   Biens nationaux, instructions et états par districts (incomplets) pour la distribution de 500 livres par chefs de famille
2Q 53   Biens nationaux, liste civile, Villepreux
2Q 55   Biens nationaux, ventes des biens provenant de la liste civile, an II–an VIII
3Q 100   Domaines nationaux, Villepreux, fabrique
4Q 178   Biens nationaux, émigrés et condamnés
5Q 244   Biens nationaux, séquestres, émigrés et condamnés
5Q 347   Biens nationaux, domaines engagés
5Q 1422   Biens nationaux, sommier des concessions

Archives Communales d'Allan, Allan

AA 8   Consultations
AA 9   Cadastre, encadastrement de biens privilégiés, 1789
AA 10   Impositions directes, 1792
AA 11   Procès avec le seigneur, 1792–1815
AA 12   Pièces diverses, 1619–1789
BB 3–4   Conseil politique, délibérations, 7 août 1768–20 février 1790
CC 8   Impositions directes, 1704–89
CC 24   Comptes consulaires, 1770–90
CC 54   Cadastre, 1780
CC 55   Dépenses, reçus, 1780–4
CC 56   Dépenses, reçus, cahier de doléances, 1788–9
DD 1   Pièces diverses
RV 1   Dossiers d'administration générale, 1789–an VII
RV 2   Délibérations municipales, 21 février 1790–27 Ventôse III; délibérations communales, 16 Nivôse IV–25 Vendémiaire VI
RV 3   Actes administratifs et de police, cahiers, Prairial IV–Pluviôse VI
RV 5   Actes paroissiaux et d'Etat-civil
RV 7   Actes paroissiaux et de l'Etat-civil, Frimaire–Germinal II

RV 11 Cadastre et mutations, encadastrement des biens des privilégiés, 21 mars 1790
RV 14 Contribution patriotique
RV 20 Nouvelles contributions directes, 1792
RV 22 Nouvelles contributions directes, 1792, an V, an VII
RV 24 Nouvelles contributions directes, 1791; emprunt forcé VII
RV 25 Administration militaire, 1793–an VII
RV 27 Sûreté générale; population
RV 39 Etats-Généraux: députation, 1789
N[on] C[oté] Contribution mobilière: mâtrice de rôle, 1792
N[on] C[oté] Délibérations municipales, 15 Floréal VIII–21 janvier 1821

Archives Communales de Châtelaudren, Châtelaudren

Municipalité, délibérations du Conseil municipal, 9 février 1790–13 Nivôse II
Municipalité, délibérations, 8 Nivôse II–23 Vendémiaire VII
Municipalité, délibérations, 23 Brumaire VII–21 mai 1822

Archives Communales de Neuviller-sur-Moselle, Neuviller-sur-Moselle

Carte Générale d'une Nouvelle Division et Distribution du ban de Neuviller, 15 décembre 1770

Archives Communales de Villepreux, Villepreux

D1 Assemblée municipale de la paroisse, délibérations, 12 août 1787–13 janvier 1790; Municipalité, délibérations, 7 février 1790–12 septembre 1791
D2 Municipalité, délibérations, 15 mars 1790–11 Pluviôse IV
D3 Conseil municipal, délibérations, 23 Prairial VIII–7 mai 1840

Archives de l'Evêche de Mende, Mende

Diocèse de Mende, registre, 1825–30

Bibliothèque Municipale de Grenoble, Grenoble

Délibération du Comité Général de Montélimar du 24 décembre 1789 à deux heures de relevée. n.p., n.d.
Fédération de Montélimart en Dauphiné. n.p., n.d. [1789]
Notes sur la commune d'Allan avant et pendant la Révolution, 1443–1789. Par J. Michel, instituteur, 1887
Procès-verbal et délibération de la ville de Montélimar, sur les événemens des 28 et 29 Juillet 1789. n.p., n.d.
Renonciation à la nobilité par les propriétaires possédans Biens Nobles, cytoyens des Trois-Ordres de la ville de Montélimar. n.p., n.d. [1789]

Bibliothèque Municipale de Nancy, Nancy

Favier, J. *Catalogue des livres et documents imprimés du Fonds lorrain de la bibliothèque municipale de Nancy.* 2 vols., Nancy, 1898
Monographies communales: Laneuveville-devant-Bayon, 1888
Monographies communales: Neuviller-sur-Moselle, 1888
Monographies communales: Roville-devant-Bayon, 1888
1360/1   Réponses faites à l'enquête ordonnée en 1761 par la Cour souveraine en vue de connaître les causes de la misère qui frappait alors le peuple lorrain, IV
2767   Neuviller-sur-Moselle 2 plans: projet de faisanderie; salon au château de M. le marquis de La Galaizière
2938   Roville Plan du territoire: projet de pont sur la Moselle

Private archives

M. Jacques Champouillon, Roville-devant-Bayon
M. Jean Renaux, Neuviller-sur-Moselle

PRINTED PRIMARY SOURCES

Almanach historique, politique et économique du département de la Lozère pour l'an IX de la République (1800 et 1801 vieux style). Mende, n.d.
Annuaire administratif, judiciaire, industriel et commercial du département de Seine-et-Oise, 1818, 1819, 1820. Versailles, n.d.
Annuaire pour l'an XII contenant des notices pour la description et la statistique du département du Gers publié par ordre du préfet. Auch, an XII
Annuaire statistique du département de la Lozère pour l'an XI. Mende, n.d.
Archives départementales de la Drôme: inventaire de la série E (supplément). n.p., n.d.
Archives parlementaires de 1787 à 1860: recueil complet des débats législatifs et politiques des chambres françaises (première série, 1787–99). 96 vols., Paris, 1862–1990
Aulard, F.-A. (ed.). *Recueil des Actes du Comité de Salut Public avec la correspondance officielle des représentants-en-mission et le registre du Conseil-Exécutif Provisoire.* 30 vols., Paris, 1889–1951
Balguière, préfet. *Tableau statistique du département du Gers.* Paris, an X
Boyd, J. P. (ed.). *The Papers of Thomas Jefferson.* 27 vols., Princeton, N.J., 1950–97
Les Bretons délibèrent: répertoire des registres de délibérations paroissiales et municipales, 1780–1800, et des cahiers de doléances, 1789. Saint-Brieuc, Quimper, Rennes and Vannes, 1990
Brun-Durand, J. *Dictionnaire biographique et biblio-iconographique de la Drôme.* 2 vols., Grenoble, 1900–1
Calmet, A. *Notice de la Lorraine.* 2 vols., Nancy, 1756
Chateaubriand, F.-R. de. *Mémoires d'outre-tombe.* 4 vols., Paris, 1948
Collection générale des loix. 24 vols., Paris, 1786–1800
Compte-rendu par la Commission des Communes de Provence. Aix-en-Provence, 1790

Coriolis, G.-H. de. *Traité sur l'administration du comté de Provence.* 3 vols., Aix-en-Provence, 1786–8

Dictionnaire géographique de Lozère. n.p., 1852

Documents relatifs à l'histoire du Gévaudan: deuxième partie: délibérations de l'administration départementale de la Lozère et de son directoire de 1790 à 1800 publiées par la Société d'agriculture, industrie, sciences et arts de la Lozère, sous les auspices du conseil général et sous la direction de M. F. André, archiviste du département. 3 vols., Mende, 1882–4

Les Economiques par L. D. H. [l'ami des hommes]. 2 vols., Amsterdam, 1769

Etienne, C. *Cahiers de doléances des bailliages des généralités de Nancy, III: Cahiers du bailliage de Vézelise.* Paris, 1930

Gazette nationale, ou Le Moniteur universel.

Guérout, J. *Rôles de la taille de l'Election de Paris conservés aux Archives Nationales (sous-série Z^{IG}) et dans les Archives Départementales.* Paris, 1981

Instruction abrégée sur le système métrique... pour le département du Gers. Auch, an X

Jollivet, B. *Les Côtes-du-Nord: histoire et géographie de toutes les villes et communes du département.* 3 vols., Guingamp, 1854

Lepage, H. *Les Communes de la Meurthe: journal historique des villes, bourgs, villages, hameaux et censes de ce département.* 2 vols., Nancy, 1853

Marquis, *Mémoire statistique du département de la Meurthe.* Paris, an XIII

Mathieu de Dombasle, C.-J.-A. *Annales de Roville: première livraison.* Paris, 1824

Mirabeau, V. de, and Quesnay, F. *Philosophie rurale ou économie générale et politique de l'agriculture réduite à l'ordre immuable des loix physiques et morales, qui assurent la prospérité des Empires.* 3 vols., Amsterdam, 1764

Miraval, P., and Monnier, R. (eds.). *Répertoire des travaux universitaires inédits sur la période révolutionnaire.* Paris, 1990

Mirouse, F. (ed.). *François Ménard de La Groye, député du Mans aux Etats Généraux: correspondance, 1789–1791.* Le Mans, 1989

Oeuvres de Maximilien Robespierre. 10 vols., Paris, 1950–67

Ogée, [J.]. *Dictionnaire historique et géographique de la province de Bretagne, dédié à la nation bretonne.* 2 vols., Mayenne, 1843 [reprinted 1973]

Paroisses et communes de France: Drôme. Paris, 1981

Paroisses et communes de France: Lozère. Paris, 1982

Paroisses et communes de France: région parisienne. Paris, 1974

Plan détaillé de topographie, suivi de la topographie du département du Gers (par le citoyen Dralet). Paris, an IX

Poitrineau, A. (ed.). *Les Anciennes Mesures locales du sud-ouest d'après les tables de conversion.* Clermont-Ferrand, 1996

Réimpression de l'Ancien Moniteur. 32 vols., Paris, 1840–7

Saint-Jouan, R. de. *Dictionnaire des communes: département des Côtes-du-Nord.* Saint-Brieuc, 1990

La Statistique agricole de 1814: Gers. Paris, 1914

Thénard, M. *Bailliages de Versailles et de Meudon: les cahiers des paroisses avec commentaires accompagnés de quelques cahiers de curés.* Versailles, 1889

Vincens, P.-P. *Dictionnaire des lieux habités*. Mende, 1879

Usteri, P., and Ritter, E. (eds.). *Henri Meister: souvenirs de mon dernier voyage à Paris [1795]*. Paris, 1910

Young, A. *Travels in France during the Years 1787, 1788 and 1789*, ed. M. Betham-Edwards. London, 1900

SECONDARY SOURCES

Anfos-Martin. *Vieux écrits: documents relatifs à l'histoire des diverses communes de l'ancien arrondissement de Montélimar*. Montélimar, 1928

Antoine, M. *Le Gouvernement et l'administration sous Louis XV: dictionnaire biographique*. Paris, 1978

Arrivets, J. 'L'Assemblée provinciale de la généralité d'Auch: essai historique', *Bulletin de la Société d'histoire et d'archéologie du Gers*, 33 (1932), 246–76, 340–95; 34 (1933), 15–61, 312–61

Aston, N. *Religion and Revolution in France, 1780–1804*. Basingstoke, 2000

Aston, N. (ed.). *Religious Change in Europe, 1650–1914*. Oxford, 1997

Aubas, E. 'La Société Montagnarde de Roquelaure', *Bulletin de la Société archéologique du Gers*, 28 (1927), 25–41, 151–64

'Monographie de la commune de Roquelaure', *Bulletin de la Société archéologique du Gers*, 34 (1933), 259–300; 35 (1934), 78–99, 289–329

Azéma, T., and Orband, H.-F. *Allan: sept siècles au jour le jour*. Montélimar, 1990

Babeau, A. *Le Village sous l'Ancien Régime*. Paris, 1915

Bardy, B. 'Les Tournées du préfet Gamot (suite)', *Revue du Gévaudan*, 1955, 61–78

'Histoires lozériennes', *Midi Libre*, 13, 20, 27 December 1992; 3, 10, 17, 24, 31 January 1993

Baumont, S. (ed.). *Histoire de Montélimar*. Toulouse, 1992

Béaur, G., and Minard, P. *Atlas de la Révolution française, X: Economie*. Paris, 1997

Bernard, R.-J. 'Les Communautés rurales en Gévaudan sous l'ancien régime', *Revue du Gévaudan, des Causses et des Cévennes*, new series, 17 (1971), 110–65

Bernard de Brye. *Un Evêque d'Ancien Régime à l'épreuve de la Révolution: le Cardinal A.-L.-H. de La Fare, 1752–1829*. Paris, 1985

Bianchi, S. 'Pouvoirs locaux et pouvoir central en milieu rural dans le sud de l'Ile-de-France, 1787–1802', *Annales de Bretagne et des Pays de l'Ouest*, 100 (1993), 519–32

Bianchi, S., and Chancelier, M. *Draveil et Montgeron, deux villages en Révolution*. Le Mée-sur-Seine, 1989

Bicenténaire de la Révolution, 1789–1989: Villepreux. n.p., n.d.

Bierschenk, T., and Olivier de Sardan, J.-P. (eds.). *Les Pouvoirs au village: le Bénin rural entre démocratisation et décentralisation*. Paris, 1998

Bodinier, B. 'La Vente des biens nationaux: essai de synthèse', *Annales historiques de la Révolution française*, 315 (1999), 7–14

Boeck, F. de. 'The Rootedness of Trees: Place as Cultural and Natural Texture in Rural South West Congo', in N. Lovell (ed.), *Locality and Belonging*. London and New York, 1998, pp. 22–52

Boehler, J.-M. *Une Société rurale en milieu rhénan: la paysannerie de la plaine d'Alsace, 1648–1789.* 3 vols., Strasbourg, 1994

Bois, P. *Paysans de l'ouest.* Paris, 1971

Bordes, M. *D'Etigny et l'administration de l'intendance d'Auch, 1751–1767.* 2 vols., Auch, 1957

La Réforme municipale du contrôleur-général Laverdy et son application, 1764–1771. Toulouse, 1968

Bordes, M. 'Le Rôle des subdélégués en Provence au XVIIIᵉ siècle', *Provence historique,* 1973, 386–403

'Consulats et municipalités en Gascogne à la fin de l'Ancien Régime', in *Recueil de mémoires et travaux publié par la Société d'Histoire du Droit et des Institutions des anciens pays de droit écrit.* Montpellier, 1974, pp. 67–82

L'Application de la réforme municipale de 1787 dans l'Election de Rivière-Verdun. Auch, 1978

Boubal, C. 'L'Affaire Charrier, 26 mai 1793–1ᵉʳ juin 1793'. Dissertation, University of Paris I, 1983–4

Bouchard, G. *Le Village immobile: Senneley-en-Sologne au XVIIIᵉ siècle.* Paris, 1972

Boulay de la Meurthe. *Notice sur l'école d'enseignement mutuel de Roville.* n.p., n.d

Bourde, A.-J. *Agronomie et agronomes en France au XVIIIᵉ siècle.* 3 vols., Paris, 1967

Bourgès, A. *Les Doléances des paysans bretons en 1789, quelques cahiers de paroisses.* Saint-Brieuc, 1953

Boutier, J., and Boutry, P. *Atlas de la Révolution française*, VI: *Les Sociétés politiques.* Paris, 1992

Bouton, C. A. *The Flour War: Gender, Class and Community in Late Ancien Regime French Society.* University Park, Pa., 1993

Boyé, P. *Les Travaux publics et le régime des corvées en Lorraine au XVIIIᵉ siècle.* Paris and Nancy, 1900

'Le Chancelier Chaumont de La Galaizière et sa famille', *Le Pays lorrain,* 28 (1936), 113–32, 441–60, 537–52; 29 (1937), 129–57; 30 (1938), 481–507

Brégail, M. 'Deux grands congrès des Sociétés populaires du Gers (juin et septembre 1793)', *Bulletin de la Société archéologique du Gers,* 1900, 126–33

'Luttes politiques des Girondins et des Montagnards dans le département du Gers', *Bulletin de la Société archéologique du Gers,* 1902, 78–97

'Un Révolutionnaire gersois: Lantrac', *Bulletin de la Société archéologique du Gers,* 1903, 18–32, 119–34, 226–44

Le Gers pendant la Révolution, 1789–1804. Auch, 1934

Brinton, C. C. *The Jacobins: An Essay in the New History,* 2nd edn. New York, 1961

Cabourdin, G. *Terres et hommes en Lorraine, 1550–1635: Toulois et Comté de Vaudémont.* Nancy, 1979

Quand Stanislas régnait en Lorraine. Paris, 1980

Chabin, M. 'La Conscription dans l'arrondissement de Marvejols à la fin de l'Empire', in *Cévennes et Gévaudan: actes du XLVIᵉ Congrès organisé à Mende et Florac les 16 et 17 juin 1973 par la Fédération Historique du Languedoc-Méditérranéen et du Roussillon.* Mende, 1974, pp. 297–307

Chapelain, E. 'Le District de Saint-Brieuc: problèmes politiques et administratifs, mars 1793–novembre 1799'. Dissertation, University of Haute-Bretagne, 1990

Cholvy, G., and Hilaire, Y.-M. *Histoire religieuse de la France contemporaine*. 3 vols., Toulouse, 1985–8

Clade, J.-L. 'La Vie municipale dans la région de Rougement (Doubs) de l'Ancien Régime à la Restauration (1720–1820)'. 3 vols., dissertation, University of Besançon, 1983

Claverie, E. ' "L'Honneur": une société de défis au XIXᵉ siècle', *Annales: économies, sociétés, civilisations*, July–August 1979, 744–59

Clémendot, P. *Le Département de la Meurthe à l'époque du Directoire*. n.p., n.d. [1966]

Constantin, C. *L'Evêché du département de la Meurthe de 1791 à 1802*, I: *La Fin de l'Eglise d'Ancien Régime et l'établissement de l'Eglise constitutionnelle*. Nancy, 1935

Contamine, H. *Les Conséquences financières des invasions de 1814 et de 1815 dans les départements de la Moselle et de la Meurthe*. Metz, 1932

Corbel, P. 'Production, pouvoirs et mentalités dans une commune rurale gallèse: Plélo'. Dissertation, University of Haute-Bretagne, 1980

'Gens de Plélo: 1600–1914: une ethno-histoire en cours'. Dissertation, University of Haute-Bretagne, 1984

Costan, Baron de. *Passage de Napoléon dans la Drôme, en 1814, et campagne du Duc d'Angoulême, en 1815*. Lyon, 1890

Coudert, J. 'La Vaine pâture dans les pays de la Meurthe au XIXᵉ siècle', in *Mélanges offerts à M. le Professeur Pierre Voirin*. Paris, 1966, pp. 130–61

Crassin-Blanc, C. *Allan: chroniques d'un village de la Drôme*. n.p., 1981

Croix, A. (ed.). *Les Bretons et Dieu: atlas d'histoire religieuse, 1300–1800*. Rennes, n.d.

Daugé, S. 'Un Physiocrate, seigneur de Roquelaure', *Bulletin de la Société archéologique du Gers*, 1905, 87–102, 196–208

Defresne, A. *Documents historiques se rattachant à la vie des villages avant 1789 et sous la Révolution*. Versailles, 1908

'Les Registres municipaux de Rennemoulin jugés au point de vue économique', in *Recherche et publication des documents relatifs à la vie municipale de la Révolution: Comité départemental de la Seine-et-Oise: bulletin de 1912–1913*. Versailles, 1913, pp. 31–69

'Mesures prises sous la Révolution pour le maintien de l'ordre dans les communes des environs de Versailles', in *Recherche et publication des documents relatifs à la vie économique de la Révolution: Comité départemental de la Seine-et-Oise: bulletin de 1922–1927*, pp. 63–71

Delacroix, M. *Statistique du département de la Drôme*. Valence, 1835

Delon, P.-J.-B. *La Révolution en Lozère*. Mende, 1922

Les Elections de 1789 en Gévaudan. Mende, 1922

Delpal, B. *Entre paroisse et commune: les catholiques de la Drôme au milieu du XIXᵉ siècle*. Valence, 1989

Demortier, M. 'Le Problème de l'union à travers le cahier de doléances et les délibérations municipales d'Allan (1788–98)', in *Les Drômois: acteurs de la Révolution: actes du Colloque de Valence*. Valence, 1990, pp. 171–8

Derlange, M. *Les Communautés d'habitants en Provence au dernier siècle de l'Ancien Régime*. Toulouse, 1987

Desan, S. *Reclaiming the Sacred: Lay Religion and Popular Politics in Revolutionary France*. Ithaca and London, 1990

Droguet, A. (ed.). *Les Bleus de Bretagne de la Révolution à nos jours: actes du colloque de Saint-Brieuc–Ploufragen, 3–5 octobre 1990*. Saint-Brieuc, 1991

Duboul, A. *La Fin du Parlement de Toulouse*. Toulouse, 1890

Dubreuil, L. *La Vente des biens nationaux dans le département des Côtes-du-Nord*. Paris, 1912

Duby, G., and Wallon, A. (eds.). *Histoire de la France rurale*. 4 vols., Paris, 1975–6

[Dumont]. *Memoirs of Mirabeau: Biographical, Literary and Political by Himself, His Father, His Uncle and His Adopted Child*. 4 vols., London, 1835

Dupuy, R. (ed.). *Pouvoir local et Révolution, 1780–1850: la frontière intérieure*. Rennes, 1995

Durand, R. *Le Département des Côtes-du-Nord sous le Consulat et l'Empire, 1800–1815: essai d'histoire administratif*. 2 vols., Paris, 1926

Egret, J. 'La Pré-Révolution en Provence, 1787–1789', *Annales historiques de la Révolution française*, April–June 1954, 97–126

Emmanuelli, F.-X. *Etat et pouvoir dans la France des XVIᵉ–XVIIIᵉ siècles: la métamorphose inachevée*. Paris, 1992

Fages, E. *L'Industrie des laines en Gévaudan au XVIIIᵉ siècle*. Mende, 1907

Faucheux, M. *L'Insurrection vendéenne de 1793: aspects économiques et sociaux*. Paris, 1964

Febvre, L. 'Que la France se nomme diversité: à propos de quelques études jurassiennes', *Annales: économies, sociétés, civilisations*, 3 (July–September 1946), 271–4

Fel, A. 'Notes de géographie humaine sur la montagne de Margeride', in *Mélanges géographiques offerts à Philippe Arbos*. Clermont-Ferrand, 1953, pp. 71–81

Forrest, A., and Jones, P. (eds.). *Reshaping France: Town, Country and Region during the French Revolution*. Manchester, 1991

Fournier, G. *Démocratie et vie municipale en Languedoc du milieu du XVIIIᵉ au début du XIXᵉ siècle*. 2 vols., Toulouse, 1994

Fréville, H. *L'Intendance de Bretagne*. 3 vols., Rennes, 1953

Gand-Gaudez, F., and Laperche-Lepape, C. 'Les Doléances politiques, administratives, militaires, économiques, sociales et religieuses des Lorrains en 1789 d'après les cahiers des bailliages'. Dissertation, University of Nancy II, 1986

Gérard, C. *Histoire d'un village lorrain, Neuviller-sur-Moselle*. Nancy, 1936

Gérard, C., and Peltre, J. *Les Villages lorrains*. Nancy, 1979

Gibson, R. *A Social History of French Catholicism, 1789–1914*. London and New York, 1989

Girard, C. 'La Catastrophe agricole de 1816 dans la Meurthe', *Annales de l'Est*, 1955, 333–62

Gomez, J.-M. 'Dartigoeyte, un représentant du peuple en mission dans les départements du Gers et de la Haute-Garonne'. Dissertation, University of Toulouse Le Mirail, 1993

Grandmottet, O. 'Histoire rurale de la seigneurie de Villepreux au XVIIIᵉ siècle'. Dissertation, Ecole des Chartes, 1951

Gross, J.-P. *Fair Shares for All: Jacobin Egalitarianism in Practice*. Cambridge, 1997

Gueniffey, P. *Le Nombre et la raison: la Révolution française et les élections*. Paris, 1995

Guionnet, C. *L'Apprentissage de la politique moderne: les élections municipales sous la monarchie de juillet*. Paris and Montréal, 1997

Guyot, C. *Des assemblées des communautés d'habitants en Lorraine avant 1789*. n.p., 1886

Hartmann, E. *La Révolution française en Alsace et en Lorraine*. Paris, 1990

Histoire de Lorraine, publiée par la Société lorraine des études locales dans l'enseignement public. Nancy, 1939

Hoffman, P. T. *Growth in a Traditional Society: The French Countryside, 1450–1815*. Princeton, N.J., 1996

Hottenger, G. *La Propriété rurale: morcellement et remembrement*. Paris and Nancy, 1914

Ikni, G.-R. 'Crise agricole et Révolution paysanne: le mouvement populaire dans les campagnes de l'Oise, de la décennie physiocratique à l'an II'. 6 vols., dissertation, University of Paris 1, 1993

Jessenne, J.-P. *Pouvoir au village et révolution: Artois, 1760–1848*. Lille, 1987

Jones, P. M. *Politics and Rural Society: The Southern Massif Central, c. 1750–1880*. Cambridge, 1985

 The Peasantry in the French Revolution. Cambridge, 1988

 'Agricultural Modernization and the French Revolution', *Journal of Historical Geography*, 16 (1990), 38–50

 'The "Agrarian Law": Schemes for Land Redistribution during the French Revolution', *Past and Present*, 133 (1991), 96–133

 Reform and Revolution in France: The Politics of Transition, 1774–1791. Cambridge, 1995

Jouhannaud, A.-M. 'La Société des amis de la Constitution de Versailles, 2 août 1790–18 Frimaire III'. Dissertation, n.p., 1970

Knittel, F. 'La Naissance de l'enseignement de l'agriculture en Lorraine, 1759–1848'. Dissertation, University of Nancy II, 1999–2000

Kwass, M. *Privilege and the Politics of Taxation in Eighteenth-Century France: Liberté, égalité, fiscalité*. Cambridge, 2000

Lacoste, M. 'La Crise agricole dans le département de la Meurthe à la fin de l'Ancien Régime et au début de la Révolution'. Dissertation, University of Paris, 1951

Lacroix, A. *L'Arrondissement de Montélimar: géographie, histoire, statistique*. Valence, 1868

Lamaison, P. 'Les Stratégies matrimoniales dans un système complexe de parenté', *Annales: économies, sociétés, civilisations*, July–August 1979, 721–43

Latour, P. de. 'Un Mouvement prérévolutionnaire: les refus de dîmes en Comminges et Gascogne', *Annales du Midi*, 101 (1989), 7–25

Lavefve, L. 'Les Comités révolutionnaires de l'an II dans le district de Versailles'. 2 vols., dissertation, University of Paris I, 1991

Le Page, R.-H. *Les Bleus du Châté: histoire des châtelaudrinais sous la Révolution.* Lorient, n.d. [1974]

Le Sage, *abbé. Notices historiques sur le diocèse de Saint-Brieuc avant, pendant et après la Révolution et sur les environs de Broons et d'Uzel.* Saint-Brieuc, 1890

Lebrun, F. 'Les Epidémies en Haute-Bretagne à la fin de l'Ancien Régime, 1770–1789', *Annales de démographie historique*, 1977, 181–206

Lefebvre, G. *Les Paysans du Nord pendant la Révolution française.* [condensed version] Bari, 1959
The French Revolution from 1793 to 1799. London, 1967

Lemoine, H. 'Notes historiques sur Villepreux (Seine-et-Oise)', *Revue de l'histoire de Versailles et de Seine-et-Oise*, 30 (1931), 66–86, 131–53
'La Condition des habitants d'un village de la région de Versailles au XVIIIᵉ siècle', in *Recherche et publication des documents relatifs à la vie économique de la Révolution: Comité départemental de la Seine-et-Oise: bulletin de 1935–1937.* Rodez, 1938, pp. 109–15
'La Vente des Biens Nationaux dans le district de Versailles, notamment à Villepreux', in *Recherche et publication des documents relatifs à la vie économique de la Révolution: Comité départemental de la Seine-et-Oise: bulletin de 1942–1943*, pp. 72–6
Villepreux au val de Gally. Versailles, 1963

Levi, G. *Inheriting Power: The Story of an Exorcist.* Chicago, 1988

Lotharingia. *Archives lorraines d'archéologie, d'art et d'histoire, VI.* Nancy, 1996

Lucas, C. (ed.). *The French Revolution and the Creation of Modern Political Culture, II: The Political Culture of the French Revolution.* Oxford, 1988

La Margeride: la montagne, les hommes. Paris, 1983

Mariolle, B. 'Le District de Versailles comme test du nouveau diocèse constitutionnel de Seine-et-Oise'. Dissertation, Institut Catholique Sorbonne IV, 1988

Markoff, J. 'Peasant Grievances and Peasant Insurrection: France in 1789', *Journal of Modern History*, 62 (September 1990), 445–76
The Abolition of Feudalism: Peasants, Lords and Legislators in the French Revolution. University Park, Pa., 1996

Martel, M. *Allan: mon village.* Le Teil, 1947

Martin, G. *Histoire et généalogie de la maison de La Tour-du-Pin.* La Ricamarie, 1985

Marwick, A. *The New Nature of History: Knowledge, Evidence, Language.* Basingstoke, 2001

Maurice, P. *La Famille en Gévaudan au XVᵉ siècle, 1380–1483.* Paris, 1998

Maurin, Y. 'La Répartition de la propriété foncière en Lozère au début du XIXᵉ siècle', in *Cévennes et Gévaudan: actes du XLVIᵉ Congrès organisé à Mende et Florac les 16 et 17 juin 1973 par la Fédération Historique du Languedoc-Méditérranéen et du Roussillon.* Mende, 1974, pp. 309–35

Meixmoron de Dombasle, C. de. *Notes et documents pour servir à l'histoire de l'établissement de Roville.* Nancy, 1844

Mijoint, O. 'Les Assemblées d'habitants sous l'Ancien Régime à travers des actes d'assemblées d'habitants du village de Chevreuse'. Dissertation, University of Paris I, 1995

Minois, G. 'Le Rôle politique des recteurs de campagne en Basse-Bretagne, 1750–1790', *Annales de Bretagne et des pays de l'Ouest,* 89 (1982), 153–64
    La Bretagne des prêtres en Trégor d'Ancien Régime. Beltan, 1987

[Morangiès]. *Essai sur l'agriculture de quelques cantons du département de la Lozère.* Lyon, 1831

Morineau, M. *Pour une histoire économique vraie.* Lille, 1985

Müller, M., and Aberdam, S. 'Conflits de dîme et révolution en Gascogne gersoise, 1750–1800'. Dissertation, University of Paris I, 1971–2

Nières, C. 'Les Villes en Bretagne: 12, 40 ou 80?', *Revue du Nord,* 70 (1988), 679–89

Orband, H.-F. *Villages fortifiés de la Drôme: histoire d'Allan en Provence.* Taulignan, 1990

Ozouf, M. *Festivals of the French Revolution.* Cambridge, Mass., and London, 1988

Pélaquier, E. *De la maison du père à la maison commune: Saint-Victor-de-la-Coste, en Languedoc rhodanien, 1661–1799.* 2 vols., Montpellier, 1996

Peltre, J. *Recherches métrologiques sur les finages lorrains.* Paris, 1975
    'Les Remembrements en Lorraine à l'époque moderne (XVIIᵉ–XVIIIᵉ siècles)', *Annales de l'Est,* 28 (1976), 197–246

Perrin, R. *L'Esprit public dans le département de la Meurthe de 1814 à 1816.* Nancy, n.d.

Peyrard, C. *Les Jacobins de l'ouest: sociabilité révolutionnaire et formes de politisation dans le Maine et la Basse-Normandie, 1789–1799.* Paris, 1996

Pezard, J.-P. 'Une Communauté villageoise à la fin de l'Ancien Régime: Chatou de 1770 à 1789'. Dissertation, University of Paris X Nanterre, 1975

Pfister, C. *Les Préliminaires de la Révolution à Nancy: l'élection aux Etats-généraux et le cahier de la ville de Nancy.* Nancy, 1910
    Les Elections à Nancy et dans le département de la Meurthe sous le Consulat et le Premier Empire, 1799–1815. Nancy, 1912

Picquet, E. 'Une Fête à Châtelaudren en 1788: le Comte de Coëttando', *Mémoires de la Société d'émulation des Côtes-du-Nord,* 49 (1911), 55–69

Pommeret, H. *L'Esprit public dans le département des Côtes-du-Nord pendant la Révolution, 1789–1799: essai d'histoire politique d'un département breton.* Saint-Brieuc, 1921 [reprinted 1979]

Postel-Vinay, G. *La Terre et l'argent: l'agriculture et le crédit en France du XVIIIᵉ au début du XXᵉ siècle.* Paris, 1998

Pourcher, P. *L'Episcopat français et constitutionnel et le clergé de la Lozère durant la Révolution de 1789.* 3 vols., Saint-Martin-de-Boubaux, 1896–1900

Pourcher, Y. *Les Maîtres de granit: les notables de Lozère du XVIIIᵉ siècle à nos jours.* Paris, 1987

Renwick, J. *Voltaire et Morangiès, 1772–1773, ou Les Lumières l'ont échappé belle.* Oxford, 1982

Richard, G. 'Nancy à la fin de l'Empire: l'entrée des alliés en 1814', *Pays lorrain*, 35 (1954), 10–24

'Nancy sous la première occupation alliée', *Pays lorrain*, 35 (1954), 50–66

'Nancy sous la Première Restauration', *Pays lorrain*, 36 (1955), 125–42

'Les Cent Jours à Nancy', *Pays lorrain*, 38 (1957), 81–96

Rives, J. *Dîme et société dans l'archévêché d'Auch au XVIIIe siècle*. Paris, 1976

Rocquain, F. *L'Etat de la France au 18 Brumaire*. Paris, 1874

Rohan-Chabot, A de. *Les Ecoles de campagne en Lorraine au XVIIIe siècle*. Paris, 1967

Rothiot, J.-P. 'La Question des communaux dans les Vosges: triage, partage, et appropriation privée', *Annales de l'Est*, 49 (1999), 211–43

Saint-Martin, G. *L'Histoire, la vie: Roquelaure près d'Auch, village de Gascogne*. Miélan, n.d. [1983]

Saint-Seine, A. de. 'Histoire de la ferme de Grand'Maisons', typescript, Villepreux, n.d. [held in A. D. des Yvelines]

Sauvageon, J. 'La Paysannerie et la Révolution dans les campagnes drômoises', in *Les Drômois: acteurs de la Révolution: actes du Colloque de Valence*. Valence, 1990, pp. 99–116

Seyve, M. *Montélimar et la Révolution, 1788–1792: audaces et timidités provinciales*. Montélimar, 1989

Shapiro, G. and Markoff, J. *Revolutionary Demands: A Content Analysis of the Cahiers de Doléances of 1789*. Stanford, Calif., 1998

Sheppard, T. F. *Lourmarin in the Eighteenth Century: A Study of a French Village*. Baltimore and London, 1971

Silbertin-Blanc, C. 'La Légende du séjour de Rousseau à Carpentras: la correspondance inédite de [Hyacinthe-Antoine?] d'Astier-Cromessière avec Jean-Jacques, 1763–1769', *Provence historique*, 13 (1963), 29–63, 160–202, 240–79

Soboul, A. 'Esquisse d'un plan de recherches pour une monographie de communauté rurale', *La Pensée*, July–August 1947, 34–48

The French Revolution, 1787–1799. London, 1974

Soulabaille, A. 'L'Evolution économique et sociale de Guingamp aux XVIe, XVIIe et XVIIIe siècles'. Dissertation, University of Rennes, 1997

Sourbadère, G. 'Quelques aspects de l'oeuvre de l'intendant d'Etigny à travers les cahiers de doléances gersois', *Bulletin de la Société archéologique et historique du Gers*, 1996, 361–4

Sutherland, D. M. G. *France 1789–1815: Revolution and Counter-Revolution*. Fontana, 1985

Tambour, E. *Les Registres municipaux de Rennemoulin*. Paris, n.d. [1903]

Etudes sur la Révolution dans le département de Seine-et-Oise. Paris, 1913

Tarbouriech, A. *Les Cahiers du clergé et du Tiers Etat de la Sénéchaussée d'Auch en 1789*. Nîmes, 1992

'Texte pour servir à l'histoire de la Lozère en marge de la Révolution: lettre de l'abbé Béraud, curé de Saint-Alban', *Bulletin du C.E.R.*, 12 (1991), 86–7

Theo, R. 'Saint-Alban: la vie d'autrefois à travers les délibérations municipales', *Lou Païs*, May–June 1982, 72–3

Thiry, J.-L. *Le Département de la Meurthe sous le Consulat*. Nancy, 1958

Tilly, C. *The Vendée*. Cambridge, Mass., and London, 1976

Tinthoin, R. 'Saint-Alban: vie économique et démographique', *Lou Païs*, February 1959, 1–2; March 1959, 2; April 1959, 11

Tocqueville, A. de. *L'Ancien Régime*, ed. G. W. Headlam. Oxford, 1969

Tournès, R. *La Garde nationale dans le département de la Meurthe pendant la Révolution, 1789–1802*. Angers, 1920

Touzery, M. *L'Invention de l'impôt sur le revenu: la taille tarifée, 1715–1789*. Paris, 1994

Atlas de la généralité de Paris au XVIIIe siècle: un paysage retrouvé. Paris, 1995

Dictionnaire des paroisses fiscales de la généralité de Paris d'après le cadastre de Bertier de Sauvigny, 1776–1791. Caen, 1995

Trevedy, J. *Le Déluge de Châtelaudren en 1773*. Saint-Brieuc, 1891

Troux, A. *La Vie politique dans le département de la Meurthe d'août 1792 à octobre 1795*. 2 vols., Nancy, 1936

Viot, C. *Vie de Antoine Bertier de Roville*. Paris, 1875

Vivier, N. *Propriété collective et identité communale: les biens communaux en France, 1750–1914*. Paris, 1998

Wylie, L. (ed.). *A Village in Anjou*. Cambridge, Mass., 1966

Zink, A. *Azereix: la vie d'une communauté rurale à la fin du XVIIIe siècle*. Paris, 1969

Clochers et troupeaux: les communautés rurales des Landes et du Sud-Ouest avant la Révolution. Bordeaux, 1997

Index